THE WORLD ECONOMY

PATTERNS OF GROWTH AND CHANGE

B. J. McCormick

Philip Allan/Barnes & Noble Books

First published 1988 by

PHILIP ALLAN PUBLISHERS LIMITED
MARKET PLACE
DEDDINGTON
OXFORD OX5 4SE

First published in the USA 1988 by

BARNES & NOBLE BOOKS
81 ADAMS DRIVE
TOTOWA
NEW JERSEY 07512

© Brian J. McCormick, 1988

British Library Cataloguing in Publication Data

McCormick, B.J. (Brian Joseph), *1931–*
 The world economy: patterns of growth
 and change.
 1. Economic conditions, 1970–1987
 I. Title
 330.9'047

ISBN 0-86003-076-8
ISBN 0-86003-179-9 Pbk

Typeset by MHL Typesetting Ltd., Coventry
Printed in Great Britain at the Alden Press, Oxford

To David P. Saca

Contents

Acknowledgements

In so far as books have origins, the beginnings of this one can be found on the tablets of stone handed down by the Manchester School of Lewis, Devons, Martin, Coppock and Johnson fortified by discussions with Beryl Barber, John Bochel, Gordon Bridger and Patricia Longbottom. As they were passing through Sheffield, Colin Leys and Teodor Shanin forced me to think about Africa and peasants. I am also indebted to Eric Owen Smith (Germany), Joseph Harrison and Harold Blakemore (Spain and Latin America), K.J. McCormick, D.W. Anthony and Kazutoshi Koshiro (Japan), Charles Blake (the USA) and Peter Reynolds (post-Keynesian economics). The libraries of Sheffield University, Sheffield Polytechnic, Sheffield City, Manchester and Leeds Universities provided the raw materials for the studies of Europe, Asia, Latin America and Africa. The persistent and nagging criticisms of my pen mistress, Hilary Scannell, have converted an unreadable manuscript into something reasonable, for which eternal thanks. Monica abstained from comment and Paul sat this one out as the manuscript slowly engulfed every room in the house. Finally, the dedication acknowledges a friendship which began at school and has continued for forty years.

An earlier version of the chapter on Japan appeared in the University of Buckingham's discussion papers in economics.

Sheffield, 1988   Brian McCormick

1

Introduction

The trebling of the price of wheat and rice between 1972 and 1974 and oil price increases in 1973 and 1979, with attendant rises in the prices of other raw materials, marked a turning point for the world economy: it had been preceded by twenty years of unparalleled prosperity and was followed by a depression. Soviet purchases from the United States triggered the increase in the price of wheat; but the context of that increase was the reliance of the Third World on foodstuffs produced in the advanced countries. The rise in food prices acted as a stimulus (although it was not the only one) to the rise in oil prices imposed by the Arab oil producing states — themselves important importers of grain. This rise interrupted the expansion of the advanced economies and left the non-oil producing less developed countries facing increased food and raw material prices; in an attempt to overcome their difficulties many of them borrowed heavily. But the reaction of the advanced countries to the second oil shock, in 1979, was to deflate and throw the world economy into the disarray of the 1980s, with consequent disagreement between the advanced and the developing countries. The fall in the demand for foodstuffs and raw materials by the advanced countries led to falling prices, which in turn in 1986 were fed back to oil prices (Figure 1.1). The world economy responded weakly: it was expected that oil prices might fall further. In some countries the fall in oil prices was not passed on to consumers but was used by governments as a means of restoring revenues.

Oil and grain price rises marked the end of an era; but they were symptoms, not causes. Other aspects of the world economy were causing concern before 1972. In the early 1960s there had been indications of a new industrial revolution — automation — and there were fears of technological unemployment. Opinion was divided as to the causes of rising unemployment: was it due to the new technologies or deficient aggregate demand? In retrospect those fears seem premature. But they were allayed by the increase in aggregate monetary demand which was to lead to the worldwide inflation of the 1960s and 1970s. The relative

1

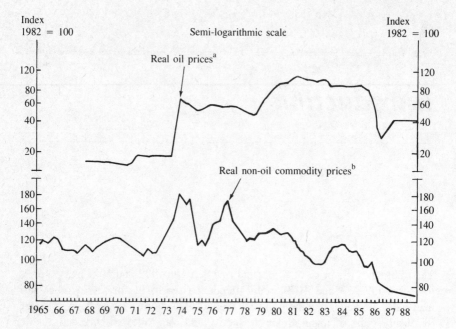

Index
1982 = 100   Semi-logarithmic scale   Index
                                                                       1982 = 100

Real oil prices[a]

Real non-oil commodity prices[b]

Source: OECD (1987)
Notes: (a) OECD import price index deflated by OECD manufactures
              export prices.
        (b) Weighted average of food, tropical beverages, vegetable
              oilseeds and oils, agricultural raw materials, minerals,
              ores and metal prices deflated by OECD manufactures export
              prices.

Figure 1.1

economic fortunes of the major powers diverged, with Japan and West Germany
undergoing a revival and displacing Britain from its political and economic leadership. Reduced tariff barriers led to an influx of goods from the newly industrialising
countries. There were signs of a new mercantilism. There were wars, of which
Vietnam was the most significant. Living standards in many parts of the world,
especially in Africa, deteriorated. In this context the oil price rises were merely
another turn of the screw.

What are the Questions?

That turning point in the 1970s is the subject of this book. Why did it happen
when it did? Was there anything unusual about the prolonged boom which had
stretched from the post-war 1940s to the 1960s and about the persistent recession
which began in the 1970s and continued into the 1980s? Did these events form
part of a 'long wave', a phenomenon whose shadowy existence in the eighteenth

and nineteenth century had been charted by Kondratieff (1979)? But if there was a 'long wave' — and clearly there had been a long boom — why had so few countries in Africa, Latin America and Asia taken off in the 1960s into self-sustained growth? There are further questions that need answering. Is economic development an inherently inegalitarian process? Was a polarisation of the world economy into an advanced North and an underdeveloped South inevitable? Were there particular reasons for Europe's economic development in the nineteenth century? Do those reasons also account for the success of the industrialising countries of South-east Asia and the relative failure of those in most parts of Africa and Latin America? Has the creation of the European Community impeded the development of former colonial areas? How can we account for the apparent paradox of developing countries becoming importers of foodstuffs? Why have the centrally planned economies of Eastern Europe been so unsuccessful in their attempts to modernise their societies? Was it, indeed, the increasing inequalities between and within the North and South which led to the end of the boom?

The Plan of the Book

The questions raised in the previous paragraph form the substance of the book. Chapter 2 attempts to measure the differences in the national incomes of countries and seeks to find out if development is a necessarily inegalitarian process. Chapter 3 concentrates upon the problems of agrarian economies: it considers the difficulties of stabilising prices and incomes of primary products and producers, examines the reasons for the prevalence of sharecropping and draws attention to the implications of the rising agricultural productivity of the advanced economies. The main features of advanced countries are described in Chapter 4, with the emphasis upon fix price markets, while Chapter 5 examines the interactions between advanced and less developed countries, beginning with a reconsideration of the Prebisch—Singer thesis on the alleged deterioration of the terms of trade of developing countries and asking whether there is a technological gap between the advanced countries.

We move on to a more detailed analysis of the post-war economy in Chapter 6, looking at the experiences of individual countries and regions. In their studies of 'long waves' Lewis (1978) and Rostow (1978) emphasised the importance of movements in raw material prices; this chapter therefore analyses the factors responsible for changes in oil prices and this leads on, in Chapter 7, to an examination of the impact of those changes upon Japan, which has few natural resources. Chapter 7 also considers the factors involved in the emergence of the newly industrialising countries of South-east Asia and asks whether trade is an engine of growth. But Japan's success may have been due to the policies of its largest trading partner, the United States, and Chapter 8 looks at supply-side economics, Reaganomics and the rise and fall of the dollar. Despite the rise in oil prices the US economy managed to create some 10 million jobs during the 1970s, while

Western Europe lost an equivalent number. Chapter 9 therefore analyses the workings of the European Community and contrasts its performance with that of the United States as well as non-European non-members, such as Sweden, Austria and Switzerland; the impact of the Common Agricultural Policy upon the less developed countries is also discussed. In the nineteenth century the areas of white settlement, Australia, Canada and Argentina, enjoyed high standards of living; Chapter 10 concentrates upon the changing fortunes of Australia and Canada and points to the similarities between the Australian experience and that of some less developed countries. The centrally planned economies of Eastern Europe, their failure to gain parity with the advanced market economies and their search for methods of introducing acceptable market socialism, are the subject of Chapter 11. China has attempted to follow a different path to development from that pursued by the East European countries and Chapter 12 outlines the various Chinese strategies and compares them with those adopted by India. In Chapter 13 attention is focused on Latin America, dependency theory, hyper-inflation and debt and it concludes with a comparison of the economic performance of the large Latin American economies and the newly industrialising countries of South-east Asia. In Chapter 14 we turn to Africa, comparing the prevalence of famine there with its relative absence in Latin America and Asia. The weaknesses of African agriculture are then considered and the policies of some African states are analysed. Finally we draw the various strands together, and ask whether we have advanced our understanding of economic development since Lewis wrote *A Theory of Economic Growth* (1955).

But to set the scene we need to describe the main features of the world economy as it emerged from the Second World War, and identify some of the forces that have been operating on it over the last forty years. We shall attempt to relate that discussion to an analysis of the 'long waves' of economic growth and development since the Industrial Revolution.

The International Economy

At the end of the Second World War the international economy split along ideological lines into a core of advanced market economies surrounded by a periphery of less developed countries, and a core of centrally planned economies with their own associated periphery. Through the 1950s and 1960s the core of advanced countries (previously the United States, Western Europe and the former white colonies of Australia, Canada, South Africa and New Zealand) was enlarged by the inclusion of Japan. From a pre-war situation of 'socialism in one country' — the USSR — the sphere of the planned economy was extended to most of the countries of Eastern Europe — Poland, Hungary, Czechoslovakia, Romania, Bulgaria, Albania and the Baltic states Estonia, Latvia and Lithuania, as well as a portion of Finnish Karelia. The periphery of less developed but centrally planned economies came to include China, Cuba, Vietnam and Angola with the rest of the world forming a penumbra of less developed market economies.

Simple classifications are useful, but they fail to capture political reality:

Yugoslavia, for instance, occupies an intermediate position between the market and the planned economies. In the 1950s many developing countries, with differing political and economic systems, attempted to distance themselves from the superpower Cold War by forming an alliance of Third World countries — the Non-Aligned Movement. But these countries were united only in opposition; their economic systems, to take only one example, placed different degrees of emphasis upon planning and the price mechanism. To illustrate the complexity further, most advanced countries are mixed economies within which planning and the market complement each other. Within the less developed countries the prescriptive Marxian stages of evolution through feudalism, capitalism and socialism were challenged by politicians who saw capitalism and socialism as alternatives, not a necessary sequence. China and Cuba chose socialist routes, India and South Korea capitalist, although they also saw some virtue in planning. Trade was the link between these heterogeneous systems (although trade between the market and centrally planned blocs only started to become significant in the 1970s).

The Structure of Trade

Trade between the developed countries declined from 70 per cent of all trade in 1970 to 64.4 per cent in 1983 under the impact of the oil price rises and the need to export more to the OPEC countries. But it rose to 74.5 per cent between 1984 and 1986. Oil producers export some 68 per cent of their total output to the advanced countries. Only the planned economies attempted at first to insulate themselves from the advanced market economies, although the 1970s and 1980s have seen an increasing openness.

Developed countries tend to trade with each other and a large part of their trade is, in fact, intra-industry trade. Germans sell cars to Italians and Italians sell cars to Germans. Different countries may specialise in producing different components for the same car — a form of international division of labour by the manufacturers. There have, however, been significant changes in the importance of manufacturing in the core countries in the 1960s and 1970s. As Table 1.2 shows, manufacturing in the United States and the United Kingdom has declined, while impressive increases have occurred in West Germany and Japan. The importance of primary products in the exports of the less developed countries has been falling. The relative importance of manufactures in less developed countries is still low, as Tables 1.3 and 1.4 indicate; but much of their industrial capacity is already in medium technology industries, such as cars and electrical engineering.

Armaments

The framework of international trade depends on political stability and political stability has been assumed to depend on defence spending — which, paradoxically, has tended to undermine political stability. Figure 1.2 shows military expenditure since the end of World War 2. According to the Institute of Strategic Studies

Table 1.1 Patterns of Trade Among Developed, Less Developed and Planned Economies (Average Annual Value of Exports 1984−86, Milliards of Dollars)

	World	Developed economies	OPEC	Other less developed economies	Planned economies Eastern Europe	Asia
World						
$	1,991.4					
%	100.0	67.1	7.4	15.5	7.8	1.9
Developed economies						
$	1,324.7					
%		74.5	5.3	14.3	2.7	1.6
OPEC						
$	147.7					
%		64.1	2.9	29.6	2.0	0.1
Other less developed economies						
$	310.6					
%		63.0	6.0	20.0	5.5	3.2
Planned economies Eastern Europe						
$	177.9					
%		25.5	2.7	11.3	53.7	3.3
Asia						
$	30.6					
%		39.5	2.2	41.5	11.8	

Source: UNCTAD (1987)
Note: Detail does not add to total due to errors and omissions in underlying data.

Table 1.2 The Changing Patterns of Manufacturing within the Core, 1963−81

	Share of world manufacturing output (%)	
	1963	*1981*
United States	40.3	29,4
West Germany	9.7	12.4
United Kingdom	6.5	3.8
France	6.3	7.0
Japan	5.5	15.7
Italy	3.5	4.5
Canada	3.0	2.4

Sources: OECD (1979), World Bank (1983)

Table 1.3 Manufacturing in the Periphery, 1970−80

	Share of world manufacturing output (%)	
	1970	1980
Low income countries	1.6	1.7
Middle income countries	10.9	13.4
Capital-surplus countries	0.2	0.3
Total share	12.8	15.3

Source: World Bank (1983)

Table 1.4 The Growth of Manufacturing Output in the Leading Newly Industrialising Countries, 1963−81

	Share of world manufacturing output (%)	
	1963	1981
Hong Kong	0.08	0.27
Singapore	0.05	0.16
South Korea	0.11	0.22
Taiwan	0.11	0.23
Brazil	1.57	3.01
Mexico	1.04	1.95
Spain	0.88	2.24
Portugal	0.23	0.40
Greece	0.19	0.31
Yugoslavia	1.14	0.89
Total of the above	5.40	10.54

Sources: OECD (1979), World Bank (1983)

(1986) the two superpowers are responsible for between 55 and 60 per cent of all global defence spending, with the USA accounting for 30 per cent and the USSR for about 25 per cent. If spending by NATO and the Warsaw Pact countries is included the total spending rises to between 75 and 80 per cent. The Middle East accounts for a further 9.5 per cent and China for between 5 and 6 per cent; the Far Eastern countries are responsible for another 5 per cent, Latin America for 2.5 per cent and Sub-Saharan Africa (mainly South Africa, Ethiopia and Nigeria) spends about 1.5 per cent.

Since the 1960s Third World countries have been the world's most important buyers of conventional weapons and have accounted for about three-quarters of

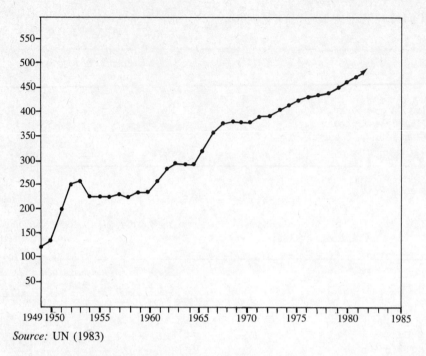

Source: UN (1983)

Figure 1.2   World Military Expenditure, 1949−82 (US $ billion in constant (1978) prices and exchange rates)

trade in them. Third World spending reached a peak of $43.6 billion in 1982 and then fell to $28.2 billion in 1983 as a result of the world slump and the saturation caused by heavy spending in the 1970s. There has been a shift away from spending on high-tech weapons such as planes and tanks and rockets to small arms for counter-insurgency operations. The arms trade between the North and the South has been influenced by the emergence of Third World arms producers such as Brazil, Taiwan and India.

Transnational Corporations

Trade flows in goods and services have been influenced by changes in communications. The post-war period has witnessed a rise in the importance of transnational corporations. In the nineteenth century transnational corporations were involved mainly in the extractive industries and in agricultural commodities; financial flows tended to pass through specialist finance houses. In the post-war period multinational corporations have become important in manufacturing (especially cars and electronics as is indicated by Table 1.5) and even in banking (Table 1.6) and tourism (Table 1.7).

Table 1.5 Leading Transnational Corporations in Manufacturing, 1980

Corporation	Country of origin	Total sales ($ million)	Foreign content as a percentage of	
			Assets	Employment
General Motors	United States	57,728	12	31
Ford Motor Co	United States	37,086	40	58
IBM	United States	26,213	46	43
General Electric	United States	25,523	28	29
Unilever	UK/Netherlands	24,161	36	48
ITT	United States	23,819	33	53
Renault	France	18,958	..	24
Phillips	Netherlands	18,377	26	79
Volkswagen	West Germany	18,313	..	38
Siemens	West Germany	17,583	..	32

Source: UNCTNC (1983)

Table 1.6 Leading Transnational Banks, 1975

	Home country	Total assets ($ billion)	Foreign assets	
			Developed countries	Developing countries
Bank America	United States	94.9	85	174
Citicorp	United States	87.1	67	167
Deutsche Bank	West Germany	80.3	28	37
Banque Nationale de Paris	France	78.2	37	60
Crédit Lyonnais	France	74.1	26	38
Société Générale	France	66.9	29	32
Dai-Ichi Kangyo	Japan	73.3	17	16
Dresdner Bank	West Germany	61.6	29	37
Chase Manhattan	United States	61.2	59	128
Fuji Bank	Japan	61.2	17	19
Sumitomo	Japan	63.6	18	13
Mitsubishi	Japan	62.7	16	16

Source: UNCTNC (1981)

Several explanations have been put forward to account for the rise of transnational corporations. One runs in terms of product cycles. New inventions occur
in the advanced countries and are initially produced there. But high labour costs
lead to a search for cheaper centres of production. This need not mean that firms
set up factories in low wage cost countries: they could lease the manufacturing
rights to indigenous firms. However, the problems of ensuring a return on R&D

Table 1.7 The Ten Major Transnational Hotel Chains, 1978

Corporation	Home country	Number of transnational associated hotels abroad in		
		Developed countries	Developing countries	Total
Holiday Inn[a]	USA	67	47	114
Inter-Continental	USA	28	46	74
Hilton International	USA	33	39	72
Sheraton Hotels	USA	34	30	64
Club Méditerranée	France	30	26	56
Trust House Forte	UK	37	16	53
Novotel	France	27	18	45
Travelodge[b]	UK	31	3	34
Ramada Inns	USA	25	8	33
Hyatt International	USA	6	20	26

Source: UNCTNC (1982)
Notes: (a) Excludes Canadian hotels of Commonwealth Holiday Inn.
(b) Owned by Trust House Forte (UK).

and the need to maintain quality control and promote sales can lead to firms deciding to control production directly by building their own plant abroad. This shift to direct foreign investment has been encouraged by the tariff barriers that have arisen from customs unions and the political independence of many developing countries.

Labour Migration

Goods move and resources move. The post-war period has seen enormous flows of labour between countries. The 1986 *Report of the US Council of Economic Advisors* revealed that some 500,000 people emigrate to the United States annually. Although not as large as the nineteenth-century migrations, this annual influx has enhanced the labour force. There has been a notable change of origin, with about half the migrants coming from Asia in the 1960s. As Tables 1.8 to 1.10 indicate, there have been substantial flows of labour into Western Europe from Southern Europe and North Africa, into Argentina from Bolivia, Chile and Paraguay and into Venezuela from Colombia. The Arab oil states have received labour inflows from surrounding states. Labour migration has not only increased output in the host countries but also provided, through remittances, an important flow of income into the source countries (Table 1.11).

Labour migration may be classified as (i) legal or illegal; (ii) skilled or unskilled; and (iii) permanent or temporary. The distinctions have a bearing upon the question of who benefits from migration. Illegal immigrants do not enter into the tax base of the host country except through the payment of expenditure taxes;

Table 1.8 Selected West European Countries: Recorded Number of Migrant Workers, 1980 (000)

Out-migration country	In-migration country					
	Belgium	France	West Germany	Netherlands	Switzerland	UK
Algeria	3.2	322.7	1.6	—	—	—
France	38.5		54.0	2.0		14.0
Greece	10.8	3.0	138.4	1.2		6.0
Italy	90.5	146.4	324.3	12.0	301.0	73.0
Morocco	37.3	116.1	16.6	33.7	—	—
Portugal	6.3	430.6	59.9	4.2	—	5.0
Spain	32.0	157.7	89.3	10.4	85.7	17.0
Tunisia	4.7	65.3	—	1.1	—	—
Turkey	23.0	20.6	623.9	53.2	20.1	4.0
Yugoslavia	3.1	32.2	367.0	6.6	62.5	5.0
Other	83.2	192.4	490.1	70.2	237.0	804.0
Total	309.6	1,487.0	2,165.1	194.6	706.3	928.0

Source: ILO (1985)

Table 1.9 South American Region: Estimated Number of Migrant Workers in 1974 (000)

Out-migration country	In-migration country					
	Argentina	Brazil	Chile	Colombia	Peru	Venezuela
Argentina			3		25	20
Bolivia	500	45	70	4	60	10
Brazil	70			5	5	20
Chile	250			5	10	20
Colombia			7		5	605
Ecuador			8	60	20	20
Paraguay	470	70				
Peru			40	4		20
Uruguay	80	3				
Venezuela			5	33		
Other		22	2	9	20	40
Total	1,370	140	135	120	50	755

Source: ILO (1985)

skilled emigrants may deprive the source country of a return on public invest-ment in health and education. Temporary migrants — guest workers — may solve the problem of how to cope with fluctuations in economic activity and return migra-tion may be an alternative to dumping goods on foreign markets or dumping a country's own nationals into unemployment.

Table 1.10   Arab Region: Estimated Number of Migrant Workers in 1980 (000)

Out-migration country	In-migration country					
	Iraq	Kuwait	Libya	Oman	Saudi Arabia	All countries
Democratic Yemen		9.5		0.12	6.5	83.845
Egypt	100.0	85.0	250.0	6.3	155.1	695.65
India	2.0	45.0	32.0	35.6	29.7	280.0
Iraq		40.0			3.25	44.76
Jordan (in Palestine)	7.5	55.0	1.5	2.25	140.0	250.35
Lebanon	4.5	8.0	5.7	1.5	33.2	61.05
Oman		2.0			10.0	33.45
Pakistan	26.16	34.0	65.0	44.5	29.7	371.63
Somalia		0.5	5.0	0.4	8.3	19.7
Sudan	0.5	5.5	21.0	0.62	55.6	89.22
Syrian Arab Republic		35.0	15.0	0.6	24.6	83.15
Yemen		3.0		0.12	325.0	336.145
Other Arab		0.3	65.6	0.12	0.5	66.52
Other Asian	1.5	10.0	27.0		93.5	168.5
Other	2.0	45.9	44.2	4.67	49.8	237.3
Total	125.0	378.0	545.0	96.8	1,023.25	2,821.72

Source: ILO (1985)

Table 1.11   Flow of Workers' Remittances and its Share in Total Exports and Imports of Goods in Selected Labour Exporting Countries, 1977

	% exports	% imports
Algeria	4	3
Bangaldesh	18	9
Egypt	66	27
India	22	20
Jordan	186	38
Morocco	44	18
Pakistan	88	40
Syria	9	7
Tunisia	16	8
Turkey	56	17
Yemen Arab Republic	5,449	139
Yemen PDR	352	49

Source: Russell (1986)

Bretton Woods and the Post-war International Economic Order

The pattern of trade and investment has been strongly influenced by the institutional financial framework created at the end of the Second World War. The long and severe depression of the 1930s had caused many countries to pursue beggar my neighbour policies, with high tariffs and competitive devaluations. The result was a contraction of world trade and a reversion to self-sufficiency and bilateral deals. In response, in a rejection of protectionism — seen as one of the causes of the Second World War — a new international trade and financial regime was established in 1944 at Bretton Woods, New Hampshire. This established (i) an International Monetary Fund (IMF) whose tasks were to stabilise exchange rates and to supply short-term credit to member countries to finance balance of payments problems; (ii) a General Agreement on Tariffs and Trade (GATT) which sought to remove obstacles to trade; and (iii) an International Bank for Reconstruction and Development (known as the World Bank), whose tasks included the provision of assistance to developing countries. Domestically, the advanced countries were supposed to regulate aggregate money demand to avoid inflation and unemployment; internationally, they were to adhere to IMF pronouncements on exchange rate adjustments, reduce trade barriers and avoid balance of payments surpluses/deficits.

The Bretton Woods system collapsed in the early 1970s. It had been coming under strain since the mid-1960s when GATT instituted the so-called Kennedy round of tariff reductions which enabled the developing countries to gain greater access to the markets of the advanced countries. The re-emergence of West Germany and Japan created tension between the major trading countries. And, finally, there was the 'American problem'. At the end of the nineteenth century the United States was visibly a great power, but was concentrating its efforts upon the exploitation of its own hinterland. After its involvement in the First World War it had retreated into splendid isolation. But the Second World War led to the USA taking on extensive world commitments. There were no other contenders for its role: Europe's per capita income was about a half that of the USA and the USSR's about a quarter. The war had led to the emergence of two super-powers and the eclipse of Britain's sea power and colonial empire.

But in the 1950s and 1960s the US advantage was gradually eroded by the slow growth of its national income and the growing strength of other countries. US aid and currency devaluations in the 1940s and 1950s enabled Europe and Japan to recover. Then the expense of US involvement in Vietnam and the civil rights programme to combat poverty and discrimination led to financial strains which were exacerbated by printing money. These inflationary pressures on the United States were transmitted to the rest of the world; in Europe they were further fuelled by an increase in public sector spending. In the 1970s the United States could no longer sustain the role of the world's banker and the dollar was unhitched from the gold standard and devalued. The rest of the world's currencies followed suit and a floating exchange rate regime ensued.

The Third World

If the events of the 1970s raised doubts about past and future policies in the advanced countries, there were even more acute misgivings in the less developed countries (in what has come to be called the Third World, as opposed to the First

World of advanced countries and the Second World of the centrally planned economies). The end of the Second World War had seen the collapse of the colonial empires of Britain, the Netherlands and France. But the disappearance of the empires did not mean the end of dependency. Few of the newly independent countries seemed able to take off into self-sustained growth, despite the long boom of the 1950s and 1960s; the absence of any mass advancement of the less developed countries raises questions about the relationship of the economic development in the nineteenth and early twentieth century with the long booms of those earlier periods. What were the factors responsible for Europe's 'take off' in the nineteenth century? Has any country ever 'taken off' on the basis of free trade or have the early stages of industrialisation always required a policy of protectionism? To answer these and other questions we need to return to 'long waves' and the evidence for them in the post-war period.

Cycles and Long Waves

Economists have attempted to identify patterns in the fluctuations of economic activity according to their periodicity and causation: these are called 'cycles' and 'long waves'. We will now look at the most important of these.

Kitchin Cycles

These are fluctuations in inventories (stock holding) and have a periodicity of about four years. In the 1950s and 1960s they attracted a great deal of attention. In Britain they were identified with the so-called 'stop go' cycles and with political activity. It was alleged that before elections governments would boost demand in order to influence voting behaviour. The result would be a pre-election boom which would suck in imports, increase inventories and lead to a balance of payments crisis. After the election a deflationary policy would be pursued, imports would fall and stocks would return to normal levels.

Juglar Cycles

The Juglar cycle is a cycle in fixed capital formation and was the classic nineteenth-century trade cycle which was perceived to dominate British economic activity in the first three-quarters of the nineteenth century; it had a periodicity of about ten years and was associated with credit crises. An expansion of demand due, say, to a rise in exports or an invention would be financed by an increase in trade credit. Overexpansion of credit would then lead to a fall in the reserves of the commercial banks and the Bank of England would attempt to protect the fragile financial system by raising interest rates. The rise in interest rates would then choke off the boom, bankruptcies might occur and equilibrium would eventually be restored. The instability of credit provoked controversies over the appropriate method of controlling the money supply (discussed further in Chapter 4).

Between 1870 and 1914 the peaks of Juglar cycles could be observed in 1872, 1882, 1889, 1906 and 1907; but in Britain these were less pronounced than those of previous years. From the 1880s onwards the British problem seems to have been one of prolonged depression, stemming from international competition and rising protectionism. Booms were weak and attention was directed at possible causes, such as the lack of profitable investment opportunities. The inter-war years also presented a complicated picture; but the notion that booms and slumps were due to real, as opposed to financial, factors persisted, despite Hayek's attempts (1932) to explain the ending of booms in terms of credit squeezes.

After the Second World War the theory of cycles became more firmly based upon the interaction of the multiplier and the accelerator (Samuelson 1939) and the presence of a full employment ceiling, as elaborated by Hicks (1950). A rise in, for example, government spending would lead via the multiplier to a general expansion of incomes and hence of consumer spending. The rise in spending would induce an increase in investment (the accelerator effect) and the rise in investment would then lead to an increase in incomes which would in turn be spent (the interaction effect).

Two questions then arise. First, does a boom create full employment? Second, is it possible to maintain that full employment? The answer to the first question depends upon the strength or weakness of the multiplier and accelerator effects. If they are weak then weak booms will result, and vice versa. But even a strong boom will not enable an economy to stay at the full employment ceiling. This ceiling is dictated by the size of the labour force. When the boom hits this ceiling further investment is constrained and therefore declines. The multiplier effect of falling incomes then carries the economy down to a floor set by autonomous investment. An economy may never reach full employment if there is a credit squeeze which chokes off a boom (a monetary ceiling) or if the real forces embodied in the multiplier and accelerator are weak.

The theory of Juglar cycles needs considerable qualification to fit the observed data since 1945. In the post-war period economies were more stable than the theory predicted; they were able to maintain full employment for at least two decades. It was not until the 1970s that a decline in fixed investment occurred. The long boom of the 1950s and 1960s suggests that it is possible by skilful demand management — or luck — to stay at the ceiling. After the First World War monetary controls were scrapped, creating an immediate violent boom, which was followed by collapse. After the Second World War the controls stayed in place until the mid-1950s and there seems to have been a gradual movement on to a stable growth path. There was a monetary ceiling but it was more flexible than the old gold standard; there was much more information available for investors to use to plan decisions. Political cycles did exist; but in so far as there was a ceiling it was controllable by governments. But it is arguable that government policies influenced

growth rates rather than cycles. In the end the boom was merely delayed: it was
ended by a new ceiling — in raw materials.

This brings us on to a consideration of longer cycles (or waves). In Hicks's
view (1977) autonomous investment has a beneficial effect upon an economy.
But what if autonomous investment fluctuates independently? (Autonomous investment is not geared to immediate profit prospects.) And what if population cycles
or variations in the availability of raw materials or technological progress are
also fluctuating and creating differing ceiling constraints at different times? What
if the growth that is actually observed is the result of countries pursuing a variety
of heterogeneous growth paths which interact? In other words, does the theory
of 'long waves' impose a regularity on the data which does not stand up to close
inspection? We will try to find some answers by looking at two longer cycles
— the Kuznets and the Kondratieff.

Kuznets Cycles

Kuznets cycles were first postulated when it was recognised that alternate
nineteenth-century US Juglar cycles were particularly severe. Similar severe recessions were then identified in Britain, France and Germany, although the timing
of the peaks and troughs differed from country to country. Kuznets cycles appeared to be associated with swings in construction activity (railways, roads,
housing). The construction boom accounted for the relative mildness of the
coincident Juglar recession while the subsequent Kuznets slump accentuated the
coincident Juglar downturn. US Kuznets cycles alternated with those in Western
Europe in the nineteenth century. O'Leary and Lewis (1955) have suggested that
the lack of synchronisation may have been an effect of the Napoleonic Wars which
had temporarily detached American economic development from that of Europe.
However, they also went on to note that the Second World War disrupted the
pattern and caused all economies to enter a construction boom in the 1950s. Brinley
Thomas (1954) has linked these alternations in US and European construction
to movements of labour and capital from Europe to the USA. In the USA the
boom would cause a rise in interest rates which would depress investment in
Europe and create a flow of resources and people across the Atlantic. When the
US boom petered out interest rates would fall and a boom would then begin in
Europe. Easterlin (1968) has traced links between marriage and birth rates and
changes in construction activity and earlier writers, such as Robertson (1915),
have linked construction activity with the expansion of the American frontier.

Kondratieff Waves

The Kondratieff long wave was first detected in a time series of prices, not production. Kondratieff (1925/1979) claimed to have found two and a half cycles

between 1780 and 1920 (1789—1849, 1849—96 and 1896—1920). Kondratieff noted that the turning points of the waves did not always coincide in all countries and he suggested as possible causes: (i) technological change; (ii) wars and revolutions; (iii) the opening up of new countries to the world economy; and (iv) gold discoveries. He also postulated a more general theory that monetary disturbances lead to investment booms and slumps: monetary overinvestment increases the money supply, permitting increases in investment which then have to be checked by a rise in interest rates. Subsequent writers, such as Rostow (1978, 1980) have attempted to bring the chronology up to date by identifying cycles for 1890—1933 and 1933—70. Figure 1.3 presents a stylised picture of long waves based upon movements of the US wholesale price index. Table 1.12 draws attention to the links between long waves in industrial production in the advanced countries and variations in the volume of world trade. Although based upon a non-random sample Table 1.13 attempts to shed some light upon Kondratieff's conjecture of a link between long waves and the opening up of new territories to the world economy by suggesting that most countries take off on the upswings of long waves. Table 1.14 also suggests a possible link between the upswings of long waves when, as Kondratieff inferred, the scramble for markets and the rise in raw material prices was likely to bring countries into conflict, and wars.

Kondratieff's thesis about technological progress was elaborated by Schumpeter (1939) who suggested that long waves might derive from the clustering of innovations. The first long wave could be attributed to the impact of inventions in textiles, the second to the coming of the railways and the third to the emergence of the chemical and electrical engineering industries. More recently, Mensch *et al.* (1984) have examined the pattern of innovation clusters and Freeman *et al.* (1982) have looked at the innovations which have dominated the post-war boom. Perez (1985) has suggested that long waves are associated with changes in the institutional framework of economic activity; for example, the Bretton Woods regime was essential to the development of the post-war boom because it permitted an expansion of trade.

In Hicks's theory of the trade cycle autonomous investment plays a role similar to that assumed in long waves. In Lewis's work on growth and fluctuations in the nineteenth century a rise in raw material prices provided a check to the growth of the advanced countries in the 1880s; Rostow elaborated this theme by indicating the links between economic development in the periphery: the rise in raw material prices would cause a check to expansion in the advanced countries and result in increased investment in the periphery. And as we noted above, earlier writers such as Robertson (1915) emphasised the role of the frontier of development in determining economic activity in Europe.

But what is the nature of the evidence for long waves? Two or three scattered observations do not add up to satisfactory proof of their existence. Kondratieff's thesis was challenged at the outset by Soviet writers who disputed his methodology and its apparently capitalist apologetics which suggested that the collapse of capitalism was far from inevitable, downswings being merely part of long waves

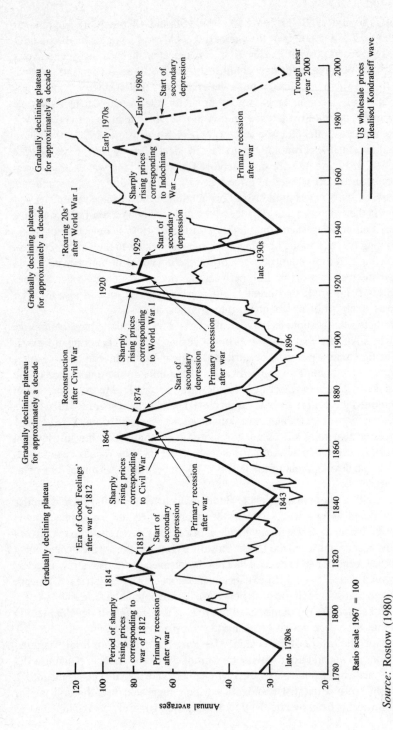

Figure 1.3   The Kondratieff Wave

Source: Rostow (1980)

Table 1.12 World Trade and Industrial Production, Selected Industrial Countries, 1820−1980 (average annual percentage rates of growth)

Period	World trade volume	UK	Industrial production Germany[a]	France[b]	USA
1820−40	2.1	3.2	. . .	. . .	. . .
1840−70	3.5	4.6	4.5	. . .	5.4
1870−90	2.2	1.2	2.5	. . .	4.9
1890−1913	3.7	2.2	4.2	3.9[c]	5.9
1913−38	0.4	2.0	2.2	0.9	2.0
1938−48	. . .	2.2	5.8	0.8	7.4
1948−71	7.3	3.1	8.4	6.0	4.0
1971−80	5.8[c]	1.0	2.0	2.4	3.0

Source: UNCTAD (1981)
Notes: (a) In the boundaries of the period considered. From 1948 refers to the Federal Republic of Germany only.
   (b) 1901−13.
   (c) Excluding the trade of the socialist countries.

(Garvey 1943). The Kondratieff long wave is essentially derived from data on the *world* economy: this inevitably raises questions about the existence of such waves in individual countries and about the methodology of aggregating times series from different countries each of which may be at a different stage of economic development. To identify his long wave Kondratieff fitted a trend by ordinary least squares and then used a nine-year moving average to eliminate the Juglar cycle. Now Slutsky (1937) had demonstrated much earlier that the application of a moving average to random numbers will generate a cycle where none had previously existed and that when applied to cyclic data would generate a longer cycle. (A similar criticism of some of Kuznets's techniques had been advanced by Howrey (1968).)

In attempting to resolve the arguments of the previous paragraph Solomou (1986, 1987) has reappraised the evidence for the world economy and for the advanced countries for the period 1850 to 1973. He concludes that for the classic period of capitalist development, running from c.1850 to 1913, the Kuznets cycle could indeed be observed in the world economy, but the Kondratieff wave could not. After 1892 there was a distinct acceleration in the world growth rate as compared with the period 1872−92; but this upswing in growth after 1892 does not follow a Kondratieff downswing in the period 1872−92.

In the inter-war years the world economy failed to maintain its pre-1913 long-run growth path. There was some catching up in the period 1924−29 but the overall trend for 1913−29 failed to match the prewar trend. In the period 1929−37 the downswing in the world economy was strongly influenced by the fortunes of dominant economy, the United States. The most important features of the inter-war period stemmed from the first World War which ended previously alternating patterns of home and overseas investment and increased the influence of the US

Table 1.13 Approximate Timing of Turning Points and Take-Off of Leading Sectors in Various Countries, 1870–1970

	Turning point	*Industrial take-off*
First Kondratieff upswing 1780–20		Great Britain
First downswing 1820–40	Chile	USA, France, Belgium
Second upswing 1840–70	Brazil, Malaysia, Thailand Argentina	Germany, Sweden, Norway, Denmark
Second downswing 1870–90	Burma, Mexico, Algeria Japan, Peru, Sri Lanka Colombia	Japan
Third upswing 1890–1920	Taiwan, Ghana, Ivory Coast Nigeria, Kenya, Uganda, Zimbabwe, Tanzania, Philippines, Cuba, Korea	Russia, Italy, Canada, Australia
Third downswing 1920–33	Morocco, Venezuela, Zambia	
Fourth upswing 1933–70	India, Pakistan, China, Iran, Iraq, Turkey, Egypt, Indonesia, Afghanistan Bangladesh, Ethiopia, Mozambique, Nepal, Sudan, Zaire	Argentina, Brazil, Mexico, Turkey, India, China, Taiwan, Thailand, South Korea

Sources: Reynolds (1983), Rostow (1978)

economy. After the Second World War a prolonged boom stemmed from the dominant position of the United States, the catching up process in Europe and Japan and favourable raw material prices.

Solomou rejects the Kondratieff wave in favour of a historical analysis of specific periods. This takes us back to the second question we posed at the beginning of this chapter: why did some countries enter the world economy in particular periods and others fail to do so? Kennedy (1988) analyses periods in terms of the rise and fall of great powers. Thus, Britain's hegemony extended from 1815 to 1885. Between 1885 and 1942 a bipolar world began to emerge as Britain's power (based upon maritime strength) gave way to the rise of the continental powers. After 1942 (the Battle of Stalingrad and the entry of the United States into the Second World War) there began a period of political domination by the USA and the USSR. Towards the end of the 1970s this bipolar world began to change after the rise of Japan, the emergence of China and attempts to reconstitute Europe as the EEC. But a strong case can be made for partitioning history into shorter

Table 1.14 Long Waves and Wars

First Kondratieff upswing	French wars 1788−92
First downswing	
1820−40	No substantial wars
Second upswing	
1840−70	Crimean War 1854
	Indian Mutiny 1857−58
	American Civil War
	Three Prussian campaigns
	Taiping Rebellion
Second downswing	
1870−90	Relative peace
Third upswing	
1890−1920	Boer War,
	Spanish-American War
	Balkan conflicts
	Russo−Japanese War
	First World War
Third Downswing	
1920−33	Relative peace
Fourth upswing	
1933−51	Spanish Civil War
	Sino−Japanese War
	Italian campaign in Ethiopia
	Second World War
	Korean War, Malaysia

Source: Rostow (1978)

periods: this allows for a more detailed consideration of successful and unsuccessful developments and for those institutional changes (neglected by Solomou but stressed by Perez) which had a decisive effect upon shaping the evolution of the world economy and which accounted for the differential growth rates (stressed by Solomou) which shaped variations in the overall growth rate of the world economy. We shall therefore retain the traditional Kondratieff partition of history (while remaining sceptical about long waves) in order to bring out the factors operating in specific historical periods.

The First Long Wave 1780−1848

The Upswing 1780−1815.   This period was dominated by Britain's industrial revolution and rising population, as well as by the French wars. The antecedents of Britain's early start were previous centuries of political stability and agricultural improvement. The defeats of the Dutch and Spanish navies had provided Britain with access to overseas territories and this naval supremacy was reinforced by the defeat of the French naval and land forces. Alongside these long-run developments were changes in the industrial structure of the economy. Crafts (1985) has observed that there was a considerable shift of population out of agriculture and into the towns as early as the seventeenth century. Agricultural improvements helped to offset some food shortages, but food was also imported from Eastern Europe. However, the French wars tended to restrict the movement of ships in the Baltic and real wages were checked by food shortages and consequent price increases. The factory system was extended to incorporate technical innovations and the growth in the demand for textiles. But the favourable effects of the industrial revolution were reduced by the considerable borrowing required to finance the war. Elsewhere in Europe the impetus to industrialisation was delayed until well after the French Revolution had abolished serfdom and created free labour markets — a process that was to be repeated in various countries, ending with the abolition of serfdom in Russia in the 1860s. In America the dislocation of trade by the French wars provided a boost to local industries.

The Downswing 1815—48. The coming of peace in 1815 produced a significant change in the institutional framework of industry and trade. The Congress of Vienna has been regarded as an attempt to restore the *status quo ante* in Europe. Its implementation and enforcement did signal an attempted return to the *ancien régime*; but its real importance lay in the fact that it enabled market forces to effect a peaceful conquest of Europe with new technologies and thereby undermined the social and political fabric. In Britain there were two railway booms in the 1830s and 1840s. In Prussia and Russia there was an emphasis upon road building. In France there was a systematic extension of the canal system which was so thorough that it probably delayed the development of the railways.

There were nationalist stirrings in the 1820s and in the 1830s and revolts against the rigidities imposed by conservative policies adopted in 1815. In the Netherlands a successful revolt against the Dutch created Belgium. In France, Switzerland, the Italian States, Poland and Portugal there were uprisings. In Britain public pressure won a Reform Act, although this was accompanied by stern measures against Chartism. The effect of these rumblings was to create a new alignment in Europe between the conservative German and Italian states, Poland and Austro-Hungary, where the diktat was imposed by Prussia and Russia, and the new liberalism in Belgium, Switzerland and France which was influenced by developments in Britain. The Rhine came to mark a political division in Europe.

In 1848 there were further disturbances. Rapidly increasing populations put food supplies under pressure and crop failures provoked unrest in Austro-Hungary, France and the Italian and German states. In France the ideas of 1798 enjoyed a revival. In Ireland there was famine. But at either end of Europe, in Britain and Russia, there was apparent political stability.

Tables 1.15 and 1.16 reveal the large gap that opened up between Britain and the rest of the world in the late eighteenth and nineteenth centuries. According to Bairoch's tantalising estimates the Third World was responsible for three-quarters of the world's manufacturing output in 1780; by 1900 this figure had

Table 1.15 Relative Shares of World Manufacturing Output, 1750–1900

	1750	1800	1830	1860	1880	1900
Europe	23.2	28.1	34.2	53.2	61.3	62.0
United Kingdom	1.9	4.3	9.5	19.9	22.9	18.5
Habsburg Empire	2.9	3.2	3.2	4.2	4.4	4.7
France	4.0	4.2	5.2	7.9	7.8	6.8
German states (Germany)	2.9	3.5	3.5	4.9	8.5	13.2
Italian states (Italy)	2.4	2.5	2.3	2.5	2.5	2.5
Russia	5.0	5.6	5.6	7.0	7.6	8.8
Unites States	0.1	0.8	2.4	7.2	14.7	23.6
Japan	3.8	3.5	2.8	2.6	2.4	2.4
Third World	73.0	67.7	60.5	36.6	20.9	11.0
China	32.8	33.3	29.8	19.7	12.5	6.2
India/Pakistan	24.5	19.7	17.6	8.6	2.8	1.7

Sources: Bairoch (1982), Maddison (1983)

Table 1.16 Per Capita Levels of Industrialisation, 1750–1900 (relative to UK in 1900)

	1750	1800	1830	1860	1880	1900
Europe	8	8	11	16	24	35
United Kingdom	10	16	25	64	87	100
Habsburg Empire	7	7	8	11	15	23
France	9	9	12	20	28	39
German states (Germany)	8	8	9	15	25	52
Italian states (Italy)	8	8	8	10	12	17
Russia	6	6	7	8	10	15
United States	4	9	14	21	38	69
Japan	7	7	7	7	9	12
Third World	7	6	6	4	3	2
China	8	6	6	4	4	3
India/Pakistan	7	6	6	3	2	1

Source: Bairoch (1982)

fallen to 11 per cent. On a per capita basis there was only a small gap between Britain and the Third World in 1780; by 1900 the gap had grown alarmingly. And the gap between Britain and the rest of continental Europe was no less significant. Bairoch's estimates raise two questions. First, was the whole of the gap attributable, as he infers, to industrialisation or should some of the rising gap be attributable to colonisation and plunder? And was the large gap observable before 1780 not itself the result of colonisation and plunder? This issue must remain unresolved because of the difficulties of obtaining reliable data for the pre-industrial period (although Maddison has made some tentative explorations). Second, why did so few countries join Britain in industrial development in the peaceful period after Waterloo? To answer this we must look at individual countries.

In France the Revolution and the wars had complex effects. The new legal framework put in place by Napoleon might have been conducive to free enterprise; but its main effect was to give land to the peasants and increase the weight of forces against industrialisation. France failed to develop mass markets for manufactures and continued to cater for elites who demanded *objets d'art* rather than standardised products. The wars had destroyed the French fleet and removed the colonies and above all they led to the determination of other European powers to check any further French attempts at expansion.

In the German states there was the problem of unification and its implications for the balance of power between the Habsburg Empire and Russia. Although Prussia was industrialising, it was a pigmy compared with other countries and had problems coordinating activities in the annexed Rhineland. For the Habsburg Empire the problem was to cope with its role as the fulcrum of the balance of power in Europe. Military demands reduced the resources available for industrialisation. Finally, Russia maintained its position as a military power but declined economically through the combined effects of population growth, a failure to reform agriculture and a tendency to rely upon imports of manufactures.

We must now consider Britain's place in the world economy. Despite industrial superiority, mercantilist attitudes prevailed until the second half of the nineteenth century. There were controls on exports of machinery and restrictions on the migration of skilled labour. There were also informal controls operating through the insistence of goods being carried in British ships and through the 'cultural imperialism' which induced foreigners to imitate the English way of life. Finally, there was the direct control of political rule. Free trade was not an obvious element in Britain's expansion and when, in the second half of the ninteenth century, it became a dogma it was often promulgated on the basis of tit for tat and to overcome food shortages. It seems doubtful whether any economy, after the seventeenth century, has developed on the basis of free trade without a prior period of restricted trade. Even the United States required not merely the protection of distance from European competition but also tariffs.

The Second Kondratieff Wave 1848–96

The Upswing 1848–73.   The second Kondratieff upswing coincided with an important era of liberal free trade policies in Europe and the United States. In Britain the removal of trade barriers had begun earlier with the recognition that it was difficult to control exports of machinery and the migration of skilled labour; it concluded with the abolition of the Corn Laws. In the 1840s America reduced tariffs and trade liberalisation policies continued until the Civil War forced the use of tariffs as a means of war finance. In 1860 the Cobden—Chevalier Treaty removed tariffs between Britain and France. The Zollverein removed trade restrictions between the German states and was a prelude to political union. The effect of trade liberalisation policies, coupled with the intensification and spread of industrialisation, was that four countries became responsible for some three-quarters of the world's output of manufactures: Britain (32 per cent); USA (23 per cent); Germany (13 per cent); and France (10 per cent).

The second Kondratieff upswing was punctuated by wars, gold discoveries and an increase in the acreage under wheat in the American Mid-West.

Behind the wars lay the spread of the railways which made it feasible for countries to be enlarged and for political, as well as economic, gains to be realised. The Crimean War was ostensibly about the custody of the Holy Places in the Middle East and about Russia's interest in the Balkans and the Middle East. Its outcome was twofold. It removed Russia from Europe and enabled the remodelling of Germany and Italy to proceed. The ability of Britain and France to conduct a war many miles from their own territories forced Russia to consider modernising and industrialising. Railroads enabled Prussia to bring about a unification of the German states and to conduct successful campaigns against Denmark, Austria and France. Railroads also enabled the Northern states to conquer the Southern states in the American Civil War and that war and the subsequent unification of the country opened up the West, providing the impetus for an upsurge of industrialisation and an extension of the farming frontier.

From 1850 to 1873 Britain enjoyed a prolonged boom. The repeal of the Corn Laws did not, as some prophesied, lead to a collapse of agriculture. Indeed, agriculture enjoyed a 'golden age' — a result which had been anticipated by Ricardo, Malthus and Torrens. The feared flood of agricultural imports did not take place until the revolutions in transport brought a lowering of costs in the 1870s. Instead there was an expansion of the demand for agricultural commodities in Europe and a restriction of supply from Eastern Europe as a result of the Crimean War. Some adjustment did take place: agriculture's contribution to the national income fell from 20 per cent in 1851 to 14 per cent in 1871 and there was a switch from arable to meat and diary farming; but the rise in real incomes in industry transmitted itself to farming.

The period from 1850 to 1870 was one of rising prices which acted as a stimulus to economic development. Rising prices can be attributed, in the first instance, to gold discoveries, but industrial expansion also led to an increase in money and credit. Railway construction in Europe and America provided an important source of demand and required increased raw materials. Population pressures led to a demand for more houses and there was also a rise in overseas investment.

The Downswing 1873—96.   The second Kondratieff upswing had been marked by revolutions in transport and increasing trade liberalisation. The second downswing introduced a second industrial revolution coupled with a waning of economic liberalism. In the steel industry the Gilchrist—Thomas process enabled the phosphatic ores of Alsace—Lorraine to be exploited. It was a period in which there was an emphasis upon scientific research and this was most manifest in Germany and the United States. The second industrial revolution produced new products and processes and the demand for raw materials pulled more countries in the periphery into the world economy (for example Burma, Sri Lanka and Colombia). In the advanced countries there was a move to protectionism to nurture infant industries (the United States) and to defend agriculture (France and Germany) against the flood of cheap grain from the New World.

Increased investment in the previous upswing had led to a fall in grain prices and other raw materials. Freight rates tumbled and produced an agricultural depression in Europe. The British response was to reduce the acreage under crops and to switch to dairy farming. But Britain had a well developed industrial base which other European countries did not. France and Germany resorted to protection but the Scandinavian countries devised other responses. During the previous upswing the Nordic countries had entered the world economy by exporting primary products; in the downswing they were faced with competition from the New World. However, the Scandinavian countries possessed, in varying degrees, features which were to make them resilient. In the second half of the eighteenth century a free peasantry owning medium sized farms had emerged in Demark. The contrast with England and France is therefore instructive.

In England the peasantry was dispossessed and agriculture came to be dominated by the landed aristocracy and capitalist farmers. In France the Revolution produced smallholdings which inhibited progress. The Danish reaction to falling grain prices was to shift to dairy farming and to food processing. Instead of exporting grain, grain was imported and fed to pigs. Meat, bacon and butter began to be exported. This strategy of diversification was assisted by the social cohesion resulting from moderate income inequality and high educational standards. In the slump of the 1930s these same factors were to assist in the switch away from farming and into engineering. And what was true of Denmark was also true later in Sweden, Norway and Finland. In Sweden the switch to food processing pulled women into market jobs. In Finland the effect of the fall in freight rates was to cause a switch away from exporting tar and timber to wood processing (cellulose and paper). But Finland's engagement with the world economy was to begin in earnest only after the upsurge of nationalism (Sibelius and Nurmi), independence from the USSR after the First World War and the payment of reparations after the Second World War. In Norway the response was slower and had to wait for the development of hydroelectric power. But in all these Scandinavian countries the adverse effects of the agricultural depression were reduced by migration to the United States, by measures to prevent industrialisation increasing income inequalities and by an emphasis upon high educational standards which later permitted a trained and flexible workforce to switch to new industries.

The relevance of the small open Scandinavian economies to the problems of the larger European economies might, however, be questioned. We need therefore to consider Germany, whose defeats of Austria and France had ensured its political unification and stability but whose industrialisation had begun earlier. German industrialisation went through three phases. The first, running from about 1720 to about 1790, involved the recruitment by the state (essentially Prussia) of competent businessmen as managers for the industries in which the state had an interest. The second, from about 1790 to about 1840, saw the state — again, primarily Prussia — providing its own industrial experts for a select range of strategic industries. In the third phase, from 1840 to 1914, the private industrialist and financier became important more or less independently of government interest or intervention. Significantly, it was only this final entrepreneurial phase, which was accompanied by pronounced economic and social adjustments, which produced an extensive range of industrial activity in Germany.

German development differed in many respects from Britain's. Germany had fewer natural resources. Coal existed but it was not plentiful nor was it of high calorific value, and stocks of other minerals were limited. Financial assistance was provided by the landowners and through a banking system which tended to emphasise long-term lending rather than, as in Britain, short-term lending. The banks encouraged the formation of cartels which imposed uniform manufacturing conditions and eliminated obsolete plant; they also made available the new ideas which were implemented by the college graduates emerging from the technical high schools. These new ideas were acquired from the exploitation of foreign discoveries: 'Aniline dyes, the generation of electric power, the Gilchrist—Thomas process for iron manufacture — each basic to Germany's late nineteenth century pre-eminence — were French and British, not German discoveries. The essential connection between foreign invention and domestic innovation was the German research team' (Trebilcock 1981).

There were also profound differences in the organisation of firms. German company law had, in the 1870s, begun to find a formal place for workers in the managerial structure through the device of works' councils. Bismarck was later to introduce a social security system in an attempt to check the rise of trade unions.

German policies were influenced by the ideas of Friedrich List. In his book, *The National System of Political Economy,* published in 1841, List had argued that Britain's espousal of free trade was merely the means by which it maintained its control of the international economy. Britain's industrial revolution, List stressed, was a product not of free trade but of protection. Thus, the successful growth of the Lancashire cotton industry had demanded the destruction of the Indian textile industry.

> Had they sanctioned the free importation of Indian cotton and silk goods, the English cotton and silk manufactories must of neccesity come to a stand. India had not only the advantage of cheaper labour and raw materials, but also the experience, the skill and the practice of centuries. The effect of these advantages could not fail to tell under a system of free competition. But England was unwilling to found settlements in Asia in order to become subservient to Asia in manufacturing industry ... Accordingly England prohibited the import of Indian cotton.

Nor were the Indians the only recipients of British economic policy. As we have noted earlier, there were attempts to restrict exports of machinery and emigration of skilled labour. And having achieved pre-eminence it was inevitable that Britain should seek to prevent other countries from using protection to develop manufacturing industries.

> Any nation which by means of protective duties and restriction on navigation has raised her manufactuing power and her navigation to such a degree of development that no other nation could sustain free competition with her can do nothing wiser than to throw away these ladders of greatness and preach to other nations that she has hitherto wandered in the paths of error and has now, for the first time, succeeded in discovering the truth.

List did not deny that free trade could stimulate efficiency and promote capital accumulation and he saw the unification of Germany as a means of creating a large competitive economy. But he also argued that domestic manufactures should be protected against foreign competition. Free trade might benefit everyone but restricted trade might be even better for individual countries.

The backward areas of Europe must now be considered. Why did Spain, Italy and the three dynastic empires which had not been involved in the political settlements of 1871 (Austro-Hungarian, Russian and Ottoman) fail to achieve a self-sustaining growth in this period? At the turn of the century a group of writers, known collectively as the Generation of 98, pondered the reasons for Spanish stagnation. Some traced Spain's decline to the defeat of the Armada by a Catholic admiral. Others located the cause of weakness in the loss of the colonial empire; but they were opposed by those who argued that Spanish imperialism had exhausted itself in changing the spiritual values of the natives whereas the English had merely and cynically taken their wealth. The geographical problems eluded them although they were later emphasised by Carr (1982). Spain is the most mountainous country of Europe and is subject to centrifugal pressures for separatism which created problems in Catalonia and in the Basque region. But a more potent factor was the failure to develop a law of property rights which would have permitted the growth of markets. The Castilian kings were not under any pressure to offer commercial rights to the gentry and to merchants in return for funds with which to finance the monarchy and maintain defence. Finance came from plundered American treasure, and a vast bureaucracy developed to administer it. In Britain the conflict between the crown, which wanted finance, and the gentry, who could provide it, had led to the civil war of the seventeenth century, the victory of parliament over the crown and the extension of property rights, vital to the development of markets.

Spain failed to achieve a land reform; in contrast the Austro−Hungarian Empire carried through a land reform but its effect on the crucial Hungarian farmlands was to create large-scale farms and a landless, dependent peasantry. And although Austria produced more iron per head than the German Customs Union in 1840, the momentum of early industrialisation was not maintained because of a lack of coal and other minerals; progress up to 1914 was slow.

According to Gershenkron (1962) and other observers Russia was a backward country at the turn of the century. This verdict has been disputed by Gattrell (1986) who denies that Russian agriculture was backward and that the commune stood in the way of progress, offering as evidence an index of grain production in 50 provinces of European Russia which reveals a threefold rise in output between 1851 and 1914 which was associated with a high rate of population growth between 1850 and 1914 — which might indicate that there was no agrarian problem before the First World War.

Yet there were peasant protests in 1917 and after the Revolution in 1929: figures do not tell the whole story. The emancipation of serfs averted unrest and stemmed from a recognition that peasant armies could not, of themselves, defeat the more professional armies of the Western powers. But the terms of emancipation were onerous and many peasants were forced into debt; they were rescued only by starvation and death. Agricultural output barely kept pace with the rise in population. The problems were intensified by the lack of educational reforms which might have provided avenues of escape for peasants into industry. But labour was tied through debts to the land and hence there arose the paradox of a capital-intensive industrial development in a country with an abundance of unskilled labour which was untrained to produce the equipment required for a less capital-intensive technology. Russia, in fact, relied on the West for its industrial equipment and had to accept Western technology. It was, paradoxically, cheaper to import equipment from the West than to build up a labour-intensive industrial base. But as long as agriculture failed to produce a sizable surplus and as long as the labour force was ill educated it was impossible to promote self-sustaining industrialisation.

This brings us to the success story of Japan. The Japanese industrial take off is associated with the Meiji Restoration of 1868 (although the civilising influence of the previous Tokugawa period should not be overlooked). But the Meiji Restoration served to emphasise the confrontation with and response to Western culture. The response was fourfold: a land reform which compensated the former owners with bonds and gave the peasants an incentive and the government a source of revenue; the introduction of technical colleges and a Ministry of Industrial Affairs which anticipated the post-Second World War Ministry of Industry and Trade; a currency reform which removed inflationary pressures; and the selling off by the state of many assets to the private sector.

The comparisons and contrasts with advanced and backward countries are instructive. Japan, like Sweden and Germany, emphasised the importance of education and vocational training. Japan, like Britain, developed as a result of trade which grew at 7 per cent per annum between 1870 and 1913. But Japan's exports were primary products whereas Britain's were manufactures. And unlike Britain the state intervened to direct and subsidise industry. Finally, the contrast with Russia is striking; the Japanese managed to obtain an agricultural surplus whereas the Russians struggled to keep agricultural production in line with the advance of population.

Japan succeeded, China and India did not. China's problem was that modernisation had to take place within the context of a cultural tradition which resisted change and of an empire which had experienced considerable historical continuity. Now some of these characteristics could be found in Japan. But there were differences. China was caught in a high level, pre-steam engine equilibrium trap in which muscle power was always cheaper than the steam engine. Political continuity and stability had been associated with an expansion of population. In 1700 the population was about 150 million; by 1850 it had reached 430 million. Political stability had allowed China to become a huge free trade area in which muscle power made machinery unnecessary and capital accumulation in fixed capital irrelevant. Capital was absorbed by the need to keep food output in line with the increase in population and to enable trade and transport networks to be created and maintained between regions. There were, of course, tensions within this economic system. The elaborate bureaucratic form of government gradually lost contact with the masses. Entry to government was based upon performance in examinations but the education system placed a premium upon classical learning and was failing to produce enough openings for the increasing numbers of well educated children. When confronted by Western traders and governments, the ruling classes made concessions which ensured their own permanence but did not acknowledge the need for modernisation.

Japan succeeded; China was caught in a high level equilibrium trap; but what of India? Did all India's problems stem from the British Empire? The fact that China did not 'take off' into growth is a warning against such a simplistic assumption. Land reform and increased agricultural productivity might even have helped industrialisation in India. Britain's land policy was designed to raise tax revenue and may have increased land turnover and concentrated holdings. Rich peasants emerged; but rich peasants existed in Japan and invested in industry and commerce. But India's rich peasants did not engage in such productive activities. A lack of domestic investment was complemented by lack of foreign investment. Britain did invest in India, but mainly in infrastructure such as railways. The big problem was that there was too little foreign investment in relation to the size of the economy and the low stage of development. However, there was always the possibility of investing the surplus from trade.

India's trade was dominated by the imperial connection. In the early nineteenth century India's opium paid for Britain's imports of China tea. In the third quarter of the nineteenth century, when Britain found in increasingly difficult to sell goods in Europe and American markets, there was a switch of manufactures to India. In 1870 India was Britain's third most important customer; in 1913 it was *the* most important customer. Exports of manufactures from Britain, espically textiles, led to a displacement of Indian exports of manufactures and to increases in exports of agricultural commodities. Yet despite the growing importance of the Indian market, Britain's share of that market fell from 84 per cent in 1870 to 62 per cent in 1910. India's trade was growing faster than its trade with Britain and the trade surplus was increasing. Between 1861 and 1895 the net inflow of silver into India accounted for about one-third of the world's output of silver. But the treasure did not have an expansionary effect: it was hoarded.

The failure to expand aggregate demand did not arise out of political uncertainty — the imperial connection ensured stability. But the imperial ties may have inhibited drive and dynamism. Unlike Japan, India felt no need to respond to the challenge posed by the West. Unlike France and Germany, India could not erect tariffs to keep out British goods and protect infant industries; the link with Britain also inhibited the development of a separate banking and financial system. Britain's domination of India therefore led to a paradox; it was too weak to provide a boost to the local economy and it was too strong politically for the Indians to fear any threat of foreign competition. Not until the First World War reduced trade with Britain did local industry receive the necessary stimulus. Even then a lack of national identity and an absence of xenophobia distinguished India from both Russia and Japan. Not until independence was political will concentrated on modernisation.

The Third Kondratieff 1896—1933

The Upswing 1896—1920. The third upswing was marked by rising food prices and raw material prices and adverse terms of trade for manufactures. The response was further European investment in the periphery — in Argentina, Australia, Canada, South Africa and Brazil. The expansion of investment to and exports from the periphery was associated with the development of the staple theory of trade whereby exports of primary products from developing countries were assumed to yield a surplus which could be used to transform an economy — in other words, export-led growth. The thesis was partially supported in Canada, Australia and New Zealand but not in Latin America. The differences in development stemmed from differences in political structures.

Spanish bureaucracy and landholding rights were transmitted to Latin America and persisted after independence. Opinions differ as to the continent's subsequent development. Some maintain that the continent became detached from the world economy until the last quarter of the nineteenth century; others aver that an informal empire through trade was established by Britain. These views may refer to different time periods. In the short run there was an influx of English traders and capital in pursuit of an imagined vast market. But as expectation evaporated there was a collapse of trade and investment in the 1820s which had a deleterious effect upon local industries. Latin America's absorption into the world economy had therefore to await the rising raw material prices of the last quarter of the nineteenth century.

Table 1.17 shows the impact of rising prices and falling transport costs on the export performances of the Latin American countries. Argentina experienced the most spectacular growth as capital and labour poured into the country. But the growth of exports did not lead to the growth of other sectors. This was not because of foreign domination of economic activity: foreign ownership was prevalent in Chile, Cuba, Mexico and Peru but not in Argentina, Brazil and Colombia. A strong rebuttal of the foreign domination thesis is provided by the fact that Britain

Table 1.17 Annual Rate of Growth of Exports 1883–1913 (current US dollars)

Argentina	7.6	Ecuador	5.1
Brazil	4.5	Mexico	4.3
Central America	3.7	Peru	3.7
Chile	2.1	Uruguay	3.6
Colombia	4.1	Venezuela	3.6
Cuba	2.9		

Source: Lewis (1978)

dominated Australia, Canada and New Zealand and yet they were able to use export revenues to change the bases of their economies and render them less vulnerable to trade fluctuations. The difference was political. In Australia power rested with the urban dwellers who were able to impose tariffs on manufactures and so to raise real wages and expand industry. In Argentina political power rested with the rural landowners — the legatees of Spanish rule.

The First World War.   Although public finance was originally to do with the raising of money for defence, the study of war has tended to occupy a peripheral place in neoclassical economics. This is in contrast to its role in Kondratieff long waves and its importance in Marxist thinking. The First World War was a consequence of the uneven development of the advanced countries and the increasing economic strength of Germany; the fear of German domination of Europe by France and the possible challenge to Britain in the world economy; the aspirations of the Italians following unification and the increasing weaknesses of the Habsburg and Ottoman Empires.

German economic expansion required markets; but Germany entered the game too late to acquire colonies. There was, therefore, a preoccupation with a central European policy (*Mitteleuropa*) which could provide markets for raw materials and goods. The attempt failed and in failing it led to a reconstruction of Europe. In Russia the Romanov dynasty fell and was replaced by the Union of Soviet Socialist Republics. The Habsburg and Ottoman Empires disintegrated into numerous countries, each with its own tariff wall. France, through reparations and annexations, sought to prevent a third Franco-Prussian War and despite being a victor Britain's economic and political empires collapsed with a subsequent undermining of the gold standard and the displacement of sterling as the key currency. Canada and Latin America became more dependent upon the United States. In India the war fuelled demands for independence. The United States emerged out of the war as the strongest nation but failed to impose its desired policies upon Europe. The Treaty of Versailles provided no solutions to the causes of the war.

The Downswing 1920–33.   The third Kondratieff downswing saw the collapse of economic liberalism and the world economy, concluded with the greatest slump in history and sparked off a search for new theories of economic activity. But the causes of the slump are still the subject of controversy between those who attribute the downturn to monetary factors and those who emphasise real forces.

The monetarist explanation, as put forward by Friedman and Schwartz (1963), is that a contraction in the US money supply converted a minor recession into a major slump. There had been recessions in the United States in the 1920s, but these were inventory cycles from which the economy quickly recovered. Indeed, throughout the 1920s the US economy appeared to be generally buoyant. There was an expansion of new industries: cars and trucks, chemicals and chemical engineering and electricity. New managerial control systems were introduced and Taylorism and Fordism became more widely used. But in 1929 a recession was intensified by the contraction in the money supply and transmitted to the rest of the world by the decision to call in loans.

The monetary explanation of the slump draws upon US experience. The analysis which is based upon the workings of real forces derives from European experience and from Keynesian economics. This points to weaknesses in the American economy before 1929. The construction industry began to slow down in 1927 and Temin (1976) has emphasised the weak state of agriculture. One consensus now appears to be that the changes in the money supply aggravated an existing weakness in the farm sector. (A similar explanation is put forward for the depressed condition of many of the primary producers on the periphery.) There had been an expansion of agriculture during the war which led to a fall in prices in the 1920s. But the fall in the total value of world production of primary products was only 3 per cent between 1925 and 1929, less than the fall in the price of manufactured goods (technological progress was one contributory factor). It seems doubtful, therefore, whether the declining aggregate purchasing power of primary producers can be regarded as the main cause of the Great Depression (Aldcroft 1977).

In Britain an immediate post-war boom was followed by the loss of overseas markets and the collapse of the staple trades. Production of staples had been adjusting gradually to overseas competition before the war; for example, exports of cotton yarn had been declining. But the pace of adjustment was too slow and British entrepreneurs have been accused of being myopic in failing to switch early enough into the newer electrical and chemical engineering industries. In the end the degree of reconstruction required to accommodate to the post-war world was too large to be carried through by the price mechanism. A surgical operation was required to remove excess capacity; but that was delayed by the return to the gold standard at pre-war parity. In Germany there was a further problem of war debts. In both Germany and Britain social security systems were extended during the 1920s and increased the incomes of those out of work and relieved the trade unions of the burden of coping with their own unemployed members. Benefits were sufficiently high to contribute to continuing high unemployment in both countries.

During this period monetary instability characterised most of the European countries and Germany, Hungary, Poland and Austria experienced hyperinflation: hence the search for a new monetary standard. Unfortunately the new gold standard was imposed upon countries with extremely fragile economies. The United States was strong in the 1920s and it has been customary to attribute the breakdown of the international monetary system to the failure of the Americans to follow the rules of the gold standard and to inflate their economy when they received gold inflows. This failure was, Friedman and Schwartz argue, to reduce the world's money supply and to cause deflation in other parts of the international economy. But this argument presupposes that there was a decline in the reserves of other countries whereas reserves in the rest of the world were increasing as a result of mining and the conversion of existing private gold stocks into currency. Furthermore, other countries, notably France, were not observing the rules of the gold standard either. This is not to say that the United States could have prevented or mitigated the slump through appropriate monetary policy; but it does caution against assuming that the slump was transmitted in a simple fashion from the United States to the rest of the world. US and British tariffs may indeed have had a much greater effect upon Europe than monetary events.

The Fourth Kondratieff 1933–72

The Fourth Kondratieff Upswing 1933–51.   The collapse of the world economy was followed by a revival around 1933. In the United States this began with the New Deal. In Britain it was associated with the emergence of new industries in the Midlands and the South and with a housing boom financed by monetary expansion. The expansion in the South was, however, in sharp contrast to the depression in the North. There was a problem of insufficient profits. Under the impact of the slump product prices had fallen but wage rates showed remarkable rigidity and, as a result, real wages rose. The 1931 devaluation gave a temporary stimulus to exports but by 1937 other countries had devalued and parity with sterling had been restored. Further devaluation might have led to capital flight, and expanding the money supply might have been construed as inflationary. An excise tax whose proceeds could have been paid to industry might have helped but was not considered. The multiplicity of firms made it difficult to reach agreements on rationalisation; each firm hoped that others would volunteer for redundancy; freedom of entry even meant that the restoration of profits attracted newcomers.

In Japan it was the agricultural areas which experienced the greatest hardship with the loss of markets for textiles and the fall in the price of rice. The response was devaluation of the yen and deflation. Japanese wages and prices were remarkably flexible and the agricultural depression released large numbers of

women for factory work; expenditure reduction was accompanied by diversification and expenditure switching. There was a contraction of the numbers in
textiles and agriculture and an expansion of engineering and chemicals, including
artificial fibre manufacture. Japan became the largest producer of artificial silk
in the world. The economic policies did, however, have political repercussions.
Deflation meant cutting government spending and the militarist groups resented
such measures and mobilised popular support to secure an expansion of spending
on armaments. Rising profits not only prevented inflation but served to finance
an armaments drive. The huge devaluation of the yen by 65 per cent between
1929 and 1933 stimulated exports but also created resentment in the major powers.
They promptly started to close the doors on Japanese exports to the colonies and
that led the Japanese to consider the advantages which might accrue from having
an empire of their own. But what stands out is the remarkable degree of flexibility
of Japanese prices. Japan's problems were similar to those of Britain but (setting
aside rearmament) they were solved by the remarkable programme of production and trade diversification whereas Britain's problems continued to linger on
up to and even beyond the Second World War.

The contrast with France is also instructive. The 1929 slump had less effect
on France than most other advanced countries — it was the British devaluation
of 1931 that had an impact on France. But competitive devaluation was rejected
because, as in the case of Germany, there was a fear of inflation; deflation and
import controls were used instead. But some prices were more flexible than others
so that the economy became distorted. Agricultural prices fell more than manufacturing prices; wages were inflexible as compared to product prices. Attempts to
maintain the same deflationary policies through the 1930s led to continual political
crises. Eventually in 1936 a Popular Front government was returned to power
and introduced an increase of wages of 12 per cent and a reduction of weekly
hours from 48 to 40. The result of these changes was to increase hourly wages
by about 60 per cent. Farm prices were also increased. In theory increasing wages
should have increased aggregate money demand and stimulated output and employment. But wages are also costs and French prices moved rapidly out of line with
world prices. In an attempt to avert crisis the franc was, at last, devalued. The
results must be deemed a mixed blessing. Full employment was restored but industrial production in 1937 was 20 per cent below its 1929 level. Many workers
returned to the agricultural sector and France entered the Second World War with
a rural economy and considerable numbers subsisting in underemployment in the
farm sector.

Before the First World War the German economy was expanding and chal-
lenging Britain's leadership of the world. The war checked that advance and left
the country bereft of gold, many domestic and foreign assets and export markets,
and created a reparations problem. The immediate response was inflation which
lasted until the second half of the 1920s. Thereafter the economy improved until
1928 when foreign funds were withdrawn to fuel the US stock market boom and
because the French sought to discourage a proposed customs union between Austria

and Germany. At the beginning of the world slump there was a reluctance to devalue the currency because of the fear that devaluation was synonymous with inflation. Instead attempts were made to deflate the economy; but exports continued to decline as a result of the severe competition from a devalued sterling.

In an attempt to stabilise the economy import licences and exchange controls were introduced and there were experiments with bilateral trade agreements with Southern European and Latin American countries. But none of these policies proved successful in reducing unemployment and in 1933 there was a change of emphasis and public works programmes were introduced. The possible impact of these policies on private investment was overtaken by the switch to the war economy which the National Socialists brought about.

By 1926 the USSR was recovering from the aftermath of the October Revolution and the period of war communism. The lesson from (civil) war communism seemed to be that workers' control at the level of the enterprise was incompatible with either effective state planning or efficient management within the enterprise. But the period of war communism can also be looked upon as an experiment in the first steps of transition to socialism and when the civil war ended there was, under the new economic policy, a serious attempt to introduce a kind of socialism in which the state was prepared to accept the market as its partner in economic development. The result was that the pre-war agricultural acreage was restored (although there was a reduction in productivity). But a return to pre-war standards was not the objective of the leadership. Instead, they saw the need to catch up with the advanced economies and to industrialise in order to protect the USSR from further invasions. But industrialisation and modernisation required finance.

Finance was obtained through forced savings and an increase in the money supply. The lack of an efficient tax system and an enforced isolationist policy made this inevitable. For many developing countries, customs duties provide a source of revenue; but this route was denied to the USSR by the enforced severing of trade contacts; hence, the expansion of aggregate money demand which led to full employment by 1930 and inflation in 1936 and resulted in shortages of raw materials and labour. Increased agricultural productivity was sought through collectivisation and the liquidation of the kulaks: by 1936 about 90 per cent of all peasants were organised into collectives. The immediate effect of collectivisation was a fall in output as the peasants slaughtered their livestock and reduced their efforts; the ultimate effect was a rise in output and the appropriation of the surplus by the state. The means by which rural savings were extracted were the cadres, the disgruntled sons of peasants, who hated the social mores of the villages and, being loyal party members, were intolerant of inefficiency. Collectivisation achieved some of its objectives: it reduced rural inequality, it accelerated the growth rate of output, it released labour for the factories and it helped to finance industrial development. The cadres succeeded, after a fashion, where the tsars had failed and they provided a lesson for the Chinese experiments after 1949.

Solving the problems of agriculture went hand in hand with industrial reconstruction. The system of workers' control was abolished by the simple expedient of dismissing the old trade union leaders and integrating the trade unions into the state machine. The task of the unions then became that of organising productivity drives. And the efforts of the workers were further harnessed by the use of piece rates and the inculcation of the principles of American scientific management.

Among other primary producing countries fortunes were mixed, outcomes being dependent upon exports of raw materials and foodstuffs. In Eastern Europe there was a decline in exports of grain and attempts to revive the trade with Western Europe proved abortive. In Latin America many countries defaulted on their loans and became ineligible for private loans until the 1970s. The first steps towards import substitution industrialisation were undertaken in the larger Latin American economies and the process was assisted by currency depreciations, tariffs and, in the case of Brazil, by reductions in coffee production.

The fourth upswing was associated with a number of wars of which the Second World War was the most important. But there had been other preceding conflicts. In the Far East the Japanese began their conquest of China and their plans for the establishment of a sphere of influence throughout South-east Asia. In Africa the Italians invaded Abyssinia. In Spain there was a civil war which many saw as a testing ground for the larger war to follow.

The Second World War.   The Second World War arose because three countries — Germany, Italy and Japan (the Axis Powers) — saw possibilities of gain. In the case of Germany there was an ideological factor: the war was seen as a means of purifying Europe from the corrupting influence of Jews, communists and the baleful effects of Britain, France, the USSR and USA; and of restoring national pride. Gains were to arise from the correction of injustices imposed after the First World War and from extensions of territory. In Germany the idea of living space (*Lebensraum*) was revived and there was a desire to create a self-sufficient economic unit within which Germany could exploit the resources of conquered territories. During the war the new economic order was imposed upon defeated nations. In Japan a similar set of ideas led to the formulation of a Co-Prosperity Sphere. (In Italy the ideas were not so strongly expressed.)

Because the Axis Powers had limited resources they conceived of the war as short in duration. They relied upon the possession of an initial military superiority (combining tanks, planes and infantry in a unique fashion which came to be known as the *Blitzkrieg*). In contrast, the Allies (Britain, France, the USSR and the United States) had to plan for a longer war in order to mobilise their resources. In the clash of strategies the long view triumphed: Germany had hoped to achieve a quick knock out blow against Russia and failed, while Japan hoped that Pearl Harbour would convince the United States of the futility of retaliation and ended up by rousing a sleeping giant.

The war was a total war in the sense that it directly involved civilians as well as military personnel and it was fought on all continents (except the Americas) and in all oceans. Its outcome was the complete destruction of German and Japanese ideas of reconstructing the world economy and their replacement by

American ideas. The war led to the demise of the British Empire and the decline of the British navy.

The United States had the opportunity to impose its ideas upon the world. There was a greater emphasis upon free trade and the independence of colonies. The American occupation of Germany and Japan resulted in both countries being 'Americanised' industrially and in the destruction of monopolies and concentrations of political power. Soviet influence dominated the developing countries of Eastern Europe and partitioned Germany. The Germany which Bismarck had succeeded in creating was effectively destroyed.

The Second World War led to the reconstruction not only of Europe but also of the rest of the world; its repercussions were to continue through the next downswing. In Europe spheres of influence for the principal victors, the United States and the USSR, arose by accident but were not seriously disputed. Britain made only a mild protest at the installation of a pro-communist government in Romania and the USSR did not demur when Britain took control in Greece. The European buffer zone gave the USSR some security. Eastern Europe achieved the political stability which it had previously lacked. This stability and the formation of the Council of Mutual Economic Cooperation was counterbalanced by the formation of the European Economic Community.

In the Far East there was the resurgence of China, the rehabilitation of Japan and the independence of India and Pakistan. The Japanese occupation of Southeast Asia had loosened most of the imperialist bonds and in the 1950s and 1960s independence movements arose throughout the area. In the Middle East the state of Israel was created — the source of much subsequent instability in that region. (In Africa independence movements came later and were to meet difficulties because the old colonial boundaries had cut across recognisable ethnic and religious boundaries.) Having been relatively insulated from the Second World War, Latin America was to prove an area of political and economic instability in the post-war period.

But the main effects of the Second World War upon Asia, Africa and Latin America were to create a mood of unity and to direct attention to the problem of inequality. Seeking to avoid partisanship for either of the superpowers, Nehru sought to unite the newly independent countries in a Non-Aligned Movement which could exert an influence through the United Nations and draw attention to the disparities in the world distribution of income which had been ignored under colonialism.

The Fourth Downswing 1951−72. The fourth downswing led to the most prolonged boom in world history. The fall in primary product prices after the Korean War was intensified by improvements in agricultural and mining techniques. In the late 1950s there was a dramatic fall in energy prices. The boom in the advanced countries was assisted by the development of the Cold War which led to a rearmament drive. In Europe reconstruction was assisted by Marshall Aid, although Millward (1984) has argued that recovery was already under way. The boom in the advanced countries was assisted by the reduction in farm populations and the rise in industrial activity was propelled by the diffusion of the new industries of cars, electrical engineering and chemicals from the USA to Western Europe and Japan. Multi-divisional companies became common and multinational corporations began to emerge. The institutional framework for trade proved to be remarkably resilient until the late 1960s, when competition from newly industrialising countries brought the system under strain.

The Fifth Kondratieff

The Fifth Upswing 1972. The fifth upswing began in the middle of the 1970s following the sharp rise in the prices of grains and oil which were in turn, accompanied by a worldwide inflation. The decision of the advanced countries to deflate their economies following the second oil price rise led to a collapse of primary product prices.

Summary and Conclusions

The rise in raw material prices in the 1970s marked a turning point in the world economy. Before the rise in raw material prices there had been an expansion of trade between the advanced countries marked by the emergence of multinational corporations. Substantial flows of labour had entered the growing economies from poorer countries.

The end of the boom raised questions about the previous economic policies which had been pursued and why they had brought prosperity to so few countries in the southern hemisphere. Was free trade a deterrent to their growth? Did they need to protect their infant industries? The boom and the subsequent slump revived interest in Kondratieff long waves. However, the evidence is suggestive rather than conclusive; the evidence for Kuznets cycles and alternating patterns of home and foreign investment in the nineteenth century is more plausible. The discussion of long waves drew attention to the nature of the shocks imposed upon economies and, in particular, the importance of political factors: the two world wars exerted crucial impacts. The discussion of long waves was also useful in drawing attention to the forces which assisted or hindered the development of economies in the nineteenth and early twentieth century.

Bibliography

Abramovitz, M. (1968) 'The passing of the Kuznets cycle', *Economica*, vol. 35, pp. 234–241.

Aldcroft, D.H. (1977) *From Versailles to Wall Street*, Allen Lane.

Bairoch, P. (1982) 'International industrialization levels from 1750 to 1980', *Journal of European Economic History*, vol. 11, pp. 153–210.

Bordo, R. and Schwartz, A.J. (1981) 'Money prices in the nineteenth century. Was Thomas Tooke right?', *Explorations in Economic History*, vol. 18, pp. 92–127.

Carr, R. (1982) *Spain 1808–1975*, Clarendon Press.

Crafts, N.R.F. (1985) *British Economic Growth during the Industrial Revolution*, Clarendon Press.

Cronin, J.E. (1979) *Industrial Conflict in Modern Britain*, Croom Helm.

Easterlin, R. (1968) *Population, Labor Force and Long Swings in Economic Growth: The American Experience*, Columbia University Press.

Freeman, C. *et al.* (1982) *Unemployment and Technical Innovation: A Study of Long Waves and Economic Development*, Francis Pinter.

Friedman, M. and Schwartz, A.J. (1963) *The Monetary History of the United States, 1860–1960*, Princeton University Press.

Garvey, G. (1943), 'Kondratieff's theory of long waves', *Review of Economic Statistics*, vol. 25, pp. 203–219.

Gattrell, P. (1986) *The Tsarist Economy*, Wheatsheaf.

Gerschenkron, A. (1962) *Economic Backwardness in Historical Perspective*, Harvard University Press.

Gordon, D., Weisskopf, E. and Bowles, S. (1983) 'Long swings and the nonreproductive cycle', *American Economic Review*, vol. 68, pp. 251–261.

Hansen, A.H. (1939) 'Economic progress and declining population growth', *American Economic Review*, vol. 29. pp. 1–18.

Hartley, C.K. (1980) 'Transportation, the world wheat trade and the Kuznets cycle 1850–1913', *Explorations in Economic History*, vol. 17, pp. 218–250.

Hayek, F. (1932) *Prices and Production*, Routledge and Kegan Paul.

Hicks, J.R. (1950) *The Trade Cycle*, Oxford University Press.

Hicks, J.R. (1965) *Capital and Growth*, Oxford University Press.

Hicks, J.R. (1973) *Capital and Time*, Oxford University Press.

Hicks, J.R. (1977) *Economic Perspectives*, Oxford University Press.

Howrey, E.P. (1968) 'A spectrum analysis of the long swing hypothesis', *International Economic Review*, vol. 9, pp. 228–252.

ILO (1985) *World Labour Report*, ILO.

ILO (1986) *World Labour Report*, ILO.

ISS (1986) *The Military Balance 1986–1987*, International Institute for Strategic Studies.

Juglar, C. (1862) *Des crisis commerciales et leur retour periodique en France, en Angleterre et aux Etats Unis*, Hachette.

Kennedy, P. (1988) *The Rise and Fall of the Great Powers*, Unwin Hyman.

Kitchin, J. (1923) 'Cycles and trends in economic factors', *Review of Economic Statistics*, vol. 5, pp. 10–16.

Kondratieff, N.D. (1979) 'The major economic cycles', translation, *Review*, vol. 2, pp. 519–562. First published (1925) in *Vopost kon'iunktury*, vol. 1, pp. 28–79.

Koombs, J. (1981) 'Economic growth and industrialization in Hungary, 1831–1913', *Journal of Economic History*, vol. 20, pp. 105–146.

Lewis, W.A. (1955) *A Theory of Economic Growth*, Allen and Unwin.

Lewis, W.A. (1978) *Growth and Fluctuations, 1870–1913*, Allen and Unwin.

List, F. (1841) *National Systems of Political Economy*, Longman Green (English translation 1904).

Long, J.B. and Prosser, C. (1983) 'Real business cycles', *Journal of Political Economy*, vol. 91, pp. 39–69.

Lucas, R.E. (1986) *Models of Business Cycles*, University of Chicago Press.

Maddison, A. (1983) 'A comparison of levels of GDP per capita in developed and developing countries, 1700–1980', *Journal of Economic History*, vol. 43, pp. 78–85.

Marglin, S. (1974) 'What do bosses do?', *Review of Radical Political Economics*, vol. 6, pp. 60–113.

Mensch, G. *et al.* (1984) 'Changing capital values and the propensity to innovate', in C. Freeman (ed.) *Long Waves in the World Economy*, Francis Pinter.

Millward, A.S. (1984) *The Reconstruction of Western Europe, 1945–51*, Methuen.

OECD (1979) *The Impact of Newly Industrializing Countries on Production and Trade in Manufactures.*

OECD (1987) *Economic Outlook,* June.

O'Leary, P.J. and Lewis, W.A. (1955) 'Secular swings in production and trade, 1870–1913', *Manchester School,* vol. 23, pp. 113–151.

Perez, C. (1985) 'Microelectronics, long waves and world structural change', *World Development,* vol. 13, pp. 441–463.

Reynolds, L.C. (1983) 'The spread of economic growth to the Third World', *Journal of Economic Literature,* vol. 21, pp. 941–980.

Robertson, D.H. (1915) *A Study of Industrial Fluctuations,* Staples.

Rostow, W.W. (1978) *The World Economy: History and Prospect,* Macmillan.

Rostow, W.W. (1980) *Why the Poor Get Richer and the Rich Slow Down,* Macmillan.

Russell, S.S. (1986) 'Remittances from international migration: a review in perspective', *World Development,* vol. 14, pp. 677–696.

Samuelson, P.A. (1939) 'Interactions between the multiplier analysis and the principle of acceleration', *Review of Economic Statistics,* vol. 21, pp. 75–78.

Schumpeter, J.A. (1939) *Business Cycles,* 2 vols, McGraw-Hill.

Slutsky, E. (1933) 'The summation of random causes as the cause of cyclical processes', *Econometrica,* vol. 5, pp. 105–146.

Solomou, S. (1986) 'Non-balanced growth and the Kondratieff wave in the world economy', *Journal of Economic History,* vol. 46, pp. 165–171.

Solomou, S. (1987) *Phases of Economic Growth 1850–1973,* Cambridge University Press.

Temin, P. (1976) *Did Monetary Forces Cause the Great Depression?,* Norton.

Thomas, B. (1954) *Migration and Economic Growth,* Cambridge University Press.

Trebilcock, C.J. (1981) *The Industrialization of the Great Powers,* Longman.

UN (1983) *Economic and Social Consequences of the Arms Race and of Military Expenditures,* United Nations.

UNCTAD (1981) *Trade and Development Report,* United Nations.

UNCTAD (1987) *Handbook of International Trade and Development Statistics, Supplement,* United Nations.

UNCTNC (1981) *Transnational Banks: Operations, Strategies and their Effects in Developing Countries,* United Nations.

UNCTNC (1982) *Transnational Corporations in International Tourism,* United Nations.

UNCTNC (1983) *Transnational Corporations in World Development, Third Survey,* United Nations.

World Bank (1983) *World Development Report 1983,* United Nations.

2

Incomes and the Welfare of Nations

This chapter addresses the difficulties of measuring the differences in the economic welfare of countries or differences in economic welfare within countries and directs attention to two questions: first, how do we measure differences in economic welfare? Second, what happens to the distribution of income as economic development proceeds? This latter question is, in effect, two questions because it can be posed at the level of the world economy (the world distribution of income) as well as the individual country. Both sub-questions have been of intense interest to economists. Thus, Lewis (1976) has argued that 'Development must be inegalitarian because it does not start in every part of an economy at the same time'. And according to Kuznets (1955), 'in the early phases of industrialization, income inequality becomes strong enough first to increase and then reduce income inequalities'. The Kuznets thesis can be extended to the international distribution of income to become what has been called the *convergence thesis,* whereby early developers and late starters are presumed to eventually attain the same growth rate of incomes — a thesis which has been subjected to criticism by Myrdal (1957) and Kaldor (1970), who have both pointed to the possibility of cumulative divergence. Even economic maturity may not be without its attendant problems of income distribution within industrial sectors. However, that issue is deferred until Chapter 4.

Measuring Income: Measuring Welfare

Economic welfare (ecfare) is concerned with those aspects of welfare to which economic factors can contribute and which can be measured with money. We can therefore approximate economic welfare by the following equation:

42

*Ecfare = Consumption enjoyment from the use of labour, capital
and natural resources + Leisure*

This definition has not been adopted by any of the standard economic measures
of value: classical, Marxist or neoclassical. Classical economists have excluded
leisure because they assumed that life was lived out at the subsistence level, and
Marx took a similar view. Neoclassical economists tended to exclude leisure
because they approached the problem of income measurement from the point of
view of the businessman so that consumption enjoyment represented payment to
resource owners. Of course, in developing countries there is a strong case for
excluding leisure because much leisure is really idleness enforced by lack of
resources. In advanced countries leisure might be measured by the wage foregone
if it could be assumed that work was available if wanted.

However, it is the neoclassical approach to ecfare which has been generally
adopted; it has been measured in national income terms as the flow of goods and
services during a period. The link between income and ecfare is then established
and qualified as follows.

It is assumed that the price paid by an individual for the last unit of a commodity measures the utility (ecfare) he places upon that good. In other words,
price measures marginal utility. But an individual might have been prepared to
pay more for the intra-marginal units (which cost him the same as the final unit)
and it is therefore assumed that the consumer surplus (the utility derived over
and above the money outlay) can be measured by subjecting the individual to
an act of extortion whereby he is asked the maximum price he would be prepared
to pay for each unit. From this the total utility derived from a good could be
calculated, However, this procedure is subject to qualification. The utility derived from the first glass of water may be infinite; it therefore becomes meaning-
less to add the utility from the second glass of water to that from the first. The
procedure cannot be used to measure the utility or ecfare from necessities and
another starting point has to be adopted. From this qualification a set of consequences follows. The total utility derived by an individual from all the goods he
consumes may not be measurable; the total of totals of utility derived from all
the goods consumed by an individual may not be measurable, and therefore the
total of totals of utility derived from all goods consumed by a group of individuals
(that is, the national income or output) may also not be measurable.

Behind the qualification to the utility approach to ecfare lies a distinction between utility and the structure of wants. It has been customary to regard utility
as homogeneous. But the utilities derived by an individual from different goods
may be different. There may be a hierarchy of wants with each level being
associated with different utilities. The early neoclassical economists, such as
Marshall, recognised the hierarchy of wants and concentrated upon those wants
which were not associated with necessities. They then went on the assume that
there was a law of diminishing marginal utility of real income which implied that
taking a pound from a rich man and giving it to a poor man would lead to an

increase in total ecfare. This was the rationale behind interpersonal comparisons
and income redistribution.

Subsequently, some neoclassical economists denied interpersonal comparisons
and in effect argued that the hierarchy of wants was different for different individuals (although they did tend to assume that it was possible for one individual
to substitute one good for another and still remain at the same level of utility).
In unravelling this controversy Georgescu Roegen (1966) has drawn attention
to the following points. There is a hierarchy of wants and each individual attempts to satisfy high order wants before going on to satisfy low order wants;
it must not therefore be assumed too readily that it is always possible to substitute
one good for another — a dipsomaniac would not be prepared to give up his last
bottle of whisky for a limitless quantity of cigarettes. Second, the high order wants
may be the same for all individuals in a community and therefore interpersonal
comparisons may be attempted. Third, low order wants may be so idiosyncratic
as to defy comparison. It may not thus be possible to say whether depriving one
person of the ability to go yachting in order to allow someone else to go pony
trekking will improve community ecfare. The upshot of all this is that national
income statistics need to be treated with caution and may need to be supplemented
with information on basic wants such as life expectancy. Indeed, it may be more
important to judge ecfare in terms of the percentage of the population engaged
in agriculture since that measures a community's command over food. What we
shall now do is consider the refinements that statisticians make in order to provide a more acceptable measure of ecfare.

Purchasing Power Parity

Table 2.1 shows that gross domestic product (income) per capita in the developing countries was less than one-twelfth of that in the advanced countries and in
the planned economies of Asia it was one-fiftieth of that of the advanced countries. Such disparities would seem to suggest the well nigh impossibility of the
developing countries ever catching up with the advanced.

However, before jumping to such a conclusion we must note that international
comparisons presuppose that the official exchange rates provide a common

Table 2.1 Per Capita Gross Domestic Product in Economic Blocs, 1985 (US dollars)

Developed market economies	11,080
Developing countries	884
Socialist countries	
Eastern Europe	. . .
Asia	288

Source: UNCTAD (1988)

denominator whereby all goods and services in all countries can be measured in dollars. In other words, the figures in the table assume that the same good will sell for the price in every country when allowance has been made for the fact that different countries use different currencies. Thus, if $1 = £2 then a commodity priced at $1 in the United States would cost £2 in Britain. This is the law of one price which assumes that if there were differences in prices then consumers would switch from the dear market to the cheap market until the price levels or exchange rates adjusted so as to yield purchasing parity across countries.

There may, however, be divergences between a country's exchange rate and its purchasing power, the most obvious being the existence of non-traded goods. As Marris (1984) observed, 'It is not impossible for a hairdresser to commute between London and New York. It has been done by Mr Vidal Sassoon — but it is expensive.' And it is those goods which require direct personal contact which tend not to be traded and whose prices will not be reflected in exchange rates. In the case of developing countries there is the added complication that many services are not provided outside households.

An attempt to overcome some of the limitations of national income data has been made by Kravis et al. (1984). For a limited number of countries and for the year 1975 they have produced purchasing power parity measures of GDP

Table 2.2   Per Capita GDP and Price Levels, 1975, Six Groups of Countries by Income Class

	Income class					
	1	2	3	4	5	6
Per capita quantity converted by exchange rates (US dollars)						
GDP[a]	177	939	1,587	2,985	5,376	7,176
Purchasing power parities (international dollars)						
GDP[b]	646	1,660	2,577	3,737	5,454	7,176
Price levels (US=100)						
GDP	40.7	51.7	64.5	73.6	107.4	100.0
Tradables	60.7	70.7	86.6	97.9	118.5	100.0
Non-tradables	24.9	37.2	46.5	58.4	96.7	100.0
Exchange rate deviation index[c]	3.64	1.76	1.62	1.25	1.01	1.0

Source: Kravis et al. (1984)
Notes: The class intervals (with US per capita GDP of $7,176 equal to 100) and the countries in each real income class are:
  1. 0–14.9 Malawi, Kenya, India, Pakistan, Sri Lanka, Zambia, Thailand, Philippines
  2. 15.0–29.9 South Korea, Malaysia, Colombia, Jamaica, Syria, Brazil
  3. 30.0–44.9 Romania, Mexico, Yugoslavia, Iran, Uruguay, Ireland
  4. 45.0–59.9 Hungary, Poland, Italy, Spain
  5. 60.0–69.9 UK, Japan, Austria, Netherlands, Belgium, France, Luxembourg, West Germany
  7. 90.0–100.0 USA
  (c) is (b) divided by (a).

per capita. The results are presented in Table 2.2. When comparisons are made on the basis of the official exchange rates the income per capita of class 1 countries was 3.2 per cent of the income of class 5 countries whereas a purchasing power comparison revealed that class 1 countries earned 11.8 per cent of class 5 incomes. But the main finding in Table 2.2 is that the exchange rate comparisons of GDP per capita (line 4) systematically understate real incomes per capita and yield a rough trend in the exchange rate deviation which diminishes as the level of incomes of countries rises. The existence of this systematic relationship is useful because it makes it possible to produce a time series of real (purchasing power parity) incomes per head for different countries and then to observe the changes in the distribution of world income — on the assumption that non-traded goods are relatively unimportant.

Growth and Convergence

We have taken a snapshot of incomes at a point of time. But what does a long-run analysis of the world distribution of income reveal? Is there a tendency for a convergence of real incomes. Table 2.3 taken from Maddison (1982) presents some evidence for a group of industrialised market economies. All countries show some advance in productivity; but the range of productivity increases is considerable. Indeed, the rate of productivity increase seems to be inversely correlated with the levels of real income prevailing in the nineteenth century. Thus, Australia

Table 2.3   Percentage Increase in Productivity, GDP per Capita and Exports of 16 Industrial Countries, 1870–1979 (1970 US$)

	Real GDP per man hour	Real GDP per capita	Volume of exports
Australia	398	221	—
UK	585	310	930
Switzerland	830	471	4,400
Belgium	887	439	6,250
Netherlands	910	429	8,040
Canada	1,050	766	9,860
USA	1,080	693	9,240
Denmark	1,098	684	6,750
Italy	1,225	503	6,210
Austria	1,270	643	4,740
West Germany	1,510	824	3,370
Norway	1,560	873	7,740
France	1,590	694	4,410
Finland	1,710	1,016	6,240
Sweden	2,060	1,083	5,070
Japan	2,480	1,661	293,060

Source: Maddison (1982)

had the highest real income per capita in 1870 and the lowest growth rate between 1870 and 1979. Conversely, Japan had a low real income per capita in 1870 and a high growth rate between 1870 and 1979.

How, then, can we explain the tendency to convergence? Capital accumulation, education and technological progress suggest themselves as possible causes and they can be incorporated in the model of optimal capital accumulation first proposed by Ramsay (1928). Assume, initially, that a country's capital stock is small and the marginal product of capital is high; there will then be an inducement to save and invest. As the capital stock increases, the marginal product of capital will fall and there will be a slowing down of the growth rate of the economy.

Is the tendency to convergence universal? Data collected by Summers *et al.* (1986) for the post-war period suggest not. Figure 2.1 derived from Baumol (1986) reveals three zones of economic growth. At the top the elongated zone contains the advanced market economies with the United States having the highest real income per capita in 1950 and the lowest growth rate thereafter. Below lies a zone embracing the planned economies with lower real incomes and lower growth rates but still exhibiting some tendency to convergence. Finally, there are the developing countries whose growth rates bear no relationship to initial incomes.

Can we explain the differences between the three zones? In the case of the advanced economy we might use Ramsay's theory plus the diffusion of US knowhow through aid and trade. A similar process might be at work for the planned economies, with their failure to use markets resulting in lower growth rates and the devastation of the Second World War explaining their lower initial incomes. But what of the developing countries? One explanation for lack of convergence

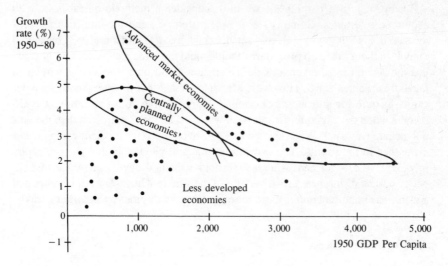

Source: Baumol (1986)

Figure 2.1 Growth Rates, 1950–80, GDP Per Capita Compared to 1950 Level, Advanced Market Economies, Centrally Planned Economies, Less Developed Economies

Table 2.4   Growth Rates of Population and GDP, 1965–80 (%)

	Population	GDP
Low income countries		
China and India	2.1	6.1
Other	1.9	6.8
Middle income countries		
Lower middle income countries	2.3	4.1
Upper middle income	2.1	4.1
Developing countries		
Oil exporters	2.7	3.9
Export manufacturing	1.9	5.9
Highly indebted	2.4	3.2
Sub-Saharan	3.0	2.3
High income oil exporters	4.8	2.6
Industrial market economies	0.7	3.0

Source: World Bank (1978)

may lie in different population pressures and the existence of low level equilibria traps. As real incomes rise they may be pulled down by the growth of population. Thus, Table 2.4 suggests that the developing countries do have high population growth rates and may therefore never reach a threshold income for growth. In Britain population growth persisted in keeping real wages constant until the middle of the nineteenth century. The information in Figure 2.1 needs to be taken in conjunction with the data presented in Chapter 1, which suggests a long-run failure of the Third World to catch up.

But by way of a parenthesis we must consider a methodological issue with economic overtones. Summers *et al.* measured national income (that is, they measured spending on goods and services) whereas Maddison (1983) measured output. In theory the two procedures should yield the same results because national income accounting conventions define spending and output in such a way as to make their values equal. However, Maddison noted that in 1965 the average per capita income for a group of developed countries was 56.2 per cent of the US income when the expenditure approach was used but 58.2 per cent when the output method was used. When applied to the developing countries there was a greater difference in the results. The expenditure method yielded an average per capita income of 16.73 per cent whereas the output method gave an average of 11.3 per cent. The differences arose because of the way in which services were treated and this has important implications for estimating the income gap in earlier periods.

The Kuznets Process

International comparisons of real income per head are a measure of inequality in the world distribution of income but, because they are averages, they tend to ignore intra-national dispersions of income. National movements in incomes are the result of complex intra-national changes in income distribution.

This brings us to the Kuznets thesis: 'in the early phases of industrialization, income inequality becomes first strong enough to increase and then reduce income inequalities'. Kuznets based his conclusion on a cross-section study of five countries — the United Kingdom, the United States, India, Sri Lanka and Puerto Rico — and his findings gave rise to the U-shaped pattern of income inequality first increasing and then decreasing with economic development. Kuznets's finding has attracted considerable attention and debate. Fields (1981) has suggested that increasing inequality may not be an inevitable concomitant of economic development and the concept of equity growth has been canvassed. But before examining the Kuznets thesis and its alternatives we need to consider some measures of inequality.

Measures of Inequality

The Lorenz Curve

The simplest measures of inequality are the Lorenz curve and the Gini coefficient. Figure 2.2 illustrates a Lorenz curve. Along the horizontal axis the number of income recipients is measured and along the vertical axis incomes are measured cumulatively. Both incomes and income recipients are expressed in percentage terms. A perfectly equal distribution of income would therefore be represented by the diagonal. In the diagram the curved line traces out the degree of income inequality.

Gini Coefficient

A method of summarising the degree of inequality displayed by the Lorenz curve is provided by the ratio of the shaded area under the line of perfect equality to the entire area under the diagonal: that is $A/A + B$. This measure is known as the Gini coefficient. But although it is widely used, it is impossible to capture a whole curve with a summary statistic. It is, for example, possible for two income distributions to yield the same Gini coefficient and yet for the distributions to be considerably different, as in Figure 2.3. Only if one distribution lay outside another would it be possible to say that one distribution were more equal than another.

The Atkinson Measure

To resolve the problem posed by intersecting Lorenz curves Atkinson (1987) has suggested the introduction of a social welfare function which specifies the welfare

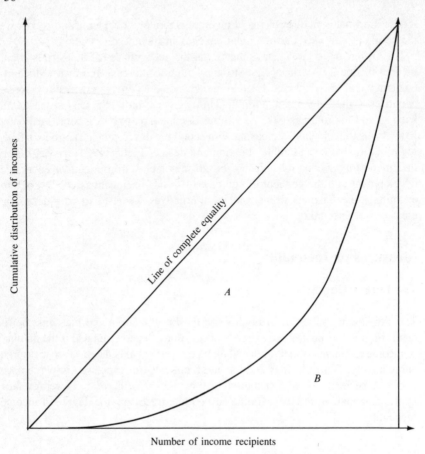

Figure 2.2 Cumulative Distribution of Income Recipients (%)

which society would attach to varying degrees of inequality. Such a parameter, ϵ, would take on values from zero (society is indifferent about the distribution of income) to infinity (when society is concerned only about the condition of the lowest income group). What the Atkinson measure does is to force us to consider what the desired distribution of income is and thereby eliminate the problem posed by intersecting Lorenz curves. In other words, is the greater equality at lower incomes presented by curve *A* preferable to the greater equality at high incomes presented by curve *B* in Figure 2.3?

The Theil Index

In comparing Lorenz curves two sources of inequality have to be considered: one is the degree of inequality within a given Lorenz curve and the other is the

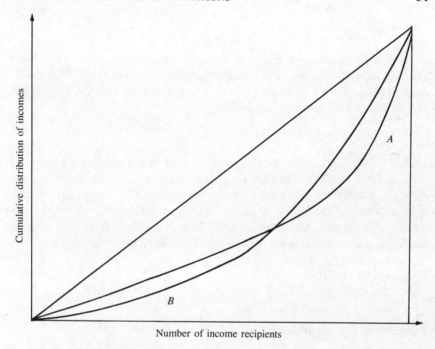

Figure 2.3 Intersecting Lorenz Curves

degree of inequality between two curves. Theil (1967) has proposed an index which attempts to incorporate both these factors.

Poverty

Absolute poverty may be defined by a head count ratio, Pn.

$$Pn = q/n$$

where

q = the number in poverty with income $y \leq z$
z = the poverty line
n = the population

But absolute poverty does not consider the extent to which individuals fall below the poverty line. Sen (1984) has therefore proposed a relative poverty index which measures the total income required to bring people up to the poverty line, Pg:

$$Pg = g_i$$

$$g_i = y_i = z - m$$

where z is the poverty line and m is the mean income of the poor. In addition Sen has sought to measure the distribution of poverty by means of a Gini coefficient and to produce a synthetic index Ps which measures both the poverty gap and its distribution between individuals:

$$Ps = Pn \, [g_i + (1 - g_i) \, G]$$

where G is the Gini coefficient. Ps should vary between 0 and 1; when everyone is above z then Ps is zero and when Ps is 1 then everyone earns nothing. However, Kakwani (1980) has drawn attention to the fact that when Ps is differentiated with respect to I and G the derivative implies that the larger the inequality of income among the poor the smaller the increase in poverty when I increases; whereas the result should be the other way round. Therefore, he suggests

$$P_s = P_n g_i \, (I + G)$$

Economic Development and Income Distribution

We can now return to the Kuznets thesis. Tables 2.5 and 2.6 present cross-studies of Gini coefficients around 1970. In Table 2.5 the degree of inequality tends to become greater as we move from the industrialised countries through the middle income countries to the low income countries — which would seem to confirm the Kuznets thesis.

Table 2.6 reveals considerable differences among countries in the degree of income inequality, with the highest coefficients being recorded in the African and Latin American countries. What stands out are the sharp differences in income inequality in various parts of the Third World, with Asia showing more equality than Africa and Latin America. The developed economies show more equality than the developing countries. The results seem to confirm the Kuznets thesis; but when the Gini coefficients are regressed against the income levels then only about 20 per cent of the variation in inequality is explained.

Table 2.5 Gini Coefficients for the World and Selected Regions, c. 1970

Low income countries	0.461
Middle income countries	0.544
Industrialised countries	0.393
Oil states	0.544
World	0.677

Source: Grosh and Nafziger (1986)

Table 2.6 Gini Coefficients for 50 Countries, c. 1970

		Developing countries			
Asia		*Africa*		*Latin America*	
Indonesia	0.462	Madagascar	0.562	Argentina	0.437
India	0.467	Ivory Coast	0.456	Chile	0.506
Pakistan	0.33	Dahomey	0.467	Venezuela	0.622
Malaysia	0.504	Malawi	0.470	Costa Rica	0.416
Sri Lanka	0.378	Chad	0.369	Colombia	0.557
Hong Kong	0.430	Tanzania	0.503	Brazil	0.574
Korea, South	0.360	Senegal	0.587	Mexico	0.524
Taiwan	0.329	Uganda	0.401	Dominican Republic	0.493
Philippines	0.494	Sierra Leone	0.612	Panama	0.557
Thailand	0.385	Sudan	0.446	El Salvador	0.539
				Ecuador	0.526
				Barbados	0.426
Average	0.407	Average	0.487	Average	0.515
		Developed countries			
Denmark	0.386	Norway	0.362	Finland	0.406
West Germany	0.334	France	0.518	UK	0.362
Netherlands	0.449	Spain	0.393	Greece	0.381
Hungary	0.251	Yugoslavia	0.347	Japan	0.393
Australia	0.318	New Zealand	0.371		
Canada	0.33	Sweden	0.406		
		Average	0.380		

Source: Kakwani (1980)

What happens to the degree of inequality as economic development proceeds? Consider, for example, the case of an economy consisting of an agricultural sector and a manufacturing sector. Let us also assume that within each sector there is complete equality of incomes but that the average income is higher in the manufacturing sector. Labour will then flow from the rural to the urban sector and as the manufacturing sector expands it will draw more labour from the countryside until incomes are equalised between the sectors.

In this simple example, which lies at the heart of the Kuznets process, the question of whether there are inequalities of incomes within the sectors is assumed away. It is also assumed that there is no technological progress in the farm sector, no programme of land reform and no rural industrialisation. When the problem is set in a realistic context the distinction between an agricultural sector and a manufacturing sector may be false. It is thus conceivable that a programme of providing small-scale industries in rural areas could reduce income inequality as in Taiwan, where, throughout the post-war period of accelerated growth, there has been a continuous progress towards greater equality of income distribution, making it an exception to the Kuznets thesis. Indeed, once we allow for change in the rural sector then many possibilities emerge. On the one hand, agricultural innovations, such as a Green Revolution, could lead to a displacement of labour and the emergence of rich farmers and landless labourers — an English type of agricultural revolution. The landless labourers might then migrate to the towns and form a subsistence sector of workers in personal services. The degree of income inequality could then widen in both sectors. Extended to the world economy, the movement of labour from developing countries to the advanced countries in the 1960s could have increased inequality. On the other hand, a programme of land reform could reduce the size of landholdings, increase productivity and create more equality. Thus, Berry and Cline (1979) have found strong evidence for an inverse relationship between productivity and farm size in Brazil, the Philippines and India.

Latin America

In assessing the effect of economic development on income distribution there is a need to take account of demographic changes. Brazil presents an apparent paradox of economic growth with a worsening size distribution of incomes. Between 1967 and 1981 Brazilian GNP grew at a rate of 8.1 per cent per annum, a slightly faster rate than the 7 per cent growth rate achieved between 1947 and 1967. But this growth rate was accompanied by increasing inequality. The World Bank *Development Report* of 1987 revealed that in 1972 half of household income was received by the top decile and two-thirds by the top quintile; the poorest quintile received 2 per cent.

But increasing inequality seems to have been an inevitable consequence of Brazil's surplus labour economy and Morley (1983) has argued that the measures of inequality used are inappropriate in a dynamic economy because they measure an individual's or household's income in a single period rather than lifetime income. If the poor can expect their incomes to rise then the fact that there are substantial numbers of poor people may be unimportant. To be born at all gives the possibility of betterment in a society with substantial mobility between rural and urban areas. Brazilian experience, therefore, indicates the difficulties of making any welfare comparisons of income distribution when the composition of the population is changing. If the population is increasing and the increase varies with the level of income of different groups in society, then the dispersion incomes of various groups will alter and can result in intersecting Lorenz curves. Hence, it may be difficult to make unambiguous welfare statements and it may not be necessary to explain increasing inequality as the result of wage controls or authoritarian capitalism. Instead, increasing inequality could be the consequence of a continuous labour surplus and a skill-intensive pattern of growth — although the skill-intensive pattern of growth would need explanation in the presence of surplus unskilled labour. But we conclude with the observations contained in Table 2.7 which reveal that between 1960 and 1980 the Gini coefficient rose, the share of the lowest 40 per cent fell and the share of the top decile showed little change, which would seem to suggest that only a few of the very poor had rising lifetime incomes.

Table 2.7 Income Distribution in Brazil, 1960—80

	1960 Langoni	1970 Langoni	1970 Adjusted[a]	1980
Cini	0.50	0.565	0.580	0.590
Percentage share of lowest 40 per cent	11.57	10.03	9.74	9.72
Share of the top decile	39.66	46.67	48.03	47.89

Sources: Langoni (1973), Denslow and Tyler (1984)
Note: (a) Earlier data not strictly comparable due to truncation of upper tail of data, hence the adjustment.

Another Latin American country whose income distribution has been intensively analysed is Colombia. According to Berry and Urrutia (1976) income distribution was about the same in the 1960s as it was in the 1930s. There was a deterioration up to the 1950s and thereafter an improvement which gave a time path conforming to the Kuznets process. Urrutia has suggested that, as in the case of Brazil, many of the social measures introduced may have long-term effects which cannot be measured by simple snapshot statistics. Foxley (1976) has edited a volume of papers which has dealt with other Latin American countries. Cuba managed to bring about a redistribution of income after the revolution of 1959. The major contributing factors were land reform and employment policy which resulted in a shift in income distribution until the 1970s. There was also an attempt to reduce the influence of Havana upon the distribution of income. Taking Latin America as a whole it would appear that Colombia might have passed the turning point in the Kuznets process and Cuba may have achieved some improvement in equality. But for the remainder it would appear that there has been no major deterioration in the incomes of the poor although their relative position may not have improved. In some countries the absence of improvement may reflect the persistence of large landholdings and the tendency of the urban rich to prefer imported goods, with the result that there is little development of domestic manufacturing and the exchange of raw materials for manufactures becomes a permanent state of affairs. In other cases the decision to pursue a policy of import substitution industrialisation has meant that incomes have been kept unequal in order to create a market for manufactures; not only have the poor been kept in poverty but manufacturing industries have been unable to enjoy economies of scale.

Asia

Poverty rather than inequality has characterised much of Asia, especially India. According to Dandekar and Rath (1971) the consumption of the bottom 20 per cent of the rural poor increased by only 2 per cent between 1960 and 1968 while there was a marked deterioration for the bottom 20 per cent of the urban poor.

However, the results are affected by the choice of terminal years and 1960 was a good year for agriculture. What happened in the 1960s seems to have been an export of the poor from the rural to the urban areas. In the second half of the 1960s high yielding varieties of rice and wheat were introduced to Asia; but the available evidence seems to suggest that this produced an increase in inequality as only the richer farmers were able to take advantage of the innovations. In Malaysia Lee (1981) found that inequality fell between 1957 and 1959 and fell in Sri Lanka between 1963 and 1973. Since the end of the Second World War successive governments in Sri Lanka have pursued policies of food subsidisation, free education and free health care. However, these policies could be maintained only by curtailing investment in physical capital and as a result growth has slowed down and balance of payments difficulties have occurred. In 1977 a newly elected government placed greater emphasis upon growth and investment and substituted means tested food stamps for subsidised food. The resulting increase in inequality was greatest in the urban areas.

Some Asian countries managed to achieve high degrees of income equality as well as high economic growth rates (sometimes called growth with equity). In the case of Hong Kong, Hsia and Chau (1978) found that the economy had a growth rate of 10 per cent between 1967 and 1982 and this transformed a labour surplus economy into one with labour shortages. Over the period 1961 to 1971 income dispersion narrowed. In Taiwan the Kuznets turning point was reached about 1968 (Feis, Ranis and Kuo 1979) and Taiwan appears to have achieved a high degree of equality through land reform and rural industrialisation. Finally, South Korea appears to have achieved growth with equity in the 1950s and 1960s. However, inequality started to emerge in the 1970s as a result of governments fostering the growth of heavy industry. In the 1980s the world depression began to slow down economic growth but rising expectations served to bring about political unrest as a result of the lag of political freedoms behind the rise in incomes.

The Japanese experience is perhaps the most interesting, not only because of the existence of statistics to measure inequality which go back into the nineteenth century, but because it has been considered to be a forerunner of developments in the other Confucian societies of Asia. The evidence for the early periods is based upon wage data; household data is available only for later years. But splicing the two sources together suggests that the rural/urban differential remained constant before World War 1, widened in the 1920s and narrowed after 1960. For China information is limited; but the emphasis there since the Revolution upon establishing basic needs suggests that income inequality may have been less than in many other developing countries. There is the supporting evidence that life expectancy and literacy rates have been much higher than in India.

Centrally Planned Economies: USSR

Because of the substantial replacement of private by public ownership of the means of production, the planned economies might be supposed to exhibit more equality than the market economies. Yet information to support this is surprisingly sparse. There is also the complicating problem of the relationship between money incomes and real incomes in economies where consumer goods are priced below market clearing prices and there are continual complaints of empty shelves and a persistent tendency for goods sold in collective farm markets to command higher premiums than those sold in official retail markets. A rationing system might favour the low paid because they might be presumed to have a low cost of waiting; but this may be offset by the fact that the well paid seem to have better access to better quality goods through sources of supply not available to the low paid. Finally, there are exchange controls which tend to make puchasing power comparisons difficult.

Drawing upon various sources, Bergson (1984) has compared wage inequality in the USSR and Western European countries and concluded that there are striking similarities; but when the stage of economic development is taken into account (the Kuznets factor) then there may be less inequality. When analysed over a long period there appear to have been three cycles in the movement of income dispersion. In the first period, after the Revolution, inequality fell. It then rose in the Stalin period and started to decline in the post-war period until relatively recently. Real incomes are, however, affected by the peculiarities of the Soviet retail market and the highest income groups have greater access to goods.

The United States

In colonial and pre-revolutionary America there was a high degree of income equality, the product of a relatively homogeneous population and an open frontier. From the Civil War to the Great Crash (1860–1929) the degree of inequality seems to have increased and its cause appears to have been the rapid rise in total productivity in manufacturing which agriculture did not manage to emulate until much later. After 1929 the impact of the New Deal seems to have brought a greater equality which lasted until the end of the Second World War. As a result of equilibrium between opposing forces the degree of inequality remained constant through the 1950s to the 1970s. On the one hand, changes in the age distribution of the population, more single parent families and changes in living arrangements whereby older children moved out of the parental home were factors promoting inequality. On the other hand, social security benefits tended to redress many of the emerging inequalities. But since the 1970s there has been a questioning of social security benefits on the grounds that they reduce the willingness to work and save and result in a slower growth rate. Hence, there have been moves to deregulate the economy which may increase inequalities (Table 2.8).

Non-economic Indicators

So far we have concentrated upon those aspects of economic welfare which can be brought within the ambit of the measuring rod of money. However, as we

Table 2.8 Gini Coefficients of the Distribution of Incomes of Families and Unrelated Individuals, USA

1929	0.49	1947	0.418
1935–36	0.47	1952	0.408
1941	0.44	1962	0.407
		1970	0.419

Source: Blinder (1980)

Table 2.9 Selected Indicators of Living Standards for Economic Blocs

	Population (millions)	Growth 1970–82	GNP per head ($)	Growth 1960–82 (%)	Inflation (%) 1960–77	Inflation (%) 1970–82	Life expectancy	Higher education (%)
Low income countries	2,266.5	1.5	280	3.6	3.2	11.5	59	4
China and India	1,785.2	1.7	290	3.5	—	—	62	4
Other	541.3	2.6	250	11.1	3.2	11.7	52	2
Middle income countries	1,158.3	2.2	1,520	3.6	3.0	12.8	60	11
Oil exporters	519.5	2.5	1,260	3.6	3.0	13.9	60	8
Oil importers	638.8	2.0	1,710	3.5	3.0	12.7	63	13
High income oil exporters	17.0	5.0	14,820	5.6	—	16.0	58	8
Industrial market economies	722.9	0.7	10,108	3.3	4.3	9.9	75	37

Source: UNCTAD (1986)

noted in the case of Brazil, it is important also to consider non-economic factors. In Table 2.9 we draw attention to other aspects of the world distribution of well being, life expectancy, literacy and population growth. The average life expectancy figure of 62 years for India and China conceals an expectancy of some 66 to 69 years in China and 52 years in India.

Conclusions

Economic welfare is one aspect of welfare; but using national income data as a measure of ecfare is fraught with difficulties. Even comparisons between individuals within a country run into difficulties. Economists have sought to surmount the obstacles by assuming that there is a relationship between the prices of goods and the utility (ecfare) which is derived from those goods. But in the final analysis interpersonal comparisons would seem to require some homogeneity of individuals within a community or the introduction of an ethical yardstick. Despite these strictures, national income statistics are used to suggest international comparisons of welfare and given the willingness to use such information two questions suggest themselves. First, is the gap between rich and poor countries narrowing? Second, is the gap between rich and poor within a country an inevitable result of economic development? There were signs of convergence between the advanced and planned economies, but further discussion is deferred until the chapter on the USSR and Eastern Europe. For the developing countries there are no signs of convergence. Our answer to the second question is agnostic. Economic development may or may not be associated with increasing equality and inequality may not be necessary for economic development. The economies of South-east Asia have demonstrated that it is possible to take off into growth and maintain equality; and the centrally planned economies have always tended to place emphasis upon equality.

Bibliography

Adelman, I. and Morris, C.T. (1973) *Economic Growth and Social Equity in Developing Countries,* Stanford University Pres.

Ahluwalia, M.S. (1976) 'Inequality, poverty and development', *Journal of Development Studies,* vol. 3, pp. 340–384.

Arnott, R.J. and Gersovitz, M. (1986) 'Social welfare underpinnings of urban bias and unemployment', *Economic Journal,* vol. 96, pp. 413–424.

Atkinson, A.B. (1987) 'On the measurement of poverty', *Econometrica,* 55, pp. 742–764.

Bairoch, P. (1983) 'International industrialization levels, 1750–1980', *Journal of European Economic History,* vol. 11, pp. 269–333.

Baumol, W.J. (1986) 'Productivity growth, convergence and welfare: what the long-run data show', *American Economic Review,* vol. 76, pp. 1072–1086

Bergsman, J. (1985) *Income Distribution and Poverty in Mexico,* World Bank Staff Working Paper, No. 395.

Bergson, A. (1984) 'Income inequality under Soviet socialism', *Journal of Economic Literature,* vol. 22, pp. 1052–1095.

Berry, A.R. (1983) 'Predicting income distribution in Latin America during the 1980s', in
   A.R. Ritter and D.H. Pollock (eds) *Latin American Prospects for the 1980s*, Praeger.
Berry, A.R., Bourguinon, C. and Morrison, E. (1983) 'The level of world inequality: how
   much can one say?', *Review of Income and Wealth*, vol. 29, pp. 217–242.
Berry, A.R. and Cline, W.R. (1979) *Agrarian Structure and Productivity in Developing
   Countries*, Johns Hopkins.
Berry, A.R. and Urrutia, M. (1976) *Income Distribution in Colombia*, Yale University
   Press.
Bienen, H. and Diejomaoh, V.P. (1981) *The Political Economy of Income Distribution
   in Nigeria*, Holmes and Meier.
Blinder, A. (1980) 'Income distribution', in M. Feldstein (ed.) *The American Economy in
   Transition*, National Bureau of Economic Research.
Castro, A.P. *et al.* (1981) 'Indicators of rural inequality', *World Development*, vol. 9,
   pp. 401–408.
Dandekar, V.M. and Rath, N. (1971) 'Poverty in India', *Economic and Political Weekly*,
   vol. 6, pp. 32–40.
Denslow Jr, D. and Tyler, W. (1984) 'Perspectives on poverty and income inequality in
   Brazil', *World Development*, vol. 12, pp. 1019–1025.
Feis, J.C., Ranis, G. and Kuo, S. (1979) *Growth with Equity: The Taiwan Case*, Oxford
   University Press.
Felix, D. (1983) 'Income distribution and the quality of life in Latin America: patterns,
   trends and policy implications', *Latin American Research Review*, vol. 18, pp. 3–33.
Fields, G.S. (1981) *Poverty, Inequality and Development*, Cambridge University Press.
Foxley, A. (1976) *Income Distribution in Latin America*, Cambridge University Press.
Friedman, M. and Friedman, R. (1984) *Free to Choose*, Secker and Warburg.
George, V. and Lawson, R. (1984) *Poverty and Inequality in Common Market Countries*,
   Routledge.
Georgescu Roegen, N. (1966) *Analytical Economics*, Harvard University Press.
Griffin, K. (1974) 'The international transmission of inequality', *World Development*, vol.
   2, pp. 3–16.
Grosh, M.E. and Nafziger, E.W. (1986) 'The computation of world income distribution',
   Economic Development and Cultural Change, vol. 34, pp. 347–360.
Horvat, B. (1987) 'The welfare of the common man in various countries', *World Develop-
   ment*, vol. 2, pp. 29–39.
Hsia, R. and Chau, L. (1978) 'Industrialization and income distribution in Hong Kong',
   International Labour Review, vol. 117, pp. 316–324.
Kakwani, N. (1980) *Income Inequality and Poverty*, Cambridge University Press.
Kaldor, N. (1970) 'The case for regional policies', *Scottish Journal of Political Economy*,
   vol. 20, pp. 17–25.
Kravis, I.B. *et al.* (1984) 'Comparative studies of national incomes and prices', *Journal
   of Economic Literature*, vol. 22, pp. 1–39.
Kuznets, S. (1955) 'Economic growth and income inequality', *American Economic Review*,
   vol. 45, pp. 18–25.
Langoni, C.G. (1973) *Distribuicao da Renda e Desenvolimento Economico do Brasil*,
   Expressao e Cultura.
Lee, E. (1981) *Export-led Industrialization and Development*, ILO.
Lewis, W.A. (1955) *A Theory of Economic Growth*, Allen and Unwin.
Lewis, W.A. (1976) 'Development and distribution' in A. Cairncross and M. Puri (eds)
   Employment, Income Distribution and Development Strategy, Macmillan.
Lewis, W.A. (1978) *Growth and Fluctuations 1870–1913*, Allen and Unwin.
Maddison, A. (1982) *Phases of Capitalist Development*, Oxford University Press.
Maddison, A. (1983) 'A comparison of levels of GDP per capita in developed and develop-
   ing countries, 1700–1980', *Journal of Economic History*, vol. 43, pp. 78–85.

Marris, R. (1984) 'Comparing the incomes of nations: a critique of the international comparisons project', *Journal of Economic Literature*, vol. 22, pp. 40–57.

Morley, S. (1983) *Labor Markets and Inequitable Growth: The Case of Authoritarian Capitalism in Brazil*, Cambridge University Press.

Myrdal, G. (1957) *Economic Theory and Underdeveloped Regions*, Duckworth.

Nugent, J. (1979) 'The distribution of income and its determinants', *Latin American Research Review*, vol. 14, pp. 239–245.

Ramsay, F.P. (1928) 'A mathematical theory of saving', *Economic Journal*, vol. 38, pp. 543–559.

Sen, A.K. (1984) *Resources, Value and Development*, Blackwell.

Smith, J.D. (1984) 'Trends in the concentration of personal wealth in the United States, 1958–1976', *Review of Income and Wealth*, vol. 30, pp. 215–224.

Stewart, F. (1984) *Planning to Meet Basic Needs*, Macmillan.

Streeten, P. (1980) 'Basic needs and human rights', *World Development*, vol. 8, pp. 107–111.

Summers, R., Kravis, I. and Heston, R. (1986) 'Changes in world income distribution', *Journal of Policy Modelling*, vol. 6, pp. 237–269.

Theil, H. (1967) *Economics and Information Theory*, North Holland.

UNCTAD (1986) *Handbook of International Trade and Development Statistics*, United Nations.

UNCTAD (1988) *Handbook of International Trade and Development Statistics*, United Nations.

Urrutia, M. (1985) *Winners and Losers in Colombian Economic Growth*, Oxford University Press.

Williamson, J.G. (1985) *Did British Capitalism Breed Inequality?*, Allen and Unwin.

World Bank (1978) *World Development Report*, United Nations.

3

Agrarian Economies

Most Third World countries are agrarian societies; some are mineral producers; all are classed as primary producers. But the United States, Canada, Australia, New Zealand and Western Europe have large farming sectors and are not usually considered to be poor. Therein lies the paradox. Are Third World peasants irrational and inefficient in allocating their resources or does their poverty stem from a lack of resources which requires foreign aid to alleviate it? Is there a problem of price instability which leads to income instability and poverty — a poverty which is more easily dealt with in the advanced economies through the use of farm subsidies? Are Third World agricultural institutions efficient but second best responses to the risks inherent in the environment? Do those risks explain the predominance of sharecropping (profit sharing) as opposed to wage contracts? Are the high interest rates charged nationally and internationally by money lenders a reflection not merely of the scarcity of finance but a means by which lenders screen borrowers in order to produce an acceptable level of risk and default? Have the agricultural policies of the advanced countries had such an adverse effect upon Third World agriculture that the less developed countries should dissociate themselves from the international economy? Has integration into the world economy compelled Third World farms to produce cash crops (pineapples, for example) and reduced their capacity to produce basic foodstuffs?

Agrarian economies display a variety of contractual relationships and outcomes: shifting cultivation, plantations and agribusinesses; self-proprietors, sharecroppers and wage labour; concealed unemployment and underemployment. We begin with an examination of the problems of self-proprietors and the risks they face in product markets. We then move on to sharecropping and wage labour. The types of employment contract are influenced by population pressures and the availability of land. We therefore need to consider the theory of population and migration as responses to both population pressures on the available land and the need to industrialise in order to diversify the economy. Then we touch upon the issue of land reform. Finally, we consider the impact of the advanced countries upon Third World agriculture.

Self-Proprietors

The self-employed farmer faces risks from the supply side and from the demand side; both risks may affect his income. Supply-side risks comprise floods, drought, diseases and pests. Demand-side risks include the possibility that consumers may choose substitutes (soft drinks instead of coffee or tea). If all risks emanate from the supply side and the demand curve has a unit price elasticity then all risks can be accommodated through price adjustments since total revenue remains constant under a unit price elastic demand curve. But if the demand curve is not unit elastic, then a farmer may attempt to insure against risks. Diversifying crops is possible if all crops are not subject to the same risk. If diversification is not possible then a farmer may attempt to accommodate risks by variations in his permanent or lifetime income or by insuring with merchants or with government. The effect of such insurance schemes is to superimpose a unit price elastic demand curve upon the actual demand curve. In Figure 3.1 the unit demand curve is $D'D'$ and the actual demand curve is DD. Suppose that $S''S''$ is the unexpected short-run supply curve. Merchants or government could maintain a price OP'' by buying up what the market will not purchase — cd units — and farmers' incomes would be $OP''.OQ''$ ($= OP.OQ$). Now suppose the unexpected supply curve is $S'S'$. This time there is a market shortage of ab and the merchants or government could again act as a buffer by selling off an amount ab of their stocks. In this case the farmers' incomes are equal to $OP'.OQ'$ which is again equal to $OP''.OQ''$ and $OP.OQ$ because $D'D''$ is a rectangular hyperbola. (A similar analysis might be conducted for demand shifts.)

Under what circumstances will farmers enter into such insurance contracts? The most widely used model of decision making under uncertainty embodies what is known as the expected utility theorem. The essence of the theorem is that an individual will estimate the utility he will obtain from each possible state of the world and the probability that each state of the world will occur. The utility associated with each outcome is then multiplied by the probability that it will occur and the expected utility is the sum of these weighted probabilities:

$$EU = p.U(A) + (1 - p)U(B) \tag{3.1}$$

where EU is the expected utility, A and B are the states of the world, p is the probability of A occurring and $(1 - p)$ is the probability of B occurring.

Suppose that a farmer bets £100 at odds of 5 to 1 that there will be a drought and that the probability of drought is 1/15. The expected utility of the gamble is calculated by finding the farmer's wealth in the event of a drought and in the absence of a drought. The expected utility is

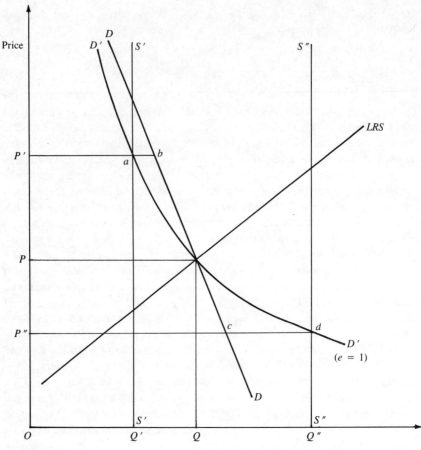

Figure 3.1

$$EU = 1/15. \ U \ (W_0 + 500) + 14/15 \ (W_0 - 100) \tag{3.2}$$

The first term on the righthand side of the equation is composed of the probability of winning (1/15) and the utility associated with the final wealth (W_0 + 500); that is, the initial wealth plus the amount received from the insurer if there was a drought. The second term gives the probability of there not being a drought (of losing the bet) which is (1 − 1/15) and the loss of utility associated with the initial wealth being reduced by the gamble. Now most individuals are risk-averse and will undertake a gamble only if the expected utility from the gamble exceeds the utility that might be expected from the initial wealth. In this case the gamble would be rejected because the expected gain is negative.

$$500.1/15 \; - \; 100.14/15 < 0 \qquad\qquad\qquad (3.3)$$

Under what circumstances might insurance arrangements break down? The obvious answer is where the expected gains are less than the costs of insurance; for fluctuations in income which are expected to be small a farmer may not take out insurance. Instead, he may insure with himself through variations in his lifetime consumption. A more cogent reason for the breakdown of insurance schemes is the insurer's fear of moral hazard: farmers may be tempted into imprudence because they believe that they can claim on their insurance policies. Thus, farmers may be tempted to overproduce because they know that the surplus will be bought up by governments.

International Commodity Agreements and Compensatory Finance

This has a bearing upon the case for international commodity agreements, which seek to soften fluctuations in price by the fixing of export prices and the creation of buffer stocks. History has not been kind to such agreements. The International Sugar Agreement, signed in 1977, failed to stabilise world sugar prices. For most of the period of its operation the world price was below the minimum price of the Agreement. A similar story can be told of the Cocoa Agreements, the first of which was negotiated in 1972, and which repeatedly failed to keep the cocoa price within the target prices. In 1980 a new agreement was reached but it contained no production or export quotas and neither the United States, a major importer, nor the Ivory Coast, a major exporter, joined the scheme. In coffee markets there have been attempts to control prices by commodity agreements between producers and consumers and cartels of producers. But the attempts to control prices were undermined by the expansion of output in Africa and had to be accommodated by reductions in Brazil's output.

Given the difficulties of securing commodity agreements it is tempting to consider an alternative approach of seeking to try and increase the level and stability of earnings from total commodity exports by providing compensatory finance. One such scheme is contained within the Lomé Convention which is an agreement designed to give some African, Caribbean and Pacific countries access on favourable terms to the highly protected European Community. The main stabilising element of the convention, called Stabex, applies only to exports to the EEC of a number of tropical agricultural commodities plus iron ore and simple processed goods. However, the funds have not always been adequate for the objectives and the distribution of the compensation has been uneven, with richer countries tending to get the largest share. Furthermore, the benefits from Lomé have been nullified by the dumping by EEC countries of substitute commodities, such as sugar beet, in third markets; this has resulted in lost earnings to developing countries. A more general scheme operated by the IMF enables countries to borrow up to 125 per cent of their IMF quota. However, payments by the IMF have not always been readily forthcoming, even in periods when the export earnings of the Third World countries have been high and the repayment of loans feasible. Third World countries have pressed for a more universal approach in terms of tariff concessions as well as compensatory finance.

Pastoralism

In semi-arid areas self-proprietorship may give way to pastoralism and common property rights in which graziers share an area of land. Such common property rights systems have been criticised on the grounds that they provide no protection against overgrazing. In other words, a form of moral hazard may emerge: the cost to each farmer of putting extra animals on the land is less than the cost he imposes on others. But the persistence of pastoralism and the pattern of shifting cultivation should warn against such criticisms. The persistence of pastoralism suggests that it may contain methods of preventing such an abuse of common property rights. What may undermine such systems are population growth; differences between rich and poor farmers; and the breakdown of trust when property rights are uncertain.

Population Growth, Sharecropping and Wage Labour

In an economy with plentiful land an individual might be indifferent between self-employment, partnership (sharecropping) and wage labour. At the margin the returns on each form of activity would be equalised. But when population pressure increases and land becomes scarce the urge to accumulate and own land becomes important. The question then arises as to what form contracts between landlords and landless labourers should take. Table 3.1 throws some light upon the prevalence of wage labour in the less developed countries. With the exception of some parts of Latin America and Sri Lanka — in both regions plantation agriculture is common — there is a relative lack of wage labour and a predominance of self-employment and sharecropping, although it is possible to find the three forms of contract coexisting. It is also common to find that markets are interlocked, so that landlords supply credit, food and other inputs as well as land.

How can we account for the prevalence of sharecropping? Earlier economists, such as Adam Smith, regarded sharecropping as a form of tax and as such inferior to a fixed rental contract — thereby suggesting that peasants were irrational. But the persistence of sharecropping suggested to Cheung (1969) that the classical analysis was flawed.

In Figure 3.2 the vertical axis measures the marginal and average products of

Table 3.1 Developing Countries: Share of Wage Labour in Agricultural Employment

	Year	%	Year	%	Year	%
Argentina	1960	50.0	1970	53.2	1980	53.0
Bolivia	1950	10.0	1976	11.7		
Brazil	1960	25.5	1970	25.4		
Chile	1960	67.0	1970	61.8	1983	45.1
Costa Rica	1963	52.8	1973	59.7	1983	63.3
Dominican Republic	1960	24.6	1970	29.7	1981	19.4
Ecuador	1962	39.9	1974	36.7	1981	29.3
El Salvador	1961	63.8	1971	47.4		
Honduras	1961	27.5	1974	29.0		
Mexico	1960	53.6	1970	50.0		
Nicaragua	1963	48.1	1971	45.7		
Panama	1960	15.5	1970	20.8	1980	27.6
Uruguay	1962	53.6	1975	50.8		
Venezuela	1961	33.0	1971	27.7	1984	33.1
Algeria	1966	59.3	1977	48.3		
Egypt	1960	34.7	1976	49.9		
Morocco	1960	34.7	1977	52.0		
India	1961	23.1	1971	36.5		
Indonesia	1964	20.4	1971	23.6		
Iran	1960	25.2	1976	18.6		
Korea (South)	1960	9.7	1976	9.1	1984	12.0
Pakistan	1961	14.0	1976	8.0	1985	11.0
Philippines	1960	11.1	1075	17.1	1983	15.2
Sri Lanka	1963	54.8	1971	51.0	1981	45.0
Syria	1960	37.5	1970	18.6		
Thailand	1960	3.1	1970	4.1	1980	9.0

Source: ILO (1965–85)

labour and the horizontal axis measures the quantities of labour applied to a given quantity of land. Under a sharecropping system the landlord would obtain a share denoted by the difference between MP_L, the marginal product of labour, and $MP_{L(1-s)}$ where $MP_{L(1-s)}$ is the tenant's income after paying the landlord the share s. Now if the tenant had an opportunity cost wage of OW then it would be optimal for him to supply OL labour, which is less than the amount OL_1 which would maximise the landlord's rent. This is the tax analogy; but it can be misleading. If the tenant could rent land on these terms he could obtain for himself a rent measured by the area A over and above his opportunity cost and this would conflict with the assumption of perfect competition in the labour market. The landlord could try to insist upon the tenant providing OL_1 amount of labour but this would be agreeable only if the area B were equal to area A. If B were greater than A then the landlord could offer to increase the amount of land and decrease the rent share, while insisting upon an increase in the amount of labour

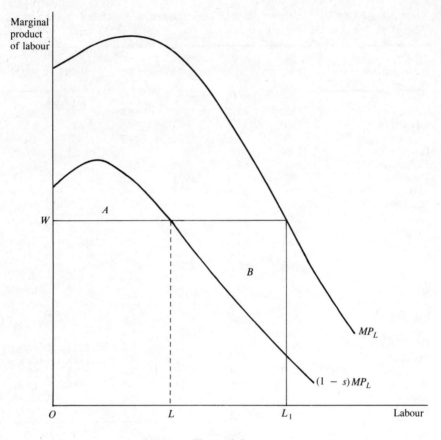

Figure 3.2

supplied. And if *A* were greater than *B* then it would be profitable for him to reduce the amount of land offered.

What Cheung's analysis suggests, therefore, is that the landlord could obtain the same return under a fixed rental system as he could obtain under a share-cropping system, provided that he could fix both the amount of land leased to the tenant and the amount of labour the tenant must supply. If there were free competition then a fixed rental system and a sharecropping system would be equally efficient — a conclusion which follows from the Coase theorem, which states that if property rights are clearly defined and negotiations are costless, then exter-nalities can be internalised. (The Coase theorem suggests that if there are unrealised gains from trade then attempts will be made to realise them. Landlords may bribe or penalise workers and workers may offer more effort for greater rewards. A revised contract will be made if the potential gainers can compensate the poten-tial losers and still be better off or if the potential losers from a change can bribe the potential gainers not to press for a change and still be better off.)

Cheung suggested that the type of contract adopted would depend upon the attitude to risk. (Hence, different marginal product curves could be drawn in Figure 3.2 to denote different states of nature.) If the labourers were risk-averse then they would choose wage contracts; if landlords were risk-averse then they would choose fixed rental contracts; and if both landlords and tenants were risk-averse then they would share risks through sharecropping. But negotiations may not be costless. A landlord who offers workers a fixed wage may have to employ supervisors to make sure that they do not shirk. The problems of supervision can therefore lead to two-tier markets in which some workers are offered permanent contracts (salaried contracts) with a large differential in order to supervise others; the incentive to supervise efficiently would be ensured by the large drop in earnings that would occur if they were dismissed and became wage labourers. We may also observe that in villages where labour mobility is low it might be possible to accumulate information about the qualities of workers over the year. But in conclusion we should recognise that sharecropping may not be the only means of resolving the problem of what to do about the tenant who shirks and the fact that landlords often provide credit and other inputs (because of their easier access to other markets) may strengthen the case for sharecropping.

Employment Contracts: A Digression

Although we have been concentrating upon employment contracts in agriculture, the analysis should not be seen in parochial terms. Stripped of fine detail the structure of employment contracts carries over into an industrial setting. Thus, Markusen (1979) has distinguished between wage contracts, salary contracts, and profit sharing contracts, with the choice of contract being dictated by the following factors:

1. the degree of risk-averseness of employers and workers;
2. the ease of access to information of employers and workers;
3. the work—leisure preferences of workers;
4. existence of unemployment benefits;
5. methods and costs of enforcing contracts;
6. transactions costs associated with hiring, training and dismissing workers.

Under a wage contract management may offer workers a fixed payment and no job security if workers are no more risk-averse than management are, if unemployment benefits exist and if workers are prepared to accept the bunching of leisure periods. When workers are extremely risk-averse then they will prefer salaried contracts under which they are guaranteed a wage and employment. Whether management will offer such contracts will depend upon its attitude to risk and its ability to spread risk through the capital market. A profit sharing contract is one in which employment is offered but the reward may be variable and its acceptance may depend upon whether workers can exercise some control over decision making.

Of course, a crucial factor governing the type of contract adopted is the ease of enforcement. If workers cannot assess the state of trade and fear that employers may renege then they will opt for wage or salary contracts. They may also seek to assess the state of trade through strikes or voluntary stoppages. But we should not jump too readily to the conclusion that workers will reject profit sharing. In regular trades where there is an expectation of continuity then neither employers nor workers will risk their reputations by reneging on contracts. In such trades realised profits will represent that portion of quasi-rents which had not been anticipated but which both parties recognised might become available for distribution.

Credit Policies and the Rationality of Peasant Societies

What has been said about employment contracts can be extended to the analysis of the terms of credit. In economies characterised by scarcity of finance, we would expect interest rates to be high; but it is also suggested that the rates are often extortionate and (paradoxically) that there may be a fringe of unsatisfied borrowers. Resolution of the paradox can be achieved by recognising that lenders may need to screen would be borrowers and safeguard themselves against defaulters.

This brings us to the assertions of irrationality and inefficiency. Many institutional practices in agrarian societies may simply be the second best response to risks. Thus, as we have noted, sharecropping may be a perfectly sensible approach to the problems of wage labour and the absence of large farms. Of course, there may be other aspects of peasant life which differ from what is commonly accepted in industrial societies. The tendency of neoclassical economics to assume that economic agents pursue their own self-interest and are indifferent to the welfare of others may reflect life in cities; but it is less likely to be an accurate description of rural communities, where interdependence is a fact of life. Schultz's assertion that peasants are rational and also poor may be an accurate insight into peasant societies and one which carries radical implications. Peasants may seem to lack entrepreneurship because the costs of removing risks may exceed the expected benefits. Therefore there may be risks without entrepreneurship. But those risks could be removed by foreign aid or even by appropriate state intervention.

Unemployment

Agrarian economies tend to suffer from unemployment because activities are sequential, there are climatic disturbances and because demand and supply elasticities tend to be low. Between sowing and reaping there may be bouts of idleness and although it may be possible to fill them with domestic industries such work may be inefficient as compared to factory trades. Changes in climate can give rise to floods, drought and pests from which factory trades may be immune. Low demand elasticities can mean that very sharp price falls are required to stimulate demand during recessions. Low supply elasticities may signify immobile resources.

Agrarian unemployment may be concealed or open. Concealed unemployment may be deduced from the coexistence of positive wage payments to workers and a zero marginal product of labour, a situation that may be incompatible with a wage system but may be feasible in a regime in which the total product is distributed according to some ethical share rule. Casual evidence should, however, be treated with caution. There may be bouts of idleness between sowing and reaping; but all workers may be fully employed at seasonal peaks of activity. Surveying the available literature, Jorgenson (1967) came to the conclusion that there was little support for a belief in a zero marginal product. Yet it may be possible to draw a distinction between 'heads' and 'hours'; the marginal product of heads may be zero but the marginal product of hours may be positive. If some workers on farms were removed then it might be possible for total output to be maintained by the remaining workers working longer hours or working more intensively. Evidently, there may be a trade off between consumption and leisure. Conceivably productivity may not be independent of income so that at low levels of income productivity is low. But the benefits of increased incomes and food intake may take a long time to become evident and it may profit an employer to offer slightly higher wages to a better fed worker and entice him away from his existing employer. So a situation analogous to the poaching of apprentices in in-

Table 3.2 Developing Countries: Open Unemployment as a Percentage of Labour Force, 1980

	Total	Male	Female
All developing countries	6.0	5.2	7.8
Latin America and Caribbean (low income countries)	8.1	7.4	10.3
Latin America and Caribbean (middle income countries)	5.6	7.8	8.4
China	. . .	. . .	. . .
India	4.6	3.3	7.3
Asia (other low income countries)	4.5	2.3	10.2
Asia (middle income countries)	3.4	3.4	3.4
Africa and Middle East (low income countries)	14.8	15.9	12.6
Africa and Middle East (middle income countries)	7.7	4.7	8.7
Africa and Middle East (capital surplus oil producers)	5.4	6.1	4.0

Source: ILO (1965–85)

dustrialised countries may obtain and the labour force remains low paid, with low productivity.

Population

Irrespective of whether unemployment is open or concealed, a model of an over-populated agrarian economy requires a theory of population. Malthus put forward the thesis that a rise in real wages would lead to an increase in population — a thesis which seems to have been refuted by the experience of the advanced countries. However, Becker (1981) has proposed a neo-Malthusian theory based upon a distinction between the number of children and the quality of children. Thus, parents may have a demand for children but the income elasticity of demand for children may be lower than the pressure to increase spending on the education and training of children and the demand for children may also diminish as the potential market earnings of wives increases.

Becker's thesis may involve a distinction between the short- and long-run effects of increases in real income. In the short run an increase in income in less developed countries may lead to an increase in population. There may be a low level equilibrium trap into which less developed countries fall. The demand for 'quality' may be a long-run response and may be linked to the educational standards of parents and the provision of state education for children as well as the job opportunities for women. Thus, Schultz (1985) has suggested that the changes in the prices of grains and animal products in Sweden between 1860 and 1910 raised the price of butter, improved women's wages relative to men's and contributed to the long-run decline in fertility. More recently, Richtering (1986) used cross-section data for 100 countries in the mid-1970s to isolate the crucial influences upon fertility and mortality rates. He found that between 80 and 90 per cent of the cross-country variation in fertility and mortality behaviour could be explained by a set of only six exogenous variations. Education was found to be an important determinant of both fertility and mortality whereas economic performance, as measured by GDP per capita, did not prove to be significant in multiple regressions. This indicates that a more favourable social setting may be more important than economic growth in controlling fertility and mortality rates.

Becker's thesis has received added impetus from Easterlin's evidence of long swings in population growth. When real incomes were high it was found that the number of children increased; but when those children entered the labour market they depressed earnings and hence they tended to have fewer children than their parents; this could mean a labour shortage and higher earnings in the future. Casual observation would suggest the existence of long swings in the world economy in the post-war period. The effect of the inter-war years slump was to cause a fall in birth rates which led to a rise in birth rates in the 1940s and 1950s. In mining areas the rise in the birth rate occurred much earlier than in non-mining areas because miners were exempt from armed service. Elsewhere

Table 3.3

Country	Crude birth rate per population (1978)	Crude death rate per population (1971)	Urban population as % of total (1980)	Adult literacy rate (%) (1975)	Daily calorie intake (1977)	GNP per capita ($) (1978)	Population per physician (000) (1977)
Malawi	52	20	9	25	2,066	180	48
Sri Lanka	26	6	27	78	2,126	190	6
Algeria	48	14	61	37	2,372	1,260	5
Malaysia	29	6	29	60	2,610	1,090	4

Source: World Bank (1980)

the war delayed the rise in the birth rate and because of wartime deaths the baby boom of the late 1940s and 1950s was accentuated. The baby boom of the 1940s subsequently gave rise to an 'echo boom' in the 1960s and those children entered the depressed labour market of the 1970s and 1980s. But the determinants of population growth in developing countries are not always easy to unravel. Thus, in Table 3.3 all the countries listed have comparable calorific intakes per head despite widely ranging real incomes.

Labour Migration

In the Lewis model of economic development the supply of labour from the agricultural sector to the industrial enclave is perfectly elastic. Employment in the capitalist sector is therefore not constrained by supply but by demand; there are unlimited supplies of labour. Therefore, given the wage and the technology prevailing in the capitalist sector, profit maximisation determines the capital— labour ratio and the capital stock determines the volume of employment. If all wages are consumed and profits are the sole source of savings then growth is determined by the rate of profit and the propensity to save out of profits (a theory of growth which is similar to that advanced by post-Keynesians such as Kaldor and Joan Robinson).

But how can the model be reconciled with the existence of urban unemployment and the fact that in some less developed countries the supply curve of labour to the capitalist sector is upward sloping? The first question raises another: should the agricultural sector be taxed in order to subsidise jobs in the industrial sector? In other words, does the price ratio between the two sectors need correction? This question has a long history in political economy. In the aftermath of the Russian revolution it was known as the 'price scissors' — a metaphor which likened the movements of the prices of manufactures and food to the blades of a pair of scissors. More recently, Sah and Stiglitz (1984) have attempted to unravel the issues involved in the problem of the scissors and concluded that the determinants of the optimal tax depend upon the social valuation of the welfare of the peasants and the industrial proletariat as compared to the social valuation of investment. Thus, if, as in the Stalin period, the priority is to industrialise then the consumption of both peasants and proletarians may be penalised. But if the welfare of the proletariat is ranked higher than that of the peasants then the whole of the tax burden could fall on the peasantry.

However, any tax policy would have to take account of the reactions of both the peasants and proletarians. Thus, Harris and Todaro (1970) have suggested that the migration of peasants might be based not upon current wages but upon the difference between the net present values of the urban and rural income streams. The fact that a migrant may not immediately get a job in a town may be less relevant than the fact that his eventual employment may yield relatively higher earnings. In other words, relative earnings need to be weighted by employment prospects. Furthermore, there may be both casual and regular jobs in towns. What matters, therefore, is whether output in the towns is expected to be greater than in the agricultural areas. If it is expected to be higher then there may be no need to subsidise jobs in the towns (which could lead to higher unemployment) or impose controls on migration from the farms.

Urbanisation

Labour migration raises the question of urbanisation in developing countries. Table 3.4 reveals that the largest cities are in the Third World and they are projected to increase up to the year 2000. Urbanisation is, in fact, a phenomenon of developing countries; the shift *out* of cities is more pronounced in the advanced economies. Urbanisation is associated with industrialisation and with different forms of socialisation. It can be strongly influenced by the greater increase in productivity in manufacturing than in farming. These differences may owe much to national economic policies. If governments tax agriculture in order to subsidise industry then there will be a shift out of agriculture. If governments pursue import substitution policies then there will be an incentive to move into industry. Urbanisation may therefore be a conscious economic policy and it may offer the possibilities of release from rural poverty (although these possibilities may be an illusion). Urbanisation may, in fact, result in an increase in the demand for fuel (implying deforestation) and a demand for foreign foodstuffs, such as wheat.

Land Reform

Table 3.5 gives the per capita agricultural growth rates in various regions. The low growth rate of the less developed countries is clearly highlighted and raises

Table 3.4 Populations and Projected Populations of the Mega-Cities (Millions)

	1980	2000
Mexico City	15.0	26.3
Sao Paulo	9.2	24.0
Tokyo	17.0	17.1
Calcutta	7.1	16.6
Bombay	8.5	16.0
New York	15.6	15.5
Seoul	8.5	13.5
Shanghai	11.8	13.5
Delhi	5.9	13.3
Rio de Janeiro	9.2	25.0
Buenos Aires	10.1	13.2
Cairo	7.3	13.2

Source: World Bank (1983)

Table 3.5 Annual Average Growth Rates per Capita of Agricultural Production

	1961–70	1970–80
Developed manufacturing areas	0.8	1.1
Developing countries	0.1	0.4
Socialist, Eastern Europe	2.1	0.7
Socialist, Asia	2.5	1.4

Source: UNCTAD (1985)

the question whether the problem of agrarian economies can be solved through industrialisation and tariffs restricting imports of manufactures or whether, as Lewis (1978) suggests, import substitution should begin with an improvement in agricultural productivity. Import substitution became fashionable during the 1930s because of the dramatic fall in the incomes of primary producers. Some countries, such as Brazil and Mexico, began a vigorous policy of restricting imports of manufactures and in the 1960s they were joined by many African countries. In the case of Brazil and Mexico imports as a percentage of GDP fell from 12 per cent in 1950 to 8 per cent in 1965. In India the decline in imports was much less but still significant. However, import substitution turned the terms of trade against agriculture, encouraged a movement to the towns and slowed down economic growth. There were declines in the world market shares of meat (Argentina), coffee (Brazil) and tea (India).

The case for improving agricultural productivity therefore rests upon its influence upon the market share of agriculture and in releasing resources to create an efficient manufacturing sector. The case for land reform rests upon the observation that there is a negative correlation between farm size and productivity.

However, the cause of such improvement is not always obvious. A greater willingness to work on the part of small proprietors may be an important factor but there may also be differences in crops grown. However, before jumping to any conclusions about agricultural policy in the developing countries we need to consider farm policies in the advanced economies.

The International Wheat Market

Differences in food production and productivity in food production are strongly influenced by pricing policies in both the advanced and developing countries. Wheat, which accounts for the greater part of world trade in cereals, is exported by the advanced countries and is imported by Third World countries many of which lie in the tropics and have never been wheat producers.

With the exception of the USSR, the advanced countries tend to produce in excess of their domestic requirements (Table 3.6). The USA accounts for about 12 per cent of the world's output but 43 per cent of the world's exports, with the other major producers being Canada, Australia, France and USSR. The anomaly is the USSR which produces about 25 per cent of world output; but harvests are variable and in 1973 a fall in domestic production led to an increase in imports which, coupled with the drought in Africa, resulted in a fall in world stocks and a sharp rise in prices. Since 1974 Soviet wheat production has improved, largely as a result of better weather conditions.

There have been significant changes in the importers since the end of the Second World War. In the late 1940s and early 1950s Europe was a major importer;

Table 3.6 Self-Sufficiency Rates, 1979–81 (Average Percentage)

	USA	Canada	EEC 10	Japan	Australia
Butter	112	98	118	94	123
Cheese	100	94	106	13	148
Skimmed milk	150	216	126	54	134
Wheat	299	390	118	9	484
Barley	110	162	112	16	314
Maize	151	97	66	—	107
Oats	90	95	98	—	125
Sugar	58	10	124	31	411
Beef and veal	91	102	102	72	217
Pork	99	113	101	88	101
Poultry	106	97	108	94	102
Lamb	93	28	73	—	219
Rice	256	—	72	95	852
All	129	170	101	57	262

Source: OECD (1987)

but by the 1980s it had not only become self-sufficient but was a major food exporter. And by the 1980s the Third World countries accounted for two-thirds of world food imports. Hence the paradox that the world exporters are the developed industrial countries and the wheat importers tend to be the developing countries whose 90 per cent of food imports are wheat. Furthermore, 80 per cent of all cereal aid is in the form of wheat.

The paradox can be explained by the interplay of political and economic forces. In the advanced countries technological progress (often induced by government subsidies) has boosted the productivity of wheat producers. But this rise in productivity has not led to a substantial reduction in acreage. Instead, subsidies have led to an expansion in total output. In Europe food shortages in the 1930s and 1940s led to an emphasis upon self-sufficiency. In the United States rural poverty in the 1930s led to the adoption of farm support programmes. The result has been that wheat production has greatly exceeded domestic consumption and has led to a rise in exports.

The emergence of markets in the Third World countries arose from a variety of influences. First, import substitution arose out of the experiences of depressed markets in the 1930s and led to tariffs on manufacturing imports and subsidies to domestic firms. The subsidies were financed by taxes on domestic agriculture which led to a contraction of domestic agriculture and a growing dependence upon food imports. In urban areas rising real incomes led to a movement away from local grains to wheat and this substitution was reinforced by the fall in the price of wheat relative to the prices of other grains. The situation was aggravated by the fact that about 80 per cent of cereal food aid has been in the form of wheat and wheat flour, which has reduced the incentive to engage in farming in the developing countries.

The contraction of Third World agriculture has been dictated by productivity advances in the manufacturing and service sectors of the advanced countries. As urban earnings rose they pulled up the earnings of domestic farmers because farm price support schemes were geared to ensuring equity between the earnings of urban and rural workers (Lund et al. 1982). As subsidies to farmers increased they produced more, thereby increasing the flow of exports and aid with consequent pressure upon the earnings of Third World farmers.

Nor has the problem been confined to trade between the advanced and developing countries. The effect of increased agricultural protection in Europe has been to reduce imports from Canada, Australia, New Zealand and the United States. Canada and the United States therefore switched some of their resources into manufacturing and services and exported surplus foodstuffs to the Third World. But Australia and New Zealand, with their smaller domestic markets, faced the problems of finding alternative outlets and found diversification much more difficult. Australian farmers suffered a double loss: first, they suffered from the effect of the Australian tariff which raised the price of manufactures; second, they suffered from the loss of European markets as a result of the Common Agricultural Policy.

In 1987 the world wheat market came under strain. The prolonged recession and the rise in the dollar in the 1980s had led to a sharp fall in wheat imports by the developing countries and created problems for American farmers. On both continents, Europe and America, there were signs that urban dwellers might no longer be prepared to support buffer stock schemes. With a contraction of farm acreage perhaps the prairies will be returned to the buffalo and house prices fall in Europe as more land is released for housing. Above all a change in the relative prices of foodstuffs in the advanced and developing countries might lead to more efficient industrialising programmes in the Third World.

Summary and Conclusions

Agrarian economies have faced two problems: low productivity in producing foodstuffs and low prices for commercial crops. The two problems are intertwined, although there has been a tendency to attribute low productivity to the irrationality of peasants as compared with the efficiency of farmers in advanced countries. Yet many of the institutions of agrarian economies are an efficient response to situations where a complete set of markets do not exist. Economic theory has tended to view the world from the standpoint of a general equilibrium model in which it is implicitly assumed that the wages of workers are sufficient to afford them at least a subsistence income. In other words, it is assumed that labour is scarce. Yet in many parts of the world there is overpopulation in the sense that the marginal product of labour is below that level which would yield a subsistence wage. Hence the absence of wage systems and their replacement by ethical share rules. These share rules (sharecropping) can be demonstrated to be efficient in that they lead to a sharing of risks and provide incentives. Low productivity may therefore be the result of lack of complementary resources. But low productivity can also arise through the policies of domestic governments seeking to industrialise and imposing taxes on farmers in order to subsidise manufacturing. This can lead to a diminution of effort and a drift to the towns. Low productivity may also arise from the policies of the advanced countries who, in their pursuit of self-sufficiency, impose tariffs on food imports and dump surplus food on world markets. Accentuating these problems are the substitution of man made substitutes (plastics, etc.) for natural products (jute, for example). Finally, cyclical fluctuations in the advanced countries can lead to price and income instability in the developing countries.

Bibliography

Amin, S. (1978) *Modern Migration in West Africa,* Oxford University Press.

Balassa, B. (1975) 'Reforming the system of incentives in developing countries', *World Development,* vol. 3, pp. 365–382.

Becker, G.S. (1981) *A Treatise on the Family,* Columbia University Press.

Berry, A.R. and Cline, W.R. (1979) *Agrarian Structure and Productivity in Developing Countries,* Johns Hopkins.

Bhagwati, J.D. (1985) *Essays in Development Economics,* Blackwell.

Boserup, E. (1965) *The Conditions of Agricultural Growth: The Economics of Agrarian Change under Population Pressure,* Allen and Unwin.

Cheung, S.N.S. (1969) *The Theory of Share Tenancy,* University of Chicago Press.

Cole, W.E. and Sanders, R.D. (1986) 'Internal migration and urban employment in the Third World', *American Economic Review,* vol. 75, pp. 481–494.

Easterlin, R. (1968) *Population, Labor Force and Long Swings in Economic Growth: The American Experience,* Columbia University Press.

Georgescu Roegen, N. (1972) *Energy and Economic Myths,* Pergamon.

Harris, J. and Todaro, M.P. (1970) 'Migration, unemployment and development', *American Economic Review,* vol. 60, pp. 126–142.

ILO (1965–85) *Yearbooks of Labour Statistics,* ILO.

Jorgenson, D.W. (1967) 'Testing alternative theories of the development of a dual economy', in Adelman, I. and Thorbecke, E. (eds) *The Theory and Design of Economic Develoment,* Johns Hopkins.

Lewis, W.A. (1978) *Growth and Fluctuations 1870–1913,* Allen and Unwin.

Lund, P.J. *et al.* (1982) *Wages and Employment in Agriculture: England and Wales, 1960–81,* Government Economic Working Paper No 52, Ministry of Agriculture, Fisheries and Food.

Markusen, J.R. (1979) 'Personal and job characteristics of employee–firm contracts', *Quarterly Journal of Economics,* vol. 93, pp. 346–358.

Newbery, D.M.G. and Stiglitz, J.E. (1981) *The Theory of Commodity Price Stabilization,* Oxford University Press.

OECD (1987) *National Policies and Agricultural Trade,* OECD.

Robertson, A.C. (1987) *The Dynamics of Production Relationships: African Share Contracts in Perspective,* Cambridge University Press.

Richtering, J. (1986), *Modelling Fertility and Mortality Rates in the Framework of a Demographic Model,* Discussion Paper 15, UNCTAD.

Sah, R.K. and Stiglitz, J.E. (1984) 'The economics of the price scissors', *American Economic Review,* vol. 74, pp. 125–138.

Schultz, T.W. (1964) *Transforming Traditional Agriculture,* Yale University Press.

Schultz, T.W. (1985) 'Changing world prices, women's wages and the fertility transition: Sweden 1860–1910', *Journal of Political Economy,* vol. 93, pp. 315–326.

UNCTAD (1985) *Handbook of International Trade and Development, Supplement,* United Nations.

World Bank (1980) *World Development Report,* United Nations.

World Bank (1983) *World Development Report,* United Nations.

4

Advanced Economies

Advanced economies supply the motive power for the world economy. Agrarian economies may supply raw materials and provide a check to economic growth when, as in the 1890s and 1970s, raw material shortages developed, primary product prices rose and growth in the advanced economies slowed down. But the links between the advanced countries and the Third World have been diminishing and advanced countries are now capable of providing their own obstacles to growth through the exhaustion of investment opportunities, underconsumption and monetary constraints.

The outstanding feature of the advanced countries is (and has been) their dependence upon manufacturing. The exploitation of the benefits of manufacturing depends to a large extent upon the growth of demand and this issue is highlighted in the classical, neoclassical and post-Keynesian economic models. However, a concentration upon the real forces of consumption, investment and technological progress should not detract from the role of monetary factors and we devote some space to the problem of introducing money into an economy, the reasons for holding money and the difficulties of controlling the supply of money.

In the 1960s attention was concentrated upon the importance of monetary disturbance in creating inflation and the resulting analysis formed the basis of the monetarist and new classical models of macroeconomic activity. However, the 1980s have presented new problems stemming from the rise in unemployment and its persistence. Theory predicted that there should have been a rise in unemployment and then a shift away from energy-using to labour-using activities. But unemployment has persisted and, in Western Europe, wages have shown a tendency to rise despite high levels of unemployment, contrary to Marx's prediction of the effects of a reserve army of unemployed and its modern counterpart, the Phillips curve. This has led to a revival of interest in wage determination under trade unions. The sluggish response of the advanced economies has been put down to the existence of large public sectors which were unresponsive to market forces and to the existence of social security benefits and employment protection legislation. But as the 1980s draw to a close a new problem of falling labour forces has begun to emerge. However, the peculiarities of manufacturing must first be examined.

Agriculture v. Manufacturing

Agrarian economies tend to be sequential economies, where elementary processes are conducted in parallel but sowing always precedes reaping. Advanced manufacturing activities may be conducted in line. Figure 4.1 illustrates the distinction. In 4.1a we observe four farms on which activities, such as sowing, weeding and reaping, are conducted in parallel. (Although conducted in parallel the institutional arrangements for risk sharing and the distribution of the product may show some variations. Thus the four farms or strips may be rotated between the farmers in order to share out the risks from poor sites. But the essential point is that sowing must precede reaping.) Moving to 4.1b we observe that production by craftsmen may be organised in series.

However, the decisive shift comes with the introduction of a factory system in which activities are carried out in line. We can observe activities, a_1, b_2 and

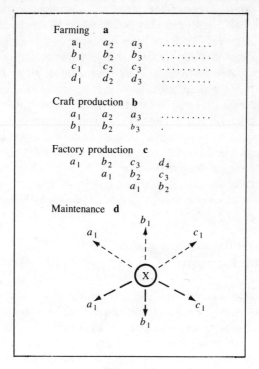

Figure 4.1

c_3 being performed simultaneously. In other words, we may observe all the parts of a motor car being produced simultaneously whereas we seldom observe (except at the Equator or in chicken farms) the simultaneous sowing and reaping of crops. The separation of tasks — the division of labour — that we observe in 4.1c results in several advantages. It reduces capital costs because every worker need not be equipped with a complete set of tools. It reduces idle time; no one has to wait for the harvest to ripen under the sun. It can increase speed and accuracy. In a nutshell, it can promote economies of scale and increasing returns.

Nor is the rearrangement of activities confined to products. Economic development — economic growth — is not merely the production of more and more products using the same processes; an adult is not simply a large baby. Development extends to the rearrangement of processes and factories, which largely falls to the construction industry which, although dispersed, operates as if it were a factory. It is the construction industry — the infrastructure — which dictates the take off (or not) of a developing country.

Agrarian economies can dispense with idle labour but they cannot dispense with idle capital. Surplus labour can be absorbed into cottage industries; there can be a dovetailing of the agricultural system with the domestic system — spinning and weaving can be carried out between spells of sowing and reaping. But horses and ploughs cannot readily be converted into spinning frames and looms (and vice versa). An agrarian economy may seek to overcome the problems of overpopulation but it will almost certainly be an overcapitalised economy.

An elaborate division of labour can bring disadvantages. It can lead to deskilling and to the displacement of labour from simple tasks. It can result in a loss of promotion and lack of opportunities for advancement. In Western economies the division of labour has proceeded so far that it has removed even maintenance tasks from the shopfloor. Thus, in Figure 4.1d we observe two assembly lines maintained by a common work station. This procedure can result in a concentration of skilled personnel on research and development and maintenance; it can also lead to delays when breakdowns occur. In Japan there has been a greater tendency for maintenance work to be carried out by assembly line workers, giving rise to greater job satisfaction as well as a reduction in delays and inventories. The Western style of shopfloor organisation may require greater coordination than that practised in Japan.

Economic Development

Economic development involves the transformation of an economy from dependence upon agriculture to a greater emphasis upon manufacturing and services. Unless workers in manufacturing work harder or work longer hours, economic development requires the transformation of agriculture in order to release labour for the industrial sector. In the process of transformation the enclosure movement in Europe led to a break up of the communal system of farming and its replacement either by family farms or by the creation of an agricultural labour market composed of landless labourers dispossessed of the social obligations inherent in feudalism. In contrast, manufacturing involved the displacement of the dispersed domestic system by the concentrated factory system.

A classical distinction has been made between diminishing returns in agriculture and increasing returns in manufacturing; some aspects of the transformation are captured in Lewis's (1954) classical model of economic development. This assumes that there is an unlimited supply of labour at the prevailing wage and as capital accumulation proceeds and the industrial enclave expands it absorbs surplus labour from the farm sector. When the labour reserve is exhausted then the take off of the economy is completed. If population expands then the economy may be caught in a Malthusian low level equilibrium trap. However, not all developing countries have surplus labour: slavery made labour scarce in Africa. The model was, in fact, based upon the evidence that real wages tended to remain constant in Britain in the first half of the nineteenth century. It also owed much to observations of the West Indies and South-east Asia. It was applied by Patrick and Rosovsky (1976) to Japan. It was also applied by Kindleberger (1967) to the post-war boom in Western Europe when many countries drew upon surplus labour in agriculture and foreign migrants. Kindleberger obtained mixed results. West Germany, Italy, Switzerland and the Netherlands had high growth rates and large increases in labour and capital. The UK, Belgium, Sweden, Norway and Denmark had low growth rates and low increases in capital and labour. A third group, Spain, Portugal, Southern Italy, Greece, Yugoslavia and Turkey had high growth rates and large increases in labour supplies but had low investment rates. Finally, France and Austria had high growth rates and low increases in their labour forces.

When the supply of labour becomes less elastic we move from Lewis's classical model to a neoclassical model of the kind portrayed by Solow (1956) in which growth is governed by the real forces of technological progress, investment and the relatively slow growth of the labour force and in which full employment equilibrium is maintained by the flexibility of wages and interest rates. Early tests by Denison (1967) suggested that capital accumulation accounted for only a small part of economic growth and that there was a large residual which may have been due to education, research and development. Subsequent tests by Jorgenson and Griliches (1967), which took account of such factors as hours of work and education, suggested that most of the residue could be accounted for and that there was no free lunch.

The Solow model is a real model — it does not contain any money. To introduce money into such an economy we need to recognise that exchange takes time and that there may be uncertainty as to the future capital value of the fixed interest bearing government debt known as a bond. The time factor encapsulates many issues. If there were perfect certainty then there would be no need to hold money since all transactions could be conducted at one point in time. Likewise if there were trust then a seller might agree to repayment at a later date or be willing to accept the quality (salability) of any article offered in exchange. But why hold money which yields no income when governments also offer bonds? The answer is that changes in interest rates can affect the capital values of bonds. This is the essence of Keynes's speculative motive for holding money and stems from uncertainty as to the future interest rate. In the 1960s and 1970s it fell into disfavour and neither Laidler (1983) nor Cuthbertson (1988) found strong evidence for the speculative motive. But following the stock market crash of October 1987 the percentage of cash holdings of the big institutional investors rose from 3 per cent in September 1987 to 8 per cent in March 1988 (Sarjeant 1988).

Once money is introduced into an economy then there is a simultaneous determination of the general level of prices and the money rate of interest, and with flexible prices the price level can move in any direction as productivity increases. In other words, it is possible to have an economy in which the price level remains constant as productivity and wages increase or it is possible to have an economy in which wages are constant and the price level falls as productivity increases. The behaviour of the price level is compatible with equilibrium as long as the money rate of interest is adjusted to keep it in line with the real rate of interest; the achievement of such a policy may require the payment of interest on cash balances (Gilbert 1957).

New Classical Economics

The model we have just sketched out is an example of what has come to be called new classical economics or rational expectations economics. In such a model people use all the information that is available to them and the theory which yields the best predictions given that information. If all trends are foreseen and foreseeable all prices adjust to the available information. There can be disturbances only if there are surprises and prices do not adjust rapidly to the 'news'.

The Business Cycle (Kitchin and Juglar)

In its initial formulation new classical economics set out to describe the consequences which might follow from monetary surprises. It sought therefore to explain the following stylised facts.

1. The outputs of all sectors tend to move together.
2. Production of capital goods shows a greater amplitude of fluctuation than consumer goods.
3. Prices move pro-cyclically.
4. Money measures move pro-cyclically.
5. Profits fluctuate more than wages.

6. Short-term interest rates move pro-cyclically; long-term interest rates show a slight pro-cyclical movement.
7. The production of agricultural goods and raw materials shows a lower than average conformity with the cycle in manufacturing.

Suppose then, that there is an unanticipated increase in the money supply. Initially individuals will not be able to distinguish between the monetary disturbance and, say, a change in tastes. Money will enter the economy at a particular point and drive a wedge between relative prices, and the movement of relative prices will be regarded as due to real forces, such as a change in tastes. Hence, economic agents will respond to the increase in demand by increasing factor supplies and output. Prices, output and employment therefore move together (facts 1 and 3). In the short run, and because of the surprise, there is a trade off between unemployment and inflation and it is this trade off which was traced out by the Phillips curve (which was originally derived from observations of changes in the rate of money wages and the level of unemployment in the UK between 1867 and 1957). But it disappears once individuals realise that prices as well as wages are rising: the Phillips curve becomes vertical in the long run.

Although we have discussed the business cycle in terms of an unanticipated monetary disturbance, it would have been possible to conduct the analysis in terms of a real disturbance, such as an oil shock or a good harvest. Thus, a rise in oil prices leads to a revision of expected permanent or lifetime income and then the initial change in income and its effects upon consumption are transmitted to subsequent periods. The change in relative prices brought about by the oil shock causes substitution effects to take place between goods and a revision of investment decisions. But the development of the theory proceeded in terms of monetary disturbances because of the need to explain the inflation of the 1950s and 1960s. The recognition of changes in raw material prices in the 1970s has caused the theory to be re-worked in terms of real shocks.

Ceilings and Floors: Real and Monetary Disturbances

Real and monetary explanations of fluctuations in economic activity need not therefore be mutually exclusive. In the nineteenth century business cycles tended, until the 1870s, to be dominated by British experience and the apparent existence of a ten-year cycle (the Juglar cycle). Such cycles were explained in terms of credit crises. An expansion would begin with, say, a rise in exports or an invention and be financed by trade credit. Eventually prices would start to rise and reserves would fall. The Bank of England would then increase interest rates in an attempt to control a fragile credit and banking system and the boom would collapse.

In the 1870s the pattern began to change as a result of increasing international competition. Booms began to peter out before a credit crisis arose. Real forces, such as a diminution of profitable investment opportunities, seemed to explain such cycles; there was a theory of weak booms. In the 1920s and 1930s the causes of crises became more complex, although the notion of a monetary ceiling seemed to be rejected in favour of the fragile nature of the real structures of economies resulting from the war. Writing just before the Second World War, Harrod suggested (1939) that the limit to growth of an economy might be set by a full employment ceiling dictated by the growth of the labour force but that it might be difficult to reach and maintain a movement along the ceiling because of the instability of investment (that is, demand). Hicks (1950) subsequently elaborated this theory. However, the remarkable feature of the post-war period, until the 1970s, was that economies did seem to move along stable growth paths with aggregate demand being matched by the growth of labour supplies. Why this occurred is still a mystery. It may have been because there was a much slower movement from a system of wartime controls to a peacetime system of market prices and the use of Keynesian demand management policies. There were, of course, fluctuations, but these were the minor Kitchin (inventory) cycles and were explained by governments trying to maintain power by increasing demand before elections. In the mid-1960s the monetary restraints exercised by the Americans were abandoned and in the 1970s a new ceiling — a raw materials ceiling — emerged and resulted in a downturn of economic activity.

Discretion, Monetary Rules and Competitive Banking

The inflation of the post-war period appears to have been associated with the use of Keynesian demand management policies in which it was assumed that money did not matter and that the task of the authorities was to steer economies through the use of discretionary fiscal policies. The apparent discrediting of Keynesian policies in the 1970s led to the proposal that discretion should be replaced by rules whereby the money supply increased in line with increases in factor supplies and technological change and unforeseen disturbances would be accommodated by automatic fiscal stabilisers. However, the revolutions in financial institutions and the deregulation of financial markets, as well as the suspicion that monopoly central banks could never be trusted to obey rules, led to the advocacy of competitive banking.

The idea of competitive banking might seem unusual but for a revival of interest in eighteenth-century Scottish banking and nineteenth-century banking in some American states. In Scotland trust in a competitive banking system was fulfilled by the fact that it offered: (1) unlimited liability; (2) freedom of entry; (3) direct customer redemption of notes for full bodied coins; and (4) a note exchange system which operated like a clearing house system. Overissue by a bank would therefore have led to a decline in reserves and a contraction of its note issue.

The fact that the Scottish system was small-scale also suggests that customers may have had considerable knowledge of each others' financial circumstances. And, finally, the fact that Scotland was a small open economy on a fixed exchange rate meant that an overissue by all the banks would have led to an outflow of gold.

But if a competitive banking system were introduced what would be the nature of the convertibility which it offered? If banks offered convertibility into gold then there would be a return to a gold standard, with all the disadvantages experienced in the past. If the banks offered convertibility into a bundle of commodities then there would be a problem of storing the buffer stock. And how would services be stored? A competitive banking system might therefore offer all the disadvantages of a commodity money. Furthermore, the Scottish system was small-scale in its operations and would seem to suggest that a competitive banking system might not be able to reap the benefits of economies of scale. There could be a large number of competitive banking systems between which there were floating exchange rates and the benefits accruing from the existence of a fixed exchange rate operating over a large area might not be obtained. What a central bank offers, therefore, is the possibilities of large-scale commercial banking coupled with the presence of a lender of last resort and a protection (a penal discount rate) against commercial banks which overissue.

However, the last word on central banking versus free banking has still to be written. Proponents of free banking take the view that money is no different from any other commodity and that the market will provide safeguards against depreciating currencies as well as against defective secondhand cars. They argue that depreciating currencies and monetary disturbances can arise only from government intervention through a central bank. Opponents agree that governments may make mistakes but maintain that there is still a case for discretionary policies. Not all disturbances are monetary in origin and in the depths of a slump it may be desirable for the money supply to be increased in order to influence real variables.

Unemployment

So far we have concentrated upon the demand side of an economy but the persistence of severe unemployment in the 1980s compels us to examine the supply side. Why did wages and prices not fall sufficiently to clear markets? Why does output fluctuate more than employment? And why have wages tended to rise despite high levels of unemployment?

To answer these questions we have to go back to the nature of the firm and manufacturing. Production involves the realisation of a surplus through the use of complementary factors, labour and capital, under the supervision of a monitoring agent. Because of the complementary nature of teamwork it becomes difficult to ascertain the productivities of factors. Thus, A's productivity depends not merely upon his own efforts but also those of B. There is therefore a bargaining problem of determining productivities and rewards. Owners of specialist machines might dismiss workers in an endeavour to find out how much they should be paid but the tactic can work in reverse: specialist machines may find it difficult to re-employ workers. Historically, the resolution of the problem seems to have been attempted by the formation of a firm in which the owners of capital hired labour at a fixed wage and the residue accrued to the capitalists in the form of dividends, with the dividends being influenced by the efforts of managers. The control of the surplus by the capitalist then led to a countervailing power — the trade union — to protect the interests of the workers.

But what do unions maximise? A model which has found some attraction to theorists is one that stresses the political nature of unions. Union members, it is argued, cannot sell their membership and therefore unions act like political agencies. Hence a median or senior voting model emerges in which the preferences of senior members acquire greater weight. Faced with a fall in demand the union will resist wage cuts because they would lead to a fall in the return on human capital by senior members and redistribute income to junior members. A similar argument applies to the resistance of unions to increase in membership during booms. The political model of unions suggests why unions will resist wage reductions and increases in membership but it does not tell us what wage level will be sought. Two possibilities suggest themselves. One is that a union sets the wage and allows the employer to fix the level of employment. This is the so-called union monopoly model; but it is much more likely to apply to weak unions which have no control over labour supply and set the wage in order to find out who is eligible for employment at that wage. A more efficient policy would be to seek to set both wage and employment as an all or nothing offer. The difficulty is to devise tests of such policies, although there is some evidence that unions do attempt to control labour supply and manning practices.

But neither the monopoly nor efficient bargaining model throws much light on wages policy. A union would like to set a real wage but may have no control over the prices of products. It would like to set a wage which is fair in relation to the wages obtained by other unions but in a decentralised bargaining situation that is difficult to achieve. A further reason for union wage resistance may therefore arise because sectional wage cuts imply a redistribution of income.

For a period before the first oil price rise (1973) Batstone (1986) attempted to correlate collective bargaining and productivity growth with the age and stability of institutions and the scope and degree of sophistication of unions and employers. (Scope covered whether unions and employers had narrow sectional interests and sophistication concerned the ability of bargainers to coordinate strategies.) Britain was assumed to have bargaining machinery which was narrow in scope (being confined to wage increases) and unsophisticated (because it lacked any coordination of the wages policies of various unions and employers). In contrast Sweden

Table 4.1 Collective Bargaining and Productivity Growth 1950−1973 (GDP per man hour)

a)	Broad scope, high sophistication		b)	Narrow scope, low sophistication	
	Netherlands	4.4		Canada	3.0
	Norway	4.2		USA	2.6
	Sweden	4.2		UK	3.1
	Belgium	4.4		Australia	2.6
c)	Narrow scope, high sophistication		d)	Broad scope, low sophistication	
	Austria	5.9		Japan	8.0
	Finland	5.2		France	5.1
	West Germany	6.0		Italy	5.8

Source: Batstone (1986)

had a collective bargaining machinery which attempted to coordinate wages policies even though the country's institutions had undergone no major disturbances for a long time. Table 4.1 suggests some correlation between productivity growth and institutions although some of the results have been undermined in the post-oil shocks period.

Product Prices

Wage rigidity need not lead to price rigidity. Overtime and shiftworking may impart a degree of flexibility to labour costs. Because of fixed hiring costs firms may hold on to labour during recessions, with the result that costs rise. In the boom periods such labour may be worked more intensively and so costs may not rise proportionately. The number of workers who are regarded as overheads may be varied. Since the 1970s the effect of high fixed costs in the form of social security payments has caused firms to hire more part-time and temporary workers. So in order to examine the reasons why product prices may be fixed we must examine other factors and consider the behaviour of profits.

Price rigidity may arise through the demands of consumers. Fix prices began to emerge in Britain in the 1980s and were associated with a relative decline in agriculture. By the 1890s the value of agriculture output was some 15 per cent of manufacturing output and Britain was becoming a fix price economy. In West Germany and France the same relative decline in agriculture was not reached until the 1950s and in Japan it was not attained until the 1970s.

Manufacturing economies tend to be high income economies. So the existence

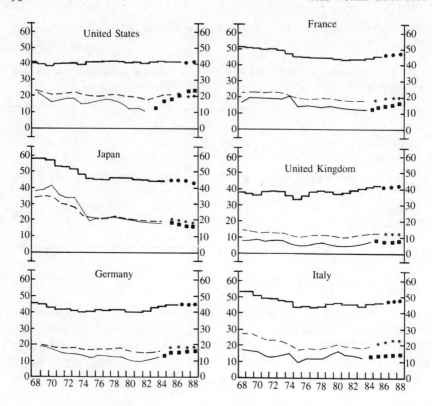

Estimate of profit share in business sector
● ● ● Projection of profit share in business sector
---- Rate of return in business sector
★ ★ ★ Projection of rate of return in business sector
—— Rate of return for manufacturing
■ ■ ■ Projection of rate of return for manufacturing

Source: OECD (1987)

Figure 4.2 Profits and Rates of Return

of fix prices may arise because shoppers attach a high opportunity cost to shopping around and value the convenience of standardised branded goods. Fixed prices may therefore be compatible with competitive conditions. But manufacturing economies are also subject to increasing returns, concentration and oligopoly. The simplest model of concentration is one which assumes that firms' growth is independent of their initial size and that all firms grow or contract by the same percentage. In such circumstances there will be a tendency to increasing concentration because the larger will grow by larger *absolute* amounts. Such a simple growth process would explain the observed skewed size distribution of firms which consist of a large number of small firms and a few large ones. A tendency towards oligopoly would explain price rigidity as a byproduct of a situation in which firms are conscious that their price decisions will cause other firms to react.

Mark-Ups

The next step is to consider the behaviour of mark-ups over the long run and over the cycle. Firms will normally fix their prices by adding a mark-up to cover overheads and profits to unit wage and raw material costs. The size of the mark-up will then be dictated by the expected price elasticity of demand and the need for profits to be sufficient to finance investment. Over the long run the profit rate might be expected to fall with increasing capital accumulation. What happens to the profit share will, however, depend upon the ease of substitution between capital and other factors. What happens to profits will depend upon the ability of firms to pass on wage increases during the upswing and to cut wages in recessions. Before the 1970s profit rates and profit shares showed some tendency to decline but the squeeze was not severe until a hard market was created by the rise in raw material prices and the reluctance of workers to accept cuts in real wages. In the 1980s there has been a tendency for profit shares to show some return to their pre-1970 levels, but profit rates have shown some variability. In Japan the fall in profits has been remarkable because it has not been accompanied by a rise in unemployment. Despite wage flexibility there has been some burden in maintaining high levels of employment (Figure 4.2).

Summary and Conclusions

Advanced economies are predominantly manufacturing economies which means that they may be subject to increasing returns stemming from the ability to re-arrange activities so that they can be conducted in parallel. They may also derive increasing returns from volume effects as in the case of boilers whose dimensions can be doubled with the result that the volume is cubed without any consequent increase in cost. Increasing returns may depend upon the size of the market. As markets expand activities can be split up and rearranged. If the rearranged activities become separate units then it may be possible to maintain competitive conditions. Thus, as Chapter 7 will indicate Japan, West Germany and the United States have maintained a large sector of small firms which work in conjunction with the large firm sector whereas Britain has tended to reduce the small sector through mergers.

The existence of increasing returns carries certain implications for macro-economic activity. Reducing demand may increase costs and prolong the unemployment of highly specialised workers. And unless the demand curve cuts the falling supply curve from above then there may be market instability. Furthermore, if increasing returns give rise to concentration and oligopoly then price rigidities may occur as firms believe that the elasticity of demand has fallen and that other firms will follow their price cuts, with the result that both prices and revenues fall — hence demands for protection and orderly marketing. This is also a reason why trade unions may resist wage cuts in order to protect the return on human capital of their older members.

Immobility of resources and price rigidities have implications for trade between advanced and developing (agrarian) economies because they provide an explanation for the movement of the terms of trade. They also provide the rationale for supply-side policies designed to improve the mobility of resources.

Bibliography

Batstone, E. (1986) 'Labour and productivity', Oxford Review of Economic Policy, vol. 3, pp. 35–46.

Cuthbertson, N. (1988) The Demand for and Supply of Money, Blackwell.

Denison, E.F. (1967) Why Growth Rates Differ, Brookings Institution.

Gilbert, J.C. (1957) 'The comptibility of any behaviour of the price level with equilibrium', Review of Economic Studies, vol. 27, pp. 177–184.

Harrod, R.F. (1939) 'An essay in dynamic theory', Economic Journal, vol. 49, pp. 14–33.

Hicks, J.R. (1950) The Trade Cycle, Oxford University Press.

Jorgenson, D.W. and Griliches, Z. (1967) 'The explanation of productivity change', Review of Economic Studies, vol. 34, pp. 249–283.

Kindleberger, C.P. (1967) Europe's Postwar Growth: The Role of Labor Supply, Harvard University Press.

Laidler, D.E.W. (1983) The Demand for Money: Theory and Empirical Evidence, Harper and Row.

Lewis, W.A. (1954) 'Economic development with unlimited supplies of labour', Manchester School, vol. 26, pp. 139–191.

OECD (1987) Economic Outlook, OECD.

Patrick, H. and Rosovsky, H. (1976) Asia's New Giant: How the Japanese Economy Works, Brookings Institution.

Sarjeant, G. (1988) '£10bn wiped off shares. Currency instability triggers market fall', The Times, 25 March, p. 25.

Solow, R. (1956) 'A contribution to the theory of growth', Quarterly Journal of Economics, vol. 70, pp. 65–94.

5

Interactions of the Core and the Periphery

In this chapter we shall be concerned with the effects of economic activity in the industrial countries upon the developing countries and the effects of the industrial countries upon each other.

There are two main links between the advanced countries and the developing countries: that established through trade in goods and services and the tie created through financial markets. In the 1970s and the 1980s the importance of financial markets has increased as a result of the external debt burdens of the developing countries and their dependence upon loans from private sources. But it is trade in goods and services which has traditionally attracted most attention: the Prebisch—Singer thesis on the terms of trade between developed and developing countries seemed to explain what had happened in the inter-war years. Prebisch and Singer argued that: (1) there is a long-run deterioration in the terms of trade of the primary producers; and (2) primary product prices relative to the prices of manufactures fall during downswings by more than they rise in upswings. Although the Prebisch—Singer thesis can be applied to the developed countries, it is normally assumed that any adverse effects will be corrected by central governments pursuing income redistribution measures. However, we should note, in parenthesis, that the Prebisch—Singer thesis might be considered to run counter to the Kuznets thesis (which stated that economic development would eventually lead to increasing equality). To the extent that terms of trade determine incomes the Prebisch—Singer thesis postulates increasing income inequality, with the economic development of the advanced countries leading to greater relative deprivation for primary producers.

Trade in Goods and Services

We noted in Chapter 1 that the importance of advanced countries in world trade
in manufactures has been declining. Nevertheless, they are still the major suppliers of such goods to the developing countries. Changes in their economic activity
therefore have an important influence upon the prices and exports of developing
countries. The advanced countries are also important exporters of primary products, especially foodstuffs and agricultural raw materials, and these products compete with the primary products of the less developed countries. In the light of
these facts we can now consider the conditions which might give rise to the predictions of the Prebisch—Singer thesis.

Ricardian Theory

In the political economy of the Third World it is customary to emphasise the existence of a fundamental asymmetry between the conditions of the advanced and
developing countries. Developed and less developed countries, it is argued, do
not possess the same access to technology and have different product and labour
markets. The benefits of free trade cannot accrue to the Third World: the gains
from free trade tend to be distributed in favour of the advanced countries and
the developing countries become unequal partners in international trade.

To illustrate the case of unequal exchange we can make use of the Ricardian
theory of international trade. In Table 5.1 we assume that North and South can
produce both steel and food but because of differences in knowhow North has
a comparative advantage over South in the production of steel; that is, it takes
relatively less labour to produce steel in North than in South. We may further
suppose that exchange takes place at the rate of 5 units of steel for 1 unit of food.
Since 5 units of steel require 20 units of Northern labour and 1 unit of food requires 20 units of Southern labour there is an equal exchange of labour.

Suppose, then that there are labour saving inventions in Northern steel production so that 1 unit of labour can produce 1 unit of steel and that the terms of trade
change to 10 units of steel for 1 unit of food. Since 10 units of steel require 10
units of Northern labour but 1 unit of food still requires 20 units of Southern
labour there is now an unequal exchange of labour. But it is still possible to argue
that there is a gain from trade since the South would still require 40 units of labour

Table 5.1 Units of Labour Required to Produce 1 unit of Steel or Food in North and South

	Steel	Food
North	4	20
South	40	20

to produce 1 unit of steel if it resorted to domestic production rather than engaging in trade.

A similar model has been proposed by Lewis (1978). Suppose that the North produces steel and food and the South produces coffee and food and that the outputs are proportional to labour inputs. The North is assumed to have a comparative advantage in steel production and the South in coffee production and the North therefore exchanges steel for coffee. However, any deficit in the trade balance of either country is met by exporting food.

Now suppose that productivity in food production rises in the North and productivity in coffee production increases in the South; the South will then export more coffee in order to obtain its steel, unless it increases its own consumption of coffee. We now have another hypothesis to add to the Prebisch–Singer thesis. The Lewis example attributes the deterioration in the terms of trade to difference in the industries in which productivity advance occurs in the North and South.

Although we have referred to the above examples as Ricardian, they are not the conclusions which Ricardo drew from his own analysis. In the *Essay on the Corn Laws* (1819) he argued that as the manufacturing sector expanded there would, as a result of the tendency of population to increase as real wages rose, be a greater number of people who would be demanding food. But as the amount of land was limited this would then lead to a rise in food prices relative to those of manufactures and this could lead to a check to the growth of manufacturing and the ability of Britain to support a larger population. The only gainers from the expansion of industry would therefore be the landlords who would 'reap where they never sowed'. This was the substance of Ricardo's case for the repeal of the Corn Laws and the importing of cheap grain.

Neoclassical Theory

The fact that Lewis's result depends upon whether the North increases its consumption of food or the South increases its consumption of coffee provides an introduction to the neoclassical (sometimes called Heckscher–Ohlin) theory of trade in which countries have equal access to all technologies but differ in their quantities of factor endowments. Countries are therefore qualitatively similar but quantitatively different. Of course, a theory which assumes that all countries have access to the same technology might seem very long-run in its perspective; and it might seem strange to assume that resources are immobile while technologies are transferable. It is usually the case that technologies are embodied in, for example, the managers or the skilled personnel of transnational corporations. Indeed, considerable amounts of capital may flow through transnational corporations to countries which are deficient in capital and technology but which possess cheap labour. The issue is one of degree: factors tend to be more immobile than technologies and national governments attempt to control immigration of labour.

The advantage of this theory is that it brings together factor supplies, technologies, inventions and changes in demand and considers their impact upon product and factor prices and can allow for short-run rigidities.

Neoclassical theory is usually presented as a series of propositions.

1. The Stolper—Samuelson theorem (1941) states that a tariff placed upon imports of a commodity which uses a country's scarce factor will raise the absolute as well as the relative reward of that factor.
2. The Rybczynski theorem (1955) states that an increase in the amount of a factor, when the terms of trade and factor prices are constant, will cause an absolute increase in the production of the good using that factor and an absolute decrease in the commodity using other factors.
3. The factor price equalisation theorem (1949) states that free trade can bring about not only an equalisation of commodity prices but also an equalisation of factor prices.
4. The Heckscher—Ohlin theorem (1919, 1933) states that countries will export those goods which use their most abundant factor intensively and import those goods which embody their least abundant factor.
5. The Findlay—Grubert theorems trace out the consequences of changes in technologies upon the production of goods, commodity prices, factor prices and the pattern of imports and exports. (The Findlay—Grubert theorems may be regarded as extensions of the Rybczynski theorem to the extent that inventions may be regarded as increasing the supplies of factors.)

The theorems are interrelated and are usually presented for the case of two countries (North and South) producing two goods (food and steel) and using two factors (capital and labour). This is the $2 \times 2 \times 2$ model which also assumes that: (1) consumers' preferences are identical in both countries; (2) North has more capital than South and South has more labour than North; (3) production functions exhibit constant returns to scale and diminishing returns to proportions. The properties of the production functions are important. By excluding increasing (internal) economies of scale it is possible to confine the effects of changes in the marginal products of factors solely in terms of changes in factor supplies and since marginal products are measured by factor prices under perfect competition it is possible to establish a link between factor prices and factor supplies. By invoking Euler's theorem on homogeneous functions it is possible to ensure that the sum of factor payments is equal to the value of the product. But for the non-mathematician the exhaustion of the product theorem can be derived by recognising that under perfect competition the firm's average cost curve will be tangential to its average revenue curve. And although the theorems exclude internal economies of scale, it is possible for them to encompass external economies of scale so that the expansion of markets can permit a division of labour and falling costs, which permit the retention of perfect competition.

We will now look at the theorems in more detail. The Samuelson—Stolper theorem can be described as follows. Suppose that labour is scarce in North and that farmers manage to impose a tariff on food imports from South. Food output will increase in North and steel output will contract. Because the steel industry uses relatively more capital than labour the discharged capital will have to accept a lower return in order to be absorbed into food production. Since labour is employed in both industries and since perfect competition prevails in factor markets then wages will rise in both industries and the return to capital will fall in both industries. Since labour is employed in both industries its absolute share may rise even though total income falls as a result of protectionism.

Figure 5.1 illustrates this argument. The horizontal axis measures the total amount of capital available and the vertical axis measures the amount of labour. The output of steel is measured from O and the output of food is measured from O'. Initially, North produces at A where the steel isoquant is tangential to the food isoquant. The tangency denotes that A is an efficient point of production in the sense that it is impossible to produce more steel (food) without reducing the output of food (steel). The locus of all efficient points such as A will lie on a contract curve which is shown by the dashed line joining O and O'. The fact that the contract curve is bowed towards the bottom axis indicates that at all efficient points of production steel production will require more capital than labour. In other words, steel is always capital-intensive and food is always labour-intensive.

When a tariff is placed on food imports then food production will expand and steel production will contract and the final point of production will be a point such as B. Now consider the rays OA and OB which trace out the scale of output of steel. Because of the assumption of constant returns to scale and diminishing

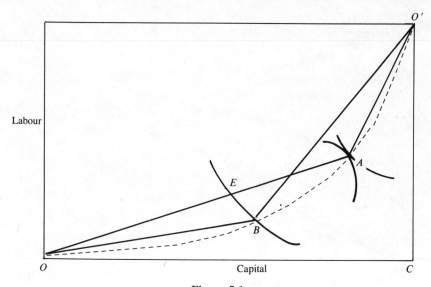

Figure 5.1

returns to proportions, the ratio of labour to capital used in steel production will
be given by the angles AOC and BOC. Since BOC is less than AOC then the
ratio of labour to capital in steel production will have fallen. In order to maintain
the same input ratio at the low output, steel production would have had to take
place at E which lies on the same ray as A. Extending the analysis to food production at A and B would also reveal a fall in the amount of labour to capital
in food production. Since the factor ratios determine the marginal products and
factor prices then we can conclude that the wage has risen and the return to capital
has fallen.

The Rybczynski theorem is demonstrated in Figure 5.2. To simplify the diagram
we have omitted the contract curves and the isoquants. Initially, production takes
place at A. An increase in the amount of labour with the factor price ratio constant will then result in an expansion of the output of steel along the ray OA and
a contraction of the amount of food production until point B is reached. Since
the factor price ratios are constant $O''B$ is drawn parallel to $O'A$. By varying
the factors which increase supply and by assuming that inventions are tantamount
to increases in factor supplies, it is possible to extend the analysis to incorporate
a range of possible effects upon exports and imports as well as product prices
and factor prices when the assumption of constant terms of trade is relaxed.

The factor price equalisation theorem is illustrated in Table 5.2 and Figure 5.3.
In the table we assume that 1 unit of steel requires 100 units of labour and 50
units of land and food requires 50 units of labour and 100 units of land; these
factor proportions are assumed to be required in both countries because the same
technologies are used. Now assume that product prices are equalised through free

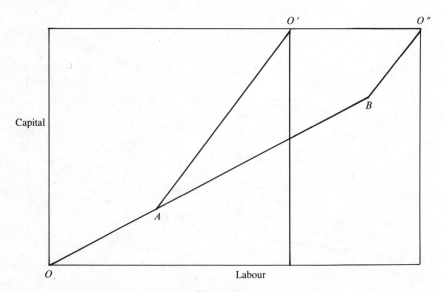

Figure 5.2

Table 5.2 Production and Trading Conditions in North and South

North	
Steel	100 units of labour × £0.50 + 50 units of land × £1.00 = £100
Food	50 units of labour × £0.50 + 100 units of land × £1.00 = £125
South	
Steel	100 units of labour × £0.50 + 50 units of land × £1.00 = £100
Food	50 units of labour × £0.50 + 100 units of land × £1.00 = £125

trade and that trade also brings about an equalisation of factor prices, i.e. assume that 1 unit of labour costs £0.50 and 1 unit of land costs £1.00 in both countries. The unit cost of steel production will then be £100 and that of food production will be £125. Since product prices equal average costs then the price of steel will be £100 and food will be £125. Now assume that product prices are equalised but that factor prices are not. Thus, suppose that the wage is £0.75 and the rental is £0.25; the unit cost of steel will then equal its product price but the unit cost of food will be less than the food price. Exports of food will therefore increase and a balance of payments surplus will result. On a fixed exchange rate system the surplus could lead to a rise in prices and costs until they were equal to those

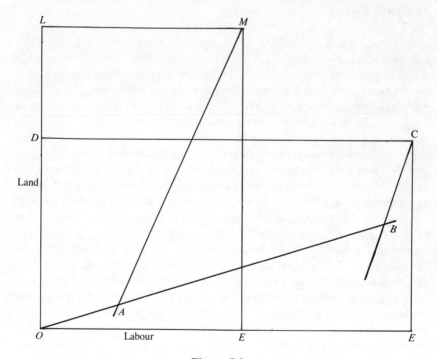

Figure 5.3

obtaining in South. On a flexible exchange rate system the exchange rate could rise until the prices were equalised.

An arithmetic example tends to give the impression that production coefficients are fixed whereas trade causes prices and outputs as well as factor proportions to vary. By juxtaposing Figures 5.1 and 5.2 in 5.3 it is possible to provide a more general proof of the factor price equalisation theorem using a theorem of corresponding points. The box *OLME* contains North's factor endowments of labour and land and the box *OECD* contains South's factor endowments. After trade the equilibrium positions of North and South are given by *A* and *B* respectively. Now both *A* and *B* lie on the ray from *O* which denotes the scale of output of steel in the two countries and since there are constant returns to scale the marginal products (and hence factor prices) are the same at *A* and *B* in steel production. Turning to food production we observe that the rays *MA* and *CB* are parallel and therefore the ratios of the marginal production of labour and land in food production are the same in both countries. Finally, since the sum of factor payments is equal to total revenues absolute factor prices are equal. Figure 5.3 also enables us to illustrate the Heckscher—Ohlin theorem. Since the length of the production rays in each country denotes the scales of output, we can see that each country produces more of the commodity which uses its most abundant factor intensively.

Empirical Evidence

Does neoclassical theory shed any light upon the determinants of trade? There are many reasons why the pattern of trading predicted by the Heckscher—Ohlin theorem might not occur in the real world. For example, there may be distortions in factor markets so that commodity prices do not reflect factor prices. Tariffs and quotas may exist. It may also be difficult to obtain information on factor endowments. How, for example, do we measure capital endowment? Consider the evidence assembled in Table 5.3 which indicates the labour-intensiveness of exports and imports for a group of developing countries. The evidence is a snapshot. It assumes that developing countries have an abundance of labour, especially unskilled labour. It assumes that there are few market distortions, such as tariffs, minimum wage legislation etc. Nevertheless, despite the qualifications that might be advanced, the information does permit a comparison between the labour contents of exports and imports. For example, in the most striking case, Indonesia, exports to developed countries used 2,176 man days compared to the 994 man days needed to generate equal value in the industries competing with imports from developed countries. In other words, Indonesia's import competing industries were using less labour because the corresponding industries in developed countries were not labour-intensive and were more efficient than industries which attempted to use labour to compensate for scarce capital and land. Although the differences are not as striking, Hong Kong uses 75 man days in exports as compared with 62 man days in import competing industries. Similarly, Chile's exports to

Table 5.3   Direct Labour Coefficients per Unit of Domestic Value-added by Direction of Trade (in Man Years)

Country	Period	Heckscher—Ohlin exportables			Heckscher—Ohlin import competing products		
		Developed countries	Developing countries	Total	Developed countries	Developing countries	Total
Chile	1966—68	61	29	34	43	43	43
Hong Kong	1973	75	67	73	62	55	60
Indonesia	1971[a]	2,176	2,149	2,175	994	1,117	1,038
Pakistan	1969—70	90	88	88	70	120	71

Source: Krueger *et al.* (1981)
Note: (a) Date for total man days

developed countries are relatively labour-intensive. Nor are the differences in factor intensities confined to trade between developing and developed countries. To take one example, Indonesian exports to developing countries use 2,149 man days to generate equal domestic value-added compared to 1,117 man days used in import competing industries.

Further evidence on the role of factor endowments is available from a study of the changing composition of South Korea's exports. Initially, exports were labour-intensive and used unskilled labour. But as a result of trade a surplus was created and investment in human and physical capital enabled a shift to take place towards the export of goods with a greater capital content (Table 5.4).

Is there any evidence to refute the Heckscher—Ohlin theorem? Are there other theories which can explain the same data? The most widely cited example is the

Table 5.4   South Korea: Percentage Share of Manufacturing Exports of Selected Commodities, 1965 and 1980

	1965	1980
Food	10.60	2.62
Textiles	26.41	14.16
Apparel	15.65	17.13
Wood products	14.27	3.01
Total declining industries	66.93	36.92
Industrial chemicals	0.23	4.69
Electrical machinery	1.46	12.12
Transport equipment	1.25	7.34
Total increasing industries	2.94	24.15
Total all selected commodities	69.87	61.07

Source: Khanna (1985)

so-called Leontief paradox which purports to show that the United States exported labour-intensive goods and imported capital-intensive goods (Table 5.5).

Various attempts have been made to resolve the paradox. It has been suggested that it ignores land, of which the United States has an abundance. The failure to recognise the importance of human capital has been put forward as a reason for the incongruous result. Factor reversals have also been used to explain the paradox. Suppose that the United States produces steel and food and that inputs of labour and capital cannot easily be varied in steel production whereas factor substitution is more easily accomplished in food production. Then, if wages are high relative to interest rates, food will be produced by capital-intensive methods and if wages are low then farmers will choose labour-intensive methods. But steel producers may not easily substitute between the factors when factor prices change. Hence, as factor prices change the factor intensity of food production will change relative to that in steel production. At some factor prices food will be capital-intensive and at other factor prices it will be labour-intensive.

Now suppose before trade takes place that the United States has an abundance of capital and that wages are high relative to capital charges in the rest of the world. Let us also suppose that the US and the rest of the world are separated by a factor reversal such that food is capital-intensive in the United States and labour-intensive in the rest of the world. Then the Heckscher–Ohlin theorem predicts that the US would export the capital-intensive good (food) and the rest of the world would export the labour-intensive good (food), which would seem to refute the thesis. A similar explanation might be advanced for demand reversals with the Americans importing capital-intensive goods because they have a strong preference for them. But before we multiply the qualifications we should note that Leontief's test did not include factor endowments but inferred them from factor intensities and that it applied to only one country (which may mean that the results cannot be extrapolated to a multi-country, multi-factor world). A recent attempt by Brown et al. (1987) to provide a world test of the theory concluded that the evidence did not support the Heckscher–Ohlin hypothesis of an exact relationship between factor contents and factor supplies. The lack of predictive power of the theory may have been due in part to the quality of the data and in part to the existence of different technologies. But Brown et al. were not able to put forward an alternative hypothesis.

Table 5.5 Domestic Capital and Labour Requirements per Million Dollars of US Exports and of Competitive Import Replacements (of Average 1947 Composition)

	Exports	Import replacements
Capital (dollars, in 1947 prices)	2,550,780	3,091,339
Labour (man years)	182.313	170.004

Source: Leontief (1953)

Growth and the Terms of Trade

But our main interest is in the relevance of the Heckscher−Ohlin theory for the Prebisch−Singer predictions which concern the effects of growth upon the terms of trade. It is agreed by protagonists that trade will improve the terms of trade of a country even if factors are immobile and factor prices are rigid. (In other words, because trade permits a country to obtain commodities at different prices from domestic prices there can be an exchange gain (whose distribution will depend upon the social welfare function adopted). This exchange gain is separate from any further gain from specialisation in production (Johnson 1962). But critics argue that the gains from trade may be unequally distributed between rich and poor countries and that distribution may become more unequal with economic growth. Now what the Heckscher−Ohlin theorems (or more precisely the Findlay−Grubert theorems) enable us to do is to isolate the effects of changes in factor supplies, technical change and changes in demand conditions upon the terms of trade. Thus, Figure 5.4 enables us to classify the consumption effects of growth. Initially, North is consuming at *C* where the community indifference curve is tangential to the price line *PP'*. Growth then shifts the price line to *P"P'''*. Now if food is the import good and the new consumption point is between *P"* and *K* then trade is ultra anti-trade biased; between *K* and *L* trade is anti-trade biased; at *E* growth is neutral; between *E* and *M* growth is pro-trade biased; and between *M* and *P'''* growth is ultra pro-trade biased.

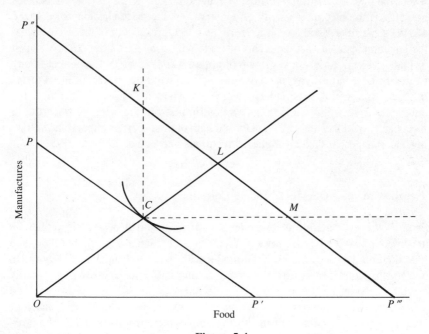

Figure 5.4

A similar exercise can be conducted for the production effects resulting from inventions or increases in factor supplies on the export (steel) and the import competing industry (food). The production and consumption effects can then be combined to produce an overall trade effect. Thus, suppose that there is a land saving invention in the food industry, i.e. an invention which is equivalent to an increase in the amount of land available. Its effect will be to cause an expansion in food production and it will therefore be ultra or merely anti-trade biased. But the effect upon food consumption will depend upon the income elasticity of demand for food resulting from the increase in incomes arising out of the use of the invention. The overall effect upon trade will therefore depend upon the relative strengths of the production and consumption effects. Conceivably, the consumption effect could be so strong as to outweigh the production effect and result in an increase in food imports despite the emergence of a land saving invention in food production. It is also possible to have a condition of immiserising growth in which an expansion of steel output leads to the need to lower the export price and turn the terms of trade against North.

The following equation encapsulates the results of an exercise along the lines suggested in the previous paragraph and incorporates possible changes in the various parameters.

$$\dot{p} = \frac{\epsilon_N \hat{Y}_N - \epsilon_S \hat{Y}_S}{(\eta_N + \eta_S - 1)} \tag{5.1}$$

where the 'hat' refers to proportional changes, p is the terms of trade, Y denotes output, ϵ is the income elasticity of demand, η is the price elasticity of demand and the subscripts N and S refer to North and South respectively. In essence what the equation states is that the terms of trade will turn against the country which has the greatest proportional growth of output weighted by the income elasticity of demand. A more dynamic economy would face a deterioration in its terms of trade and could experience balance of payments difficulties unless the denominator was positive. Whether a deterioration in the terms of trade did in fact occur would then depend upon the strength of the export or import bias following the changes in factor supplies, inventions and demand.

Neoclassical and Classical Models Combined

It is, however, possible to combine the classical and neoclassical models by postulating that the North grows in a neoclassical manner à la Solow (1956) and that the South grows in a classical model with unlimited supplies of labour. In the North labour is scarce and the labour supply is assumed to grow exogeneously at rate n. Savings are assumed to be determined by the savings propensity and are automatically invested. For simplicity of exposition, technological change is assumed to be autonomous. Finally, full employment is guaranteed by the flexibility of wages and interest rates. In the North growth leads to rising real wages

and some of the increase in incomes is spent on imports from the South. Employment in the South expands but, because there are unlimited supplies of labour,
there is no rise in real wages, so a widening wage differential results.

Increasing Returns and Infant Industries

The Heckscher—Ohlin model assumes that diminishing returns obtain in industries
and, as a result, there is incomplete specialisation in production in countries. But
manufacturing, as the classical economists observed, is subject to increasing returns
and a distinction can be drawn between external and internal economies. External
economies are those which lie outside the ability of any firm and can be realised
only by an expansion of the market which permits further specialisation and the
division of labour, and can lead to the hiving off of activities. External economies
can therefore be incorporated into the Heckscher—Ohlin model while retaining
the assumption of constant returns to scale. However, internal economies are those
which can be achieved by the individual firm. Now if the market in the North
expands and firms obtain economies of scale it may be difficult for Southern firms
to enter the market and trade. This could lead to demands for protection for
Southern infant industries. But if such protection is given then it should take the
form of a subsidy financed from a lump sum tax rather than a tariff on imports
which would raise prices to consumers.

Capital and Labour Mobility

Trade theory tends to assume that goods are mobile but that resources are immobile. Relaxing this assumption, if labour moves from the labour abundant South
to the North then the effects can be mutually beneficial. Migrants receive higher
wages and total output in the North increases. Out of the higher incomes there
may be remittances to the South as well as increased exports to the North. The
effects of capital mobility may, however, be ambiguous. It is normally assumed
that capital will flow from the North to the South and increase output and employment. But, conceivably, Northern capital could crowd out Southern capital.
Adverse effects may also follow from technological transfer via transnational corporations if they manipulate transfer prices. If the prices of new technologies
and knowhow (that is, royalty payments) are not determined in markets then it
may be possible for multinational corporations to conceal the returns they get
on their foreign investment by charging inflated prices for their resources.

An outflow of Northern capital could conceivably cause a deterioration in the
South's terms of trade. For example, suppose that there are three factors of production, labour, capital and land, which are used to produce two goods, steel
and metals. Suppose that steel is labour-intensive and metals are capital-intensive.
If the amount of capital in the North increases then the output of metals and
minerals increases and the South's terms of trade will rise. Now let us introduce

the possibility of Northern investment in the South. If both countries have identical production functions then the terms of trade will be unaffected. But suppose we then introduce a third factor of production, land, and assume that the South is land abundant. Land can be introduced into the production function but a three-factor analysis can be complicated and it is simpler to postulate that the introduction of land is equivalent to a change in technology. In other words, metals are capital-intensive *vis-à-vis* steel but the South's abundance of land means that it has lower costs per unit. In these circumstances the return on capital would be higher in the South and there would be capital investment by the North. The outflow of capital would reduce the output of steel in the North. At the same time it would increase the demand for steel by the South because of rising real incomes and the terms of trade would turn against the South.

Aid and Loans

In 1961 the advanced markets economies agreed to donate 1 per cent of their GNP to the developing countries. Few countries in fact donated 1 per cent and aid has tended to dwindle in importance. There has been a period of disenchantment, with aid seeming to be ill used; some right-wing economists have stated that aid tends to reduce the efforts of the developing countries to better themselves. However, less use has been made of the fact that aid might turn the terms of trade of the developing countries against them if it raises the demand for industrial goods to such an extent that it raises their prices. Similarly, loans could cause a deterioration in the terms of trade of the developing countries.

Cyclical Fluctuation in the Terms of Trade

So far we have been discussing models which deal with trends in the terms of trade. But another strand of the Prebisch—Singer thesis deals with the greater amplitude of flunctuations in the terms of trade of primary producers.

Suppose that a boom in the North is brought to an end by a rise in raw material prices. In response to those rising prices increased investment may have taken place in the South, but because of a lag the output of raw materials may not have expanded before the boom breaks. The rise in raw material prices then encounters real wage resistance and results in a profits squeeze. The effect of the fall in profits is to cause a fall in investment and output tends to fall more than prices. The reduction in investment and output in the North then causes a contraction in the demand for raw materials. The low demand and supply elasticities in the South then cause a fall in the prices of raw materials and turn the terms of trade against the South. The price fall will be intensified by the emergence of increased output from the investment undertaken in the boom. There may then be a long delay before excess capacity is removed. When the recovery takes place in the North it will result in an improvement in the terms of trade of the South. However, any gains could be dissipated by an increase in the population, in which case the South would find itself caught in a Malthusian low level equilibrium trap.

Empirical Evidence on the Terms of Trade

Theory must eventually confront reality. We have two predictions: a thesis on the secular terms of trade, and a prediction that the amplitude and duration of fluctuations in the prices of primary products is greater than that for manufactures.

At the outset we are faced with two difficulties, one theoretical, the other statistical. The bulk of international trade theory devoted to growth and the terms of trade is couched in terms of competitive models. The inclusion of monopoly into general equilibrium models is not easy to formulate and yet the Prebisch–Singer model emphasises the importance of product monopolists and trade unions. The second problem arises from the nature of the data. Prebisch based his conclusions upon the British barter terms of trade between 1876 and 1938. Now the barter terms of trade measure the ratio of export and import prices and some writers prefer to use the factoral or double factoral terms of trade which allow for changes in labour productivity. Unfortunately, information on the factoral terms of trade is not always available. Another criticism of Prebisch's finding is that it may depend crucially upon the time period adopted. In Prebisch's work the terminal date coincided with the depression of the 1930s. Had a longer timespan been taken then commodity prices would have shown a rise in the 1940s, a fall in the 1950s and 1960s, a rise in the 1970s and then a fall in the 1980s. And even within the aggregate time series attention must be paid to the movements in the price of oil and the prices of minerals which are influenced by governments' stockpiling policies. Qualitative changes in products must also be considered, although it is more convenient to assume that there are qualitative changes in both manufactures and primary products which somehow cancel each other out. Furthermore, there is the criticism that the decline in shipping freight rates in the nineteenth century resulted in a valuation bias in the terms of trade statistics since the British statistics valued imports cif (cost insurance freight) and exports fob (free on board). Finally, there is the possibility in the post-war period that the domination of world trade by multinationals with transfer prices designed to maximise global profits may have obscured movements in the terms of trade.

Figure 5.5 shows the movement of the terms of trade of non-oil commodities and manufactures between 1900 and 1985. In contrast to the upward trend found by Sarkar (1986) between 1800 and 1860, the trend is downwards. But equally striking is the long swing in the terms of trade with a downturn in 1918 followed by an upswing in 1975 and with minor fluctuations in the intervening period. But taking the period as a whole Evans (1987) suggests that the evidence is not consistent with an ultra anti-trade bias or anti-trade bias in agricultural productivity in the North. Instead he finds that the rate of technical change in Northern

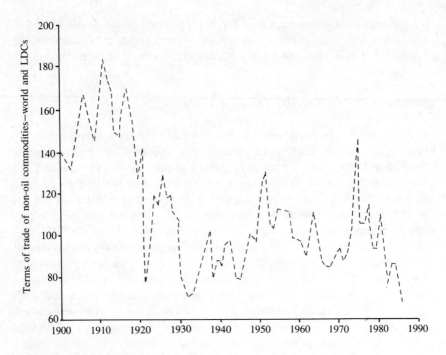

Source: Grilli and Yang (1986)

Figure 5.5   Terms of Trade of Non-oil Commodities Versus Manufactures of World
and LDCs, 1900–83

agriculture is comparable with that in manufactures. Hence, it is the lower income elasticity of demand (the Engels curve) for agricultural goods which is the
crucial factor and which exerts a depressing effect upon the terms of the South
and reduces the effects of diminishing returns to natural resources as population
expands in the North. The empirical evidence on bias in the South he found to
be too sketchy to reach any firm conclusions. However, the Engels curve effect
does point to the problems created by the large income gap between the North
and the South. Evans's work is complemented by that of Ngyuen (1987), who
has found that countries which have relatively high rates of deterioration of their
terms of trade experience low growth rates. Finally, Thirlwall and Bergevin (1985)
have found evidence which supports the Prebisch–Singer thesis that the amplitude
and duration of fluctuations in primary product prices is greater than that for
manufacturing prices.

South–South Trade

The prolonged recession of the 1970s and 1980s in the advanced countries led
Lewis (1980) to explore the possibility that trade between developing countries

might provide an engine of growth. In the 1950s trade between developing countries grew at about 1 per cent per annum, at 5 per cent from 1960 to 1965 and at 8.3 per cent between 1965 and 1970. However, trade between the advanced countries grew at a faster rate from 1950 to 1970 with the result that the share of trade among the developing countries in world trade fell from 6 per cent to 3.5 per cent. But after 1970 trade between the developing countries grew at a faster rate than trade between the advanced countries. Some part of the increase was due to the rise in the price of oil; but even when oil is excluded from the calculation then their share of world trade rose to 4.2 per cent, with the main developments taking place in South-east Asia, where one-third of the exports are to other developing countries, and in Latin America (one-quarter). There has also been a noticeable expansion in manufacturing activity. Unfortunately, the prolonged slump of the 1980s has tended to check the growth of mutual trade. There are, however, difficulties in using mutual trade as an engine of growth. Most developing countries use tariffs as an important source of government revenue and, being former colonies, are tied to advanced countries through language and culture.

Supporting evidence for pessimism also comes from studies of customs unions and free trade areas between developing countries. The creation of a customs union involves the abolition of tariffs between member countries and the erection of common external tariffs; free trade areas permit the retention by each country of its own external tariffs. But irrespective of the method of integration adopted there may be trade creation and trade diversion in the sense that some members may find that they are paying higher prices for some goods than they would have paid to non-members (who are now excluded by tariff barriers). The overall effect will, of course, depend upon the relative strengths of the trade creation and trade diversion effects. But the theory has been established upon the assumption that there will be changes in the pattern of trade which, in turn, rests upon an assumption that there is an existing pattern of production, whereas the gains for developing countries may lie in the possibilities of creating a new production system. In other words, customs unions may influence the development path.

Table 5.6 indicates the extent of intra-group trade among developing countries. Whereas intra-group trade accounts for some 50 per cent of the trade of advanced countries (and is discussed in Chapter 9) the significance of intra-group trade for developing countries seldom rises above 20 per cent. Another feature of the table is the stagnation of intra-group trade during the 1970s and 1980s, despite the initial low levels of such trade.

Differences in income between North and South are an important element in explaining differences in the volume of trade between North and South and between countries in the North. However, there are other contributing factors which account for the large amount of intra-trade in the North, such as preferences for manufactured goods over primary products and preferences for variety as incomes increase, which leads to product differentiation, economies of scale and expenditure on research and development. R & D expenditure leads to new processes

Table 5.6 Intra-trade of Developing Countries by Territories and Regions

Region	Value of intra-trade (millions of dollars)				Exports to developing countries as a per cent of total group exports				Intra-trade of group as a per cent of total exports of each group			
	1960	1970	1980	1984	1960	1970	1980	1984	1960	1970	1980	1984
A. Groupings which extended and implemented mutual trade preferences before 1970												
Association of South-east Asian Nations, 1967[a]	839	860	11,918	14,428	32.8	31.7	35.6	37.5	21.7	14.7	17.8	18.5
Bangkok Agreement	—	47	517	1,758	—	20.4	31.7	27.6	—	1.5	1.8	4.3
Customs and Economic Union of Central Africa, 1964	3	33	200	100	8.3	11.9	22.5	10.0	1.6	3.4	4.1	3.5
Central American Common Market, 1960	33	299	1,141	780	10.0	29.6	30.8	30.2	7.5	26.8	22.0	19.7
Caribbean Community, 1968; (Eastern Caribbean Common Market is not included.)	27	73	354	316	12.2	16.6	20.0	12.0	4.5	7.3	6.4	4.2
Latin American Integration Association, formerly LAFTA, 1960	564	1,290	10,270	8,120	19.4	21.2	28.1	25.1	7.7	10.2	13.5	9.2
of which: Andean Group, 1969	25	109	955	772	28.8	29.3	31.6	31.4	0.7	2.3	3.5	3.3

Region	Value of intra-trade (millions of dollars)				Exports to developing countries as a per cent of total group exports				Intra-trade of group as a per cent of total exports of each group			
	1960	1970	1980	1984	1960	1970	1980	1984	1960	1970	1980	1984
A. Groupings which extended and implemented mutual trade preferences before 1970												
West African Economic Community, 1959 (initially West African Customs Union)	6	73	296	306	14.8	15.1	15.9	18.5	2.0	9.1	6.9	7.4
Total excluding ASEAN and Bangkok Agreement	633	1,768	12,208	9,622	18.1	21.0	27.0	23.7	7.2	10.8	12.8	9.0
Total	—	2,675	24,643	25,808	—	19.8	30.7	29.2	—	8.8	12.9	11.4
B. Other groupings												
Economic Community of West African States, 1975	17	61	1,056	500	6.7	8.6	6.2	17.0	1.2	2.1	3.9	2.5
Economic Community of the Great Lakes Countries, 1976	—	2	5	10	0.0	6.5	49.7	10.0	0.0	0.2	0.2	0.7
Mano River Union, 1973	—	—	2	4	0.6	4.4	8.7	23.7	0.0	0.1	0.1	0.4
Regional Cooperation for Development, 1964	36	43	500	2,510	22.5	18.6	34.0	39.0	2.2	1.1	2.7	11.0
Total	53	106	1,563	3,024	10.0	8.6	18.9	28.0	1.8	1.5	3.1	6.5

Source: UNCTAD (1986)

Note: (a) Figures adjusted to exclude entrepôt trade. Figures for Singapore exports to Malaysia and Thailand are derived from import statistics of these two trading partners.

and products which give rise to product differentiation and the exploitation of economies of scale. Technological gaps may emerge which may take time to erase and for countries to converge.

Advanced Economies

So far we have concentrated on the trade problems of the less developed countries; but two-thirds of international trade is conducted between advanced countries. While trade between less developed or between less developed and advanced countries may seem compatible with the factor endowments theory, it is not obvious that trade between advanced countries rests upon observable disparities in factor endowments.

Four facts figure prominently in any explanation of trade between advanced countries. First, a considerable amount of trade is dependent upon investment in research and development, and changes in technology. Second, there is a considerable amount of intra-industry trade (Table 5.7). There is trade in variety: countries export to each other cars, electrical and household goods. There is also trade in components: Ford and General Motors produce engines and car bodies in different countries. Third, manufacturing tends to be subject to economies of scale. Taken in conjunction, product variety and economies of scale suggest that markets may be monopolistic or oligopolistic. Fourth, trade between advanced countries has tended to grow at a faster rate than that between developing countries and trade in manufactures has been the subject of trade liberalisation and quasi-liberalisation measures, such as customs unions and free trade areas.

Table 5.7   Intra-trade of Developed Countries by Region

Region	Value of intra-trade ($ billion)					Share of intra-trade as % world exports 1980
	1960	1970	1972	1980	1982	
EEC	10.3	43.4	61.4			
European Free Trade Association	2.9	9.4	12.9			
EEC (expanded)			110.5	347.2	298.9	52.8
Trade in manufactures between expanded EEC and residual EFTA				105.9	85.3	12.3
Intra-trade of the residual EFTA member countries				14.8	11.9	12.8
USA—Canada (preferential)		5.1		15.7	25.9	5.7
CMEA	8.1	18.4	24.2	79.2		51.0
Total	21.2	76.1	106.2	562.4	515.1	46.7

Source: UNCTAD (1985)

Research and Development and Changing Technologies

The most significant feature of trade between advanced countries is that it is increasingly influenced by investment by firms in research and development. Firms can accordingly be classified as follows.

1. Supplier dominated firms are to be found mainly in agriculture, traditional manufacturing (such as textiles) and services in which the innovations originate from the suppliers of equipment and raw materials.
2. Production-intensive firms are involved in the mass production of standardised bulk materials (such as iron and steel), or in consumer durables (cars) in which process innovations stem from the pressure to exploit economies of scale.
3. Science based firms can be found in electrical and electronics industries and chemicals which require the prior development of theoretical concepts which can be applied over a wide range of products.

Research and development within the groupings gives rise to process and product cycles or trajectories in which there is a systematic and progressive exploitation of economies of scale or uses in a wide variety of fields. Thus, the 1970s gave rise to the pressure to introduce innovations which reduced the materials content of processes and the exploitation of cheaper and more compact electronic information processing devices which increased the ability of firms to handle large amounts of information, increased the flexibility of processes and integrated a wide range of functions, such as marketing, product design and production.

Although discovery may be a random process success is linked to the amount spent on R&D. In 1983 the world spent about 265 billion dollars on research and development, double the amount spent in 1970. Of the total, 70 per cent was spent by the advanced market economies (33.4 per cent by the USA, 26.9 per cent by the EEC and 12.6 per cent by Japan) and 24.2 per cent by the centrally planned economies of Eastern Europe (18 per cent by the USSR). And although not all firms patent their ideas some 32 per cent of all patents applied for in 1980 were sought in the USA, 17.9 per cent in West Germany and 12.9 per cent in Japan. There is therefore a concentration of research activity in a limited number of countries and this may be related to productivity as measured by GDP per person employed at purchasing power parity exchange rates. Table 5.8 throws

Table 5.8 GDP per Employed Person and Productivity Levels in the Advanced Market Economies Compared with their US Levels (US in each year = 100)

	Japan	France	West Germany	UK
1950	16.6	41.2	37.0	57.8
1960	25.6	52.3	55.7	58.3
1970	49.5	69.2	69.4	61.5
1980	67.5	87.6	85.4	67.6
1984	72.0	89.0	86.9	70.8

Source: US Congress (1986)

Table 5.9 Shares of World Exports of Manufactures by Advanced Countries

	1970	1985
High R&D intensity		
USA	29.59	26.79
Japan	8.29	18.33
West Germany	16.29	13.85
UK	10.46	9.15
Medium R&D intensity		
Japan	9.36	20.17
West Germany	21.33	17.92
USA	19.88	15.66
France	7.84	7.32
UK	10.77	7.18
Low R&D intensity		
West Germany	12.47	13.44
Italy	7.21	10.21
Japan	11.16	9.66
France	8.99	9.13
USA	11.02	8.98

Source: UNCTAD (1987)

some light upon the issue. What it reveals is that the USA had the highest level of productivity in 1950 but that the productivity gap narrowed between 1950 and 1970 and then slowed down.

Table 5.9 carries the analysis a step further by indicating market shares of countries according to the research intensity of industries. High R&D intensity industries comprise computers, drugs and aerospace. Medium R&D industries include cars and chemicals. Low R&D industries include shipbuilding, glass, food processing, paper and printing, textiles, clothing and footwear. What the table reveals is that the USA tends to dominate world trade in industries involving high R&D intensity, Japan is significant in medium R&D industries and West Germany heads the rankings of the low R&D industries. However, the rise in Japan's share of world trade in high-tech industries during the 1970s is striking.

Technology Gaps, Monopolistic Competition and Trade

R&D can give rise to monopoly advantages in trade and to the exploitation of scale economies and the segmentation of markets through product differentiation. If we assume that markets can be characterised by duopoly (a euphemism for oligopoly) then it should be possible to apply the standard theories of duopoly to markets in which a product is produced in two countries. Each firm will then decide how much to produce on the assumption that its rival's behaviour can be taken as given and that transport costs can be ignored. In the Cournot model an equilibrium is reached with each firm producing one-third of the competitive output. If transport costs or a tariff are introduced then domestic firms will get a larger share of the market.

If product differentiation is introduced and there are large numbers of firms then Chamberlin's theory of monopolistic competition can be applied. Consumers will balance the gains from lower prices as a result of increasing returns and against the gains from variety; not all varieties may be produced. It is also possible to have both inter-industry trade and intra-industry trade, depending upon the relative strengths of the desire for variety and the lower costs from increasing returns.

Product variety is likely to be profitable when incomes are rising and new wants are emerging. Table 5.10 indicates the expansion in differentiated products between 1970 and 1982. What the table reveals is that there was a threefold expan-

Table 5.10 Diversification and Concentration in the Trade of the Developed Countries[a]

Country or area	1970 Number of commodities exported	1970 Diversi- fication index	1970 Concentration index	1982 Number of commodities exported	1982 Diversi- fication index	1982 Concentration index
Faeroe islands	..	..	..	7	0.966	0.857
Iceland	30	0.922	0.652	37	0.912	0.675
South Africa	65	0.589	0.136	171	0.779	0.518
Norway	49	0.591	0.162	159	0.528	0.309
New Zealand	20	0.809	0.368	144	0.757	0.252
Israel	16	0.679	0.307	142	0.661	0.222
Japan	66	0.431	0.131	162	0.499	0.205
Finland	45	0.646	0.261	150	0.567	0.193
Canada	67	0.486	0.184	165	0.476	0.180
Australia	68	0.657	0.191	173	0.674	0.168
Sweden	70	0.423	0.142	174	0.412	0.147
Gibraltar	..	..	..	65	0.635	0.145
Portugal	47	0.607	0.115	147	0.564	0.145
Netherlands	73	0.364	0.075	174	0.429	0.143
West Germany	78	0.338	0.133	180	0.328	0.142
Greece	12	0.727	0.162	147	0.639	0.139
United Kingdom	78	0.310	0.098	181	0.237	0.139
Switzerland	65	0.547	0.142	163	0.563	0.123
Ireland	39	0.626	0.165	166	0.532	0.122
Belgium-Luxembourg	76	0.362	0.099	178	0.391	0.118
Italy	70	0.370	0.113	179	0.398	0.104
Spain	62	0.502	0.109	174	0.390	0.104
United States	80	0.326	0.099	179	0.366	0.100
Denmark	71	0.505	0.103	170	0.486	0.092
France	81	0.248	0.087	180	0.282	0.089
Austria	59	0.450	0.081	168	0.451	0.080
Yugoslavia	59	0.508	0.095	162	0.456	0.079

Source: UNCTAD (1985)

Note: (a) The concentration index discriminates between countries which are relatively concentrated in their export structure; the diversification index discriminates between countries which are more diversified. Both indexes range between zero and 1.0, with the latter representing the most extreme concentration.

Table 5.11 Indices of Prices of Manufactured Exports in a Common Currency and Shares
of World Trade in Manufactures: 1970−85

	Export prices 1970 = 100			Share of world trade		
	UK	West Germany	Japan	UK	West Germany	Japan
1970	100	100	100	10.8	19.8	11.7
1971	102	105	100	10.9	20.0	13.0
1972	99	108	105	10.0	20.2	13.2
1973	94	112	113	9.4	22.1	12.8
1974	92	113	126	9.8	20.7	14.5
1975	94	112	108	9.3	20.3	13.6
1976	90	114	102	8.8	20.5	14.6
1977	94	115	105	9.4	20.7	15.4
1978	105	116	117	9.5	20.7	15.0
1979	113	113	107	9.7	20.7	13.6
1980	125	107	101	9.7	19.8	14.8
1981	120	99	107	8.6	18.3	18.0
1982	113	100	99	8.5	19.6	17.9
1983	112	99	93	8.0	19.1	19.0
1984	107	88	93	7.6	18.0	20.5
1985	110	90	91	7.8	18.6	19.7

Source: NIESR (1975, 1980, 1987)

sion in the number of products exported and concentration indices declined. But
incomes do not increase at a regular rate; there are cycles around a rising trend.
What may be crucial, therefore, is the ability of a country to exploit the surges
in incomes through expanding variety and obtaining any increasing returns which
may result in order to consolidate gains in the subsequent recessions.

The apparent unimportance of price as opposed to variety and availability is
suggested by Table 5.11. The fall in UK export prices of manufactured goods
between 1971 and 1977 could not prevent a decline in the share of world trade.
Indeed the continuing downward trend in the UK manufacturing share seems to
have been uninfluenced by rising or falling prices while the West Germans and
Japanese appear to have been able to increase or maintain market shares despite
rising prices. Of course, the problem with simple price and quantity data is that
in a period when there is considerable change in the qualities of products price
reductions are hidden in the improvements in quality and income elasticities of
demand tend to be a mixture of price and income effects.

Conclusions

Trade theory suggests that trade takes place because of differences in comparative
advantage. In Ricardian theory the differences in comparative advantage stem

from differences in technology; what then has to be explained is why differences in investment and research and development take place. In neoclassical theory trade takes place because of differences in factor endowments. This theory is useful in explaining the general pattern of trade between the labour abundant South and the capital abundant North. However, it needs to take into account changes in technologies and the behaviour of product and factor prices in order to explain the long-run decline in the terms of trade of the South and the tendency for the South's terms of trade to show considerable fluctuations during trade cycles. It also needs to incorporate the possibilities of increasing returns and product variety in order to explain trade between advanced countries. External economies are compatible with the competitive assumptions of the factor endowments theory. As the scale of trade expands economies which are not available to the individual trader become available to all traders. The division of labour is limited by the size of the market and as the market expands firms may split off activities which can be performed by new firms or by new process and product divisions. Intra-industry trade may in this way be compatible with the factor endowments model. But increasing returns due to internal economies of scale may lead to monopoly situations and arise out of differences in spending on research and development. The short-run advantages stemming from differences in R&D spending may give rise to technological gaps which may be prolonged by differences in the methods of production management. Thus, Japan's comparative advantage is in work organisation (discussed in Chapter 7). Whether that advantage will persist will depend upon the responses of other countries. At the end of the Second World War there was a dollar shortage arising out of the superiority of American industry in producing import competing goods; but that advantage lasted only twenty years. As a result of catching up by Japan and Western Europe and the American diversion of resources into defence the dominant position of the United States started to crumble in the 1970s. But the relative advantage of Japan and Western Germany could undergo a similar transformation over the next twenty years.

Bibliography

Beckerman, W. and Jenkinson, T. (1986) 'What stopped the inflation? Unemployment or commodity prices?', *Economic Journal,* vol. 96, pp. 158–167.

Brown, H.P. *et al.* (1987) 'Multicountry and multifactor tests of the factor abundance theory', *American Economic Review,* vol. 77, pp. 791–810.

Evans. D. (1987) 'The long run determinants of North–South terms of trade and some recent empirical evidence', *World Development,* vol. 15, 657–711.

Findlay, R. and Grubert, H. (1959) 'Factor intensities, technological progress and the terms of trade', *Oxford Economic Papers,* NS vol. 2, pp. 111–121.

Grilli, E.R. and Yang, Y. (1986) 'Long term movements of non-fuel primary commodity prices: 1980–1988', World Bank.

Heckscher, E. (1919) 'The effect of foreign trade on the distribution of income', *Ekonomisk Tidskrift,* vol. 21, pp. 497–512 reprinted in H.S. Ellis and L.A. Metzler (eds), (1949) *Readings in the Theory of International Trade,* Blakiston, pp. 272–300.

Johnson, H.G. (1962) *Money, Trade and Economic Growth*, Unwin University Books.

Khanna, A. (1985) 'A note on the dynamic aspects of the Heckscher—Ohlin model: some empirical evidence', *World Development*, vol. 13, pp. 1171—1174.

Krueger, A.O. *et al.* (1981) *Trade and Employment in Developing Countries*, University of Chicago Press.

Kuznets, S. (1955) 'Economic growth and income inequality', *American Economic Review, Papers and Proceedings*, vol. 48, pp. 21—33.

Leamer, E.E. (1980) 'The Leontief paradox reconsidered', *Journal of Political Economy*, vol. 88, pp. 495—503.

Leontief, W.W. (1953) 'Domestic production and foreign trade: The American capital position re-examined', *Proceedings of the American Philosophical Society*, vol. 97, pp. 21—45.

Lewis, W.A. (1978) *Growth and Fluctuations: 1870—1913*, Allen and Unwin.

Lewis, W.A. (1980) 'The slowing down of the engine of growth', *American Economic Review*, vol. 70, pp. 555—564.

MacBean, A. (1966) *Export Instability and Economic Development*, Allen and Unwin.

MacBean, A. and Nguyen, D. (1987) 'International commodity agreements: shadow and substance', *World Development*, vol. 15, pp. 575—90.

NIESR (1975, 1980, 1987) *Economic Review*, National Institute of Economic and Social Research.

Nguyen, D.T. (1987) 'Movements in the terms of trade of commodities versus manufactures: effects on less developed countries', mimeo.

Ohlin, B. (1933) *Interregional and International Trade*, Harvard University Press.

Prebisch, R. (1950) *The Economic Development of Latin America and its Principal Problems*, United Nations.

Ricardo, D. (1819) 'Essay on Profits', in *The Works and Correspondence of David Ricardo*, Sraffa edition (1951), Cambridge University Press.

Rybczynski, T.M. (1955) 'Factor endowments and relative commodity prices', *Economica*, vol. 84, pp. 336—341.

Samuelson, P.A. (1949) 'International factor price equalization once again', *Economic Journal*, vol. 234, pp. 181—197.

Sarkar, P. (1986) 'The Singer—Prebisch hypothesis and statistical evidence', *Cambridge Journal of Economics*, vol. 10, pp. 355—372.

Singer, H.W. (1950) 'The distribution of gains between investing and borrowing countries', *American Economic Review*, vol. 40, pp. 473—485.

Solow, R. (1956) 'A contribution to the theory of growth', *Quarterly Journal of Economics*, vol. 70, pp. 65—94.

Spraos, J. (1980) 'The statistical debate on the net barter terms of trade between primary commodities and manufactures', *Economic Journal*, vol. 90, pp. 107—128.

Stolper, W.F. and Samuelson, P.A. (1941) 'Protection and real wages', *Review of Economic Studies*, vol. 1, pp. 58—73.

Thirlwall, A.P. and Bergevin, J. (1985) 'Trends, cycles and asymmetries in the terms of trade of primary commodities from developed and less developed countries', *World Development*, vol. 13, pp. 805—817.

UNCTAD (1985) *Handbook of International and Development Statistics, Supplement*, United Nations.

UNCTAD (1986) *Trade and Development Report*, United Nations.

UNCTAD (1987) *Trade and Development Report*, United Nations.

US Congress, Joint Economic Committee (1986) *Technology and Trade: Indicators of US Industrial Innovation*, US Government Printing Office.

6

OPEC

The quadrupling of oil prices between 1973 and 1974 marked a turning point in the expansion and evolution of the world economy; but the causes of the rise in oil prices are still in dispute. It has been described as a blunder by the oil cartel, OPEC, and it was predicted that it would not last long because cartels cannot control their members or prevent the intrusion of new sellers. Core sector inflation tended to erode real gains so that continued price increases were needed in 1978 and 1979. But if it was a blunder it has been suggested that it arose from the incompetence not of the oil states but of successive US administrations and of the oil companies. Opposed to these hypotheses, which invoke the myopia of oil states and the advanced countries, are those which assume rational behaviour by competitive or monopolistic sellers. We shall review these alternative explanations and consider the effects of the 1973 oil price rise, the doubling of oil prices in 1978–79, and the fall in oil prices in 1986.

Alternative Explanations of the 1973–74 Oil Price Rise

The Myopic Cartel

At the time of the 1973 oil price rise it was widely stated that OPEC had made a mistake, that the trend of oil prices was downwards and that the cartel would disintegrate as members reneged and new entrants came into the market. This thesis faces two problems: it does not explain why a cartel formed in the 1960s took so long to raise prices and nor does it explain why the cartel managed to hold prices up until 1986 — 12 years is a long time in the life of a cartel.

The US Administrations

The alternative theory of incompetence places the blame upon successive US administrations and the oil companies. During the 1950s and 1960s oil played an important part in the geopolitical strategy of US governments. This strategy was effective because the United States was not only the world's greatest producer of oil but was itself independent of sources of oil outside the Western hemisphere and maintained a spare capacity of some four million barrels a day. The USA was the world's greatest producer of natural gas and the largest depository of coal supplies. But oil played a part not only in domestic policy but also in foreign affairs. Through the 1950s and 1960s the foreign policy goals were: (1) to provide a steady flow of oil to Europe and Japan; (2) to maintain stable governments in non-communist, pro-Western oil producing countries; and (3) to make American based firms the dominant influence in the world oil trade.

These domestic and foreign policy goals were served by the oil companies, seven of which dominated the market: five were American and two were British. The task of the domestic producer was to ensure an adequate supply of oil through the exploitation of existing sites and the exploration of new fields; to achieve this latter end the government provided generous subsidies in the form of depletion allowances. In the international sphere the problem was to achieve stability by avoiding a market shortage, which would provoke international intervention, and preventing a glut being created by the oil states and independent companies, who wanted to expand production to increase revenues.

But there were underlying tensions. The provision of generous domestic depletion allowances had three effects. First, they enabled the oil companies to pay virtually no taxes. Second, because they were generous, they allowed the companies to be lazy and discouraged the search for oil in the United States. Third, because they could be used abroad, they permitted companies to undertake foreign ventures in the more easily exploitable Middle East fields and they encouraged the companies to supply the non-American market. These effects upon US production were reinforced by the conservation movement which began to gather momentum in the 1960s and held back the development of the Alaskan oil field. The result was that by the end of the 1960s US domestic consumption was outstripping domestic production and from a position of being 90 per cent self-sufficient in oil supplies the US moved to importing 50 per cent of its needs. In 1971 legislation limiting oil imports was repealed and by the end of the 1970s the US was importing 30 per cent of OPEC output.

Arab Nationalism

Foreign policy was also being undermined by the pressure in the oil states for increased revenues (especially in those which wanted to industrialise) and for independent control of the oil fields. Both of these goals were strongly influenced by Arab nationalism and conflicts with Israel. In the seventh century an Arab empire, united by language and religion, had stretched from the Pyrenees to Central Asia. Although this empire had been eroded it had never completely disappeared: hopes of a revived Arab culture were never extinguished. The collapse of the Ottoman Empire after the First World War led to hopes of a revival. However, these aspirations were dashed by the creation of many protectorates and by the involvement of the British and French in the Middle East. After the Second World War many of the protectorates gained their independence, but conflicts still pervaded the Arab world. There were persistent discords between the two wings of Islam, the 'authoriarian' Shi-ites who advocated rule by charismatic *imams* and the 'libertarian' Sunnites who placed less emphasis upon the individual and more on the consensus of a community of believers. (These differences emerged with particular intensity in Iran during the 1970s.) There were conflicts over the leadership of the Arab World with Egypt, Syria, Lybia, Iraq and Iran each vying for control. And there were conflicts over the existence of Israel which made for difficulties with the United States.

Conflicts between the Arab states enabled the oil companies to play one off against the other throughout the 1950s and 1960s. In 1951 the Iranians, under Mossadegh, had nationalised the Anglo-Iranian Oil Company but were frozen out of world markets by the major companies. Iranian oil production fell from 665 million barrels a day in 1950 to 21 million barrels in 1953. In 1964 the Kuwait National Assembly threatened to nationalise the Kuwait Oil Company but withdrew its threat when oil revenues were cut to one-fifth of what they had been. In 1967 the Israeli victory in the June War propelled the Arab countries to come together and impose an oil embargo, which was broken by the companies drawing on supplies from non-Arab countries.

However, the crises in the Middle East caused a shift in policies by the oil companies and by Western governments. The closure of the Suez Canal in 1956 led to the use of supertankers to bring oil round the Cape of Good Hope. Continuing political instability in the Middle East led to a shift of investment in other countries, notably Libya and Algeria. However, in 1969 King Idris of Libya was deposed and his place was taken by Muamma el Quadaffi who soon made it apparent that he was not prepared to accept the terms suggested by the oil companies. He reduced his dependence on the major companies by granting more rights to independent companies, and despite attempts by Western governments to create conditions for a global negotiation of oil supplies which would have prevented the oil states dividing the companies, there was a collapse of negotiations in 1971 at the Tehran and Tripoli conferences, as a result of which separate (and subsequently leapfrogging) bargains were made which broke what powers the buyers possessed. The 1971 price rise led inexorably to the quadrupling of prices in 1973 — a rise which was intensified by the decision of the Arab states to bring pressure on Western governments to end the Egypt–Israeli War.

Inflation and Property Rights

So far we have concentrated upon explanations of oil price movements which have rested upon politics (the foreign policies of the United States and those of the Arab oil states) and neglected market forces. Now we must deal with the effects of inflation and its interaction with Arab nationalism.

The owner of a non-renewable resource (such as oil) who is intent on maximising his income has a choice between leaving the resource intact until a later date or selling it and investing the proceeds in assets which will yield a stream of income. The policy pursued will then depend upon the expected movement of prices and the rate of interest upon assets. If the price change is expected to be greater than the rate of interest then it will pay to leave the asset untouched and sell it at a later date. If the rate of interest is expected to be greater than the expected price change then it will be more advantageous to sell the asset and invest in other assets. The optimum policy is therefore determined by the expected price change and the rate of interest for a group of independently competitive producers (and for a monopolist the marginal revenue will be substituted for price).

During the 1950s and 1960s there were good reasons for selling oil which made it difficult for the oil states to obtain higher prices. Prices were, in fact, falling as more and more fields were developed. But from the middle of the 1960s inflation started to accelerate and this gave an incentive to producers to restrict production and allow prices to rise. The shift of ownership from the major companies to the Arab oil states, as a result of nationalisation, had the effect of changing the interest rate used in conservation calculations. Fearful of nationalisation the oil companies had tended to discount the future heavily and go for short-run profits by pursuing high extraction rates. With the change in ownership there was a move to lower extraction rates — a policy which was helped by the small consuming populations of the Arab states. There were therefore reasons independent of the use of oil as a political weapon during the Egypt—Israeli War which accounted for the rise of oil prices. These reasons also accounted for the fact that although the OPEC was formed in the 1960s it did not have any effect on oil prices until the 1970s.

The 1979 Oil Price Rise

In neoclassical economics the rise in oil prices was a change in relative prices with the price of oil rising while other prices were presumed to remain constant. It should not have led to inflation, which is a rise in the general level of prices. However, politics dictated to economics and the 1973 price rise became inflationary.

Within the advanced countries there was a fear that, because of the small consuming populations of the Arab oil states, the price rises would lead to a reduction in aggregate money demand. Indeed, there was a problem of what the Arabs would do with their increased revenues. In order to maintain high levels of employment some countries increased their aggregate money demand. There were attempts to recycle the Arab oil revenues, especially to the developing countries. Hence, there was monetary accommodation and inflation. By 1978 the real price of oil had fallen to its pre-1973 level. The result was a further increase in oil prices and the response of Western governments was deflation. There was an attempt to control aggregate money demand and to allow a switch to less energy-intensive activities to take place.

Entry Deterring Strategies and the 1986 Price Fall

We have now to account for the successful maintenance of a high price for some years. Confident predictions that prices would fall quickly were not borne out, despite the fall in demand from the industrial countries and the expansion of supplies from Mexico and Britain as well as increases in coal supplies from South Africa, Australia and the United States.

As long as inflation persisted it was sensible not to expand supplies. Second, alternative sources of supply took a long time to create. Third, OPEC was, for a time, able to operate a successful policy of maintaining the price. We must therefore look in more detail at OPEC's policies. Among non-members, Britain and Mexico showed the greatest increases in output (Table 6.1). Mexico's output increased sevenfold. From a position of being a non-producer Britain emerged to become the world's fourth largest producer. Norway's output showed a more modest expansion. The USA's output fell by some 7 per cent and the fall would have been greater but for the opening of the Alaskan oil field. Turning to the OPEC members we can observe a fall in output, with the greatest reduction being borne by a core of producers. Iraq's output fell as a result of the war with Iran while Iran's output rose in order to pay for the war. Among the other producers there were more modest reductions which reflected differences in policies. Some still wished to sell oil in order to use the revenues for industrialisation.

But what the table suggests is that a core of producers became residual suppliers in order to keep up prices when newcomers entered the market. However, there were limits to this policy. Under the impact of the higher real incomes, consumption had started to rise and when the oil revenues fell as a result of the restrictions some of them experienced balance of payments difficulties. In 1986 Saudi Arabia expanded its output and drove down the price of oil in an effort to force countries such as Britain and Iran to cut back their production. (In the case of Iran the policy may have had the effect of prolonging the war with Iraq.) But the marginal cost of continuing production for an existing producer was low as compared with the costs of stopping production and starting up again at some future date. Moreover, Britain was anxious to obtain revenue in order to escape its economic difficulties; so the fall in price did not achieve its objective.

Table 6.1 Estimated Production of Oil (000 barrels per day)

	1972	1973	1974	1975	1976	1977	1978	1979	1980	1981	1982	1983	1984
OPEC													
Indonesia	1,027	1,300	1,457	1,300	1,500	1,690	1,650	1,600	1,570	1,607	1,341	1,292	1,332
Iran	4,900	6,000	6,128	5,600	5,875	5,650	5,250	2,900	1,280	1,375	1,896	2,606	2,166
Iraq	1,500	1,882	1,829	2,400	2,070	2,150	2,500	3,370	2,600	892	914	905	1,218
Kuwait	2,750	2,890	2,600	1,950	1,820	1,700	1,900	2,210	1,400	916	675	912	925
Quatar	450	556	546	410	485	350	480	480	470	414	340	270	404
Saudi Arabia	5,255	7,418	8,400	7,000	8,570	8,950	7,800	9,250	9,620	9,642	6,484	4,872	4,545
United Arab Emirates	1,130	1,509	1,987	1,800	1,945	2,030	1,834	1,825	1,740	1,512	1,247	1,119	1,142
Algeria	1,061	1,035	889	935	950	990	1,260	1,240	1,000	750	750	687	608
Gabon	125	145	182	200	220	225	170	192	145	147	130	150	150
Libya	2,230	2,117	1,700	1,400	1,900	2,050	2,050	2,050	1,780	1,063	1,127	1,020	1,090
Nigeria	1,800	2,000	2,300	1,850	2,020	2,150	1,800	2,370	2,100	1,369	1,324	1,232	1,414
Ecuador	59	197	232	165	185	180	200	220	230	204	215	236	254
Venezuela	3,200	3,370	3,025	2,400	2,290	2,280	2,150	2,330	2,150	2,093	1,826	1,791	1,724
Total OPEC	25,487	30,419	31,275	27,410	29,830	30,395	29,044	30,037	26,085	21,984	18,269	17,092	16,972
Other non-communist	15,302	15,482	15,107	14,691	15,021	15,983	17,139	18,411	19,009	19,292	20,083	21,222	22,148
Mexico	440	478	514	710	850	990	1,270	1,490	1,960	2,390	2,734	2,702	2,743
USA	9,500	9,225	8,945	8,370	8,105	8,240	8,660	8,650	8,650	8,588	8,655	8,669	8,750
Norway	34	38	30	170	300	270	350	390	530	508	488	600	688
UK	2	2	2	40	230	775	1,100	1,570	1,600	1,790	2,050	2,260	2,452
Total non-communist world	40,789	45,901	46,382	42,101	44,851	46,378	46,183	48,448	45,094	41,276	38,352	38,314	39,120

Source: Oil and Gas Journal (various years)

The Short-Run Effects of the 1986 Price Fall

Despite the considerable fall in price in 1986, there was little immediate response by the world economy. Basing their decisions on permanent as opposed to transitory income, consumers in advanced countries hesitated. Given the large fall in price some thought there might have been an overshoot of the equilibrium price; others waited to see if there would be further price falls. In some countries governments used the price reductions to cut budget deficits by increasing taxes with the result that pump prices did not fall as much as wellhead prices. There was also a large fall in imports by the oil producers. In 1988 there were signs that the price falls were beginning to influence economic activity in the advanced economies.

Conclusions

In the 1970s the prices of raw materials rose and the advanced economies hit a raw materials ceiling and went into recession. The price rises began with a failure of the Soviet grain harvest which led the USSR to buy from the US stockpile. There was no spread effect to the other advanced countries because they were insulated by farm price support policies; but there were shortages in many developing countries which had begun importing grain. The oil shocks were a response to inflation and the growth of energy demands in the advanced countries. At the end of the Second World War it had been assumed that the main problems would be the creation of full employment and the maintenance of a full employment growth path. Those problems seemed to have been solved in the 1950s. In the 1960s the possibility of a monetary ceiling seemed to disappear, although it was eventually to produce inflation and the end of the Bretton Woods regime. It also forced the advanced economies up against the raw materials ceiling.

For owners of a non-renewable resource, such as oil, the optimum conservation policy is governed by the expected rate of change of the resource's price and the rate of interest earned on other assets. In the 1960s accelerating inflation started to reduce the income from other assets and precipitated the oil shocks of 1973 and 1979. In 1979 the advanced economies decided to reduce their energy demands by a process of deflation. The oil producers managed to maintain high prices until 1986 but were then forced to reduce them.

Although most attention has been focused on the reactions of the advanced countries to the oil shocks, many of the developing countries fared badly. For many of them oil was the main source of fuel and they were priced out of the market. There was a response from OPEC in the form of loans and grants and there were loans from the advanced countries; but when interest rates rose their problems intensified.

The long-term effects of the oil shocks will depend upon the development of alternative energy sources, such as solar energy. In the medium term the problem will be the exhaustion of sources of oil in the advanced countries and increased dependence upon the Middle East.

Bibliography

Gately, D. (1986) 'Lessons from the 1986 oil price collapse', *Brookings Papers on Economic Activity,* no 2, pp. 325–351.
Oil and Gas Journal (various years).

7

Japan and South-East Asia

One of the most remarkable features of the international economy since the oil price rises of 1974 and 1979 has been the differences in the unemployment rates of the advanced market economies. On the one hand, Japan has maintained a low unemployment rate while most Western Europe countries have stagnated. Switzerland, Austria and Sweden have had low unemployment rates but they are small market economies. The US economy enjoyed a boom in the 1970s and early 1980s but this was achieved by borrowing and running trade deficits whereas Japan increased its share of world trade. Only in 1986, as a consequence of the slide in the dollar and the rise in the value of the yen, did Japan begin to encounter trade difficulties.

These disparities in economic performance have aroused considerable interest and envy and there has been a feeling that Japan has consistently avoided problems by refusing to pursue generous import policies. Being devoid of natural resources the Japanese counter-argument has always been that it must obtain a surplus in its trade with advanced countries in order to pay for its imports of raw materials.

In seeking to unravel the causes of Japan's low unemployment we shall concentrate upon the following factors:

1. the nature of Japanese unemployment statistics;
2. the part played by monetary and fiscal policy in maintaining low unemployment since 1974;
3. wage determination and the workings of the labour markets for large and small firms;
4. the employment practices used by firms during the recession;
5. the importance of the non-tradable goods sector and the role of tariffs;
6. the rising trend of unemployment; and
7. some foreseeable problems of the Japanese economy.

Unemployment Statistics

Table 7.1 provides information on standardised unemployment statistics for some
advanced countries and shows the low unemployment rate in Japan. In attempting to obtain comparable figures it is important to note that there are some groups
of people who are difficult to classify, such as: (1) people who combine education and work; (2) discouraged workers who want work but who have stopped
looking for it; (3) people on temporary lay off or who are working short time;
(4) people on training programmes; (5) people who are above or below the normal age at which cut off points occur. These factors may influence either the
numerator (the numbers unemployed) or the denominator (the activity rate which
comprise those in jobs or seeking jobs) of the unemployment rate.

Table 7.2 provides various measures of UK activity rates and one measure for
Japan for 1981. The UK rates exhibit some slight differences due to the timing
of the surveys and also as a result of differences in the definitions adopted of
'being in the labour market'. However, the significant features of the table are
the differences in the activity rates by sex and age in Japan and the UK. Thus,
relatively few teenagers were in the labour market in Japan as compared with
the UK. At the other end of the age spectrum there were relatively more older
workers in the Japanese labour market. Furthermore, the participation rate of
women aged 25–55 was somewhat lower in Japan than in the UK.

These differences in activity rates reflect differences in preferences as well as

Table 7.1 Standardised Unemployment Rates for Selected OECD Countries, 1970–78 (%)

Year	USA	Japan	UK	West Germany	France	Sweden
1970	4.8	1.1	3.1	0.8	2.4	1.5
1971	5.7	1.2	4.0	0.9	2.6	2.5
1972	5.4	1.4	4.2	0.8	2.7	2.7
1973	4.7	1.3	3.2	0.9	2.6	2.5
1974	5.4	1.4	3.1	1.6	2.8	2.0
1975	8.3	1.9	4.7	3.7	4.1	1.6
1976	7.5	2.0	6.1	3.7	4.5	1.6
1977	6.9	6.5	3.7	4.7	1.8	1.8
1978	5.9	2.2	6.4	3.5	5.2	2.2
1979	5.7	2.1	5.7	3.2	5.9	2.1
1980	7.0	2.0	7.3	3.1	6.3	2.0
1981	9.5	2.4	12.4	6.1	8.0	3.1
1982	9.5	2.6	13.1	8.0	8.4	3.5
1983	9.3	2.6	12.5	8.0	8.3	3.5
1984	7.4	2.7	11.7	8.5	9.7	3.1
1985	7.1	2.6	11.3	8.6	10.1	2.8
1986	4.9	2.8	11.5	8.2	10.3	2.7

Sources: OECD (1967–81), OECD (1987)

Table 7.2 Labour Force Participation Rates by Age, Sex and Marital Status, Japan and UK, 1981

Age	Japan	UK census of population	Labour force survey	
Male				
15−19[a]	17.4	64.5	68.6	
20−24	70.3	89.1	90.3	
25−34	97.1	97.1	97.2	
34−44	97.6	97.8	96.9	
45−54	96.4	96.4	92.4	
55−64	85.0	83.7	69.6	
65+	41.0	10.7	10.5	
Female			*Married*	*Other women*
15−19[a]	18.0	56.3	47.8	63.6
20−24	70.3	69.3	55.6	81.5
25−34	49.4	54.3	51.3	76.5
35−44	61.6	65.6	67.5	76.6
45−54	61.9	66.0	57.7	65.5
55−64	44.9	38.0	23.2	23.6
65+	15.6	3.7	4.7	3.2

Sources: Planning Agency, Tokyo (1983), OPCS (1982, 1983)
Note: (a) The youngest age group 15−19 refers to 15−19 years for Japan and 16−19 years for UK.

opportunities. More young people leave school at the end of the compulsory period of education in the UK than in Japan. And although the introduction of various employment schemes has modified this picture it still remains valid as a generalisation for the UK. There is a higher activity rate for older men in Japan which is related to the lower provision of pensions. Finally, we may note that the lower activity rate for women stems from the fact that women are expected to leave the labour market when married and pregnant because the provision for maternity leave that obtains in Britain is lacking.

Since younger workers tend to have higher unemployment rates than older workers, some part of the difference in UK and Japanese unemployment rates might be explained simply by differences in sex and age activity rates. Thus, if we multiply the UK unemployment rates for each sex and age group by the corresponding Japanese activity rates, the UK male unemployment rate in 1981 would have been 7.9 per cent instead of 11.3 per cent and the resulting UK female unemployment rate would have been 4.5 per cent instead of 7.4 per cent. These figures may then be compared with the Japanese male rate of 2.4 per cent and a female rate of 5.3 per cent to reflect the difference in the incidence of unemployment (allowing for differences in labour force participation rates). It is useful to extend this type of analysis to other countries.

West Germany

In West Germany youth unemployment has tended to be low because: (1) legislation forces school leavers to combine school with work below the age of 18; (2) between the ages of 18 and 24 male unemployment is reduced by the existence of conscription; (3) demographic growth has been lower in West Germany than elsewhere; and (4) the use of guest workers tends to reduce unemployment during recessions.

USA

In the USA unemployment has tended to be relatively high because: (1) there is a considerable amount of geographical movement which gives rise to frictional unemployment; (2) demographic growth has been higher than in other countries; (3) many young people combine education with casual employment; (4) formal apprenticeships have not existed in the USA and therefore the channels between school and work are less clearly defined; (5) relatively high incomes have permitted a more relaxed attitude to job search; (6) there is a considerable amount of racial segmentation of the labour market; (7) the USA is on the technological frontier and job creation is more difficult than in countries which are catching up; and (8) the political commitment to a higher level of employment is lower than in Western Europe.

So far, then, we have standardised unemployment rates by adjusting the numerator of the ratio which defines the rate of unemployment. But this is not the way in which the international debate has been conducted. Instead, attention has concentrated upon the flows between employment and unemployment, especially in making comparisons between Japanese and US unemployment. Thus, Taira (1983) has argued that the differences in methods of recording unemployment mean that the Japanese rate would be double if the US criteria was used. Sorrentino (1984) and Nagayama (1984) have disagreed with Taira, arguing that the differences in recording methods are not great enough to account for the disparities.

The Japanese definition of unemployment is that a person must not have worked *at all* during the period of the labour survey. According to Woronoff (1981) this means that anyone who has worked for even one hour is counted as employed. Not only does this have the effect of reducing the unemployment figures, it also has the effect of increasing the participation rate. In addition to the low qualifying standard set for paid workers, the Japanese surveys also include unpaid family workers of whom there are about three million.

Some part of the difference in unemployment rates can also be explained by differences in the industrial distribution of the labour forces in Japan and the UK. Table 7.3 reveals that Japan has relatively more workers employed in agriculture and the distributive trades than the UK; since both sectors tend to have lower

Table 7.3 Employed Persons by Industry in Japan and the UK

	Japan	UK
Agriculture, forestry, fishing	10.7	2.5
Mining and quarrying	0.2	1.3
Electricity, gas, water	0.6	1.3
Manufacturing	23.1	26.3
Construction	9.4	6.4
Distributive trades	22.3	15.9
Transport and communication	6.1	6.0
Finance, insurance	3.5	6.0
Community, social and personal services	21.5	26.8
Not adequately described	0.1	—
Unemployed	2.5	6.3
Armed forces	—	1.2
	100.0	100.0

Source: Japan Institute of Labour (1984)

unemployment rates than manufacturing we have a further possible explanation of the lower Japanese unemployment rate.

This discussion may be summarised by saying that international comparisons of unemployment rates have to be handled carefully. The OECD and the US Department of Labor attempt to provide standardised unemployment rates but they ignore age- and sex-specific rates. Furthermore, since the 1970s international comparisons have been made more difficult because many countries have introduced community and youth employment schemes as well as a variety of other subsidies. Whether these constitute real jobs and whether the training is spurious is difficult to assess. In Sweden, for example, the effect of such schemes has been to reduce the unemployment rate from 13 per cent to 3 per cent.

Monetary and Fiscal Policies

Figure 7.1 indicates that before 1973 Japan's money supply was accelerating much more rapidly than that of the UK. After 1974 it fell and except for an increase in 1978 it continued to fall. Other things being equal, the quantity theory of money predicts that an increase in the quantity of money will lead to an increase in the price level, and Figure 7.2 shows that there was an increase in Japan's manufacturing prices. Figure 7.3 reveals that there was also an acceleration in consumer prices. After the second oil price rise the Japanese economy behaved differently: producer and consumer prices accelerated much more slowly. The behaviour of prices after OPEC III (1986) is complicated by the rise in the exchange rate as a result of US domestic policy.

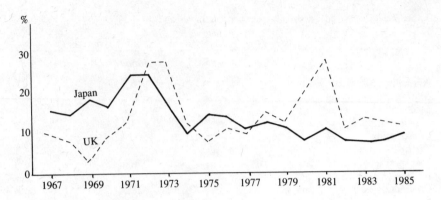

Source: OECD (1967−86), *Monthly Indicators*
Figure 7.1 Annual Percentage Changes in the Money Supply (M_1 Plus Quasi-money)
for Japan and the UK 1967−85

Some of the changes in the money supply and prices can be attributed to changes
in economic policy. Before OPEC I the Bank of Japan, as was the case with most
Western central banks, attempted to pursue the multiple goals of full employment, price level stability and economic growth. After OPEC I the Bank concentrated upon price level stability through the control of the money supply and interest
rates were allowed to rise. After OPEC II the authorities again sought to dampen
down inflationary expectations. Since OPEC III the Bank has been preoccupied
with the problems of a rising exchange rate. In the UK the money supply did
not accelerate to the same extent as that of Japan in the early 1970s and there
was a delay in the Bank of England's response to OPEC I. Then the UK money
supply continued to accelerate until 1980. Taken in conjunction with the slower

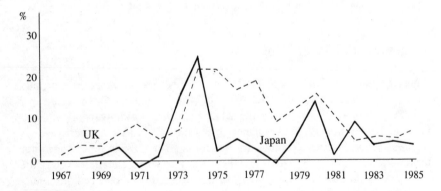

Source: OECD (1967−86), *Monthly Indicators*
Figure 7.2 Annual Percentage Changes in Producers' Prices: Manufacturing, Japan and
the UK, 1967−85

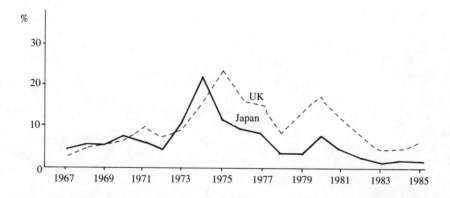

Source: OECD (1967–86), *Monthly Indicators*
Figure 7.3 Annual Percentage Changes in Consumers' Prices, 1967–85, Japan and the UK

growth of productivity in the UK, the differences in the rates of increase in money supply showed up in the movements of prices.

The effect of OPEC I was to cause a reduction in private investment. The sharp rise in energy prices cut into profits and caused a set back in investment. There was also a dislocation of trade because the USA attempted to reduce imports. But savings continued to be high and there were strong deflationary pressures in the economy. Changes in the money supply can be brought about either by open market operations or by changes in fiscal stance. After OPEC I the Japanese authorities pursued a highly restrictive monetary policy for two years but were confronted with the need for an expansionary fiscal policy because of firms' low investment programmes and the high propensity to save. There was also a need to increase government spending on social security, health and education.

The Burden of Debt

An increase in government spending financed by borrowing may or may not have beneficial effects, may or may not be a burden. We need therefore to isolate the possible effects of deficit spending: that is, spending financed not by current taxation but by borrowing. In the period when the borrowing takes place the lenders are better off because they have been willing to lend in the expectation of interest payments in the future and the borrowers are better off because they have got jobs and incomes. If there are unemployed resources, then they can be used to augment the capital stock and out of the resulting enhanced income stream the lenders can be repaid and the borrowers need be no worse off and there may be no burden on present or future generations. But if there is full employment and the loans are spent on armaments or crowd out other private spending then

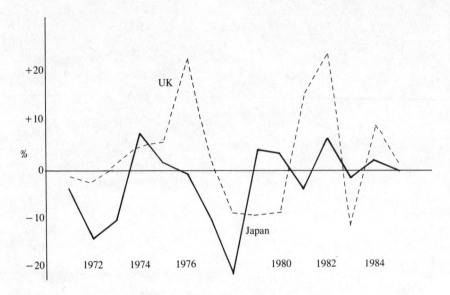

Figure 7.4 Annual Percentage Changes in Yen—Dollar Exchange Rate and the
Sterling—Dollar Exchange Rate 1970—1985

Table 7.4 Shares in World Trade in Manufactures in Selected OECD Countries 1970—83
(%)

	USA	Japan	France	West Germany	Italy	UK	Others
1970	18.5	11.7	8.7	19.8	7.2	10.8	23.3
1971	17.0	13.0	8.8	20.0	7.2	10.9	23.1
1972	16.1	13.2	9.3	20.2	7.6	10.0	23.5
1973	16.1	12.8	9.5	22.1	6.8	9.4	23.3
1974	17.2	14.3	9.3	21.7	6.7	8.8	21.8
1975	17.7	13.6	10.2	20.3	7.5	9.3	21.4
1976	17.2	14.6	9.7	20.5	7.1	8.8	22.0
1977	15.2	15.4	9.9	20.7	7.6	9.4	21.4
1978	15.1	15.6	9.8	20.7	7.9	9.5	21.4
1979	15.9	13.6	10.4	20.7	8.4	9.7	21.3
1980	17.0	14.8	10.0	19.9	7.9	9.7	20.6
1981	18.7	18.0	9.3	18.3	7.8	8.6	19.3
1982	17.8	17.9	8.8	19.6	7.8	8.5	19.6
1983	17.2	19.0	8.8	19.1	7.8	8.0	20.1

Source: NIESR (1975, 1980 and 1985)

Table 7.5 Current Balances of Selected OECD Countries 1974—86 (US$billion)

	USA	Japan	France	West Germany	Italy
1974	2.1	4.7	−3.9	10.4	−8.1
1975	18.3	−0.7	2.7	4.1	−0.6
1976	4.2	3.7	−3.4	3.9	−2.9
1977	−14.5	10.9	−0.4	4.1	2.4
1978	−15.5	17.5	7.1	9.2	6.2
1979	−1.0	−8.8	5.1	−6.2	5.4
1980	0.5	−10.8	−4.2	−16.0	−9.8
1981	4.6	4.8	−4.8	−5.7	−8.6
1982	−11.2	6.9	−12.2	3.4	−5.8
1983	−40.8	21.0	−4.2	3.6	0.5
1984	−106.5	35.0	−0.5	6.6	−2.8
1985	−117.7	49.2	0.1	13.7	−4.0
1986	−140.6	45.8	3.8	38.0	6.1

Source: NIESR (1975, 1980 and 1987)

future generations may inherit a burden — although, in the case of defence spending, there may be a problem of putting a value on freedom.

Suppose, however, that we are dealing with an open economy and that raising interest rates will induce an inflow of foreign funds. The inflow of funds will force up the price of the domestic currency and the exchange rate will rise and cause a fall in exports and an increase in imports (Figure 7.4). Hence, a surplus on the capital account (due to foreign loans) will precipitate a deficit on the trade or current account.

Despite the high savings propensity of the Japanese and the relative insulation of Japanese goods and financial markets from international competition, the trade balance did move into deficit in 1979 and 1980 (Tables 7.4 and 7.5). In this respect the Japanese experience with budget deficits anticipated the US problems of the 1980s and the European discussions of the 1980s. However, borrowing may have provided the necessary breathing space within which labour markets could adjust to the rise in energy prices.

Wage Determination

So far we have concentrated upon the part played by monetary and fiscal policies in bringing about adjustments in the Japanese economy. But in Chapter 4 we began by emphasising the problems posed by the lack of flexibility in the labour market. We must now turn to the structure of Japanese industry and the methods of wage determination. Abstracting from the problems of the agricultural sector and the

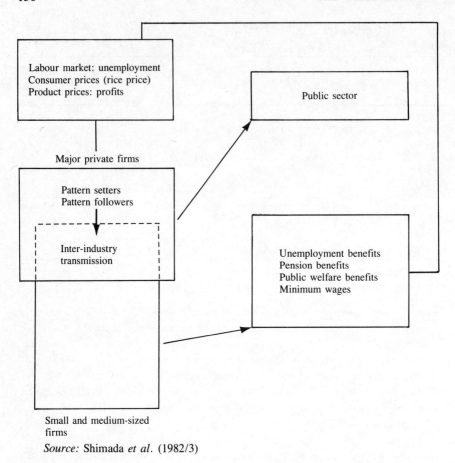

Source: Shimada et al. (1982/3)

Figure. 7.5 Determination and Transmission of Negotiated Wages in Japan

service sector, Figure 7.5 outlines the channels through which wage increases are transmitted from the large firms through to the small firms and the public sector. We begin therefore with a consideration of the private sector of large and small manufacturing firms.

Large Firms and Industrial Dualism

It is sometimes suggested that the private sector of Japanese manufacturing exhibits industrial dualism: that is, there is a sector of large firms and a sector of small firms. Tables 7.6 and 7.7 attempt to give precision to the concept of industrial dualism by comparing the size of Japanese manufacturing plants with those of the US, UK and West Germany. In the less capital-intensive industries, Japanese plants tend to be small by Western standards, employing on average no more

Table 7.6 Size of Manufacturing Plants by Capital Intensity of Industry in Selected Countries, 1969−73 (Number of Employees)

| | Less capital-intensive | | | | More capital-intensive | | | |
	UK	West Germany	USA	Japan	UK	West Germany	USA	Japan
Lower quartile	90	70	100	3	170	130	110	69
Median	360	310	360	38	600	690	420	241
Upper quartile	1,170	1,100	1,220	136	1,840	3,900	2.241	2.362

Source: Prais (1978), Japanese Ministry of Industry and Trade (1973)

Table 7.7 Numbers of Manufacturing Plants by Size of Plant in Selected Countries, 1969−73 (000)

Size (employees)	UK	West Germany	USA	Japan
1−4	30.1	147.0	99.3	350.7
5−9	20.6	43.2	43.3	213.5
10−19	19.6	28.4	41.3	83.8
20−49	19.2	25.4	47.6	59.7
50−99	9.2	11.7	24.2	18.2
100−199	6.1	7.1	16.2	8.0
200−499	4.7	4.9	11.0	4.0
500−999	1.6	1.6	3.3	1.1
1000+	1.1	1.1	2.1	0.6
Total Plants	112.2	270.4	288.4	739.3

Source: Prais (1978), Japanese Ministry of Industry and Trade (1973)

than 30 to 40 workers. In the more capital-intensive industries Japanese plants still tend to be small as compared with their Western counterparts: they employ, on average, 250 workers. However, the dispersion of plant sizes is much greater than in the West.

Japanese large plants are characterised by: (1) institutional ownership with firms tending to be owned by other firms; (2) banks providing the main source of external finance and firms having high gearing ratios; (3) the labour force of each firm consisting of a core of permanent employees and a periphery of temporary employees; (4) immobile managers who depend for their promotion on the growth of their firms; (5) enterprise or company unionism; (6) permanent workers who are paid a basic wage plus a seniority increment (*nenko*) plus a bonus, whereas temporary workers are paid only a basic wage; and (7) extensive use of job rotation and joint consultation (*ringi* or quality circles). In the small firm sector owner management is more common, workers tend to be paid a basic wage only, the distinction between permanent and temporary workers is less clear cut and joint rotation and joint consultation are not so obviously institutionalised.

Before the Second World War there were controlling groups, known collectively as the *zaibatsu,* but their involvement with the military before and during the war led to their dissolution during the US occupation. There was a further impetus to the diffusion of ownership in the 1960s when, fearful of US take over bids, Japanese firms bought each others' shares. Hence, we have the present situation in which most Japanese large firms are managerially controlled (Kono 1984). This state of affairs stands in contrast to the UK situation where in 1978, according to Nyman and Silberston (1978), one-half of the firms they sampled were controlled by groups of shareholders and, in many cases, by family groups. The UK pattern of ownership is, of course, changing under the impact of institutional shareholding but it has a long way to go before it achieves the sharp distinction between financial provision and entrepreneurial control observed in Japan.

The concept of lifetime or permanent employment may be misunderstood. It has no legal basis and arose out of full employment and skill shortages and is presumed to apply only to large firms. But since only some 30 per cent of workers are employed by large firms the numbers of workers covered by a form of permanent employment may not be exceptional. Thus, in 1979 in the UK some 16.6 per cent of the adult labour force had been in their current jobs for 20 years (Main 1982) and in the USA some 25 per cent of workers had held their jobs for 20 years or more. However, most lifetime employees in Japan held their jobs in the private sector whereas in the UK and USA there were relatively more permanent employees in the public sector.

Japanese firms have adopted company or enterprise unionism. There are national unions but within plants there is not the proliferation of unions that is observed in the UK. Craft unionism was rejected by Japanese workers after the Second World War and rival unions of right and left were virtually destroyed in the 1950s and 1960s and replaced by company unions. The causes of these changes lay partly in the effects of the US occupation and partly in the effects of the Cold War. The result was that the distinction between shop stewards and foremen has been blurred and many company board members have been former union officials. Company unionism is complemented and reinforced by job rotation, quality circles and just in time production scheduling which reduces the size of inventories.

We are now in a position to describe the nature of the wage system. The seniority wage clause, or *nenko,* may be regarded as a means of using length of service to measure on the job training and productivity as well as coping with the life-cycle of consumption and family formation in an economy where the social security system is not well developed. *Nenko* does not mean that every worker of a given age and length of service receives the same pay increase. Able workers — high fliers — can receive accelerated promotion. Furthermore, while everyone may receive status by moving up a rank, not everyone in that rank will carry the same functional position in terms of authority; the system is therefore analogous to that of army officers of the same rank carrying out different tasks and possessing degrees of authority.

The age–wage scale has undergone considerable alteration. Between 1965 and 1975 it underwent compression in the age range 35 to 55 as a result of tight labour markets and increased competition for young workers. After OPEC I there was a tendency to delay the payment of *nenko* or to reduce the amount paid in an effort to cope with the increasing burden of annual increments in an employment system which guaranteed tenure up to the age of 55. As a result of these changes some writers envisaged the end of *nenko*. However, the 1983 basic wage survey revealed a widening of differentials which may have been due to the easing of competition for younger workers and the ability of older workers to cope with technological change.

Bonuses are paid twice a year. They are separate from other wage payments and before the Second World War they were paid as a supplement to basic wages and in part as a reward for achievement. After the Second World War these features of the system were eroded and bonuses became an established part of earnings. They increased steadily up to 1975 when they approached one-third of annual earnings. They fell sharply in 1975 and 1976 and since then they have tended to form a smaller part of the increases in earnings (Table 7.8).

But as bonuses have declined in importance, so the changes in basic wages have acquired greater significance. The most important feature of Japanese collec-

Table 7.8 Structure of Annual Wage Increases in Large and Small Firms, 1973–87

Date	Shunto increase	Firms employing 30 or more workers Coefficient of variation	Bonus	Overtime	Total earnings	Small firms (5–29) wage rate increases
1973	20.1	0.05	29.5	24.8	21.5	21.1
1974	32.9	0.07	32.8	4.4	27.2	33.7
1975	13.1	0.16	6.6	1.1	14.8	14.1
1976	8.8	0.10	13.1	23.9	12.8	9.7
1977	8.8	0.07	7.1	13.5	9.2	9.4
1978	5.9	0.20	6.9	12.7	8.5	6.4
1979	6.0	0.10	6.4	12.1	6.0	6.5
1980	6.7	0.06	8.2	0.9	6.3	7.4
1981	7.7	0.06	5.6	3.6	5.3	7.9
1982	7.0	0.06	2.5	5.0	4.5	6.9
1983	4.4	0.15	2.0	5.0	3.5	4.5
1984	4.5	0.12	5.1	9.6	4.5	4.5
1985	5.1	0.09	n.a	n.a	n.a	n.a
1986	4.5	0.14	n.a	n.a	n.a	n.a
1987	3.6	0.18	n.a	n.a	n.a	n.a

Source: Japan Ministry of Labour (annual).

tive bargaining is the high degree of centralisation both in terms of the level at which negotiations take place and in their timing. Wage changes tend to be concentrated in the spring and arise out of the *Shunto* (spring offensive). The *Shunto* emerged in the 1950s to stem the decline of industry-wide collective bargaining and was initially opposed by the employers' association, *Nikkeiren*. Its subsequent acceptance owed much to the fact that because of intense competition in product markets, the major employers wished to avoid strikes disrupting work schedules. Even then the *Shunto* played a perfunctory role because bonuses were responsible for the enormous growth in earnings through the 1950s and 1960s. In fact, the Japanese wage system was evolving along lines similar to those being charted in the UK and the United States. In all three countries there had been a system of industry-wide bargaining which in the peace-time conditions of full employment had begun to disintegrate under the impact of plant level negotiations — what in the West has been called wage drift (the tendency of increases in earnings to outstrip increases in basic wage rates). But in Japan the industry-wide system persisted for much longer and was revived after OPEC I to form the basis of incomes policies on which the government could exert some influence. In contrast, the UK and US systems had disintegrated to such an extent that not only had wage determination shifted to the shopfloor but there was also a tendency for wage agreements in different firms and industries to be staggered in time — which made it impossible to get an effective incomes policy except through some form of wage tax imposed by government. Only in Japan, therefore, was it possible to get a once for all wage adjustment overnight by democratic means.

Small Firms and Minimum Wage Legislation

Figure 7.6 shows the linkages between three labour markets and it indicates that it is wage changes in the large firms which precipitate wage changes in the small firms and the public sector. One channel through which wage changes are transmitted is minimum wage legislation which operates on both a regional and an industrial basis. Being decentralised, minimum wage legislation may be more sensitive to local employment conditions than the national minimum wage systems operating in the West or in the developing countries of Latin America and it does not appear to create severe unemployment problems. Another channel through which wage increases are transmitted arises out of the extensive sub-contracting system operating in Japan. Thus, in the iron and steel, electrical and engineering industries, over 40 per cent of the small firms are engaged on contracts for other firms. The links between large and small firms are intricate and involved. Large firms may redeploy older workers to small firms and these workers may be employed in training other workers. Redeployment may also be a method by which workers are transferred to smaller firms and then made redundant by the smaller firms — a practice which enables the large firms to keep up the pretence of not

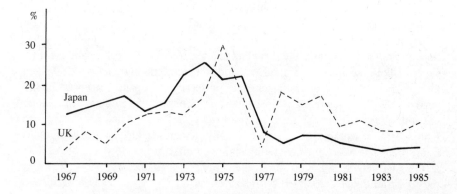

Source: OECD (1967–86) *Monthly Indicators*
Figure 7.6   Annual Percentage Changes in Hourly Earnings 1967–85,
Japan and the UK

dismissing workers. Sub-contracting may also be a means by which the brunt of the wage adjustment is borne by smaller firms: there have been frequent claims that small firms are exploited by larger firms. However, bankruptcies among small firms appear to be less common in Japan than in the UK, where employment legislation during the 1970s made it difficult for many small firms to survive.

The Industrial Relations Implications of the Japanese System

We shall now attempt to pull together the various strands of our discussion of wage determination and the part it plays in maintaining high levels of employment and productivity, making use of recent discussion of the theory of the firm.

According to Coase (1937) firms exist because of the costs of using the market and Alchian and Demsetz (1972) located an important cost in the difficulties of monitoring the efforts of workers who are engaged in team production. If A's productivity depends not only on his own efforts but also those of B, and vice versa, then there is a need for a supervisor to monitor the efforts of A and B. But Alchian and Demsetz went further and identified the supervisor with the owners of finance capital. In other words, the main risk bearers were those who supplied finance capital which was used to purchase specific, durable instruments of production; it was the capitalists who would feel the strongest need to monitor the efforts of workers who might shirk on the job. But Marglin (1974) suggested that this theory of why hierarchies exist in firms might not necessarily lead to efficiency but only increase the ability of capitalists to extract surplus value from workers. To substantiate his claim Marglin pointed to alternative and equally plausible methods of organising Adam Smith's pin factory, each of which disposed of the elaborate division of labour observed by Smith: for example, workers could be rotated between jobs or there could be batch production.

Japanese firms do practise job rotation and they also engage in joint consulta-tion. Such practices reduce the suspicion that managerial hierarchies and the divi-sion of labour have been designed to reduce the workers' knowledge of jobs and the amount of surplus value being created. Furthermore, Japanese firms are highly geared by Western standards and the annual dividends provided through the *Shunto* mean that Japanese workers are conspicuously risk bearers and make Japanese firms a form of workers' cooperative. Finally, Japanese managers see themselves as arbitrators between the competing claims of different risk bearers rather than as the guardians of the interests of the suppliers of finance capital — which is the role traditionally assumed by managers in the West.

Short Term versus Long Term

The structure of Japanese firms and their methods of organisation have a bearing upon the issue of 'short termism' which is said to characterise much of UK industry.

Briefly, it is argued that the differences in the nature of Japanese and UK capital and labour markets have led to an emphasis upon long-term profit maximisation in Japan and upon short-term profit maximisation in the UK. Because of the possibilities of take over bids UK managers, it is alleged, are reluctant to engage in long-term ventures and concentrate instead upon short-term gains. This em-phasis upon short-term gains receives added impetus from the mobility of managers who seek to increase their future earnings by pointing to the current profits of their firms as a reason why a prospective employer should make them a good offer. In contrast, Japanese managers, it is suggested, are encouraged to pursue long-term goals. They are relatively immobile and must therefore seek to increase the growth of their firms in order to increase their own earnings. Moreover the fact that firms are owned by other firms means that there is less risk of a take over bid and the existence of a bank within the industrial group means that the suppliers of loanable funds have inside information about a firm's prospects.

This argument needs to be treated with caution. There is no evidence that there is a shortage of loanable funds in the UK and the pursuit of short-term profits by individual investors is perfectly compatible with the provision of long-term finance by overlapping generations of savers who have access to a capital market which provides a source of liquidity.

However, the problem may not be that the capital market is perfect but that it is insufficiently perfect. In order to remove the problem of 'short termism' it may be necessary to provide more information, although it is doubtful whether managers would be willing to divulge information about R&D. Another possibility would be to induce institutional shareholders to take a long-term view by making an institution's tax status dependent on investment rather than trading — a move that would incline institutions in the direction of becoming, like Japanese and

West German banks, more involved in the affairs of firms. Finally, it might be possible to devise two-tier management structures with the upper tier taking a long-term view and being relatively insulated from removal by new shareholders. This would be a variation on the West German two-tier management structure — although its discussion in the context of providing workers with opportunities for greater participation was rejected a few years ago.

But many of the alleged problems of UK managers may soon descend upon their Japanese counterparts if the international deregulation of financial markets continues.

Productivity

We have two sources of information on Japanese productivity. First, there are the statistical studies by economists. Second, there are plant level studies by sociologists and economists. Table 7.9 reveals that the UK enjoyed a superior level of productivity in agriculture and construction in 1973 and 1980 and in the fuel and power industries (thanks to North Sea oil) in 1980. But the Japanese were superior in manufacturing and in services and this advantage increased between 1973 and 1980. Given the relatively greater importance of manufacturing in Japan's GDP (Table 7.10) we have an explanation of the source of overall productivity difference.

Nosworthy and Malmquist (1983) analysed the sources of differences in Japanese

Table 7.9 Output per Employed Worker Year in Japan and UK, 1973 ($000)

	Agriculture	Fuel & Power	Manufacturing	Construction	Services	GDP
Japan	2.5	15.5	9.6	7.6	9.3	8.3
UK	8.3	9.9	6.6	10.7	8.5	8.7
Japan	2.7[a]	16.6	14.5[a]	7.1[a]	10.2[a]	10.3[a]
UK	10.7	17.4	6.3	9.5	8.7	9.2

Source: Roy (1983)
Note: (a) is 1979 data.

Table 7.10 Proportion of Real Product Generated in Each Sector in Japan and UK 1973 (%)

	Agriculture	Fuel & Power	Manufacturing	Construction	Services	GDP
Japan	4.0	1.7	31.6	8.0	54.6	100
UK	2.9	3.1	24.6	9.7	59.6	100

Source: Roy (1983)

and US manufacturing productivity and concluded that the main differences lay in the rapid growth of capital and raw materials supplied to Japanese workers. However, they did acknowledge that the importance of industrial relations in Japan should not be underestimated: 'In general workers' willingness to accept and adopt new technology is an important element in the cost of introducing new capital and equipment and working techniques'. Weiss (1984) has emphasised the greater use of engineering graduates on the shopfloor.

However, detailed studies of the car industry have suggested that it was not technology but a more efficient method of production management and quality control which accounted for the greater superiority of Japanese industry. What happened was that US management techniques were adopted and adapted to Japanese cultural and economic circumstances, with the result that there was a new pattern of product development, and new forms of production organisation and new relationships were established with the suppliers of components.

The more efficient product development process reduced the lead time for developing new models from 5 years to 3.5 years and models were replaced after four years instead of eight years elsewhere. And whereas in the West the objective of mass production was to achieve the longest possible run of a standardised part, the Japanese system became geared to producing very short runs 'just in time' (*kanban*) as they were required. In 1970 it took 255 man hours to produce a car in Japan and 200 hours in West Germany; in 1981 it took 140 hours to produce a car in Japan and 195 hours in West Germany. The operations of components' suppliers also became closely linked with those of the final assembler with the result that in 1970 the Japanese had a $2,500 advantage in the US market and a $1,000 advantage in Europe. The result was a rise in tariffs against Japanese car exports; the Japanese response was to build plants in North America and Western Europe. The ability of these firms to operate successfully abroad suggests that it is possible to transplant Japanese management practices.

Methods of Employment Adjustment

Despite possessing a highly elaborate institutional framework which yields a high degree of wage flexibility in the manufacturing sector and despite the existence of the protected agriculture and distribution sectors which are capable of absorbing surplus labour, the Japanese economy has had to undertake employment adjustment policies and these have become more serious since the fall of the dollar in 1986. The methods used by the major companies have been as follows:

1. changes in hours of work;
2. changes in the number of regular full-time employees;
3. increases or decreases of part-time or temporary workers; and
4. sub-contracting.

In addition the government has assisted through measures such as the employment stabilisation schemes introduced in 1978.

Table 7.11 suggests that the Japanese work longer hours than workers in other advanced countries. There was, however, a significant reduction in weekly hours in 1975 in response to the first oil price rise and Shimada *et al.* (1982/3) have noted that variations in hours were much more common than dismissals in the early 1970s and accounted for the relative stagnation of productivity growth which can be observed in Figure 7.6. In the UK the greater attachment of the Thatcher governments to productivity regardless of what is happening to total output accounts for the differences between Japan and the UK. It is, of course, extremely difficult for a Japanese employer to reduce the number of regular employees who are recruited into the lifetime employment system other than by a suspension of recruitment at the port of entry or by a transfer to related firms before mandatory retirement (reduction at the point of departure). In 1981 94.5 per cent of firms with over 5,000 employees or more used the system of temporary detachment and 56.3 per cent used the method of retirement detachment. Since there is no principle of last in, first out, as in the UK, the burden of adjustment tends to be borne by older workers.

The social and economic restrictions placed upon reducing the numbers of regular workers do not apply to temporary or part-time workers. An employer can employ as many part-time or temporary workers as he wishes and in recent years there has been an expansion of the temporary help services with 100 dispatching agencies in 1985. These agencies have not confined themselves to conventional sub-contracting but have spread into the field of office management; they have been especially associated with the growth of female employment.

Table 7.12 shows that part of the employment adjustment process has taken the form of variation in participation rates. In the case of male workers the falls in the activity rates have been concentrated at the extremes of the working population. Until 1982 younger workers were unable to get jobs and in many instances stayed on in higher education in order to better their employment prospects. In

Table 7.11 Trends in Actual Weekly Hours of Work in Manufacturing in Selected OECD Countries 1974–81

	Japan	UK	US	West Germany	France
1974	40.3	38.1	36.8	33.5	36.2
1975	39.3	37.0	36.3	32.3	35.2
1976	40.7	37.7	36.6	31.1	35.1
1977	40.8	37.8	36.8	33.3	34.8
1978	41.1	37.7	36.9	33.2	34.6
1979	41.6	37.4	36.7	33.4	34.3
1980	41.6	36.3	36.6	33.2	34.3
1981	41.3	36.4	36.3	32.8	34.0

Source: Japan Institute of Labour (1984)

Table 7.12 Labour Force Participation by Age and Sex in Japan 1970−85

	15−19	20−24	25−34	34−44	45−54	55−64	65+
				Male			
1970	31.4	97.4	97.4	97.7	96.5	88.6	49.4
1972	27.3	81.2	97.0	98.0	97.0	86.4	47.0
1975	20.5	76.1	96.3	97.8	96.5	86.0	44.4
1977	18.2	72.3	96.4	97.9	97.9	86.0	42.4
1979	18.0	72.6	97.1	98.1	96.5	85.2	41.1
1981	17.4	70.1	97.1	97.6	96.4	85.0	41.0
1983	19.1	71.0	97.1	97.7	96.5	84.7	38.9
1984	18.9	71.0	96.8	92.7	96.4	83.9	37.6
1985	17.3	70.1	96.5	97.4	96.1	83.6	37.0
				Female			
1970	33.6	70.6	46.8	60.1	61.1	44.4	17.9
1972	28.5	67.4	43.0	50.4	60.7	43.7	15.6
1975	21.7	66.2	43.2	56.9	59.8	43.7	15.6
1977	19.8	67.6	46.0	58.1	60.0	44.2	15.2
1979	18.6	69.9	47.9	60.8	61.7	45.4	15.6
1981	18.0	70.3	49.4	61.6	61.9	44.9	15.6
1983	18.7	72.1	51.4	63.8	63.9	46.1	16.1
1984	18.5	72.4	52.6	63.7	60.1	45.0	15.9
1985	16.6	71.9	52.2	63.7	64.6	45.3	15.5

Source: Statistical Bureau (various years)

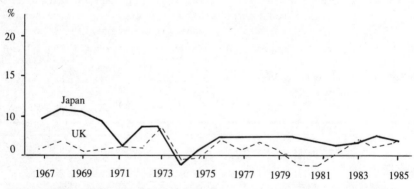

Source: OECD (1967−86), *Monthly Indicators*

Figure 7.7 Annual Percentage Changes in Real GDP per Capita 1967−85,
Japan and UK

Table 7.13 Contribution to Employment Growth or Decline by Industry in Japan 1970–80 (000 workers)

	Employees in 1970	Employees in 1980	Contribution to total change (%)
All industries	34,672	37,720	100
Industries with the largest gains			
Retailing	3,886	4,542	21.5
Business services	1,588	2,000	13.5
Construction	3,385	3,792	13.4
Medical services	1,009	1,350	11.2
Wholesaling	2,718	3,015	9.7
Industries with the largest losses			
Textiles	757	623	−4.4
Shipbuilding	312	212	−3.3
Steel, non-ferrous metals	723	641	−2.7
Lumber	369	313	−1.9
Industrial machinery	481	444	−1.2

Source: Kuwahara (1984)

1982, however, there was an upturn in the activity rates of young workers. At the other end of the spectrum older workers have found it difficult to get jobs and have been tending to drop out of the labour market.

Among female workers there has been a noticeable rise in the activity rates of women between the ages of 25 and 55. They have been returning to work because of reductions in family size, the rise in relative earnings and the availability of part-time jobs.

The final point to observe about employment adjustment is that it has been associated with an increase in the numbers of workers in the service sector and construction and with big losses in textiles, shipbuilding and iron and steel (Table 7.13).

Horizonal versus Vertical Linkages: Research and Development

We are now in a position to pull together the various strands in our discussion of the Japanese manufacturing firm. Two problems confront advanced and developing countries. First, there is the problem of how to advance the technological frontier; an issue which is especially pertinent to the USA and some Western European economies. Second, how to exploit new developments; an issue which bears upon economies seeking to catch up. Consider, then, the second problem and two differing approaches. In one procedure the firm's information structure is hierarchical. Management knows in advance the technological possibilities of workshops but may not be able to monitor unforeseen events perfectly or provide rapid corrective action. In a second procedure management does not have a complete knowledge of technologies but responds to unforeseen events by better use of on the spot knowledge.

The first approach is characteristic of firms which use job evaluation practices and the hiring of workers for specific jobs, with the jobs being classified in a collective agreement. When there are unforeseen breakdowns then remedies are provided by maintenance workers and other specialist staff. In other words, the production column tends to be lightly manned relative to the staff branches. In the second approach there is less emphasis upon the selection of workers for particular jobs and workers rotate among jobs within and between shops. As a result workers become capable of dealing with unforeseen contingencies and rely to a lesser extent upon specialist staff.

The two approaches represent different responses to the competing claims of specialisation and coordination. Specialisation, the division of labour, can increase speed and dexterity and enable the greater use of machinery. But specialisation reduces the awareness of how activities are interrelated and can give rise to alienation and loss of efficiency — hence the need to coordinate activities. The hierarchical firm attempts to solve the coordination problems through the use of specialists; the horizontal firm attempts to solve them by expanding the range of capabilities of shopfloor workers, through job rotation and the *ringi* system. And because of the heavy investment in human capital workers in horizontal firms are offered lifetime employment. The horizontal firm is most useful for exploiting the gains from technological breakthrough by a firm or an economy which is anxious to catch up with the leaders. As we have seen, the greater capabilities of the Japanese labour force have led to a significant reduction in the lead time for new models. Japanese firms have concentrated on extracting all the consumers' surplus by increasing the product range. They therefore exhibit less product diversity than their Western counterparts and more intensive product differentiation within a widely defined commodity group (e.g. watches, calculators, cameras). In contrast, Western firms tend to be multi-product firms because capabilities tend to be concentrated in specialist staffs. In the search for new markets a hierarchical firm is likely to have its strategies dictated by staff (marketing, R&D) rather than by its shopfloor. Thus, a Western brewing firm may seek new markets in catering whereas a Japanese firm may be more inclined to move into biotechnology.

But are there wider considerations which make specialisation more attractive to advanced Western economies? As specialisation increases markets for specialists develop outside the firms. Workers become committed to their occupations rather than their firms and there is a greater diffusion of new knowledge within occupations through the emergence of professional institutions and journals. Moreover, the vertical structure of firms means that it is relatively easy to add another product division.

The distinction between vertical and horizontal firms has been presented as a contrast between Western and Japanese firms but it should not be pushed too far.

Many of the ideas about industrial organisation observed in Japanese firms were pioneered by Americans. During the occupation US army engineers, former employees of such firms as Bell Telephone, introduced the Japanese to techniques such as statistical process control. Peter Drucker's *The Practice of Management* was translated and widely read and Mercer (1987) has gone further and argued that IBM was the model for Japanese firms.

Agriculture, the Service Sector and Tariffs

So far we have concentrated upon the manufacturing sector. Now we must turn to consider agriculture and the service sector. As Table 7.3 indicates, Japan still has a large number of workers in agriculture and judged by UK and US standards the level of productivity is low. In other words, agriculture absorbs a lot of workers who, in other countries, would have to be absorbed in manufacturing. One factor explaining the relatively large size of the agricultural sector is subsidies which favour small firms in general and agriculture in particular. The existence of subsidies to small firms may have political origins since the government does tend to draw a lot of political support from small businessmen. The existence of agricultural subsidies may also be due to the desire to ensure adequate food supplies and this desire to be self-sufficient in food accounts for the fact that the domestic price of rice is much higher than the world price and for the frustration of the Americans in not being able to export rice to Japan.

The service sector is also relatively large and relatively inefficient; the inefficiencies of the distribution system are one reason why foreign firms find it difficult to export to Japan. Table 7.14 throws some light upon the problem. It shows

Table 7.14 International Comparisons of Distribution Systems

	Japan	USA	UK	France	West Germany
Ratio of wholesale to retail sales [a]	5.2 (1979)	1.7 (1977)	1.5 (1974)	1.4 (1981)	1.5 (1978)
Number of shops per 1,000 persons	13.6 (1979)	5.9 (1977)	6.4 (1980)	11.3 (1979)	5.6 (1979)
Productivity in retail and wholesale trade[b] (yen per 1,000, 1980)	2,769	4,014	2,805	3,317	3,025
Small shops (1 or 2 persons) as a percentage of total shops	61 (1979)	43 (1977)	40 (1971)	66 (1980)	50 (1979)

Source: Sumitome Business Consulting Company (1984)
Notes: (a) Value of wholesale trade divided by value of retail trade. Therefore the greater the number of stages in wholesale transactions, the larger this ratio will be.
  (b) Real GDP per capita at 1975 prices.

Table 7.15 International Comparisons of Import Tariffs and Quotas

Residual Import Quotas, 1980			
	Total	*Agricultural*	*Industrial*
Japan	27	22	5
United States	7	1	6
United Kingdom	3	1	2
France	46	19	27
West Germany	4	3	1
Italy	8	3	5
Benelux	5	2	3
Canada	5	4	1

Nominal Tariff Levels 1987 [a]
(percentages: weighted by own-country imports, excluding petroleum)

	Japan	USA	West Germany	France	UK	Italy	Canada	Benelux
All industries	2.9	4.3	6.3	6.0	5.2	5.4	5.2	5.9
Textiles	3.3	9.2	7.4	7.3	6.7	5.6	16.7	7.2
Iron and steel	2.8	3.6	4.7	4.9	4.7	3.5	5.4	4.6
Electrical machinery	4.3	4.4	8.3	7.7	8.1	8.0	5.8	7.4
Non-electrical machinery	4.4	3.3	4.5	4.4	4.4	4.2	4.5	4.3
Transport equipment	1.5	2.5	7.7	7.9	7.2	8.8	1.6	7.9

Source: Cline (1985)
Note: (a) Table shows Tokyo Round tariffs to be reached in 1987.

that there are a considerable number of firms operating at the wholesale level and that the forward integration of manufacturing and wholesaling which has been undertaken in the West has not occurred in Japan. The number of retail shops is distinctly higher and their productivity is lower than their Western counterparts. It is high distribution costs rather than tariff levels which make import penetration difficult (Table 7.15).

One result of the existence of two sizable non-tradable sectors is that the wage flexibility observed in the manufacturing industries does not carry through automatically to the whole economy: at the macroeconomic level there is a divergence between sectors in economic responses to external shocks. As long as Japanese manufacturing productivity and costs are substantially lower than elsewhere then the much lower sensitivity of employment to disturbances can be accepted. However, there are signs that the scope for manoeuvre is being diminished.

An Ageing Population, Trade Surpluses and Trade Friction

The Japanese population is ageing rapidly. In 1984 some 9.3 per cent of the population was aged 65 and over and the life expectancy of women is now 80. By 1994 it is estimated that the percentage of older people will be the same as that in the United States, will be equal to that of France and the UK by the year 2000 and that thereafter Japan will become the oldest society in the world. An ageing population poses employment problems for which there may be two solutions. First, there can be a move towards earlier retirement and greater dependence upon social security payments. Second, people can work longer. The first solution has been popular in Western Europe while the second has been proposed in Japan and the USA.

The Japanese pensions system comprises both private and public schemes. In large firms permanent employment has tended to guarantee employment up to the age of 55. At 55 a worker would receive a pension plus the possibility of redeployment to a job in the small firms sector. These arrangements were created when the expectancy of life was lower than at present. The public pension scheme was formally inaugurated in 1962, although there was some coverage of employees before that date. However, Japan has an immature pensions system with benefits tending to be low because most workers have contributed for only a limited period. Thus, the average contribution period is 32 years and the corresponding benefit level is 68 per cent of the average wage of those currently employed. If the contribution period were to rise to 40 years then the corresponding benefit would be 83 per cent of the average wage. Given the speed at which the population is ageing it has become apparent that it would be impossible to maintain benefits at such levels. In 1986, the contributions and benefits were revised and greater emphasis was placed upon private pensions. The age of eligibility for both private and public pensions was raised to 60 and in line with these policies there have been steps taken by the large firms to raise the retirement age to 60. But the trouble with raising the retirement age to 60 is that it reduces the promotion prospects for younger employees in large firms and imposes difficulties in redeploying workers.

The ageing of the labour force also has a bearing upon the generation of trade surpluses. The usual argument has been that Japan has to obtain a surplus on its trade with other advanced countries in order to pay for its imports of raw materials. But this reason has been supplemented in recent years by the need to generate surpluses to cover the burden of an older population. Young people tend to save more than older people and the Japanese savings ratio has been high by Western standards. This has resulted in the need to pile up trade surpluses and financial flows to the West have shown a large increase. Indeed, many mortgages in the UK have been financed by Japanese savings. The ability of the Japanese to continue to pile up trade surpluses may, however, be sharply curtailed by the fall in the dollar and increasing protectionism in Western Europe. According to Thurow (1984) a $100 billion trade deficit has meant 2.5 million fewer jobs in the USA and, since one-quarter of the US deficit was with Japan, that implied that some 700,000 jobs were lost to Japan. Hence, the pressures for protectionism in the US and for a liberalisation of Japanese tariffs.

Export-led Growth versus Growth-led Exports

Discussion of the service sector inevitably leads on to a wider examination of the part played by international trade in Japanese economic development. We therefore begin by asking whether Japanese economic development has been export-led or whether growth has led exports. As we noted in Chapter 1, export-led growth formed the basis of the staple theory of trade which purported to explain how exports of primary products by Australia and Canada enabled them to obtain a surplus which could then be used to transform their economies and reduce their vulnerability to trade fluctuations. The theory could equally well have been applied to Japan in the nineteenth century. But can such a theory be applied to post-war Japanese economic performance?

Adjudicating between competing theories Caves (1971) has sought to apply a simple test. If both export prices and quantities increase then growth is export-led; if prices and quantities move in the opposite direction then exports are growth-led. Applied to the Japanese economy these tests suggested that trade was growth-led. Indeed, until the mid-1960s the growth of exports was sluggish. But Caves's test raises a further question: why did Japan choose to develop the newer industries? Why did Japan not continue to pursue its comparative advantage in low technology, labour-intensive goods? An explanation has been provided by Ojima, vice-president of the Japanese Ministry of Industry and Trade in 1970:

> After the war Japan's first exports consisted of such things as toys or miscellaneous merchandise and low-quality textile products. Should Japan have entrusted its future, according to the theory of comparative advantage, to these industries characterized by intensity of labour? That would perhaps be a rational advice for a country with a small population of 5 or 10 million. But Japan has a large population. If the Japanese economy had adopted the simple doctrine of free trade and had chosen to specialize in this kind of industry, it would almost permanently have been unable to break away from the Asian pattern of stagnation and poverty and would have remained the weakest link in the free world, thereby becoming a problem area in the Far East.
>
> The Ministry of International Trade and Industry decided to establish in Japan industries which require intensive employment of capital and technology, industries that are from the standpoint of comparative cost most inappropriate for Japan, industries such as steel, oil refining, petro-chemicals, automobiles, aircraft, industrial machinery of all sorts, and electronics, including electronic computers. From a short-run, static viewpoint, encouragement of such industries would seem to conflict with economic rationalism. But from a long-range viewpoint, these are precisely the industries where income-elasticity of demand is high, technological progress is rapid, and labour produc-

tivity rises fast. It was clear that without these industries it would be difficult to employ a population of 100 million and raise their standard of living to that of Europe and America (quoted by Eatwell 1982).

Japan therefore pursued an import-substitution policy. Judged in static terms such a policy might be deemed to be welfare lowering because it would reduce the level of income. But the Japanese were interested in the rate of economic growth and that depended upon the willingness to save and the rate of technological progress, neither of which is related to the type of trade policy which might be pursued in any direct manner. Thus, there is no guarantee that any surplus accruing from a free policy would be saved and invested in the acquisition of new technology. Indeed, a country might obtain new technologies embodied in imports and continue to export low technology goods which could render it open to a policy of growth immiserisation. In Japan the willingness to save was influenced by the existence of a young labour force, by a wage system which encouraged workers to base their consumption on their low permanent incomes and to save their bonuses and by an egalitarian income distribution which encouraged a sense of national identity. The pursuit of new technologies was influenced by the import substitution policy conducted in conjunction with the selective purchase and granting of licences. Because the Ministry of Industry and Trade controlled access to foreign exchange it was able to determine the firms which were granted finance for the purchase of licences. And because of the relatively equal distribution of income Japan had a mass market in which the economies of scale from the mass production of goods could be realised. Japan's comparative advantage in the efficient organisation of complex large-scale organisations was put to good effect.

Final Thoughts

Japan's low unemployment rate is due to the efficiency of its economic system. Some of the more obvious factors have been mentioned. But there are others. Japan does not have more engineers than the UK; the available statistics fail to take account of UK engineers educated in polytechnics and technical colleges. But the Japanese do have a longer, more intensive period of education. They are not obsessed with vocational education; they have not adopted the US MBA. They believe that education is about citizenship and that it is the duty of employers to train workers. They do not accept that engineers can be trained in three years and they do not allow them to escape too readily from the shopfloor into general management. They do indeed have more engineers on the shopfloor rather than in maintenance, and they have few accountants in management; in the UK the tax system has encouraged a misallocation of talent and a large number of accountants are needed in the USA because of a preoccupation with short-term gains. The Japanese work long hours. The Japanese distribution of income and wealth appears to be more egalitarian than in the UK and their education system is competitive. In short, the Japanese have created a meritocracy.

This prompts three questions. How did it arise? Can it be exported? Will it survive? It is tempting to trace the development of the Japanese economic system to history and to culture. Morishima (1982), for example, has drawn a distinction between Japanese Confuciansim and Chinese Confucianism which parallels Weber's distinction between Catholicism and Protestantism and their respective influences upon the development of capitalism. Dore (1984,1986) has also drawn attention to the Tokugawa period (roughly from the end of the sixteenth century to the middle of the nineteenth century) during which an administered society was created and contrasts the resulting view of authority which emerged in the UK where there is a public denunciation of authority and a continual assertion of individualism, where extreme class distinctions can be allied with support for a monarchy and contempt for foreigners coupled with a propensity to engage in colonial wars.

The trouble with the appeal to history is that it does not always respect the facts. Japan's low rate of inflation in the post-war period cannot be explained in terms of the past; its past inflation rate was always higher than that of the UK or the USA. Nor can industrial harmony be explained in terms of a past which has all too often been extremely militant. At the end of the Second World War a left-wing labour movement might have produced a Weimar Republic. And, of course, something has to be conceded to the US occupation which created a revolution from above in terms of both land and educational reforms and the introduction of advanced production management techniques. There is therefore no simple explanation of how the Japanese system arose. It owes something to the remote past — to the Confucian emphasis upon education and the role of women in society. It owes something to wartime planning and to the US occupation. It owes something to geopolitics and to the fact that in the 1950s Asia became a frontier of contention between the USA, USSR and China whereas Latin America and Africa were too far away to create a possible zone of Soviet influence.

This brings us to the second question: can it be exported? The obvious answer is that it has been successfully exported to other countries in South-east Asia and the final section of the chapter will discuss some of those countries. But the successful countries all share a common Confucian heritage. The real question is whether Japanese methods can be adopted in non-Asian countries. Can the successful blend of market and planning be adopted elsewhere? Are there cultural divides which permit of no transmission? One response is to point to the attempt to graft on to the UK and US systems parts of Japanese industrial practice, such as quality circles, profit sharing and small firms. The retort is that bits and pieces do not constitute a successful system. And yet the Japanese system was not created overnight. Answers to the question must therefore recognise cultural differences. Japanese management derives its authority partly from deference and partly from competence. The British rejected deference in the seventeenth century but they can still embrace competence, if they wish.

The third question is whether the system will survive. The Japanese economy took off on the back of a silkworm and then chose to use a highly trained and adaptable labour force to exploit the opportunities made available by imports of cheap raw materials — hence the move into cotton textiles. But as other countries began to industrialise the Japanese have and will continue to find that the rents which they have to pay to foreign landlords will rise. So there is a current preoccupation with information technology, ceramics, biotechnology and energy conservation. In short, Japan has the problem of most advanced countries of trying to keep ahead of the newly industrialising nations. But even if Japan could overcome the obstacle of rising import prices there would still be the problem of what goods the Japanese could purchase with their rising real incomes. In a country desperately short of land attempts to buy a larger house will simple drive up land prices and only domestic landlords will reap what industrialists have attempted to sow. In the short run the shortage of urban land can be relieved by land reform, involving a reduction in agricultural subsidies and tariffs and a transfer of land from agriculture to housing. But in the long run such a policy could aggravate the problem of increasing imports by adding food requirements to the bill for industrial raw materials.

The orthodox answer runs as follows. At the end of the Second World War the Japanese economy was devastated. The marginal product of capital was high and there was a strong inducement to save and invest. There was also the availability of foreign knowhow which could be readily imported. The high growth rate of the 1950s and 1960s was a catching up process not dissimilar to that experienced by Western Europe. But as the marginal product of capital falls and foreign technologies become exhausted, the Japanese economy will converge on a growth path similar to that of the United States or any economy which has to incur the high costs of exploring the frontier of technology. There will be resistance to change because a long period of peace will allow tensions to rise to the surface and permit society to fragment into various interest groups.

Radical analysis is more optimistic and points to the ability of the Japanese to innovate and to the possibilities opened up by the Pacific economy with its abundance of raw materials in Australia and its potential markets in South-East Asia and the western seaboard of the United States.

South-East Asia

So far we have concentrated upon Japan. Now we must turn to consider the other Asian countries. Setting aside China and India, which will be discussed in Chapter 12, attention will be concentrated upon the so-called 'baby tigers' — South Korea, Taiwan, Singapore and Hong Kong. But Table 7.16 indicates that there have been other striking performances among the other Asian countries. It must not be concluded too readily that differences in economic performances are attributable to cultural factors, and in particular the influence of Confucianism. Indeed, Table 7.16 reveals a wide range of performances. Thus, the second group comprises countries which have a favourable natural resource endowment in such things

Table 7.16 Main Economic Indicators for Various Asian Countries

	Population		GDP		Exports		
	Total (000)	Annual average growth rate	per capita (dollars)	Annual average growth rate	Annual average growth rates		
	1983	1970–83	1983	1960–84	1960–70	1970–80	1980–85
Hong Kong	5,334	2.4	5,285	7.8	14.5	22.4	9.3
Korea	40,004	1.8	1,921	6.7	39.6	37.2	4.4
Singapore	2,501	1.4	6,655	7.2	3.3	28.2	4.2
Taiwan	18,601	1.6	3,050[a]	6.0	36.5	14.3	10.0
Burma	35,777	2.2	173	1.4	−8.8	14.3	−3.9
Indonesia	160,247	2.2	489	4.1	1.7	35.9	−0.4
Malaysia	14,840	2.2	2,029	4.4	4.3	24.2	4.2
Philippines	52,025	2.5	665	2.6	7.5	17.5	−4.4
Sri Lanka	15,651	1.7	330	3.0	−1.4	13.6	5.0
Thailand	49,453	2.4	813	4.5	5.9	24.7	2.2
Bangladesh	98,567	2.2	126	2.1	5.6	6.3	5.7
Pakistan	94,885	2.9	295	2.2	10.3	13.3	3.5

Source: UNCTAD (1986)
Note: (a) 1985.

as tin, rubber, oil and agricultural goods. And even within the first group a distinction can be drawn between the city states of Hong Kong and Singapore and the larger economies of Taiwan and South Korea.

There are, however, common features which distinguish all the Asian countries from less developed countries in Latin America and Africa. First, there tends to be political continuity and effectively authoritarian governments. Second, there is a commitment to economic development. Third, although in varying degrees between groups one and two, there is an emphasis upon exports. Fourth, there is a concentrated effort to improve agricultural productivity. Between 1960 and 1985 the increase in food production per capita in Korea averaged 2.5 per cent per annum, in Malaysia 2 per cent per annum and for the whole of South-East Asia about 1 per cent per annum — the latter result being twice the average increase in Latin America and five times the average African performance. Fifth, there has been a preoccupation with mobilising domestic and foreign savings. Sixth, there has been an emphasis upon acquiring technical knowhow and combining it with an enhanced educational system to produce labour-intensive goods whose skill content is continually being increased. Seventh, there has been a willingness to use market prices as an indicator of scarcity. Of course, there has been intervention in markets; but it has been highly selective and has displayed a willingness to pass on energy price increases (and decreases) to consumers rather than indulging in subsidies. These factors have enabled many of the countries to cope successfully with the oil price shocks and with the growth of protectionism in the 1980s.

South Korea and Taiwan have some features in common. In the 1950s they both pursued import substitution policies and it was not until the 1960s that they decided to encourage exports while retaining controls in some parts of their economies. They both abandoned import duties on intermediate goods used for export and liberal credit facilities were introduced. During the 1960s exports grew at between 20 and 30 per cent. The expansion of exports was assisted by the abundance of unskilled labour at low wages. But the rural sectors were not neglected and both countries carried through land reforms which not only led to a more equal distribution of incomes in the countryside and between town and country but also raised agricultural production. Incomes in the countryside were raised through the development of industry. And the basis for a shift to goods embodying higher technologies was made possible by the expansion of secondary and higher education. Finally, the existence of economic development with unlimited supplies of labour enabled profit rates to be maintained and encouraged both technological progress and foreign investment.

Direct foreign investment by transnational corporations was more important in the case of Singapore and in the 1970s accounted for 70 per cent of manufacturing exports as compared with about 15 per cent in the case of South Korea and Taiwan. Indeed, despite the recourse to foreign borrowing in all the countries, domestic savings increased and served to underline the point that a policy of export-led growth is successful only to the extent that it raises savings and investment. In Latin America and Africa colonial habits of thinking about income distribution and savings persist and in the absence of land reform may continue to do so. But above all other contributing factors there are the organising skills which have successfully combined Western knowhow with abundant labour.

The second group of countries comprises those with relatively abundant natural resources. Their growth rates have been less spectacular than those of the baby tigers because, in some instances, they have pursued import substitution policies of taxing manufacturing imports and taxing domestic agriculture to finance domestic manufactures. There are, of course, differences within the group: Burma has been more protectionist than Thailand. In the cases of Malaysia and Indonesia performances have been affected by movements in the prices of oil and tin. But even within the second group trade has been an engine of growth. It has permitted an expansion of incomes. It has not required, but neither has it discouraged, research and development. And what has been encouraged is the acquisition of foreign knowhow to raise living standards.

The characteristics of the countries which we have discussed have been important in enabling them to cope with the oil price shocks and the increasing protectionism of the 1980s. Following the first price shock most countries made successful adjustments and achieved rapid growth, low inflation and strong balances of payments. In some cases, Sri Lanka and Bangladesh for example, devaluation was undertaken in order to maintain or strengthen their competitive positions. And although South Korea maintained its dollar exchange rate, the effect of the fall of the dollar was to improve Korea's competitive position *vis-à-vis* Japan and Western European competitors.

Economic policies in South Korea consciously attempted to cope with the oil shocks, each of which imposed a burden equivalent to about 4 per cent of GNP. During the 1960s the economy had been increasing its investment in the energy-using, heavy industries, such as chemicals and shipbuilding. After the oil price rises there was a shift from physical capital investment to investment in industries with reduced energy requirements and a need for human capital, such as electronics, telecommunications and semiconductors.

Summary and Conclusions

This chapter has dealt with the success stories of the post-war period. These are the countries which have either entered the core of advanced countries (Japan) or have lifted themselves above the periphery of developing countries into a category of Newly Industrialising Countries (NICs). It has been assumed, in contrast to Latin America and Africa, that these countries have relied upon market forces and trade oriented policies. This is a sweeping conclusion. There is considerable evidence that planning has been used in the allocation of resources and in controlling the pattern of trade. Furthermore, the importance of trade varies between them and other countries. Thus, trade as a percentage of GNP is about 8 per cent for Japan and 28 per cent for West Germany. Japan's dependence upon trade tends to be confined to the need to import raw materials (especially energy and minerals). But Japan's response to the oil shocks and the dollar fall has been impressive, as has the response of the baby tigers. We need therefore to consider those features of the South-East Asian economies which have contributed to their success. There has been an emphasis upon education — literacy levels are much higher than in Latin America and Africa. There has been land reform and an attempt to produce a more equitable distribution of income and wealth. Economic policies have been pragmatic rather than doctrinaire. Labour markets have been more responsive to shocks and incomes policies have been preferred to the indexing of wages. Stable governments and a willingness to absorb Western technology have also helped.

Bibliography

Alchian, A.A. and Demsetz, H. (1972) 'Production, information costs and economic organization', *American Economic Review*, vol. 52, pp. 211–21.

Aoki, M. (ed.) (1983) *The Economic Analysis of the Japanese Firm*, North Holland.

Aoki, M. (1986) 'Horizontal vs vertical information structure of the firm', *American Economic Review*, vol. 76, pp. 971–983.

Arai, K. (1982) 'Theories of the seniority-based wage system', *Hitotsubashi Journal of Economics*, vol. 23, pp. 15–21.

Blumenthal, T. (1981) 'Factor proportions and choice of technology: the Japanese experience', *Economic Development and Cultural Change*, vol. 29, pp. 845–868.

Caves, R. (1971) 'Export-led growth and the new economic history' in J. Bhagwati (ed.) *Trade, Balance of Payments and Growth*, North Holland.

Cline, W.R. (1985) *Trade Policy in the 1980s*, Institute for International Economics, Geneva.

Coase, R.H. (1937) 'The nature of the firm', *Economica*, vol. 4, pp. 386–405.

Dore, R.P. (1973) *British Factory—Japanese Factory*, Allen and Unwin.

Dore, R.P. (n.d.) *An Incomes Policy Built to Last*, Tawney Society.

Dore, R.P. (1984) *Authority and Benevolence: the Confucian Recipe for Industrial Success*, Pembroke College, Oxford, mimeo.

Dore, R.P. (1986) *Flexible Rigidities: Industrial Policy and Structural Adjustment in the Japanese Economy, 1970–1980*, Athlone Press.

Dore, R.P. and Sako, M. (1987) *Vocational Education and Training in Japan*, Imperial College London, mimeo.

Dore, R.P. and Sinha, R. (1987) *Japan and the World Depression*, St Martin's Press.

Drucker, P. (1946) *The Practice of Management*, John Day.

Eatwell, J. (1982) *Whatever Happened to Britain?*, BBC.

Evans Jr, R. (1984) 'Pay differentials: the case of Japan', *Monthly Labour Review*, vol. 107, pp. 58–61.

Gibb, R. (1980) *Industrial Policy in More Successful Economies*, NEDO Discussion Paper 7, National Economic Development Office.

Gordon, A. (1982) *The Evolution of Labour Relations in Japan: Heavy Industry, 1853–1955*, MIT Press.

Gordon, R.J. (1982) 'Why US wage and employment differs from that in Britain and Japan', *Economic Journal*, vol. 92, pp. 43–58.

Hall, R. (1982) 'The importance of lifetime jobs in the US economy', *American Economic Review*, vol. 72, pp. 16–22.

Hamada, K. and Kurosaka, Y. (1984) 'The relationship between unemployment and production in Japan', *European Economic Review*, vol. 25, pp. 8–15.

Hayama, Y. *et al.* (1979) *Agricultural Growth in Japan, Taiwan, Korea and the Philippines*, University of Hawaii, Honolulu.

Japanese Ministry of Industry and Trade (1973) *Census of Manufactures*, MITI.

Japanese Ministry of Labour (annual) *Monthly Labour Survey.*

Japan Institute of Labour (1984) *Monthly Indicators.*

Kato, F. (1982) 'A verification of a natural rate of unemployment hypothesis in Japan', *Bank of Japan Monetary Research.*

Kono, T. (1984) *Strategy and Structure of Japanese Enterprises*, Macmillan.

Koshiro, K. (1983) 'The employment effects of microelectronic technology', *Japan Labour Bulletin*, pp. 3–5.

Koshiro, K. (1983) 'An analysis of 1983 wage negotiations', *Japan Labour Bulletin*, pp. 7–8.

Koshiro, K. (1984) 'Unexpectedly low rates of 1984 wage hike', *Japan Labour Bulletin*, pp. 5–7.

Koshiro. K. (1987) 'Gainsharing, wage flexibility and macro-economic performance in Japan', mimeo.

Kuwahara, Y. (1984) 'Unemployment and Japan's high-tech industries', *Euro-Asia Business Review*, vol. 3, pp. 1–5.

Main, B. (1982) 'The length of a job in Britain', *Economica*, vol. 48, pp. 325–333.

Marglin, S.A. (1974) 'What do bosses do?', *Review of Radical Political Economics*, vol. 6, pp. 22–54.

Mercer, D. (1987) *IBM: How the World's Most Successful Company is Managed*, Kogan Paul.

Morishima, M. (1982) *Why Has Japan 'Succeeded'?*, Cambridge University Press.

Nagayama, S. (1984) 'Are Japanese unemployment statistics too low?', *Economic Eye*, vol. 15, pp. 27–32.

Nakamura, S. (1981) *Postwar Japanese Economy*, University of Tokyo Press.

NIESR (1975, 1980, 1987) *Economic Review*, National Institute of Economic and Social Research.

Nosworthy, J.R. and Malmquist, D.H. (1983) 'Input measurement and productivity growth in Japanese and US manufacturing', *American Economic Review*, vol. 73, pp. 947—967.

Nyman, S. and Silberston, A. (1978) 'The ownership and control of industry', *Oxford Economic Papers*, vol. 30, pp. 74—101.

OECD (annual) *Country Reports — Japan*, OECD.

OECD (1967—81) *Historical Statistics 1967—81*, OECD.

OECD (1987) *Main Economic Indicators*, January.

OPCS (1982) *Population*, Office of Population Censuses.

OPCS (1983) *Population*, Office of Population Censuses.

Planning Agency, Tokyo (1983) *Japan Statistical Yearbook*, Planning Agency.

Prais, S.J. (1978) *Productivity and Industrial Structure*, Cambridge University Press.

Roy, A.D. (1983) 'Productivity in 1980: an international comparison', *National Institute Economic Review*, vol. 102, pp. 25—31.

Sano, Y. (1977) 'Seniority based wages in Japan: a survey', *Japanese Economic Studies*, vol. 12, pp. 7—18.

Shimada, H. *et al.* (1982/3) 'The Japanese labour market: a survey', *Japanese Economic Studies*, vol. 12, pp. 135—152.

Shimada, H. and Nishikawa, S. (1980) 'An analysis of the Japanese employment system and the youth labour market', *Keio Economic Studies*, vol. 16, pp. 76—85.

Shinkai, T. (1980) 'Wage spillovers in Japanese manufacturing', *Review of Economics and Statistics*, vol. 82, pp. 66—70.

Shiriashi, T. (1983) 'Technological innovation and management problems in Japan', *Keio Economic Review*, vol. 20, pp. 48—51.

Sorrentino, C. (1984) 'Japan's low unemployment: an in-depth analysis', *Monthly Labor Review*, vol. 107, pp. 251—253.

Statistical Bureau, Management and Coordination Agency, Tokyo, (various years) *Japan Statistical Yearbooks*.

Sumitome Business Consulting Company (1984) *Report on International Comparisons of Distribution Structure and Business Practices*, BCC.

Taira, K. (1983) 'Japan's low unemployment: economic miracle or statistical artefact?', *Monthly Labor Review*, vol. 106, pp. 187—192.

Thurow, L.C. (1984) 'Economic gridlock in the offing', *Journal of Japanese Trade and Industry*, pp. 46—50.

UNCTAD (1986) *Handbook of International Trade and Development Statistics, Supplement*, United Nations.

Weiss, A. (1984) 'Simple truths of Japanese manufacturing', *Harvard Business Review*, vol. 84, pp. 87—90.

Weitzman, M. (1983) *The Share Economy*, Harvard University Press.

Woronoff, J. (1981) 'Japan's unemployment statistics are too low', *Oriental Economist*, vol. 49, pp. 108—110.

8

The United States

Emerging from the Second World War as a superpower in the context of a world short of dollars with which to buy its goods, the USA became the driving force (multiplier) of the world economy. Through the 1950s and 1960s GDP grew at an average annual rate of 1.7 per cent. Inflation was relatively low because the Eisenhower administration pursued conservative monetary policies. Some countries — such as the UK — opted for more relaxed monetary policies; but given the fixed exchange rate regime their excesses were held in check by regular balance of payments crises. The US economy experienced inventory cycles of some four years in duration, though their effects on the world economy tended to be mild — a tribute to the strong underlying growth of the rest of the world economy.

Circumstances changed in the mid-1960s. The attempt by the Kennedy and Johnson administrations to fight a major war in Vietnam and to found a great society based on a civil rights and anti-poverty programme led to an expansion in the supply of dollars. During the 1950s and 1960s the requirements of the world dollar standard had forced the USA to produce sufficient dollars for the rest of the world to use as an international medium of exchange and a store of liquidity; but not so many as to undermine international confidence. In the 1960s the confidence began to wane. There was disquiet in Europe, especially in France, over the expansion of US multinationals and US take over of domestic firms. In effect, the rest of the world was being taxed to help pay for the Vietnam War (just as it had been during the Korean War). There was pressure to raise the price of gold, implying a fall in the value of the dollar. In 1971 the dollar was finally devalued.

Following the devaluation of the dollar the US economy was hit, as was the rest of the world, first by two successive oil price rises, then by Reaganomics and by the budget deficit of 1981−2. The Carter administration had attempted to cope with the oil shocks by pursuing tighter fiscal policies than most other countries, combined with a neutral monetary policy. Interest rates fell relative to the rest of the world, although the real exchange rate continued to decline. The economy still remained sluggish despite being sustained by investment and exports. As a result of the falling exchange rate inflationary pressures increased so that consumer prices rose between 1976 and 1979. Monetary policy became tighter when Paul Volker assumed the chairmanship of the Federal Reserve Board; but the economy was then set on a different tack by the advent of Reaganomics.

Reaganomics has been called supply-side economics; in practice it contains strong demand generating forces. On the one side there is a desire to loosen up the supply side of the economy through deregulation of various sectors, such as transport and communications, reductions of income tax to create incentives and minimising minimum wage legislation and unionism. On the other side there is increased defence spending. Attempts to cut federal spending on social services met with some resistance and a budget deficit resulted. Unlike Carter and Thatcher, Reagan has pursued an easy fiscal policy and a tight monetary policy. (In contrast, Thatcher has pursued a relatively easy monetary policy and a tight fiscal policy by cutting both spending and taxes.) The effect of the US budget deficit was to increase borrowing — which affected the rest of the world.

Defence spending was increased because it was felt that the USSR was becoming superior in armed strength. The Second World War had underlined the USA's economic and military strength. Pearl Harbour had awakened a sleeping giant who then used aircraft carriers to conduct a brilliant campaign in the Pacific and provided aircraft and manpower for a land invasion in Europe. But from the 1960s onwards the USA's superiority underwent a relative decline. The fact that both the USA and the USSR had nuclear weapons produced a stalemate and an acceleration of spending on conventional weapons. But conventional weapons proved useless in Vietnam. Ultimately, Vietnam spelled the end of the Cold War in Asia as the USA and China entered a rapprochement. Military transformations were paralleled by economic changes as Western Europe and Japan closed the output gap per head and led to a further dismantling of the bipolar world. Domestic changes stemmed from attempts to found a great society and the effects of the Vietnam War on blacks who found that conscription discriminated against the uneducated ethnic minorities. By the end of the 1980s the USA was resolving the problems of military spending by attempting to reach agreement with the USSR on arms limitation. But it was increasingly being forced to reconsider the role of the state in the solving of social problems, from education and provision for the elderly, medical care and the drugs problem to the difficulties facing minority groups, some of whom, like the Mexicans, were moving freely into the USA across the southern border.

Economic Growth

Productivity might have been expected to fall following the oil price rises but Darby (1984) has argued, at least for the first oil shock, that energy price rises had only a limited impact. Once allowance had been made for demographic changes (such as age, sex, education and immigration) then the long-run trend in productivity followed a random walk about a fairly constant upward trend. There was a noticeable dip from the trend between 1929 and 1948. In that period there was a slow growth in the capital—output ratio and the subsequent sharp upward growth between 1948 and 1965 was a response to the low starting point in 1948. (Differences in growth rates between 1965 and 1973 and 1973 and 1979 were due to the underreporting of price and output changes during the Nixon price control programmes.)

Darby's findings were complemented by a study of interregional productivity growth between 1951 and 1978 by Hulten and Schwab (1984), who found that real value-added in the manufacturing industries of the Sun Belt grew at twice the rate of the Snow Belt industries and that different factors accounted for the relative growth of the two regions. Interregional differences in output growth were not due to interregional differences in productivity growth but to variations in the rates of growth of capital and labour. There was no evidence that an ageing public infrastructure, an obsolete capital stock or higher union density had slowed productivity growth in the Snow Belt. Indeed, the conclusion was that productivity rates of increase were similar in both regions. To explain the disparities in output expansion, Hulten and Schwab invoked Olson's institutional sclerosis thesis. In the Snow Belt the gradual crystallisation of interest groups, such as unions, monopolists and public authorities, tended to inhibit change and encourage the migration of resources to the Sun Belt. At the margin labour productivity was equalised across the regions but the greater readiness to absorb change and permit relatively greater increases in the employment of capital and labour accounted for the expansion of output in the Sun Belt.

Notwithstanding the absence of Darby's correction for demographic changes (which may be unimportant in the short run), Table 8.1 enables us to examine economic growth since the second oil shock. Productivity and GNP dipped in 1982 but otherwise show a continuous rise. Both consumer prices and wages also show a continuous rise, while the unemployment rate has tended to be constant, despite an increase in the labour force. Indeed, the most striking feature of the US economy has been its capacity to create jobs during a period when Western Europe has failed to do so. However, the second half of the table reveals the cost. Under the impact of a budget deficit and a rising exchange rate, the export price of manufactures has risen, imports have increased and the USA has become uncompetitive. The composition of the rising GNP has shifted away from manufactures towards services as US manufactures have come to be priced out of the domestic market. These features of the US economy during the 1980s are associated with the monetary and fiscal policies of the Reagan administration.

Reaganomics

Although Reaganomics is associated with the budget and trade deficits, it is useful to begin our analysis with the attempts at deregulating markets and their effects.

Table 8.1 Main US Economic Indicators, 1978–87

	1978	1979	1980	1981	1982	1983	1984	1985	1986	1987
GNP (constant prices) (1980=100)	97.7	100.2	100.0	101.9	99.3	102.9	109.9	113.2	116.5	119.9
Gross product per person employed (1980=100)	101.0	100.6	100.0	100.8	99.1	101.3	103.9	104.9	105.6	105.9
Consumer prices (1980=100)	79.2	88.1	100.0	110.4	117.1	120.9	126.1	130.6	133.1	137.9
Average earnings (1980=100)	84.3	91.7	100.0	108.9	115.3	120.3	126.7	133.4	138.0	142.4
Unemployment rate (%)	6.0	5.8	7.0	7.5	9.5	9.5	7.4	7.1	6.9	6.1
Volume of exports (1980=100)	81.0	91.0	100.0	99.0	89.0	86.0	93.0	96.0	102.0	117.0
Export price of manufactures (1980=100)	99.7	101.7	100.0	118.8	130.3	136.4	142.5	144.5	123.2	115[a]
Relative export performance relative to rest of world (1980=100)	87.0	91.0	100.0	101.0	91.0	86.0	86.0	85.0	85.0	93[a]
Import volume relative to domestic demand (1980=100)	108.0	108.0	100.0	100.0	98.0	106.0	121.0	123.0	135.0	139.0
Export price of manufactures (1980=100)	99.7	101.7	100.0	118.8	130.0	136.4	142.5	144.5	123.2	115[a]
Current balance of payments ($bn)	−15	−1	2	6	−8	−47	−106	−118	−141	−160
Effective exchange rate (IMF index)	102.1	99.9	100.0	112.7	125.9	133.2	143.7	150.2	122.5	108.0

Sources: OECD (1987), NIESR (1988)
Note: (a) Based on 9 months.

Deregulation in Transport and Communications

The regulation of transport and communications began in the nineteenth century to protect the public against what was regarded as the natural monopoly of the railroads. This was a problem which was not peculiar to the USA; regulation also existed in Britain. The argument for regulation was that railroads possessed a natural monopoly because the establishment of a second track alongside an existing one would result in both making losses. But in the twentieth century the railroads began to experience competition from the car and the lorry and this led to an extension of the regulatory principle to prevent unfair competition between road and rail, and later air transport.

The campaign to deregulate transport and communications began in the 1950s and accelerated in the 1970s and 1980s. It owed much to changing views on the effects of regulation and the nature of natural monopoly. Regulation, it was alleged, resulted in reduced output and the capture of monopoly profits by operators because costs were allowed to rise to produce the minimum return permitted by the regulators. It was further argued that regulatory boards were vulnerable to capture and domination by operators. A distinction was finally drawn between fixed costs and sunk costs and the concept of a contestable market emerged. An aeroplane represented fixed costs but not sunk costs because it could be flown on a variety of routes: the fact that only one plane was observed to be serving the New York to Chicago route could not be construed as a monopoly situation if it were possible for a plane operating between New York and Savannah to be switched on to the Chicago route. Aircraft on two routes represented fixed costs but not sunk costs and the small number of firms in a market was no indication of the strength of competition. Potential monopoly profits could be captured by the state if it conducted an auction of property rights. It was against this background that Congress passed the Airline Deregulation Act in 1978 and in 1980 passed the Staggers Act for railroads and the Motor Carrier Act. In 1982, as a result of an anti-trust suit filed in 1974, American Telephone and Telegraph (AT&T) agreed to divest itself of twenty operating companies which were restructured into seven separate regulated companies and allowed to buy equipment from anyone they chose.

The effects of deregulation have been qualified by the fact that there were parallel changes in technology, productivity and costs. The transport industry has had to adjust to increases in fuel costs and a severe recession. Much analysis has therefore focused on qualitative aspects, such as increases in efficiency, and whether these are consistent with the contestable markets criterion. In the airline industry there has been a shift from a system of linear routes to patterns of sunbursts and hub and spoke; operators have combined passengers on different routes and destinations in order to increase the average number of passengers per flight and reduce costs. On the railroads a similar system has evolved combining rail and road haulage. In road transport union workers have tended to earn between 30 and 45 per cent more than non-unionised drivers operating on unregulated routes. As a result of deregulation labour costs fell by about 14 per cent in 1977. To summarise a considerable literature, it would appear that efficiency has substantially increased, that cross-subsidisation has been eliminated and that a greater variety of price—service combinations has been created. The effect on the macroeconomy has been to lower inflation and increase productivity.

The Labour Market

One persistent feature of the US economy has been its capacity to create jobs: in the 1970s and early 1980s some 30 million jobs were created — compared with the loss of 10 million in Western Europe. The explanation, as we have noted, was in part fiscal expansion; but there were other impulses stemming from manpower flexibility (a willingness and ability to switch jobs) and labour costs flexibility (the movement of real labour costs to clear labour markets).

Expanding job opportunities went with declining male participation rates (although there is now an attempt to reverse this process to ease the pensions burden) and rising participation rates for young workers (an easing of youth unemployment). However, some black spots remain: ethnic minorities have tended to experience relatively higher unemployment rates and the decline of some regional industries has resulted in areas of high unemployment. Buoyant labour markets have been associated with higher labour turnover rates and a rise in frictional unemployment. In the USA about 11 per cent of workers are unemployed for more than twelve months; in Western Europe the proportion ranges between 30 and 40 per cent. Relatively high labour turnover rates do, of course, carry the disadvantage that employers may be reluctant to invest in training and workers may pick up an assortment of simple skills. Such a pattern of training and turnover may, however, be the result of a shift towards a service economy of nontradable goods induced by fiscal expansion. It places a greater emphasis upon college and university education and it may account for the US tendency to import skilled personnel from Western Europe and South-east Asia.

Manpower flexibility may be induced by the buoyant nature of the economy, which can be a potent factor in accounting for geographical mobility. But the borderline between employers and employees is, in many industries, slight and is breached by the existence of venture capital. Labour cost flexibility is promoted by the low level of social security benefits and their limited duration, as well as the low level of unionism and the comparative absence of employment protection legislation. Tax and benefit replacement ratios are much lower than in Western Europe and account for some 40 per cent of average earnings as compared with 70 to 80 per cent in Western Europe. Evidence that high nominal wages may result in high unemployment seem to be confirmed by numerous studies of the effects of minimum wage legislation and through the 1970s the legal minimum wage tended to be relaxed, easing the problem of youth unemployment.

In contrast to Western Europe, there has been a noticeable absence of laws governing the employment of workers. Unionism embraces only 16 per cent of the labour forces and is mainly concentrated in the public sector. Flexibility of labour costs has also helped to explain the USA's low productivity growth. In contrast, again, to Western European practice, Americans have tended to employ relatively larger ratios of labour to capital in production processes and to indulge in capital widening (implying a joint expansion of labour and capital) rather than capital deepening (implying a continually rising capital–labour ratio). In Western Europe labour cost rigidities have resulted in a gap between real wages and productivity and in the substitution of capital for labour. When the USA did pursue 'European' policies on wages and employment 'European' responses, in the form of diminished employment opportunities and the substitution of capital for labour, were the result.

Budget Deficits

Reaganomics is associated primarily with budget deficits and trade deficits; the deregulation measures which we have previously examined have in the main had an impact on the domestic economy and have involved the non-trade sector. We must now turn to the foreign trade sector and look at budget deficits in more detail, going beyond the nominal data. (In nominal terms the US budget has been in deficit in 50 of the 58 years between 1931 and 1988, which suggests a remarkable record of profligacy.)

We cannot establish an accurate picture by examining correlations between deficits and selected macroeconomic aggregates, such as GNP or unemployment, because it is impossible to distinguish between cause and effect. When the economy is booming tax receipts will be high and expenditure on unemployment benefits will be low. Most people would maintain that it was the boom that had caused the small deficit, not vice versa. Further complications can arise during periods of inflation because the effect of rising prices is to push more households and firms into higher tax brackets, with the result that the surplus rises. It is, of course, possible to make a correction to the income tax payments by households; but it is not so easy to do a similar exercise for firms because of the problems of deciding whether joint stock companies are owned by households or are separate legal entities. If they are separate legal entities then it is suggested that profits should be indexed against the prices of raw materials and equipment used by the firms rather than against the retail prices of goods purchased by consumers.

What we need is some measure of deficit which is independent of the effects of the economy on such a deficit. A full employment budget deficit, i.e. an estimate of the deficit that would occur if the economy were operating at full employment, would be such a measure and would be independent of fluctuations in output, employment and income. Because fluctuations in output and income tend, in the short run, to be associated with changes in unemployment the deficit needs to be defined in terms of a constant rate of unemployment. Unemployment can

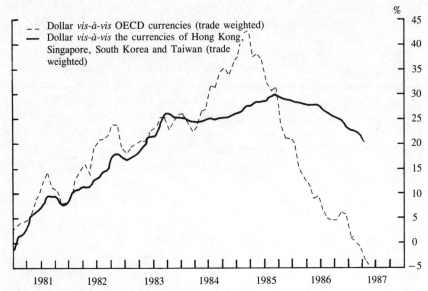

Note: (a) Deviations from 1980 levels.
Source: OECD (1987)

Figure 8.1 Exchange Rates of the Dollar[a]

be affected by changes in the size and composition of the population, so the full employment deficit needs to be corrected for demographic changes.

When all the various allowances are made it would seem that between 1955 and 1965 the full employment budget was never in deficit, although the actual budget was in deficit in five years because actual unemployment was above the target natural rate of unemployment. The Vietnam War produced a boom and as a consequence actual deficits tended to be lower than benchmark deficits. But from 1970 there were persistent actual deficits which did not result in persistent low unemployment because there was continuous inflation. In effect there were budget surpluses, which would explain the sluggishness of the economy up to the severe recession of 1981–82. The Carter administration ignored the sluggishness of the economy, concentrated upon the inflation component of stagflation and pursued tight money policies as well as, in its latter years, seeking to reduce the budget deficit. Such policies presupposed that the shocks to the economy came from the demand side and not from the supply side through oil price rises. But in 1982 there was a change in direction — a combination of major tax cuts and increases in defence spending — and the full employment budget swung from a large surplus to a very large deficit.

US macroeconomic policy has been concerned with growth, inflation and unemployment and has attempted to cope with these issues through the use of monetary policy (interest rates) and fiscal policy (taxes and government spending). Both monetary policy and fiscal policy can be used in combination to achieve a desired state of the economy: there can be a trade off between the two sets of instruments. Thus, a high tax take and low interest rates may have the same overall effect upon the economy as a low tax take and high interest rates. They can, however, produce different effects on the composition of incomes and output.

Higher real interest rates in the USA have produced an inflow of foreign capital. The fact that the United States was on a floating exchange rate meant that the foreign demand for dollars to buy securities caused the exchange rate to rise (Figure 8.1 and Table 8.1). The rise in the exchange rate caused the value of the capital stock to fall because existing plant and equipment was no longer viable at the new exchange rate. The depressing effect of the exchange rate reinforced the effect of the rise in interest rates on investment. Although it might be assumed that households would increase their savings in order to cover the loans, the opposite happened and Americans went on a shopping spree.

The expansionary stimulus of an easy fiscal policy and a tight monetary policy led to an increase in employment and a lower rate of inflation. But because of the rise in the dollar there was a fall in the exports of manufactures (tradable goods) and a rise in imports. Employment in the service sector increased.

Interregional Shifts in the Location of Industry

The substitution of foreign manufactures for domestically produced goods led many observers to conclude that the USA was going through a period of de-industrialisation. But manufacturing's share of total output has not undergone a dramatic decline; instead a shift in the composition and location of industrial activity from the North-east and the Mid-west to the South can be observed. This shift appears to have been a natural response to the high exchange rate, the liberalisation of trade barriers and labour market rigidities in Northern plants.

The influence of exchange rate movements should not, however, be pressed too far. An existing movement to the South has been accelerated; the shift began before the exchange rate changes and was prompted by the inflow of exports from the developing countries which began after the Kennedy round of tariff reductions in 1965. The decline in Northern manufacturing received a further impetus in the 1970s following the rise in energy prices.

Taken in conjunction, the supply-side shocks and tariff reforms point to the possibility of a turnaround comparable to that experienced by Britain in the 1870s when it faced severe competition from Germany and the United States, and also to that experienced by Western Europe in the 1980s. The US decline in profits as a result of competition from developing countries was accentuated by the rise in the exchange rate. Northern firms could not respond readily: not merely did they use energy-intensive technology, but they were dominated by work rules set through collective bargaining.

Unionism expanded during the 1930s under the impact of the New Deal and received a further boost during the Second World War. But after the war, the Cold War and the tendency to associate unions with communism led to their decline — a process accelerated by the Taft-Hartley Act. By the 1980s only some 16 per cent of the labour force was unionised as compared with about 40 per cent in Britain and much higher percentages in Belgium and Sweden.

Yet the response to unionism created its own rigidities in the form of managerial rules which locked in management as much as they locked out unions. The response to foreign competition has been twofold. On the one hand traditional industries have moved South in search of cheap labour and the opportunity to create less restricted workplace environments. On the other hand, high-tech industries have emerged in New England and have capitalised on the availability of well educated young people coming out of the concentration of universities in the North-east. Above all there has been a pursuit of computer-integrated manufacturing systems (CIM) which combine mass production with craftsmanship in response to consumers' tastes.

Agriculture

High exchange rates and high interest rates also had a profound effect upon agriculture. Through the 1950s and 1960s the productivity of US agriculture rose as a result of intensive research and development into new crops and better use of fertilisers. The productivity of farm labour also rose (although whether the productivity of capital rose is a moot point). Assisted by generous farm price support schemes the output of agricultural products increased to such an extent that the USA became a major exporter of cereal crops. The creation of the European Common Market in the 1960s diverted US exports to the Third World. But the overall effect of the rise in the exchange rate and interest rates has been to reduce the demand for foodstuffs by less developed countries. The world depression has also reduced demand from other countries.

As well as the fall in demand US farmers suffered a reduction in incomes as a result of the deregulation programme. Agriculture had benefited from protection in the nineteenth century when it was safeguarded against possible monopoly pricing by the railroads; as a result of the depression of the 1930s it received further protection in the form of price support schemes. Such protection was to result in a misallocation of resources as well as relatively high incomes for farmers. The Farm Bill or US Food Security Act of 1985 has sought to control the farming industry by supporting incomes in response to the fall in demand but has also attempted to reduce the surpluses of many agricultural commodities which the recession and previous farm price support schemes had fostered. But the eventual outcome will be dictated by the state of world markets as much as the resolution of the conflict between a desire to raise incomes and to lower output.

The Stock Market Crash

The stock market crash of 19 October 1987, 'Black Monday', was unexpected and its causes have not been established. It came after a period of steep rises in stock market prices during which a gap opened up between stock prices and bond prices (Figure 8.2). A correction of the gap was therefore expected but the extent of the fall was surprising. It is tempting to attribute the crash to the size of the budget and trade deficits. But if rational expectations are presumed to dominate the stock market then the deficits would have been incorporated into investors' calculations. What was the 'news' that caused investors to revise their opinions? One possibility is that disclosures about Irangate and Contragate caused investors to reconsider their views on the overall competence of the Reagan administration.

The effects of the crash are equally difficult to unravel. An immediate effect seems to have been the fear of a liquidity crisis as the Keynesian speculative motive re-emerged and the percentage of cash holdings of institutional investors rose from 3 per cent in September 1987 to 8 per cent in March 1988. However, a rise in interest rates was averted by the authorities. The fall in equity prices will have reduced the wealth of equity holders and raised the costs of investment through new issues. But since new issues form only a small part of the total financing of investment, the effects on investment costs may be slight. The effect on private consumption will depend upon whether the losses affect transitory or permanent income. However, the negative wealth effect may be presumed to be greater the larger is the proportion of equities held by households rather than held for them by institutions, and the larger is the market valuation of securities relative to GDP. Market valuation tends to be high in the USA and Canada and low in Japan. The main effects on consumption will therefore be concentrated in North America, with the impact on other advanced countries coming through foreign trade multiplier effects. The effects on the world economy will depend on the extent to which other countries can provide substitutes for domestic demand for North American imports.

Summary and Conclusions

Since the oil shocks of the 1970s US economic policy has been dominated by Reaganomics: a combination of easy fiscal policy, tight monetary policy and deregulation of markets. Reaganomics was an attempt to overcome the sluggish growth of the economy and an apparent decline in military power. Budget and trade deficits were sustained for a longer period than in Japan because of the greater strength of the US economy and the willingness of foreigners to hold dollars and US securities. There were, however, effects on the world economy. High interest rates depressed investment in Western Europe and increased the debt burden

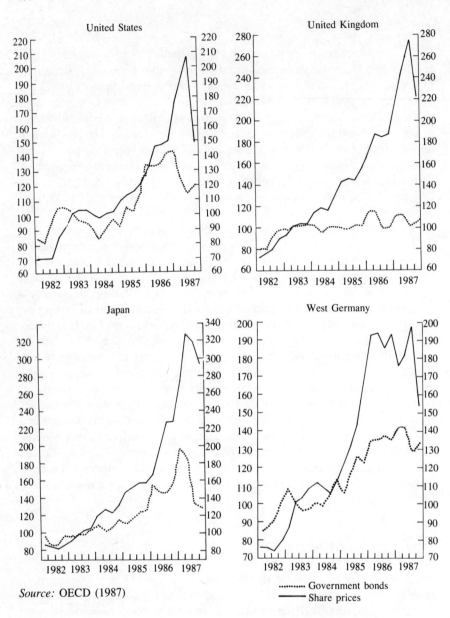

Source: OECD (1987)

.... Government bonds
———— Share prices

Figure 8.2 Stock and Bond Prices (Indices 1983 = 100)

of Latin American countries. The decision to reduce the deficits will lead to problems of choice in allocating resources. The easing of tension between the USA and USSR could lead to a reduction in defence spending and to more resources being devoted to social services and coping with an ageing population. The effects on the other advanced countries will be to reduce their trade surpluses and cause them to increase domestic demand. But the questions multiply. Has the removal of trade unions and employment legislation rested upon the power of budget deficits to provide jobs? Is there anything wrong with a situation in which the Germans and Japanese attempt to persuade the Americans to buy their goods by lending the money to buy them? Will the Americans increase their savings or will government have to generate budget surpluses in order to finance investment?

Bibliography

Darby, M. (1984) 'The US productivity slowdown: a case of statistical myopia', *American Economic Review*, vol. 74, pp. 301–22.

Hulten, C.R. and Schwab, R.M. (1984) 'Regional productivity growth in US manufacturing: 1951–78', *American Economic Review*, vol. 74, pp. 152–162.

Maddison, A. (1987) 'Growth and slowdown in advanced capitalist economies', *Journal of Economic Literature*, vol. 25, pp. 649–699.

NIESR (1988) *Economic Review*, March.

OECD (1987) *Economic Outlook*, vol. 42, December.

9

Western Europe

The sharp rise in oil prices in 1973 and 1979 and the deflationary policies pursued in the advanced countries after 1979 may have been responsible for some part of the increase in unemployment in Western Europe in the 1970s and 1980s. Yet its persistence and severity have led to a search for other causes. At the onset it is important to recognise that the performances of the European countries began to deteriorate before the oil shocks. The spectacular growth rates of the 1950s and early 1960s reflected, in large measure, a catching up process as European countries adopted US knowhow. There were, of course, differences in the successes of various countries: West Germany and the Netherlands had relatively high growth rates. International differences in growth rates owed much to differences in the availability of resources, such as the release of labour from agriculture, the effective use of monetary and fiscal policies and managerial ability to organise productive effort. Adaptability was weakest in the UK where the social structure had not been altered by foreign invasion. Even the threat of invasion had done little to shake up work methods in the UK and in the absence of a surplus of labour in agriculture, the task of redeploying workers from decaying industries and towns was never seriously tackled (Correlli Barnett 1986). But in the late 1960s and in the 1970s growth rates began to slow down (Table 9.1).

It is not obvious why the catching up process slowed down. Profit rates showed some slight fall and profit shares showed some declines, both of which were compatible with capital accumulation leading to a fall in profit rates and the elasticity of substitution being less than unity. But there were no dramatic falls until the late 1970s and early 1980s when the effect of the oil shocks and increased competition from the newly industrialising countries began to exert some influence upon economic activity in the advanced economies.

The slow down in growth was arrested by a rise in public spending. Subsequently the increase in public spending became, in the eyes of some economists such as Bacon and Eltis (1978) a major cause of the difficulties experienced in

Table 9.1 Economic Growth in the USA, Japan and the EEC, 1953–85

	1953–62	1963–69	1970–80	1981–85
USA	3.0	4.4	3.1	3.0
Japan	8.7	11.3	5.4	3.9
EEC		4.6	3.3	1.3
West Germany	6.6	4.5	3.2	1.4
France	5.1	5.4	3.6	1.2
UK	2.9	3.1	1.3	1.9
Italy	6.0	5.4	4.0	0.9

Source: OECD (1955–86)

the 1970s. They reasoned that most major economies were experiencing full employment and that the increase in public spending financed by increases in government borrowing (which in turn led to increases in the money supply, as shown in Tables 9.2 and 9.3) led to a crowding out of private investment. But it is important to realise that the expansion of public sectors took place in democratic societies and reflected real demands, even if politicians were inclined to minimise the costs of providing services. There was a rise in spending on education to cater for the increase in numbers and there was a rise in pensions and

Table 9.2 Money Growth Rates

	1969	1971	1973	1975	1977	1979	1981	1983	1985
EEC	6.1	17.8	15.0	18.2	13.9	14.4	11.4	11.5	9.5
West Germany	9.4	13.5	10.1	8.6	11.2	6.0	5.0	5.3	6.7
France	6.1	17.8	15.0	18.2	13.9	14.4	11.4	11.5	5.7
UK	2.4	13.8	26.4	10.5	10.0	12.7	13.5	11.1	12.9
Italy	7.6	14.8	17.8	13.6	13.4	12.6	10.8	10.8	11.8

Source: OECD (1955–86)

Table 9.3 Net Borrowing by Governments as a Percentage of GNP

	1971	1973	1975	1977	1979	1981	1983	1985
EEC	0.8	5.5	3.3	3.6	5.2			
West Germany	−0.2	−1.2	−5.7	−2.4	−2.7	−3.7	−3.3	−1.9
France	−0.7	−0.9	2.2	0.8	0.7	2.8	−3.1	−2.6
UK	−1.2	3.4	5.0	3.4	3.3	2.9	2.2	−4.2
Italy	4.6	5.8	13.3	9.0	9.4	11.6	11.9	−13.0

Source: OECD (1955–86)

social services to deal with the growth in the numbers of elderly people. In the UK the rise in government financed consumption (from 19 per cent of total output in 1965 to 22 per cent in 1974) was at the expense of private consumption (53 per cent to 51 per cent) rather than private investment (17 per cent to 19 per cent). Private consumption had in fact been falling since the 1920s when it amounted to some 80 per cent of total output. There may have been a substitution between private and public sources of consumer goods. The increase in public spending may have been seen as a means of mopping up any possible increase in unemployment arising from the increase in foreign competition. In other words, an increase in the non-traded sector (the public sector) may have been necessary to avoid the unemployment effects of a decline in the traded sector. But we enter one caveat. Whatever the pros and cons of a switch between private and public spending, it would appear from Table 9.4 that increased public spending led to an increase in labour costs.

Superimposed upon the increase in public spending were the oil shocks which required a shift away from energy-intensive methods of production. Substitution was, however, delayed by attempts to maintain high levels of employment through increased monetary and fiscal expansion involving the recycling of OPEC oil revenues. After OPEC II there were more conscious attempts to reduce demand. Although deflationary policies have had some influence upon wages it has to be noted that profits have not been restored to levels which would enable firms to pursue optimal debt−equity ratios. The deflationary policies of the European countries may have been prolonged by the actions of the United States, which raised interest rates and may have reduced the willingness to invest in Europe. However, the possible beneficial effects of demand side policies may have been thwarted by a lack of flexibility on the supply side. European labour markets have been dominated by strong trade unions, employment protection legislation and generous social security benefits. But there are differences in unemployment rates within the European Community and between the Community and non-members, such as Austria, Sweden and Switzerland: strong contrasts obtain in Europe as well as between Europe, the United States and Japan.

Confronted by a catalogue of problems and recognising that the structure of the European Community anticipated the recession, we argue that the benefits of the Community have not been realised and that differences in the relative

Table 9.4   Unit Labour Costs (1972=100)

	1971	1973	1975	1977	1979	1981	1983
EEC	95.2	105.9	107.4	102.5	116.3	105.7	95.7
West Germany	107.5	99.2	98.1	110.0	112.8	114.5	78.6
France	—	103.9	107.1	102.2	105.4	100.3	94.1
UK	102.2	89.3	95.5	87.0	106.8	135.7	115.4
Italy	98.0	97.4	102.0	91.2	90.2	87.4	95.7

Source: OECD (1955−86)

economic performance of the regions within the Community have not been re-
solved either by movements of resources or by the monetary and fiscal policies
available. As evidence of this assertion we shall look at the movements of incomes per capita within the Community and compare the performances of members
with non-members. We shall highlight some of the differences between member
countries in spending on education and R&D, monetary and fiscal policies and
the behaviour of labour markets. We shall additionally consider the influence of
policies which have isolated the Community from non-members and led to a reduction of incomes through, for example, the Common Agricultural Policy. However,
economic problems cannot be divorced from political problems.

If European countries combine to form a political unit, they can provide a mass
market and economies of scale comparable to those of the USA, and capable of
withstanding the competitive pressures from South-east Asia — as well as obtaining political parity with the USA, USSR, Japan and China. But this will imply
a stronger centralised political authority and a corresponding reduction of
members' sovereignty.

The European Community

The European Community is a preferential trading arrangement whereby a group
of countries accord each other favourable tariff and subsidy arrangements. More
complicated forms of integration are possible: in a free trade area the member
countries may eliminate tariffs among themselves but retain their own tariffs
against non-members; in a customs union the member countries remove all tariffs
among themselves and establish common external tariffs. At a more advanced
stage member countries may remove all barriers to factor movement between
themselves and establish a common market. Finally, members may integrate all
economic policies and form an economic union embracing common monetary
and fiscal policies. The European Community is midway between a common
market and an economic union to the extent that its members have not integrated
all economic policies; some have adopted fixed exchange rates but others, such
as the UK, have preferred to retain flexible exchange rates on the grounds that
the conjunction of North Sea oil and fixed exchange rates would have created
severe domestic problems. (With the run down of North Sea oil there has been
a move to 'shadowing' the deutschmark, implying an acquiescence in a fixed
exchange rate.) Finally, the member states still control the greater part of their
own expenditure on social policies.

The origins of the Community go back to the end of the Second World War
when most West European countries became aware of their dependence on the
United States. The war had wrought considerable destruction. It had led to the
break up of the old colonial empires, although the UK still retained some vestiges
which were to delay its entry into the Common Market. During the war European countries had lost many of their markets in the Third World to the United
States and to industrialisation in less developed countries. There was also a growing

awareness that domestic markets might be too small to bring about the growth of efficiency resulting from economies of scale.

At the end of the Second World War the Marshall Plan of aid to Europe did exert some pressure to coordinate economic and social policies, although the results were not as great as the USA desired. To the Americans there were two European problems and one domestic experience upon which they could draw for policy. First, there was the future of Germany. Germany had to be reconstructed: it could not be left to drift into totalitarianism as it did after the First World War, nor could it be left to a Communist take over bid that would leave the rest of Europe at the mercy of the USSR. There had to be a German recovery. But a German recovery could threaten Europe unless the UK acted as a counterweight. The second problem was how to bring about a united Europe which would enjoy the advantages of the USA. This was an idea which appealed to the New Deal idealism in the Congress. But it was an idea which contrasted sharply with the attitudes of the European states, each of which was intent on restoring its own autonomy behind tariff walls. What the USA sought to do with the Marshall Plan of aid to Europe was to resolve the two problems. But this required the UK to renounce its role of a world power and play a part in creating a united Europe in the image of the USA.

The UK's problem was seen as political but was, in fact, economic. It was assumed that the UK refused to enter Europe because it was a world power, or possessed the illusions of a world power. It was assumed that a Labour government wanted to create a welfare state with US dollars and was distrustful of the right-wing Christian Democratic parties emerging in Europe. But Britain's problem was a dollar problem. Britain had to obtain dollars and before the war had relied on creating a surplus in trade with Asia in order to cover a deficit with the USA. During the Second World War the surplus vanished and left the UK with a deficit greater than that of the other European countries. This had to be removed by measures which would discriminate against the dollar — the 1949 devaluation. However, the reluctance of the UK to be involved in Europe had one beneficial effect because it forced France to come to terms with its traditional enemy, Germany.

An Economic Commission for Europe was established as an agency of the United Nations and in 1948 an Organisation for European Economic Cooperation was created (later to become the much enlarged Organisation for Economic Cooperation and Development). A Council for Europe was also established. These were primarily consultative agencies, although in 1948 a small customs union was established and became known as BENELUX (between Belgium, the Netherlands and Luxembourg). Further impetus to Western European union came from the fears of a Russian invasion, the formation of a Communist Council for Mutual Economic Assistance (CMEA or Comecon) and the onset of the Cold War in 1950. In 1951 the European Coal and Steel Community was formed and this allowed both West Germany and France access to the coal and iron reserves of Alsace and Lorraine as well as determining the future of the Saar. Eventually, by the Treaty of Rome in 1957, the European Community was created. Its original members were France, West Germany, Italy, Belgium, the Netherlands and Luxembourg. Among the factors which led to its formation were the successful coalitions established by the ECSC and BENELUX, the fact that Christian Democratic governments existed in most countries and the rapid growth of all members. In 1960 the UK joined a European Free Trade Area, which included among its members the Nordic group of countries.

Preferential trading arrangements were granted by the Community to 18 African states at the Yaoundé Convention in 1963. In 1973 Denmark, Ireland and the UK left EFTA and were admitted to the European Community. Greece joined in 1981 and Spain and Portugal subsequently sought admission in 1986. In 1987 Turkey applied for entry and in the rest of EFTA there were signs of a willingness to join the Community.

Customs Union Theory

The Community has attempted to remove obstacles to trade between its members and erect common tariffs against the goods of non-members. The elimination of tariffs between members creates trade and generates gains from the production and consumption effects of trade. But if some members find that they have to pay higher prices for goods than they paid to non-members then there is trade diversion. In Table 9.5 Britain puts a tariff of £0.75 on imports of wheat from Europe and Canada. Canada is the most efficient producer and captures most of the UK market except for those consumers who prefer French wheat and are willing to pay £2.25 for it when they could obtain Canadian wheat for £1.75. Now suppose the UK and Europe abolish tariffs on each others' goods. European wheat now enters the UK duty free, and at a price of £1.50 is cheaper than Canadian wheat. Some UK consumers will switch to European wheat. This constitutes trade diversion because non-European wheat is available at lower real cost.

Table 9.5

	Canadian wheat	European wheat
World price	£1.00	£1.50
UK tariff	£0.75	£0.75
UK price (pre-union)	£1.75	£2.25
European tariff	£0.75	£0.75
UK price (post-union)	£1.75	£1.50

Empirical Estimates of the Gains from Integration

Attempts to produce reliable estimates of the effects of the Community are complicated by the problem of determining what would have happened in the absence of the Community; in other words, how can we measure the effects of changes in market shares which would have occurred in the absence of integration? Market shares in third markets are one indicator of changes in market shares resulting from integration. For example if Italy's exports to non-market countries have risen over the relevant period then it might be inferred that exports to the Community have gone up similarly.

Table 9.6 provides a range of estimates of the effects of the Community on trade flows. The differences in the magnitudes of the results stem from the choice of time periods and the methods used to compute the income elasticities of demand. But despite the wide range of estimates there is a general agreement that trade creation has been more important that trade diversion and that there may have been some external trade creation in that the formation of the Community has led to more trade with non-members. However, the results do not provide any direct evidence on the income and welfare effects of the Community. Assuming that demand functions are linear and that production is subject to diminishing returns, then the simplest method of measuring welfare gains is to multiply the volume of trade created or diverted by one-half of the tariff. Using this procedure Verdoorn (cited in Scitovsky 1958) calculated that the trade creation gains for the members of the Community in 1951 would have been 0.05 per cent of total national incomes. A later study by Petith (1977) took account of the effect of integration on the terms of trade and suggested that the gains might range between 0.3 and 1.0 per cent of aggregate national income. However, these studies were concerned with the static gains from integration and ignored any possible gains arising from increasing returns. An attempt to measure the effects of economies of scale using detailed case studies of four industries was conducted by Owen (1983) who concluded that the dynamic gains might vary between 3 and 6 per cent of aggregate GDP in 1980.

The empirical studies reach the tentative conclusion that there have been gains from integration. But what we have not examined is the gains for individual member countries — that is, the internal trade diversion or backwash effects. Before considering this issue and its possible causes in the light of the economic performances of member countries we shall examine the effects of trade diversion upon agriculture and manufacturing and the Community attempts at monetary and fiscal integration.

Monetary Union and the European Monetary System

Monetary union occurs when countries agree to fix their exchange rates and to pursue policies which will ensure that those rates will continue. Exchange rates

Table 9.6 Estimates of Trade Created and Trade Diverted in the EC (*ex post*, residual imputation)

| Author | Period | Trade created | | | | Trade diverted[b] | | | |
		All goods (US $ billion)	%[a]	Manufactures (US $ billion)	%[a]	All goods (US $ billion)	%[a]	Manufactures (US $ billion)	%[a]
Prewo	1970	19.8	23	18.0	34	-2.5	6	-3.1	15
Truman (unadjusted)	1968	—	—	9.2	26	—	—	-1.0	7
(adjusted)		—	—	2.5	7	—	—	0.5	4
Balassa	1970	11.3	13	11.4	21	0.3	1	0.1	0
Kreinen (average)	1969–70	—	—	8.4	—	—	—	1.1	—
Williamson and Bottrill	1969	—	—	11.2[c]	25	—	—	0	0

Sources: Prewo (1974), Truman (1969), Balassa (1975), Kreinen (1972), Williamson and Bottrill (1971) and Aitken (1973)

Notes: (a) Percentages relate to total and extra-area imports of all goods and manufactured products.
(b) Numbers with negative signs represent external trade creation.
(c) Unweighted average of all alternative estimates.

tend to be fixed within countries while flexible rates tend to occur between countries. So what are the conditions which must obtain for a monetary union to be successful? Why, for example, is the exchange rate fixed between England and Scotland but not between the United Kingdom and the United States?

The answer is that, if there is perfect mobility of short-term capital, then the redistribution of money cannot cause monetary disturbances. France and the United Kingdom have separate banking systems. Suppose there was a bad harvest in France which resulted in a trade deficit with the UK. Then there would be a decline in the reserves of the French banks but interest rates in France would not rise because businessmen could borrow from UK banks. Ultimately, the loans would have to be repaid but that could be done after a good harvest or a restructuring of the French economy. The mobility of short-term capital therefore removes the necessity for an integrated banking system and the possibility that local inflations and deflations can be created by the various branches of an integrated banking system. The creation of an optimal currency area therefore requires the mobility of short-term capital and price flexibility. If the latter condition is not fulfilled and resources do not migrate from the deficit area then governments may have to combat unemployment through the use of subsidies. Political union may not be necessary for the avoidance of disturbances as long as markets are capable of overcoming those disturbances; but in the absence of such markets political union may be necessary to provide a system of subsidies.

Monetary union was not contemplated in the early years of the Community because exchange rates were fixed under the IMF rules and Europe was part of a world monetary union. It became an issue only in the late 1960s when the Bretton Woods system began to break down. In 1969 the members of the Community decided to adopt monetary union as a target of economic policy; it was to be approached gradually by reducing the range of exchange rate fluctuations until rates could be fixed and the exchange reserves of all members simultaneously pooled. The first condition — reducing the range of exchange rate fluctuations — came to be known as the 'snake in the tunnel' and was introduced in 1971, although it had to be modified in 1973 and collapsed during the tumultuous years of the 1970s as several countries left the union. All that was left by the end of the 1970s was a group of countries which fixed their currencies in terms of the deutschmark because West Germany was their main trading partner.

In 1979 the idea of a monetary union was revived, with two objectives: to provide a buffer against the erratic movements of the dollar and to further the cause of economic integration.

The EMS has four elements: the European currency unit (ecu), the exchange rate mechanism, increased economic policy coordination (EMCOF) and the support measures. The ecu is a bundle of currencies with the shares of each currency weighted according to the importance of that currency. If the value of a currency changes its importance in the ecu, the value of the ecu also changes. The exchange rate mechanism consists of two systems: a direct link between currencies and the exchange rate between each currency and the ecu.

The actual performance of the EMS has been mixed and it has been strongly influenced by three factors: the effects of differences in inflation rates; fluctuations in the value of the dollar (when the value of the dollar has fallen then funds have tended to flow into deutschmarks and disrupted relationships between the currencies of member countries); and the existence of different fiscal policies operated by member countries. It has been noticeable that some non-member countries, such as Austria, have been subjected to fewer disturbances than member countries because they have used fiscal policies which have been compatible with the linking of their currencies to the deutschmark (Gilbert 1938).

This brings us to the question of whether the UK should join the EMS. Political considerations apart, the main objection has been the fact that sterling is a petro-currency with its value being determined by movements in oil prices. But with the decline in the importance of the UK as an oil producer this argument has lost much of its force and in recent years sterling has been 'shadowing' the deutschmark and exchange rate policies have been used to stabilise the economy. But the problems of the German economy in the 1980s have led to a questioning of this policy and a feeling in some quarters that the time may not be right for fixing the value of the pound in terms of the mark.

Fiscal Policy

However, the UK's decision whether or not to join the EMS is part of the much wider issue of national autonomy and raises questions about the role of fiscal policy within the Community. Since the 1970s the unemployment rates of member countries have tended to be higher than those of non-members. Later we shall consider specific aspects of non-member countries, such as Austria, Sweden and Switzerland; but at this point it is worth noting that some countries such as Austria have tied their currencies to the mark and that their relative success may come from a coordination of the monetary regime of the EMS with other instruments of economic policy. This brings us to the subject of the appropriate fiscal policies and the Community's budget.

Fiscal policy embraces three problems. First, there is the question of whether the Community's budget and those of member countries are sufficiently integrated. Are the objectives which are appropriate to the supranational authority separate from those which should be pursued by member states? Second, is there tax harmonisation in the sense that there is agreement on the manner in which each state will use a particular fiscal instrument? Finally there is the problem of fiscal coordination or avoidance of national policies which might conflict with those policies being put into effect by the supranational body.

Following Musgrave (1959) it has been customary to view the objectives of fiscal policy as: (1) the allocation of resources; (2) the redistribution of income; and (3) stabilisation and economic growth. Given these objectives the next step is to consider the appropriate level at which those objectives should be pursued.

This is decided by suggesting that whenever there are significant spill over effects the pursuit of the objective should be transferred to a higher level. Thus, if A wishes to drain a swamp, which would improve the health of its citizens as well as those in B, then a supranational authority, C, may be required to pursue that objective because A may not wish to finance the project if it believes that B will pay for it, and B will resist paying in the hope that A will pay. This is the public goods dilemma which arives when spill overs occur.

Returning to the other objectives of the budget we may note that it may be possible to subsume income redistribution under allocation if it can be demonstrated that the rich will benefit from seeing the poor better off but require an extra-market mechanism to achieve that end. The possibility of Pareto optimal redistribution raises the idea of conflating two approaches to taxation: ability to pay and the benefit principle.

To suggest certain principles of public finance is not to indicate that they have been adopted by the Community. What in fact we observe is that the number of goods and services which have a degree of 'publicness' which extends across all member states appears to be limited. Most members tend to retain control of measures for redistributing income within their boundaries, although some influence is exerted through regional grants. As Tables 9.7 and 9.8 indicate, the

Table 9.7 European Community Budget: 1986 Revenue

Source	Million ecu	%
Customs duties	9,700	29.3
Agricultural levies	1,585	4.8
Sugar and isoglucose levies	1,114	3.4
VAT	20,468	61.9
Others	190	0.6
		100.0

Source: European Commission (1986)

Table 9.8 European Community Budget: 1986 Budgeted Expenditure

Chapter	Million ecu	% share
Agriculture and fisheries	22,009	67.2
Regional policy	2,456	7.4
Social policy	2,153	6.5
Research, energy, industry and transport	762	2.3
Cooperation and development	1,172	3.6
Miscellaneous	3,159	9.6
Administration	1,049	3.2

Source: European Commission (1986)

bulk of expenditures is devoted to agriculture and fisheries and the main sources of revenue are customs duties on imports from the rest of the world and a proportion of the revenues from national VAT. The Community budget differs from national budgets in that it must balance. It cannot be used as a fiscal stabiliser except to the limited extent that a balanced budget might give rise to multiplier effects.

The concentration of the budget upon agriculture has created conflicts within the Community which have threatened its continued existence. Conflict has arisen because of the ever increasing costs of financing the budget and the need to find new sources of revenue. It has also arisen because of the disproportionate share of the budget which has been absorbed by agriculture and by the tendency of some countries to benefit more than others from outlays on agriculture. With the enlargement of the Community to include more Southern European countries political influence may be shifting from a group of Northern European manufacturing countries which were prepared to subsidise their own farming in order to achieve a degree of self-sufficiency to a group of Southern European countries for whom agriculture is the mainstay.

In theory contributions to the budget are supposed to be related to the level of GNP in each country (that is, to ability to pay); but in the case of the UK this is qualified by two factors. The UK tends to pay more because it imports more goods from non-members; and because imports are included in the tax base, there is a higher VAT contribution. Since the UK has a smaller agricultural sector it also tends to pay more in taxes than it receives in benefits (hence the 1984 Fontainebleau Agreement which attempted to reduce the British contribution).

But the long-term future of the Community is in doubt because of disagreement among members as to the role of the budget. The budget is currently devoted mainly to financing agriculture and with the enlargement of the Community to include more Southern European farm producers the agrarian interest will increase and the importance of the Northern manufacturing countries will decline. It is not easy to find non-farm issues which gain common acceptance. Energy policy is split between coal producers, such as the UK, and non-coal producers who either want to import coal or gas and oil or wish to rely upon nuclear energy. Regional policy tends either to be the same as agricultural policy or else is torn between the desire to invest in new industries and the wish to do something for older manufacturing industries through the use of tariffs.

In commenting upon the budget we have strayed from the problem of monetary and fiscal coordination. Because the budget has to balance then it has little or no stabilising role (except through the possible balanced budget multiplier effect) and this point is reinforced when it is recognised that the budget accounts for only about 1 per cent of the GNP of all the member states. This emphasises the importance of coordinating the monetary and fiscal policies of the members in order not to conflict with the workings of the EMS. Unfortunately, such coordination has not been possible.

The financing of support schemes is borne by all members through the Community budget. The cost of the programme was about £12,000 million in 1984.

Various taxes and subsidies give rise to three possible types of trade diversion:

1. diversion between the Community and the rest of the world;
2. diversion between member countries; and
3. diversion within member countries.

The Community has not published information upon relative prices of its foodstuffs since 1980. But Table 9.9 does reveal that for a range of commodities Community prices showed considerable increases between 1973 and 1980. Table 9.10 indicates that one consequence of this policy has been that the Community has achieved self-sufficiency in grains, meat and dairy products and sugar. However, the effects of self-sufficiency have also been borne by non-members, especially the USA, Canada, Australia, New Zealand and Argentina — all of

Table 9.9 Ratio of EC Prices to World Prices, 1973–80

	1973–74	1979–80
Common wheat	79	163
Durum wheat	116	159
Barley	60	161
Maize	98	190
Beef and veal	110	204
Pork	131	152
Butter	320	411
Skimmed milk	156	379
Sugar	66	190

Source: European Commission (1980)

Table 9.10 Self-sufficiency in Agricultural Products in the EC 1973–84 (%)

	1973–74	1983–84
Wheat	104	116
Barley	105	108
Oats	97	94
Maize	55	82
Sugar	90	123
Fresh vegetables	95	98
Fresh fruit	82	83
Cheese	103	107
Butter	98	147
Eggs	100	103
Beef and veal	95	105
Pork	100	102
Poultry	102	111

Source: European Commission (1976 and 1985)

whom were former major exporters of temperate zone foodstuffs to Community countries. Even tropical countries have been affected by the CAP, for the Community is now a major exporter of sugar. Finally, there is an element of unpredictability about the CAP since good harvests can lead to the dumping of agricultural commodities on to world markets as the authorities attempt to keep the butter mountains and wine lakes at reasonable levels. Community policies have thus had significant effects on other world producers (Table 9.11).

Nor is the influence of the CAP confined to the exports of other countries. As a consequence of the Community's aid programme to developing countries, production in developing countries may have fallen. Because of the availability of free food, governments in Sub-Saharan Africa have failed to provide their farmers with the incentives to expand domestic production (although, as Chapter 3 indicated, other advanced countries have pursued similar policies with the same effects).

The second and third effects of the CAP concern transfers between member countries and transfers within countries. Transfers between countries are influenced by: (1) the demand and supply of products which pass between members; (2) the amount of trade that is subject to preferential treatment; and (3) the payment flows which pass through the budget because of the common financing system. These factors become important when, for example, we consider countries, such as the UK, which have small agricultural sectors and are expected to make relatively large contributions to the CAP budget. Estimates by Rollo and Warwick (1979) avoid the influence of Community prices upon world prices and use the taxes and subsidies as a measure of the difference between Community and world prices; so the estimates measure balance of payments effects rather than the effects on price levels. What their results indicate is that the largest contributors to the CAP were West Germany, the UK and Italy, while France, the

Table 9.11 Agricultural Exports to Non-member Countries, 1974–84

	% of world exports	
	1974	1984
Wheat	8.0	14.0
Barley	25.0	22.0
Maize	1.3	3.2
Beef and veal	7.8	19.6
Pork	29.0	8.0
Poultry	5.6	23.6
Butter	28.3	50.0
Cheese	37.8	53.2
Skimmed milk powder	44.3	30.0
Whole milk powder	63.2	70.0
Sugar	5.1	15.4

Source: FAO (1976 and 1984)

Table 9.12 Real Incomes per Capita in Western Europe, 1950–86 (purchasing power
parities: UK = 100 in each year)

	1950	1960	1973	1981	1986
Austria	52	79	86	114	98
Belgium	92	91	109	126	98
Denmark	95	108	113	120	114
Finland	66	83	92	113	105
France	80	92	106	114	103
West Germany	69	106	109	125	114
Greece	34	40	55	61	54
Ireland	55	54	61	69	65
Italy	46	68	85	92	87
Luxembourg	119	129	121	114	126
Netherlands	84	92	103	108	105
Norway	90	91	107	137	132
Portugal	23	33	38	48	69
Spain	35	50	69	74	69
Sweden	110	122	133	133	140
Turkey	26	30	34	40	42

Sources: Summers, Kravis and Heston, (1986), UK Central Statistical Office (1987)

Netherlands, Denmark and Ireland received the greatest benefits. They took the
analysis a step further by providing estimates of the gains and losses within the
country resulting from the operations of CAP. Their results suggest that the gains
to producers tend to outweigh the gains to consumers. What the estimates do not
reveal, although they underline the problem, is whether rich farmers have gained
at the expense of poor farmers and whether the producer gains, in the case of
West Germany, accrue to those people who hold small plots of land, not for the
specific purpose of farming, but as a hedge against inflation.

Trade Diversion, Imports of Manufactures and Protectionism

The European Community sought self-sufficiency in food on the assumption that
it was efficient in the production of manufactures. There are some common tariffs
on imports of steel, textiles and clothing and some other manufactures but most
protectionist policies tend to be operated at national rather than at the Community
level; they are pursued through a variety of methods which tend not only to reduce
trade with non-members but also intra-Community trade. However, during the
1960s and 1970s the value of imports into the Community tended to rise much
faster than the Community's exports to the rest of the world. The reason for the
reversal of the trend was the faster growth of intra-Community trade, which tended
to suck in imports, the superior technology and low costs of Japanese engineering,

Table 9.13   Relative Real GDP per Capita in the European Community Regions, 1970–82
(all regions = 100)

	1970	1973	1982
Ile de France	160.0	164.0	163.4
'Prosperous Germany'	134.9	133.8	130.3
Luxembourg	127.0	130.0	116.8
Denmark	120.0	121.0	112.5
UK–south-east	112.0	111.0	109.6
Germany–remainder	111.0	109.0	107.9
Belgium	102.0	107.0	106.7
Netherlands	107.0	106.0	102.1
France–east and central less Paris	100.9	105.6	104.7
Italy–north-west	99.8	96.0	111.6
UK–remainder	91.0	90.6	87.1
France–west and south	83.8	87.0	88.6
Italy–north and central central	79.0	76.3	93.0
Ireland	61.0	65.0	67.6
Italy–Mezzogiorno	50.6	49.7	52.8

Source: Wabe, Eversley and Despicht (1983)

electrical and electronic goods and the cheaper costs of imports of textiles from the newly industrialising countries and Mediterranean associates, such as Portugal. In the 1980s there have been various attempts to increase restrictions on imports through the use of such devices as 'voluntary' export restraints and 'orderly marketing arrangements'. In 1982 the French attempted to stem the flow of video cassette recorders by insisting that all imports would have to pass through Poitiers, which is hundreds of miles from the ports of entry and possesses only a small customs crew. The effect was to impose a three-month delay on the clearance of consignments. But not all restrictions are successful. With the admission of Portugal, Spain and Greece into the Common Market former imports become components of intra-Community trade. Imports from the Far East are frequently 'smuggled' in via Norway and Sweden.

Intra-Community Differences in Incomes

So far we have concentrated on the gains from integration accruing to all members. But at the time of the UK entry there was a fear that the major gains would accrue to other countries, especially West Germany and France. In other words, the trade creation argument said nothing about the distribution of those gains. The argument was an extension of the analysis of the effects of free trade upon developing countries put forward by Myrdal (1957). Myrdal distinguished between spread and backwash effects. Spread effects accrue from trade creation: the availability of goods at lower resource cost, the diffusion of information about goods and technologies which would lead to changes in tastes and knowhow. Backwash effects may arise from the concentration of manufacturing industries in particular areas, which then attract resources from other regions and lead to an impoverishment of the periphery. Such polarisation can arise through the presence of economies of scale which lead to particular regions specialising in the production of certain commodities.

Tables 9.12 and 9.13 shed some light upon the distribution of real income per capita within the Community. In 1950 only Sweden and Luxembourg enjoyed higher real incomes than the UK; at the end of the 1950s they were joined by West Germany and Denmark. At the time of the first oil shock eight countries enjoyed a higher real income per capita than the UK: Belgium, Denmark, France, West Germany, Luxembourg, the Netherlands, Norway and Sweden. Between the two oil shocks they were joined by Austria and Finland. But after the second oil shock two slipped back — Austria and Belgium — and the relative differences between the UK and some of the leaders had narrowed.

(Table 9.13 extends the analysis by examining the distribution of incomes within the Community in greater detail. The highest real incomes are to be found in the so-called 'golden triangle' whose apices are Denmark, Basel and Hamburg, with an outlier around Paris.)

How can we account for the distribution of income and its movement over time? The first point to observe is that the catching up was not confined to countries within the original Community but included non-members, such as Denmark (in the 1950s) Norway (in the 1960s) and Austria (in the 1970s). The second point to note is that some countries benefited from the discovery of supplies of natural gas and oil (the Netherlands, Norway and the United Kingdom). Third, the peripheral countries (Greece, Ireland, Spain and Portugal) have shown a slight tendency to converge on the higher income countries. The fourth point is that the commonly held view that the UK has slipped badly behind the other European countries has not been so apparent since the second oil shock, the discovery of North Sea oil, increasing UK productivity and the use of purchasing power parities as a means of comparison. Finally, the comparisons need to be considered in terms of the sizes (populations) of countries and their natural resources.

But what of the effects of the Community upon individual members? Marques Mendes (1986) has attempted to shed some light upon the question by looking at the periods 1961–71 (when there were five member countries) and 1974–81 when the Community was enlarged to eight. His results are summarised in Table 9.14 and show some interesting results. In the early period it was the largest countries which experienced the lowest growth rates as a result of integration and the smallest countries which experienced the highest growth rates. In the second period the results were mixed but suggest that countries with high growth rates (pace Ireland) tended to have high growth rates as a result of integration.

What the article suggests, therefore, is that the spread and backwash effects

Table 9.14 Integration Effects on the Growth Rates of EC Countries

Contributions to growth	West Germany	France	Italy	Netherlands	Bel-Lux	UK	Ireland	Denmark
EC5 1961–71								
Actual growth	4.39	5.40	4.97	5.17	4.56	—	—	—
Growth due to EC	−0.02	−2.71	1.04	2.94	2.45			
EC8 1974–81								
Actual growth	2.65	2.66	2.74	1.99	2.03	1.24	3.84	1.98
Growth due to EC	0.91	1.57	0.42	0.53	0.71	0.37	0.31	−0.64

Source: Marques Mendes (1986)

of integration may be more complicated than had previously been thought. The small countries gained in the early period and the larger countries gained in the later period. The alleged superiority of the West Germany economy did not emerge immediately with the formation of the Community. (Of course, we need to enter a caveat. The differences in the sizes of the countries does mean that the problems of raising living standards for the larger countries may be more difficult initially, and the golden triangle does cut across national boundaries.)

West Germany

Since high incomes tend to be concentrated in West Germany we shall examine those features of the economy which might explain relative superiority in producing income. Table 9.15 provides some indicators of the structure and performance of the West German economy over the last decade. The most persistent feature of the German economy through the 1950s, 1960s and early 1970s was the undervaluation of the mark. This enabled West Germany to capture a large share of world trade in manufactures. But undervaluation raises the question of why there were no inflationary pressures, no upward push of wages and prices, comparable to those experienced by the UK after the 1949 devaluation. The usual explanation is the ingrained fear of inflation stemming from the experiences of the 1920s and the late 1940s which has led to conservative monetary and fiscal policies and a sharp distinction between the institutions responsible for monetary and fiscal policies and the government. The currency reform of 1948 led to the creation of the Bundesbank which was given the specific task of safeguarding the currency. To achieve that objective the Bank was given autonomy from the government and its policies have frequently differed from those desired by the

Table 9.15 West Germany: Main Economic Indicators, 1971–86

	GDP growth rate (%)	Industrial production growth rate (%)	Unemployment (%)	CPI (inflation rate, %)	Real wages growth rate (%)	Labour costs (1980=100)	Current balance (% GDP)	General government financial balance (% GDP)
1971	3.1	0.8	0.9	5.3	7.7	87.3	0.4	-0.2
1972	4.2	3.6	0.8	5.5	2.8	89.2	0.4	-0.5
1973	4.6	6.3	0.8	6.9	2.6	97.9	1.3	1.2
1974	0.5	-1.7	1.6	7.0	4.7	99.7	2.7	-1.3
1975	-1.7	-6.2	3.6	6.0	2.9	92.7	1.0	-5.7
1976	5.5	6.9	3.7	4.5	1.0	93.9	0.9	-3.5
1977	3.1	2.5	3.6	3.7	3.7	99.5	0.8	-2.4
1978	3.1	1.8	3.5	2.7	1.8	102.3	1.4	-2.5
1979	4.2	5.2	3.2	4.1	1.1	103.5	-0.8	-2.7
1980	1.8	0.0	3.0	5.5	0.5	100.0	-1.8	-3.1
1981	0.2	-1.5	4.4	6.3	-0.8	89.7	-0.8	-3.7
1982	-0.6	-2.9	6.9	5.3	-0.8	90.2	0.6	-3.3
1983	1.2	0.6	8.4	3.3	0.2	90.1	0.7	-2.4
1984	2.6	3.0	3.4	2.4	0.3	86.4	1.0	-1.9
1985	2.6	5.7	8.4	2.2	0.4	101.0	2.1	-1.1
1986	2.7	2.1	8.1	-0.2	0.3	101.0	4.0	-0.5

Source: OECD (1955–86)

government. The ability of the Bank to control the exchange rate has been reinforced by the special relationship established between financial and industrial
capital and by the aversion of the commercial banks to exchange rate instability.

Since the middle of the nineteenth century the banks have played an important
role in the collection and disposal of loanable funds — as compared with their
counterparts in the UK — and the German emphasis upon bank finance has provided the model for the Japanese. Not only do banks provide finance but they
also take an active part in industrial affairs. This participation is largely confined
to the three largest banks and has resulted in some 70 per cent of the shares of
the 425 largest firms being held by banks.

By virtue of their links with the banks, firms have been able to adopt much
higher gearing ratios and to obtain long-term debt finance (in contrast their UK
counterparts have relied upon retained profits for their long-term finance). Of
course, comparisons between UK and German methods of financing need to be
treated with caution. The Modigliani—Miller theorems have suggested that the
cost of capital may be independent of the method of gearing since whatever gearing ratio is adopted by firms can be undermined by lenders if they are free to
conduct their own transactions in capital markets which permit them to create
their own gearing ratios. Futhermore, even if lenders discount the future heavily
and are prepared to lend only for short periods, this does not remove the possibility
that firms may borrow for long periods if there are overlapping generations of
lenders who have access to a capital market. To suggest that British firms have
short-term horizons may be to confuse investment problems with financial problems. During the 1970s and 1980s the UK has been awash with loanable funds.
The problem may not be a lack of savings but a dearth of investment opportunities
— which may be due to the low levels of skills of the labour force. And what
the German banking system may give firms, through their greater involvement
in the affairs of firms, is a form of insider dealing which has not been available
to UK firms until the recent rise of institutional shareholding and the displacement of the traditional shareholders, the insurance companies.

We should finally observe that the powers of the banks have tended to diminish
in recent years — for two reasons. First, the great increase in company formation has tended to exceed their lending powers and there has been recourse to
the stock market. Second, there have been attempts to reduce the monopolistic
position of the banks and to compel them to reduce the values of their company
asset holdings. These two moves have tempted some to conclude that the UK
and German financial systems may be converging.

Within the manufacturing sector the striking feature is the method by which
the interests of shareholders and workers have been protected. On the one hand,
there is the distinction between the executive board (*Vorstand*) and the supervisory
board (*Aufsichstrat*). On the other hand, there is the system of codetermination
(*Mitbestimmung*) and the works' councils. And around these two interlocking
monitoring systems cluster all the accoutrements of German industrial organisation, such as the banks, the educational and vocational education systems and
the guest workers.

Whereas UK and US firms have tended to adopt a unitary management control system, with directors having to look after the interests of both financial shareholders and the general well being of the firms, German companies have adopted a two-tier system of executive and supervisory boards the origins of which go back to company legislation of 1870 and 1890. The function of the supervisory board is to provide an effective monitoring agency which is independent of the shareholders' meeting and the directors. The workers were incorporated through their trade unions into the supervisory boards through the system of codetermination in the 1950s but had been given some power on the shopfloor through the system of works' councils which were established in the 1920s. The supervisory board appoints the executive board which is responsible to the supervisory board for the management of firms. The result is a system which makes management an arbitrator between the competing claims of shareholders and workers. It therefore has advantages over the UK and US systems and even over the Japanese system of company control.

The UK system of industrial and financial controls tends to stress the conflictual nature of the relationships between managers, workers and shareholders, with the unions being a separate monitoring agency which has refused, and been refused, formal integration into the decision-making process. Like debenture holders, UK unions tend to regard their position as establishing a prior claim on the rents of firms and when offered seats on company boards have declined them. At lower levels shop stewards have been accorded limited recognition but they do not enjoy the status provided by the German works' councils.

At the end of the Second World War, German unionism was reconstructed along industrial lines — a move which elicited cautious comments from British observers. The mixture of craft, general and industrial unions prevalent in the UK was regarded as more organic. Industry boundaries, it was argued, are subject to change. Yet such generalisations ignored the point that with a system of industrial unions it becomes much easier to deal with issues at company and plant level; such unions further provide the basis of an incomes policy. German unions have been accommodated into the system of codetermination and works' councils and the fact that there were rank and file movements in the turbulent years of the 1970s should not obscure the point that the 'organic' UK system was also plagued with unofficial movements. It is, of course, possible that the decline in union membership in the 1980s and the increased power of the works' councils may lead the West German system in the direction of the Japanese model of company unionism.

But whatever direction German unionism takes, there is no doubt that industrial unionism fitted the systems of production management established after the Second World War. Under the influence of US management experts, German firms followed the same path as Japanese firms, introducing job rotation and hierarchical job ladders. In other words, they increased the capabilities of the shopfloor workers — a policy which was important for firms intent upon catching up on US firms by utilising US knowhow.

The contrast with UK firms is instructive. At the end of the Second World War the UK had much of its industrial capacity intact and its demobilisation of the armed forces was achieved quickly and easily. It also had good industrial designers. But its firms were not organised to exploit product and process inventions. The most striking example of the failure was the car industry. As Turner *et al.* (1967) observed, the UK had brilliant car designers but no production engineers. Instead, it had a system of unionism which tended to encourage sub-contracting, and diverse methods of wage payment. In attempting to achieve economies of scale, firms were encouraged to merge; but there was no attempt to rationalise production practices.

Underpinning the German institutional framework for industrial efficiency and worker participation is a well established vocational training programme where virtually all young people aged 15 to 18 years not in full-time education attend a vocational school on one day a week. At these schools they follow three-year courses which combine vocational and general core subjects and these courses lead to a final examination and recognised vocational qualifications. The German system may be regarded as a kind of apprenticeship system and can be contrasted with the relative scarcity of apprenticeships and learnerships in the UK. Even in German schools there is a greater emphasis upon vocational and technical skills which is absent in the UK; and the result is greater competence in mathematics. There is also more concern with the average and less gifted child in Germany than in the British system, which tends to create an elite, and even the French system, which tends to be intermediate between the British and German systems and puts a stress on training within firms.

The differences in educational and vocational training, as well as the emphasis upon industrial relations, has its effects upon attitudes to new technology and productivity. Even before the availability of North Sea oil, Britain tended to import skill-intensive and R&D-intensive goods and to export standardised products which were intensive in the use of unskilled labour. A National Institute study found that in 1977 German productivity was 1.4 times 'better' than in UK industry.

Yet despite the favourable organisational features of the German economy and its ability to maintain a sizable share of world trade in manufactures, the performance of the economy in the last decade (especially after OPEC II) has been disappointing. Growth rates slackened in the early 1980s, the inflation rate increased and that led to a questioning of previous policy measures. In 1978 at the Bonn Summit the German government committed itself to a series of measures which would add 1 per cent to GNP through reductions in direct taxes and increases in child allowances. The measures were seen as part of a policy to boost the world economy. In other words, West Germany, along with Japan, was to be the engine of the world economy. GNP did increase but there were numerous unfortunate side effects. Inflation increased and the current account became negative. The shift in the distribution of income led to a squeeze on profits and unemployment did not fall appreciably.

Inflation has now been checked and in 1986 the inflation rate became negative. GDP and industrial production growth rates have risen, although not to the levels of the 1960s. The profit rate has continued to show the long-run decline which became pronounced in the first half of the 1970s and has been attributed by Todd (1984b) to a rise in the strength of labour (which he found surprising in a country whose unions were traditionally docile).

During the 1970s and 1980s West Germany, along with most other industrial economies, experienced an increase in labour slack over capacity, suggesting increasing labour market rigidity. However, the U−V (unemployment−vacancy) ratio has tended to remain stable and given a fall in labour supply there has been an interest in the factors determining investment. West Germany may, in fact, have been experiencing a Minsky crisis in which debt liquidation has been aggravated by a squeeze on profits exerted by real wage rigidity.

Of course, the profitability of investment could be increased by increasing demand. But at least two factors have prevented that possibility. There is some evidence of declining consumption arising from the fact that although the population is ageing the numbers of old people are relatively low as a result of wartime deaths. Second, attempts to boost demand are still considered to be inflationary although the trade off between increases in nominal income and output is not so acute as in other countries.

Evidence on wage rigidity stems from a number of sources. Labour cost differentials are much lower in West Germany than in other countries, with the possible exception of Sweden, and have contributed to labour market inflexibility. Second, real labour cost gaps between money wages and productivity differ considerably across the economy. And in response to labour market rigidity there has been an increase in the numbers of part-time workers and a fall in full-time workers.

Attempts have been made to improve labour market flexibility. The reductions in hours which were negotiated in 1984 introduced the concept of the working year instead of the working week; this meant that daily and seasonal peaks could be worked without having to pay overtime rates. The federal government has attempted to reduce wage pressures by offering training and retraining programmes and by promoting employee participation schemes. But by way of a conclusion it would appear that West Germany has caught the 'British disease' as a result of a slow growth rate. As long as the growth rate was high workers were taken up by a fast-moving escalator and unionism tended to be weak. With the slowdown of the escalator unionism has tended to exert more influence on the economy.

France

If the German expansion of 1978 illustrated the dangers of unilateral expansion then the French policy of 1981 would seem to have provided confirmation. We begin with a discussion of some general aspects of the French economy.

From 1955 to 1968 the French economy grew at 5.7 per cent per annum — double the UK rate. The factors responsible for successful growth were a high

Table 9.16 France: Main Economic Indicators, 1971–86

	GDP growth rate (%)	Industrial production growth rate (%)	Unemployment (%)	CPI (inflation rate, %)	Real wages growth rate (%)	Labour costs (1980=100)	Current balance (% GDP)	General government financial balance (% GDP)
1971	5.4	4.5	2.6	5.5	5.4	106.2	0.6	0.7
1972	5.9	7.5	2.7	6.2	4.9	102.6	0.5	0.8
1973	5.4	7.0	2.6	7.3	6.7	112.4	0.2	0.9
1974	3.2	2.9	2.8	13.7	4.9	116.0	-2.3	0.6
1975	0.2	-7.4	4.1	11.8	4.9	116.8	0.0	-2.2
1976	5.2	9.0	4.4	9.6	4.1	116.3	-1.5	-0.5
1977	3.1	0.9	4.7	9.4	3.0	113.0	-0.7	-0.8
1978	3.8	2.7	5.2	9.1	3.6	110.3	0.6	-1.9
1979	3.3	4.4	5.9	10.8	2.1	110.1	0.0	-0.7
1980	1.1	0.0	6.3	13.6	1.3	100.0	-1.4	-0.2
1981	0.3	-0.8	7.3	13.4	0.9	114.4	-1.4	-2.8
1982	1.6	0.5	8.5	11.8	3.0	137.5	-3.0	-2.1
1983	0.7	1.0	8.7	9.6	1.5	155.1	-1.7	-3.1
1984	1.5	2.0	10.0	7.3	1.2	168.2	-0.8	-2.9
1985	1.1	2.0	10.5	5.9	0.0	178.4	-0.8	-2.6
1986	2.0	1.0	10.7	2.7	2.1	186.4	-0.9	-2.9

Source: NIESR (1970–87)

investment rate and an elastic supply of labour from the agricultural sector. A minor contributing factor was the government practice of indicative planning. But since the upsurge of strikes and student unrest in 1968 the performance of the French economy has been less impressive. Between 1974 and 1984 inflation averaged just over 10 per cent a year, with two peaks in 1974 and 1980 of 13.7 and 13.6 per cent respectively, and the growth rate fell below 3 per cent. Meanwhile unemployment continued its inexorable climb from 2.8 per cent in 1974 to 10.7 per cent in 1986 (Table 9.16).

Collective bargaining does not appear to play a significant part in wage determination in France, although appearances can be deceptive. Only about 20 per cent of the labour forces is unionised, as compared with about 40 per cent in the UK. The relative weakness of trade unionism and the radicalism of the French populace presents a paradox whose resolution depends upon drawing a distinction between the industrial working class and the peasantry. The trade union movement lacks the cohesion exhibited in the UK and is split between communist and non-communist unions and between white collar and manual workers' unions. British trade unions created the Labour Party and have tended to relegate political issues to the preserve of collective bargaining; French unionism has tended to be subservient to the syndicalist notion of political conflict and the general strike. As a consequence French unionism has not developed plant level bargaining to the same degree observed in the UK and most wage agreements tend to be negotiated at national level. But the ability to mount national strikes presupposes some form of grass roots organisation which may be present because a national minimum wage is set by the government in conjunction with unions and employers.

Since 1950 France has had a national minimum wage and between 1950 and 1968 the national minimum wage kept pace with the retail price index but increased at a slower rate than average hourly earnings so that wage differentials widened. In 1968 the national minimum wage was reformed with the aim of ensuring that the minimum increase should never be less than the increase in the purchasing power of average hourly earnings for the period in question. The law also allowed for the minimum to be raised by more than the amount justified by the automatic retail price indexation and in 1981 and 1982 it was raised on four occasions.

Information about underpayment is available from the annual declarations of wages which are legally required by the Treasury and from attempts at estimating the number of workers who are affected by the minimum wage increases. In 1977 the number of underpaid workers was estimated to be 6.5 per cent of the labour force; the majority tended to be women in the textile and clothing industries. The estimates of numbers affected by the minimum wage increases have varied with the size of the increases: between 1950 and 1984 some 4 per cent of workers tended to be affected by the wage but in 1968 some 12.5 per cent were affected by the 35 per cent wage increase. The 1977 wage survey revealed that the average degree of underpayment was 4 per cent of the minimum wage. In addition to underpayment there is also the problem of avoidance since it is possible to avoid paying the wage by employing temporary workers. The actual effect of minimum wage legislation on employment is therefore a matter of speculation. Martin (1984), for example, has suggested that the absence of any effect of the wage on youth employment might be because the wage is set at a level below the market clearing rate. Other evidence suggests that it is not the minimum wage *per se* which has led to the increase in unemployment but the existence of employment protection legislation and employment taxes which have inhibited the employment of workers (OECD 1986).

In contrast with the French situation, minimum wage legislation appears to have had significant employment effects in the Netherlands. Youth unemployment rose rapidly after the first oil price rise of 1974 and coincided with the extension of the statutory wage to young workers. However, the period 1974 to 1985 has provided only a limited number of observations and van Schaaijk (1983) assumed that a quasi-minimum wage existed for young workers from 1964 because their wages tended to be tied to the lowest wage of adult workers from that date. On the basis of data on changes in the relative wages and unemployment rates of younger and older workers he concluded that a 25 per cent reduction in the wages of young workers would correct the problem of youth unemployment. In 1981 the differential between younger and older workers was widened in the belief that such a reduction would relieve the government's budget and alleviate youth unemployment. In a subsequent study (1985) he suggested that the employment of young workers had increased and that it had been at the expense of older workers.

The UK does not have a general minimum wage. Instead it has wages councils which determine a legal minimum wage for workers who are mainly employed in retail trades, catering and agriculture. A study by Lund *et al.* (1982) of the workings of the Agricultural Wages Board between 1960 and 1981 revealed that the increases in real wage rates tended to be offset by changes in the real premium (the excess of earnings over wage rates). Lund *et al.* did not provide an explanation for the catching up process; but they did suggest that the determinants of investment should be explored. It is conceivable that investment in plant and machinery could raise the marginal product of labour and induce farmers to bid up wages. The rationale for such investment could lie in the interrelationships between rural and urban wages and agricultural subsidies. Over time the greater income elasticity of demand for manufactures and services over agricultural goods could lead to urban wages rising faster than farm wages and this, in turn, could lead to rural migration. An increase in investment could therefore be looked upon as a response to potential labour shortages. It should finally be noted that agricultural subsidies have been provided both as a means of improving efficiency by raising the capital—labour ratio and in order to ensure that farm wages do not fall behind urban wages.

A study of the effects of minimum wage legislation in the clothing industry by Morgan *et al.* (1985) revealed low demand elasticities for the period 1950—81, suggesting that a 10 per cent increase in real wages reduced employment by between 0.28 and 0.12 per cent for males and 0.28 and 0.09 for females. The higher figures were obtained from econometric models which assumed that firms were constrained in the amount that they could sell. But the most significant finding of the study was that the effects of changes in social security contributions (employment taxes) were three times greater than the effects of minimum wage changes.

In the UK there have been no studies of the employment effects of minimum wage legislation in the main sectors of retailing and catering. However, in 1986 the government did decide to remove young workers from scope of minimum wage legislation and to remove the provisions governing the payment of holiday remuneration.

This brings us to the subject of economic policy since the oil shocks. Following OPEC I there was an attempt to maintain a high level of employment. The result was an expansionary policy which led to a rise in the inflation rate, a perceptible rise in unemployment and current account deficits which caused France to leave the European Monetary System. In 1976 Raymond Barre replaced Jacques Chirac as Prime Minister and introduced a deflationary policy designed to balance the budget and moderate wage and price increases. The result was a balanced budget and a return to the European Monetary System. But rising unemployment began to undermine the economy: an increase in social transfers was financed by wage taxes which led to rising labour costs and an expansion of the welfare state.

The Mitterrand government of 1981 took advantage of the balanced budget and the fact that government spending was a low percentage of GDP to increase spending without raising taxes, to raise minimum wages, enact new labour laws and allow for monetary accommodation. The minimum wage was raised by 10 per cent in 1981 and real wages rose by 5 per cent. Weekly hours were reduced from 40 to 39 and paid holidays were increased from 4 to 5 weeks. In addition, there was a significant increase in nationalisation with 12 industrial firms, 36 banks and 2 financial corporations taken into the public sector with 2.6 per cent of the labour force becoming public employees. The share of publicly owned corporations in GDP was increased from 5 to 8 per cent.

The effects of the Mitterrand policies were to increase GDP but also to raise inflation compared with other OECD countries. Unemployment outside the large non-trading sector rose and was not reduced because of the increase in the minimum wage and the social security benefits. There was a fall in investment and a crisis of confidence which led to capital outflows. There were devaluations in 1981 and 1982.

The adverse effects of the Mitterrand policies were in part aggravated by the world recession in 1982; the overall effect was to lead to a movement to socialist austerity in 1982 and 1983. This deflationary policy has continued under the government of Chirac. But although the inflation rate has fallen and the growth rate, labour costs and the current balance improved, unemployment has risen and government expenditure still remains high by the standards of the 1970s.

Italy

Italian unemployment statistics need to be treated with caution. On the assumption that the demand for money function is stable, comparisons of the money supply required to drive the recorded goods and services round the economy suggest that there is a large underground economy operating in Italy which produces the equivalent of about 15 per cent of GDP and employs the equivalent of about 20 per cent of the labour force (Table 9.17). These figures may be compared with the findings for the UK equivalent of between 3 and 5 per cent of GDP although some estimates go as high as 15 per cent. However, for both countries the estimates vary according to the periods for which observations are made and the methods of recording transactions.

A second factor influencing the labour market is the compensation fund (*Cassa Integrazione Guadagni*) which is paid to workers who have been made redundant by their firms and who receive 80 per cent of the contractual wage from the state while still remaining, from the legal standpoint, employees of their firms. It was introduced as a method of restructuring the labour force by enabling redundant workers to be regarded as 'employed' while they found new jobs. In 1985 the number registered under scheme was equivalent to 14.5 per cent of the officially unemployed and their inclusion would have raised the official unemployment rate from 10.4 to 12.5 per cent. A third factor affecting the unemployment statistics is that the quarterly labour force surveys include 'marginal workers' in the unemployed; that is, housewives, students and pensioners who might take a job if one were offered and who comprise some 40 per cent of total job seekers. A fourth factor influencing activity rates and unemployment rates is the legislation governing the hiring and firing of workers. Firms must follow strict procedures for hiring workers which stipulate that they must hire from waiting lists (*colocamento*) which rank the unemployed according to duration of unemployment, age and family situation — a procedure which penalises the young. In addition, there is evidence of overqualification, with higher unemployment rates for those with higher education.

Between 1945 and 1965 the annual growth rate was some 5—6 per cent, which was exceeded only by Japan. This high growth rate was achieved by tapping a large labour surplus and by the discovery of new energy sources. But by 1965 there was growing dissatisfaction with wages. Real national income had grown rapidly but wages had not kept pace. In 1969 there was a major strike wave which led to wages rising by 20 per cent and there were reductions in weekly hours in 1972. In addition wages were indexed to the cost of living (the so-called *scala mobile*).

Table 9.17 Italy: Main Economic Indicators, 1971–86

	GDP growth rate (%)	Industrial production growth rate (%)	Unemployment (%)	CPI (inflation rate, %)	Real wages growth rate (%)	Labour costs (1980=100)	Current balance (% GDP)	General government financial balance (% GDP)
1971	1.6	-0.6	5.3	4.8	8.3	106.1	1.8	-5.2
1972	3.2	4.9	6.3	5.7	4.5	106.9	1.6	-7.5
1973	7.0	9.7	6.2	10.8	12.1	105.8	-1.7	-7.0
1974	4.1	4.0	5.3	19.1	2.8	101.4	-4.6	-7.0
1975	-3.6	-8.8	5.8	17.0	8.3	108.5	-0.2	-11.7
1976	5.9	11.6	6.6	16.8	3.5	97.0	-1.5	-9.0
1977	1.9	0.0	7.0	17.0	9.3	95.1	1.2	-8.0
1978	2.7	1.9	7.1	12.1	3.6	92.5	2.4	-9.7
1979	4.9	6.7	7.6	14.8	3.7	96.6	1.7	-9.5
1980	3.9	5.2	7.5	21.2	-2.2	100.0	-2.5	-8.0
1981	0.2	-2.2	8.3	17.3	4.5	100.1	-2.3	-11.9
1982	-0.5	-3.1	9.0	16.5	0.5	103.6	-1.6	-12.6
1983	-0.4	-2.4	9.8	14.6	4.3	105.3	0.2	-11.7
1984	2.6	3.4	10.2	10.8	0.6	107.7	-0.9	-13.0
1985	2.3	1.2	10.1	9.2	0.8	117.7	-0.5	-12.6
1986	2.7	2.7	11.1	5.8	3.2	123.5	0.4	-12.1

Source: NIESR (1970–86)

The initial response to the first oil shock was to seek to maintain the growth rate of the economy through borrowing and as a result GDP rose by 7 per cent in 1973. But in the following year the balance of payments deteriorated and restrictive monetary and fiscal policies had to be imposed. In 1975 an expansionary policy was resumed and between 1975 and 1978 there were rising exports and inflation.

The effect of OPEC II was to cause the terms of trade to deteriorate by about 10 per cent and there was a recession in 1980. There was another attempt to maintain a high level of employment through fiscal expansion but this led to a deterioration in the balance of payments, a devaluation of the lira and the introduction of tighter monetary controls. The persistent high level of imbalances in the government's budgets then forced an attempt at fiscal reform. Unfortunately, the political structure of multi-party coalitions and weak parliamentary majorities has always made it difficult for governments either to raise taxes or to abolish the indexing of public sector pay. The rising trend of unemployment has also made it difficult to reduce social security benefits. The overall effect has been to make monetary policy, as operated by the relatively independent Bank of Italy, the main instrument of economic policy. But given the reluctance to restructure the budget and the absence of labour market legislation, it is not surprising that the inflation rate has been high. (It might have been higher but for the restraining influence exerted by the EMS.)

The United Kingdom (Table 9.18)

The United Kingdom joined the European Community in order to revive a flagging economy. The causes of the slow rate of growth of the UK economy have been the subject of continuous discussion since the last quarter of the nineteenth century when competition from Germany and the United States begain to threaten Britain's leadership of the world economy. Kaldor (1966) has suggested that international growth rates are strongly influenced by the growth rate attained at take off and that Britain's growth rate in the late eighteenth and nineteenth century was low compared with those required from its later challengers. Lewis (1978) provided an explanation of the slow down of the last quarter of the nineteenth century and many of the factors which he isolated were still being canvassed in the post-war period.

> Britain was caught in a set of ideological traps. All the strategies available to her were blocked off in one way or another. She could not lower costs because of the unions, or switch to American-type technology because of the slower pace of British workers. She could not reduce her propensity to import by imposing a tariff or by devaluing her currency, or by paying export subsidies. She could not pioneer in developing new commodities because this required a scientific base which did not accord with her humanistic snobbery. So instead she invested her savings abroad; the economy decelerated, the average level of unemployment increased and her young people

Table 9.18 UK: Main Economic Indicators, 1971–87

Year	GDP growth rate (%)	Industrial production growth rate (%)	Unemployment (%)	CPI (inflation rate, %)	Real wages growth rate (%)	Labour costs (1980=100)	Current balance (% GDP)	General government financial balance (% GDP)
1971	2.7	-0.7	3.7	9.4	2.8	78.6	2.0	1.4
1972	2.3	1.8	4.0	7.1	6.2	77.6	0.4	-1.9
1973	7.9	9.0	3.0	9.2	3.4	69.6	-1.4	-3.5
1974	-1.1	-1.7	2.9	16.0	1.0	70.2	-4.0	-3.8
1975	-0.7	-5.4	4.3	24.2	4.7	75.8	-1.5	-4.8
1976	3.8	3.3	5.7	16.5	2.8	69.0	-0.7	-5.0
1977	1.0	5.1	6.1	15.8	-9.6	66.9	0.0	-3.5
1978	3.6	3.0	6.0	8.3	9.2	72.6	0.7	-4.4
1979	2.1	3.8	5.1	13.4	1.4	83.8	-0.3	-3.2
1980	-2.3	-6.7	6.6	18.0	-0.7	100.0	1.4	-3.9
1981	-1.4	-3.4	9.9	11.9	-1.8	104.5	2.6	-3.2
1982	-1.5	1.9	11.4	8.6	-1.4	100.7	2.0	-2.3
1983	3.4	3.6	12.6	4.6	1.0	94.9	0.7	-3.5
1984	1.8	1.2	13.0	5.0	2.5	94.4		-4.0
1985	1.5	4.7	11.3	6.1	4.9	100.0		-2.8
1986	2.6	1.7	11.5	3.3	4.6	104.8		-3.0

emigrated. . . . The British relied on the market economy to bring them into equilibrium; instead it brought them to relative stagnation.

After the Second World War the search for causes of slow growth became more intensive.

Concern with the decline of the manufacturing sector should not be taken too far. At the end of the Second World War there was a need to increase overseas earnings in order to replace the income lost from the overseas assets which had been destroyed during the war or had been sold in order to pay for the war effort. In Asia the independence of many countries led them to set up their own import competing industries. The export drive of the late 1940s and early 1950s did succeed in raising the UK's share of world trade; but it could not have continued once West Germany and Japan made the adjustment to peace-time trading. Some contraction of the UK share of world manufacturing was inevitable and by the early 1970s it had stabilised. But some further reduction was also to be expected following the discovery and exploitation of North Sea oil; it could have been averted only if there had been an inflow of other resources, such as happened in the USA, Canada and Australia.

Nevertheless there are still problems. There is the problem of what happens after the North Sea oil has been exhausted. There is the problem of whether the service sector can provide enough overseas earnings. There is the problem of whether too little is spent on R&D and whether the UK's exports embody low technology and unskilled labour and are vulnerable to competition from the newly industrialising countries. These are, in fact, the old problems because the UK has always had an abundance of natural resources — in the nineteenth century coal was a major export. When the challenge from the United States and Europe emerged in the last quarter of the nineteenth century Britain increased its exports of coal and a condition of immiserising growth developed comparable to that experienced by some developing countries in the twentieth century who find that they have to export more and more natural resources and agricultural commodities in order to pay for a given quantum of imports.

The Structure of Exports and Imports

Since the emergence of overseas competitors in the mid-1950s there have been numerous adjustments in the structure of UK's foreign trade. Table 9.19 shows the large rise in exports to Western Europe, especially to the European Community, which has been accompanied by an equally large rise in imports. But trade with North America has also increased and some 80 per cent of trade in goods is now conducted with advanced countries. The bulk of the exports tend to be engineering products, with fuel oils having become important in the 1980s. On the import side there has been a decline in the imports of foodstuffs as a result of greater self-sufficiency; but there has been an increase in imports of manufac-

Table 9.19 Destination of Exports and Origin of Imports, UK, 1955 and 1985 (%)

Regions/Countries	Exports fob		Imports cif	
	1955	1985	1955	1985
Western Europe	28.9	58.3	25.7	63.1
EEC	15.0	46.3	12.6	46.0
North America	12.0	17.0	19.5	13.8
USA	7.1	14.7	10.9	11.7
Other developed	21.1	4.8	14.2	7.5
Japan	0.6	1.3	0.6	3.4
All developed	62.0	80.0	59.4	84.3

Source: United Kingdom Balance of Payments (1986)

tured goods. Thus, the nineteenth-century situation of Britain being an exporter of manufactures and coal and an importer of foodstuffs has been replaced by one where the UK exports manufactures and fuel oils and imports manufactures. Even the trade pattern of the 1950s and 1960s has now vanished. In the first two decades after the war the UK tended to have a deficit on visibles and a surplus on invisibles. In the 1970s the deficit on visibles was transformed by earnings from oil exports and the surplus on invisibles has tended to come from services rather than profits and interest from overseas assets. However, one feature remains common to both periods: the continued role of the UK as an exporter of long-term capital.

The Effects of North Sea Oil

The short- and long-run effects of North Sea oil have been a matter of considerable controversy. It has been alleged that its effects have been to destroy the manufacturing base of the economy and to raise the level of unemployment. Others have suggested that when the oil runs out it will be a relatively simple matter to switch back to manufacturing.

The short-run effects of North Sea oil are fairly easily identified. The windfall enabled the UK to sell oil for manufactures and to expand the service sector. The export of oil caused a rise in the exchange rate; this rise made UK manufactures uncompetitive. At existing prices and the new higher exchange rates foreigners were no longer willing to buy UK goods and UK residents found it cheaper to import manufactures, causing a contraction of the manufacturing base.

The expansion of services and the contraction of manufacturing, with accompanying unemployment, has been called the Dutch disease on the grounds that a similar pattern emerged in the Netherlands when natural gas was discovered in the 1960s. Evidence of the Dutch disease has also been found in Jamaica, Norway, Australia and Indonesia. In other words, it has occurred in every country which has had a windfall of natural resources which was not subsequently accompanied by an increase in other factors of production. But, despite the presence of similar events in other countries, there are several unanswered questions. First, was the level of increase in unemployment necessary? Second, should some of the oil revenues have been used to re-equip manufacturing to ensure its competitiveness when the oil runs out?

That some rise in the exchange rate was inevitable must be accepted because there was no other way in which the gains from the oil could have been realised. But the sharp rise in the exchange rate and the severe and prolonged unemployment which resulted do seem to have been less than inevitable. The exploitation of North Sea oil should have led to a rise in national income and to some frictional unemployment. Instead, the exchange rate rose dramatically, national income stagnated and long-term unemployment increased — which suggests that there was a contraction of the money supply and aggregate money demand. It was, of course, tempting to expand oil production because of the high price of oil and that would have raised the exchange rate. But the government reduced aggregate money demand in order to curb public sector borrowing. Unfortunately, the reduction in aggregate money demand was carried too far.

Overseas Investment

Some portion of the oil revenues were invested abroad and that helped to reduce the rise in the exchange rate. However, that policy resurrected the question of whether overseas investment was desirable. The immediate issue was whether some portion of the oil revenues should be used to re-equip industry and prepare it for the day when the oil ran out. The long-term issue was whether controls should be re-imposed on capital flows on the grounds that overseas investment was diverting money from investment in UK industry.

The short-term issue hinges on the question of whether there are increasing returns in manufacturing. If there are increasing returns and they are acquired by learning by doing then there are *prima facie* grounds for investing in industry. A failure to invest would lead to a large gap in knowhow between the UK and other countries. However, even if there are learning effects it is not at all obvious which industries will be the most important in twenty years' time.

The longer-term issue concerning British overseas investment goes back to the nineteenth century when Germany and the USA were 'catching up'. In the 1920s Keynes cautioned against foreign lending on the grounds that it could lead to unemployment. More recently, the TUC has argued that foreign lending raises interest rates at home and leads to a fall in domestic investment and an increase in unemployment. But much depends upon what foreigners do with their loans. Initially, foreign interest rates must be higher than UK rates in order to induce Britons to want to buy foreign assets. The effect of exchanging sterling for foreign currencies is that the exchange rate falls. But what then do foreigners do with their sterling? Unless they want to increase their holdings of sterling they may buy UK assets. Until all the decisions have been implemented and exchange rate, asset prices and interest rates have settled into equilibrium it is impossible to say what the long-term effect on the UK economy will be. The alternative to overseas investment might have been a larger increase in imports which would have depressed manufacturing industry further. In fact, capital controls to increase employment seem to be a second best or third best policy to a fiscal expansion or wage adjustments. But having emphasised the points in contention it has to be recognised that developing countries, such as Japan, did use capital controls in the 1950s and 1960s.

Industrial Competitiveness

So far we have concentrated upon the problems associated with the discovery and exploitation of North Sea oil; but it is now time to consider the more general issues surrounding Britain's competitiveness. Table 9.20 shows that over the long run UK productivity growth has been lower than in most other countries and even the relative improvement since the second oil shock has not resulted in a significant closing of the gap in productivity levels between the UK and West Germany and the USA (Table 9.21). Of course, a breakdown between manufactures and services, as in Table 9.22, does show that the UK has tended to be more efficient in non-manufacturing than Europe and the USA. But not all services are tradable goods — even though some foreigners may come to London to buy their clothing in Marks and Spencer's shops. Nor are all jobs in the service sector full-time; nor do services bring in the same revenue as manufactures; it takes about a 3 per cent increase in the output of the service sector to compensate for a 1 per cent contraction in manufactures. We are therefore left with some awkward questions concerning the efficiency of the residual manufacturing sector.

Kaldor (1966) suggested that manufacturing is subject to increasing returns and to greater possibilities for invention. Taking up Verdoorn's Law, which postulates

Table 9.20 Growth Rates of Real Output per Worker Employed (% per Annum)

	UK	USA	France	West Germany	Italy	Japan
1873–99	1.2	1.9	1.3	1.5	0.3	1.1
1899–1913	0.5	1.3	1.6	1.5	2.5	1.8
1913–24	0.3	1.7	0.8	−0.9	−0.1	3.2
1924–37	1.0	1.4	1.4	3.0	1.8	2.7
1937–51	1.0	2.3	1.7	1.0	1.4	−1.3
1951–64	2.3	2.5	4.3	5.1	5.6	7.6
1964–73	2.6	1.6	4.6	4.4	5.0	8.4
1973–79	1.2	−0.2	2.8	2.9	1.8	2.9
1979–86	1.8	0.6	1.6	1.7	1.2	2.8

Sources: Matthews *et al.* (1982), OECD (1986)

Table 9.21 Output per Employee in Manufacturing, 1951−86 (UK 1970=100)

	West Germany/UK	*USA/UK*
1951	0.77	2.73
1964	1.10	3.04
1973	1.21	2.84
1979	1.39	2.99
1986	1.37	2.95

Sources: Prais (1981), IMF (1986)

Table 9.22 Annual Average Growth Rates by Sectors, 1961−84

	1961−72	*1972−79*	*1979−84*
Manufacturing			
UK	4.21	2.13	3.99
USA	3.10	2.00	2.67
Europe	5.27	4.27	3.71
Non-manufacturing			
UK	3.17	2.14	2.17
USA	1.91	0.51	0.13
Europe	4.51	3.05	1.48

Source: Gordon (1987)

that increasing manufacturing output is associated with increasing productivity, and recognising that there were no labour reserves in agriculture, he proposed that a tax on services (the Selective Employment Tax) and exchange rate depreciation might remove the balance of payments constraint to export-led growth. A variation on this theme was later put forward by Bacon and Eltis (1978), who suggested that it was the public sector which was crowding out manufacturing.

Most empirical work has not supported Verdoorn's Law. Rowthorn (1975) argued that Kaldor's results were significantly influenced by the inclusion of Japan. Chatteriji and Wickens (1983) took the view that UK manufacturing had been characterised by Okun's Law rather than Verdoorn's Law: there was a short-run (cyclical) relationship between employment growth and productivity but not a long-run relationship. During recessions labour hoarding rose and productivity fell; in the succeeding booms idle labour was pressed into use and productivity rose. The Selective Employment Tax did achieve some of its objectives but it was disliked and later withdrawn (Thirlwall 1987). The Bacon and Eltis theory has been criticised on the grounds that public sector spending has been at the expense of private sector consumption rather than private investment. Finally, the main obstacle to exchange rate depreciation as a means of improving economic growth appears to have been the resistance of trade unions to real wage reductions.

It is, in fact, the supply-side problems which have attracted the most attention and they have been identified as: (1) an inability to manage large plants; (2) low capital per worker; (3) low levels of education and training of managers and workers; (4) militant unions; (5) low levels of spending on R&D (except for defence spending). The problems of managing large plants have been highlighted by Prais (1981a) and by the Department of Employment's study of strike activity (Smith 1978). Large plants tend to have more strikes than small plants and more strikes than their counterparts in other countries; but the association has not been universal in the UK and there are some industries in which large plants are relatively strike free (such as food processing).

Prais (1981a) has uncovered evidence which suggests that there has been over-manning and difficulties in introducing improvements and Batstone (1986) took the view that British trade unions tended to have a narrow sectional outlook and lack an ability to coordinate and implement strategies (in sharp contrast to unions in Sweden and West Germany). However, a study by Millward and Stevens (1986) found evidence of a greater willingness of workers to accept new ideas during the recent recession.

Despite the evidence that there is no lack of savings in the UK (House of Lords 1980), the amount spent on R&D has been low and has been concentrated, in the main, upon defence. Defence contracts tend to be cost-plus and there is no great incentive to efficiency. Indeed, the contrast between ICI and GEC is instructive. GEC has relied heavily upon defence contracts and upon investing money in the City. No doubt financial prudence can be defended on the grounds that during a period of inflation a higher return can be obtained from government assets than from commercial ventures. But it does lead, in the long run, to a loss of industrial efficiency. In contrast, ICI has had a good record in research and has shown vigorous expansion in overseas markets.

Poor productivity has been attributed to fragmented unionism, concentration on defence R&D, a tendency for the capital market to tolerate inefficiency and the fact that a large part of industry is in the public sector. It has also been attributed to the poor quality of management. Industrial training has tended to lag behind that in other countries. As we noted earlier, in Japan some two-thirds of young peopld tend to continue in higher education whereas in the UK two-thirds tend to finish full-time education at the age of 16. In the USA most young people do not take up full-time jobs until they are 21 and in West Germany formal education continues up to the age of 18. These differences in the length of schooling and associated industrial training seem to be linked with the industrial structure prevailing in those countries and with the dates at which industrialisation began. In Britain an early start and abundant natural resources have led to a concentration on low technology and the use of unskilled labour — Britain's comparative advantage was in natural resources. Coming later the USA, Japan and Germany saw the need to train workers to use higher technology. In the USA there is a relative absence of apprenticeships which leads to a stress upon the acquisition of basic skills in college and university. In the UK the apprenticeship system became transformed into a method of labour supply restriction and it collapsed in the 1980s. An Industrial Training Act was passed in 1964 and then abandoned because of criticisms that it was too bureaucratic. Its successor has, however, proved to be equally weak; engineering employers have criticised their statutory training board and in other industries non-statutory boards have often been unsuccessful.

Monetary, Fiscal and Incomes Policies

So far we have neglected the role of macroeconomic policies pursued in the UK since the first oil shock and their differences from those pursued in Japan, the United States and other European countries. We begin therefore with some definitions. Following Friedman we may define a monetary policy as any policy which results in a change in the money supply. This definition tends to leave as fiscal policy only those measures which are compatible with a balanced budget. The distinction between monetary and fiscal policy therefore turns upon the channels through which the money supply is varied. In the case of monetary policy proper, the emphasis is upon open market operations and changes in reserve requirements; in the case of fiscal policy the stress is upon budget surpluses and deficits. An incomes policy is not designed specifically to change the money supply but to exert pressure upon the rate of change of money incomes. It is, however, analogous to a tax or borrowing condition since the implicit message behind an incomes policy is that a restraint on incomes today will lead to an increase in incomes tomorrow. As such, incomes policies are analogous to deficit financing and the system of post-war credits used during the Second World War.

Following OPEC I there was an attempt to maintain the level of aggregate money demand in order to counteract the possibilities of a recession. It was also difficult for a Labour government to pursue deflationary policies in the wake of the miners' strike which increased the power of the trade unions; the result was a compromise. Aggregate money demand was to be maintained and there was to be an incomes policy (the Social Contract). The policy mix was not successful. Despite the Social Contract wages rose by over 30 per cent in 1975 and the company sector, faced with increasing costs, went into deficit and began shedding labour and reducing stocks.

Faced with a loss of control over the economy the government moved to a more stringent form of demand management. Yet the economy was to be expanded by allowing the exchange rate to depreciate and another incomes policy was introduced to counteract any real wage resistance to the fall in the value of sterling. The policy failed during the so-called winter of discontent when the government tried to keep wages down to 5 per cent despite the fact that prices were increasing by 15 per cent. Strikes by local government workers were an influential factor in the election of a Conservative government in 1979.

The Conservative government introduced a shift towards supply-side economics.

There was greater emphasis on combating inflation through the control of the money supply and fiscal policy was to be used to improve the allocation of resources. In other words, fiscal policy was to be used for microeconomic objectives. income policies were abolished for the private sector although wage norms were retained for the public sector. Legislation was introduced to curb the power of the trade unions. There was, however, a noticeable gap between intentions and outcomes. In part, the divergence between grasp and reach was due to the need to honour commitments entered into by previous governments: for example, the government had to accept the payment of a 25 per cent wage increase to local government workers stemming from an arbitration award. But setting that aside wages rose in the private sector as a result of a shift from income taxation to VAT.

The more serious problems arose from the difficulties encountered in controlling the money supply. In 1979 the government introduced its medium term financial strategy which aimed to steadily reduce the rate of increase of the money supply in order to achieve a zero rate of inflation. But the policy did not work; actual increases in the money stock tended to be higher than target increases while the velocity of circulation of money tended to fall sharply. This led some observers to suggest that the target should be set in terms of both the stock and the velocity of circulation of money — which seemed to be a return to Keynesian ideas of controlling agrregate money demand. The reasons which led to the fall in the velocity are not fully established but the reduction in the inflation rate may have been a factor leading people to hold more money; changes in monetary institutions and the controls imposed upon institutions may have been another contributing factor. The problems of controlling the money supply were to lead later to a softening of the emphasis upon the money supply and the public sector borrowing requirement and to an increased interest in exchange rate management.

By 1985 the macroeconomy seemed to be in some semblance of control with inflation having fallen and wage increases being lower than in the 1970s. There were, however, some disturbing features. Despite the high levels of unemployment money wages seemed to continue increasing (that the increases were at a lower rate has been attributed to the fall in the prices of raw materials; but that they are still increasing seems difficult to assimilate). Two explanations have been put forward. The first interpretation is that there is a distinction between insiders and outsiders and that those in jobs (insiders) are not influenced by the level of unemployment but may moderate their demands if wage unemployment is increasing. The problem then becomes one of reducing the power of insiders through wage subsidies to the unemployed or legislation restricting the powers of trade unions. The second factor which has been isolated is the immobility of labour stemming from the existence of public housing and the relative absence of a market in rented properties. As a result increases in demand for labour in the South have not been matched by inflows of labour because of the housing shortage. Wages therefore rose in the South of England and have led to pressures for comparable wage increases elsewhere and to an induced increase in unemployment. Several solutions have been suggested, such as inducing firms to leave London and the introduction of subsidies for workers to move.

Ireland

So far we have concentrated upon the high- and medium-income countries of the Community. We now turn to a consideration of one of the poorer countries, Ireland. Ireland is, was and always will be a dependent economy. By the Act of Union with England it entered into a free trade area and its textile industries were destroyed. It then became an agrarian economy exporting grain to England and growing potatoes for its subsisting peasants. In the 1840s the potato blight resulted in a paradox of famine being associated with food shipments to England. The Great Hunger gave rise to a Great Anger and to a war of liberation. After independence Ireland tended to become inward looking and its economy stagnated. In the 1960s the policy began to change and foreign investment was encouraged. However, Ireland has still remained an agrarian economy although there has been some development of food processing; hence the decision to enter the Economic Community.

Although Irish farmers benefited from the CAP, the involvement in the Community led to moves to create a welfare state along the lines of those in Western Europe. To finance welfare schemes governments in the 1970s resorted to borrowing. As a proportion of gross domestic product, Ireland's debt became the largest in Europe. To meet the interest payments taxes were increased and unemployment rose to 19 per cent to become the highest in Europe (apart from Spain). In the mid-1980s, Ireland faced a crisis. It has sought to encourage foreign investment by the use of subsidies but those allowances penalised indigenous firms. It has tried to induce high-tech firms to establish subsidiaries in Ireland; but such industries can also move out. It has too small a population to provide a large domestic market and for firms seeking large markets attractive subsidies were being offered by other Community members. Ireland could concentrate upon its comparative advantage in agriculture; but it faces the possibility that CAP subsidies could be reduced and there is always the problem of competing against the new entrants to the Community, such as Spain, Portugal, Greece and possibly Norway, Austria and Turkey. There therefore remains only the historical solution — migration.

Non-EC Members: Austria, Sweden and Switzerland

By way of a parenthesis we can now consider the economic performances of three non-members of the EEC. All three countries have common features: they are small open economies; their political systems are highly democratic and they are buffer states between East and West. But thereafter the differences begin to emerge. Sweden and Switzerland managed to avoid involvement in two world wars and have enjoyed prolonged periods of peace and prosperity, while Austria was a casualty in both wars.

Austria

Austria's unemployment rate was higher than that of the UK in the 1960s; but these relative positions became reversed in the 1970s. In the 1960s Austria's unemployment rate was 2.0 per cent as compared with 1.7 per cent in the UK. But by 1985 Austria's unemployment rate was 3 per cent while that of the UK had risen to 13 per cent. However, as we observed in the case of Japan, the OECD standardised unemployment rates need qualification. The growth of the Austrian labour force has been much slower than the UK in the 1970s and 1980s and a more obvious correction arises from the Austrian use of guest workers.

But setting aside the issues of comparability we can concentrate upon the various factors which might explain Austria's low unemployment rate. There has been considerable unanimity among the different interest groups in society. The civil wars of the inter-war years and successive invasions by Germany and the USSR have promoted social cohesion; a social partnership has emerged. The Austrian political chamber system consists of chambers for the various professions, including labour, which are the legal representatives of their members in the legislative process and are involved in top level decisions about economic policy. This high degree of social cohesion is underlined by the long lasting coalition government between the Austrian Socialist Party and the Austrian People's Party.

Second, there has been agreement on the main methods of what has been called Austro-Keynesianism. Discretionary fiscal policy has been rejected in favour of setting a full employment budget balance so as to achieve long-run economic growth and ensuring short-run stability by the use of a wide range of automatic stabilisers. Fiscal policy has been allied to a monetary policy which initially tied the schilling to a European currency basket and subsequently to the German mark. The effect has been to tie the fortunes of a small open economy to what has been, until recently, the most dynamic of its trading partners. But to call the policy Austro-Keynesian may be a misnomer; although it incorporates the Keynesian emphasis upon demand management while rejecting the temptation to use discretionary fiscal policies for electoral purposes, the monetary—fiscal policy is similar to that suggested by Friedman.

The third feature of Austrian economic policy has been the emphasis upon incomes policy, with union leaders consciously pursuing a wages policy linked to the long-run growth of productivity. Austria has been notable among advanced countries for having a high degree of wage flexibility. A rise in unemployment of 0.5 per cent tends to reduce wage inflation by about 1 per cent which is close to the degree of wage flexibility observed in Japan but smaller than that of the UK (1.9 per cent).

Sweden

In the 1950s and 1960s Sweden acquired a reputation for economic growth combined with price level stability, a high level of employment and a high degree of income equality. The Swedish model was considered to be the successful outcome of a 'middle way' which steered between communism and capitalism. The origins of the model were seen to lie in the experiences of the 1930s and the thinking of a long line of distinguished economists who created the Stockholm School.

Swedish economic theory descended from Wicksell who was concerned with price level stability which he saw in terms of divergences between: (1) a money rate of interest and a natural rate of interest; (2) savings and investment; and (3) the marginal product of capital and the rate of interest. These divergences were regarded as elaborations of the quantity theory of money whereby changes in the quantity of money led to cumulative expansions and contractions and a change in the price level. An increase in the quantity of money would push the money rate of interest below the real rate, create a gap between the marginal product of capital and the money rate of interest and lead to an increase in investment over the normal flow of savings. In monetary equilibrium all these divergences would disappear and money would be neutral.

In subsequent work Wicksell provided a rule for economic stability in a growing economy whereby wages were to increase in line with productivity and the price level was to remain constant. This rule provoked Davidson to suggest that wages should remain constant and the price level should fall as productivity increased. The resolution of what came to be known as the Wicksell–Davidson controversy was subsequently found to rest upon implicit assumptions concerning expectations and the causes of productivity increases. The problem of expectations led Myrdal (1957) to draw a distinction between *ex ante* investment and savings and *ex post* investment and savings and to postulate that monetary equilibrium occurred when *ex ante* investment and savings were equal.

But the Stockholm School continued to assume full employment and their analysis contained no discussion of changes in output. Lundberg (1985) has accepted this criticism of the Stockholm School but has argued that their originality lay in their concern with: (1) the stabilisation of the price level; (2) the use of sequence analysis; (3) the international aspects of the macroeconomy; and (4) the policy conclusions to be derived from theory. But Lundberg has underestimated the strength of Keynesian economics. In his earlier works, *The Tract on Monetary Reform* and *The Treatise on Money*, Keynes tackled the problems of price stability and dealt with the issues of public finance as well as presenting an account of what later came to be called the monetary theory of the balance of payments.

Lundberg overlooks the strength of Keynes's crticism of period analysis which he had set out in correspondence with Ohlin and which argued that there were problems in coping with periods of different length (Keynes 1973b). The *General Theory* may have been addressed to professional economists but the policy recommendations had appeared in the Liberal Party's Yellow Books and in his pamphlet *Can Lloyd George Do It?*; it was from from these sources that Swedish economists drew their policy proposals.

In the 1950s and 1960s Swedish and Keynesian theorising were fused to produce an economic policy based upon the use of automatic stabilisers and a social policy which stressed equality and the extension of the welfare state. Through the 1950s and 1960s GNP grew at 3 per cent per annum. There were, of course, fluctuations, cycles of about five years in duration set in motion by fluctuations in export markets. But overall the economy experienced stable growth and price levels.

Slow growth in the 1970s has led to a questioning of Swedish economic and social policy. To what extent has slow growth been caused by international forces? To what extent have attempts to equalise incomes and maintain full employment through the use of taxes and subsidies caused a misallocation of resources? Has the long period of insulation from wars allowed the various interest groups to crystallise to such an extent that change is now prevented?

At the microeconomic level the wisdom of high marginal tax rates has been questioned, as have unemployment and early retirement subsidies which have led to a contraction of the numbers and the labour force and a fall in the numbers unemployed. If the unemployment subsidies were set at levels comparable to those in the UK then the unemployment rate would rise to about 12 per cent; if the tax rates on incomes and the subsidies to early retirement were brought into line with those in other advanced countries then the labour force would increase by about 6 per cent. The size of the public sector has also been attacked, and the view has been expressed that the pursuit of equality has led to the growth of an informal economy and a neglect of the inequalities arising from differences in needs over the lifecycle, differences in working hours and distortions arising from the effects of housing subsidies. At the macroeconomic level there has been concern that the economy is living beyond its means and a feeling that fiscal policy has to be toughened.

Above all there is the problem of societal norms. Solidarity and equality are strong forces in Swedish society and to overcome the problem of declining profits 'fund socialism' has emerged. Investment is to be increased through a system of centralised profit sharing in which a portion of the total revenue of firms is to be handed over to investment funds which are to operate on industrial and regional bases and on which representatives of the unions shall sit. In effect, the scheme represents an attempt to extend industrial democracy from the shopfloor to the board room. But whether workers will see the connection between investment decisions and shopfloor outcomes has yet to be established. But this represents an alternative approach from that operating in Japan and from that being proposed in the UK. It does, of course, rely heavily upon the establishment of credible economic policies by governments.

Switzerland

Switzerland is remarkable for having the lowest unemployment rate of all advanced countries: 0.2 per cent! (Allowance must be made for the use of guest workers as a buffer stock. During the recession of 1974–76, for example, some 300,000 workers were displaced from industry and about 180,000 foreign workers left the country with the result that about 60 per cent of unemployment was exported.) But it should be noted that Switzerland had a low unemployment rate before the Second World War.

Among the factors which seem to have contributed to the relative absence of inflation and unemployment are, first, that Switzerland is a small open economy which has pursued a hard money policy. Second, only about 30 per cent of the labour force is unionised. Third, hours of work are long by European standards and when a referendum was held to consider a reduction in working hours the result was a majority in favour of longer hours! Fourth, the coverage of the unemployment scheme is low, as are benefits. Fifth, wage determination is highly decentralised so that wages have been flexible: a 1 per cent rise in unemployment reduces wage inflation by 7.14 per cent as against an OECD average of 1.76 per cent (Grubb *et al*. 1983). However, the most interesting feature of the Swiss economy has been its ability to avoid the slowing down which Olson (1983) has maintained affects advanced countries and which appears to have been present in Sweden.

The Future of Europe

The prolonged recession of the 1970s and 1980s and the continued enlargement of the membership of the Community has forced a reconsideration of the future of Europe. In the two decades both the United States and Japan have appeared to prosper and this has raised questions concerning the policies pursued by the Community. The mass market which was supposed to be attainable at its inception does not appear to have materialised and increasing political security has reduced the pressures to relinquish national autonomy. The benefits of monetary integration have not been achieved and comprehensive social policies to deal with poverty and inequality have not emerged. The continued enlargement of the Community will bring economic benefits through the enlargement of the free trade area. However, the increase in the number of Southern European states does imply a shift of power away from the manufacturing countries which founded the Community towards agrarian interests. In the sphere of manufacturing and high technology the attempts at coordination of research activities have not been promising and there are strong possibilities that Europe will tend to slip further and further behind the USA and Japan.

Bibliography

Aitken, N.D. (1973) 'The effects of the EEC and EFTA on European trade: a temporal cross-section analysis', *American Economic Review*, vol. 63, pp. 881–892.

Allgayer, F. *et al.* (1983) *Federal Republic of Germany: Medium Economic Trends and Problems*, Economic Papers No 16, Commission of the European Communities.

Bacon, R. and Eltis, W.A. (1978) *Britain's Economic Problem: Too Few Producers*, Macmillan.

Balassa, B. (ed.) (1975) *European Economic Integration*, North Holland.

Barnett, C. (1986) *The Audit of War*, Macmillan.

Basevi, A. (1983) *Macroeconomic Prospects and Policies for the European Community*, Economic Papers No 12, Commission of the European Communities.

Batstone, E. (1986) 'Labour and productivity', *Oxford Review of Economic Policy*, vol. 2, pp. 32–43.

Blanchard, O. (1985) *Employment and Growth in Europe: A Two-Handed Approach*, Economic Papers No 36, Commission of the European Communities.

Blanchard, O. *et al.* (1983) *US Deficits, the Dollar and Europe*, Economic Papers No 24, Commission of the European Communities.

Breedveld, D.C. (1983) *Evolution et Problèmes Structurels de l'Economie Néerlandaise*, Economic Papers No 11, Commission of the European Communities.

Chatteriji, M. and Wickens, M. (1982) 'Productivity, factor transfers and economic growth in the UK', *Economica*, vol. 49, pp. 21–38.

Chatteriji, M. and Wickens, M. (1983) 'Verdoorn's Law and Kaldor's Law: a revisionist interpretation', *Journal of Post-Keynesian Economics*, vol. 5, pp. 397–413.

Christensen L.R. *et al.* (1980) 'Relative productivity levels, 1947–1973: an international comparison', *European Economic Review*, vol. 16, pp. 61–94.

Ciardelli, Q. *et al.* (1984) *Evolution et Problèmes Structurels de l'Economie Italienne*, Economic Papers No 27, Commission of the European Communities.

Daly, A. *et al.* (1985) 'Productivity, machinery and skills in a sample of British and German manufacturing plants', *National Economic Research*, vol.111, pp. 48–61.

Davies, S.W. and Caves, R. (1987) *Britain's Productivity Gap*, Cambridge University Press.

Denison, E.F. (1967) *Why Growth Rates Differ*, Brookings Institution.

Emerson, M. (1981) *European Dimensions in the Adjustment Problems*, Economic Papers No 5, Commission of the European Communities.

European Commission (1976, 1985) *Yearbook of Agricultural Statistics*, The Commission.

European Commission (1980) *Agricultural Situation in the Community*, The Commission.

European Commission (1986) *Budget of the European Communities*, The Commission.

FAO (1976, 1984) *Trade Yearbooks*, Food and Agriculture Organisation.

Gilbert, J.C. (1938) 'The mechanism for the interregional redistribution of money', *Review of Economic Studies*, vol. 6, pp. 187–194.

Gordon, A. (1987) 'Comment on "fiscal policy" ', in R. Dornbusch and R. Layard (eds) *The Performance of the British Economy*, Oxford University Press.

Grubb, D. *et al.* (1983) 'Wage rigidity and unemployment in OECD countries', *European Economic Review*, vol. 21, pp. 18–37.

House of Lords (1980) *Report of the Committee on the Functioning of Financial Institutions*, HMSO.

IMF (1986) *International Financial Statistics*, IMF.

Jacquemin, A. (ed.) (1984) *European Industry: Public Policy and Corporate Strategy*, Clarendon Press.

Kaldor, N. (1966) *Causes of the Slow Rate of Growth in the United Kingdom*, Cambridge University Press.

Kennedy, W.P. (1987) *Industrial Structure, Capital Markets and the Origins of British Economic Decline*, Cambridge University Press.

Keynes, J.M. (1970/1923) *The Collected Writings of John Maynard Keynes*, vol. 2, *A Tract on Monetary Reform*, Macmillan.

Keynes, J.M. (1971/1930) *The Collected Writings of John Maynard Keynes*, vols 5–6, *A Treatise on Money*, Macmillan.

Keynes, J.M. (1973a/1936) *The Collected Writings of John Maynard Keynes*, vol. 7, *The General Theory of Employment, Interest and Money*, Macmillan.

Keynes, J.M. (1973b) *The Collected Writings of John Maynard Keynes*, vol. 13, *The General Theory and After*, Part 1, *Preparation*, Macmillan.

Kreinen, M.E. (1972) 'Effects of the EEC on imports of manufactures', *Economic Journal*, vol. 82, pp. 897–920.

Layard, R. *et al.* (1984) *Europe, the Case for Unsustainable Growth*, Economic Papers No 31, Commission of the European Communities.

Lehment, E. (1982) 'Economic policy response to the oil price shocks of 1974 and 1979', *European Economic Review*, vol. 18, pp. 235–242.

Lund, P.J. *et al.* (1982) *Wages and Employment in Agriculture: England and Wales, 1960–1981*, Government Economic Working Paper 52, Ministry of Agriculture.

Lundberg, E. (1985) 'The rise and fall of the Swedish Model', *Journal of Economic Literature*, vol. 23, pp. 1–25.

Marques Mendes, A.J. (1986) 'The contribution of the European Community to economic growth', *Journal of Common Market Studies*, vol. 24, pp. 261–277.

Martin, J.P. (1983) 'Effects of the minimum wage on the youth labour market', in *North American*, OECD Occasional Studies.

Martin, J.P. (1984) *Youth Unemployment and Minimum Wage Legislation in the USA and France*, OECD.

Matthews, R.C.O. *et al.* (1982) *British Economic Growth 1856–1973*, Oxford University Press.

Millward, A. (1985) *The Reconstruction of Western Europe*, Allen and Unwin.

Millward, N. and Stevens, M. (1986) *British Workplace Industrial Relations 1980–1986*, Gower.

Morgan, P. *et al.* (1985) *Wage Floors in the Clothing Industry 1950–1981*, Research Paper 54, Department of Employment.

Muellbauer, J. (1986) 'Productivity and competitiveness in British manufacturing', *Oxford Review of Economic Policy*, vol. 2, pp. i–xxv.

Musgrave, R.A. (1959) *The Theory of Public Finance*, McGraw-Hill.

Myrdal, G. (1932) *Monetary Equilibrium*, Hodge.

Mydral, G. (1957) *Economic Theory and Underdeveloped Regions*, Duckworth.

Nardozzi, S. (1983) *Structural Trends of Financial Systems: France, Germany, Italy*, Economic Papers No. 14, Commission of the European Communities.

NIESR (1970–86) *Economic Review*, National Institute for Economic and Social Research.

OECD (1955–86) *Main Economic Indicators*, OECD.

OECD (1986) *Economic Survey*, OECD.

Olson, M. (1983) 'The political economy of comparative growth rates', in D.C. Mueller (ed.) *The Political Economy of Growth*, Yale University Press.

Owen, N. (1983) *Economies of Scale, Competitiveness and Trade Patterns within the European Community*, Clarendon Press.

Pavitt, K. (1980) *Technical Innovation and British Economic Performance*, Macmillan.

Petith, H. (1977) 'European integration and the terms of trade', *Economica*, vol. 87, pp. 262–272.

Prais, S.J. (1981a) *Productivity and Industrial Structure*, Cambridge University Press.

Prais, S.J. (1981b) 'Vocational qualifications of the labour force in Britain and Germany', *National Institute Economic Review*, vol. 98, pp. 134–146.

Prewo, W.E. (1974) 'Integration effects in the EEC: an attempt at quantification in a general equilibrium framework', *European Economic Review*, vol. 5, pp. 379–405.

Reati, A. (1984) *Rate of Profit, Business Cycles and Capital Accumulation in UK Industry, 1959–81*, Economic Papers No 35, Commission of the European Communities.

Reati, A. (1985) *Rate of Profit, Business Cycles and Capital Accumulation in West Germany, 1959–81*, Economic Papers No 37, Commission of the European Communities.

Rollo, J.M.C. and Warwick, K.S. (1979) *The CAP and resource flows among EEC member states*, Government Economic Service, Working Paper No. 52, Ministry of Agriculture and Fisheries.

Rowthorn, R. (1975) 'What remains of Kaldor's Law?', *Economic Journal*, vol. 85, pp. 238–240.

Rubenstein, W.D. (1981) 'Education and social origins of British elites, 1870–1970', *Past and Present*, vol. 112, pp. 163–207.

Sachs, J. and Wyplosz, C. (1985) 'The economic consequences of President Mitterrand', *Brookings Papers on Economic Acitivity*, vol. 15, pp. 83–114.

Sanderson, M. (1988) 'Education, science and research, 1890 to the 1980s', *Oxford Review of Economic Policy*, vol. 4, (forthcoming).

Schaaijk, M. van (1983) 'Loondifferentiate en werkloosheid', *Economishe Statische Berichten*, vol. 21, pp. 21–25.

Schaaijk, M. van (1985) 'Starre beloningsver houdingen, Starr werklooseheid houdingen?' *Maanschrift Economie*, vol. 49, pp. 45–59.

Scitovsky, T. (1958) *Economic Theory and Western European Integration*, Allen and Unwin.

Smith J.D. (1978) 'Trends in the concentration of personal wealth with the United States 1958–1976', *Review of Income and Wealth*, vol. 30, pp. 419–428.

Smith, A. (1981) *A Review of the Informal Economy*, Economic Papers No. 3, Commission of the European Communities.

Steinheer, A. (1982) *The Great Depression: A Repeat in the 1980s?*, Economic Papers No. 10, Commission of the European Communities

Steinheer, A. (1983) *Income Distribution and Employment in the European Communities, 1960–82*, Economic Papers No 23, Commission of the European Communities.

Summers, R., Kravis, I., and Heston, A. (1986) 'Changes in world income distribution', *Journal of Policy Modelling*, vol. 6, pp. 237–269.

Thirlwall, A.P. (1987) *The Economics of Nicholas Kaldor*, Wheatsheaf.

Todd, D. (1984a) *The Growth of Public Expenditure in the EEC Countries, 1960–81*, Economic Papers No 29, Commission of the European Communities.

Todd, D. (1984b) *Total Factor Productivity Growth and Productivity Slowdown in the West German Industrial Sector, 1970–81*, Economic Papers No 32, Commission of the European Communities.

Truman, E.M. (1977) 'The effects of European economic integration on production and trade of manufactured products', in B. Balassa, (ed.) *European Economic Integration*, North-Holland.

Truman, E.M. (1969) 'The European Economic Community: trade creation and trade diversion', *Yale Economic Essays*, vol. 9, pp. 201–257.

Turner, H.A. *et al.* (1967) *Labour Relations in the Car Industry*, Allen and Unwin.

UK Balance of Payments (1986), HMSO.

UK Central Statistical Office (1987), Press release, CSO.

Verdoorn, P.J. and Schwartz, A.N.R. (1972) 'Two alternative estimates of the effects of EEC and EFTA on the pattern of trade', *European Economic Review,* vol. 3. pp. 291–335.

Wabe, J.S., Eversley, J.T. and Despicht, N.S. (1983) 'Community regional policy in changing economic conditions', *Banca Nazionale del Lavoro Quarterly Review*, No. 145, pp. 185–209.

Wegner, M. (1983) *The Employment Miracle in the US and Stagnation Employment in the EC*, Economic Papers No 18, Commission of the European Communities.

Williamson, J. and Bottrill, A. (1971) 'The impact of customs unions on trade in manufactures', *Oxford Economic Papers,* vol. 23, pp. 323–51.

10

Australia and Canada

The nineteenth-century industrialisation of Europe brought two distinct responses in the periphery. On the one hand, there was the opening up of the tropics to provide raw materials and foodstuffs. On the other, there was the development of the temperate zones. Both responses were dependent upon the movement of capital and labour and Lewis (1978) noted that the sources of labour influenced the evolution of the two regions. In the tropics low wage labour, especially Chinese labour, flowed into South-east Asia. High wage labour from Europe flowed into the temperate zones. Low wage labour was associated with low technology and productivity and led to the persistence of traditional agriculture and the retardation of industry; high wage labour and high level technology enabled white settlers in Australia and Canada (as well as New Zealand and Argentina) to enjoy high living standards. At the turn of the century Australia and Canada ranked below the United States but above the majority of European countries in real income per capita. In 1913 Australia's output of manufactures (financed out of trade in agricultural goods) was greater than that of France or Germany. But what of the subsequent years? Have Australia and Canada maintained their relative positions or, being primary producers, have they followed the Singer—Prebisch path of other primary producers and been faced with declining prices for their exports of primary products? Or have they fulfilled the staple thesis (first outlined for Canada) which states that the revenues obtained from the sale of primary products can be used to build up manufactures and services?

Australia

Australia was the last great land mass to be discovered and the first to be integrated into the world economy. Exports of merino wool begain in the 1830s. The gold discoveries of the 1850s led to an inrush of settlers and to a boom in

222

railroad and residential construction. At the turn of the century the development of the refrigerated ship enabled exports of meat to reach Europe and the closing of the American frontier led, as in the case of Canada, to the export of wheat. However, the smallness of the domestic market and the remoteness of Australia from the main foreign markets meant that industrialisation did not take place until the inter-war years — and then the industries required protection. Between the wars there was no appreciable rise in real incomes per capita. In the immediate post-war period there was a growth in output and income but it was not as great as in most other advanced countries and since the 1950s there has been a lagging behind other countries (Table 10.1).

We need to put Australia into perspective. Australia's population is much smaller than that of Canada and the UK, although its growth rate has been comparable with that of Canada and distinctly higher than that of the United Kingdom and most West European countries. Its national income is one-half that of Canada and one-third that of the UK and the growth rate of income has not been appreciably high. In terms of structure, mining accounts for about 8 per cent of GDP, agriculture for a similar percentage and manufacturing for about 20 per cent of

Table 10.1 Real per Capita Gross Domestic Product (1975 US $)

	1950	1980
USA	4,580	8,089
Canada	3,524	7,451
West Germany	1,843	6,876
Luxembourg	2,962	6,527
Sweden	3,152	6,779
Belgium	2,469	6,084
Norway	2,415	7,026
France	2,209	6,679
Iceland	2,251	6,060
Denmark	2,831	6,636
Netherlands	2,339	5,713
Japan	809	5,735
Australia	3,630	6,188
Switzerland	3,034	6,480
Finland	1,908	5,857
UK	2,696	5,145
New Zealand	3,421	4,543
Austria	1,674	5,861
Italy	1,423	3,352
Greece	918	3,922
Spain	1,171	4,179
Ireland	1,597	3,352
Portugal	746	3,047
Turkey	695	2,048

Source: Summers, Kravis, and Heston (1986)

Table 10.2 International Comparisons of the Structure of GDP, 1970−84

	Agriculture	Mining	Manufacturing	Utilities and Construction	Services	Government
Australia						
1970−72	6.5	3.4	23.6	10.9	52.5	4.0
1982−84	4.5	6.4	17.7	9.3	59.1	4.2
Canada						
1970−72	3.6	3.1	20.1	7.9	36.1	14.4
1982−84	3.4	5.7	16.0	8.1	38.6	16.2
UK						
1970−72	2.5	1.5	28.2	8.5	36.9	11.2
1982−84	1.9	6.8	21.6	7.4	38.8	13.4
Netherlands						
1970−72	5.3	1.7	25.3	10.0	39.5	12.3
1982−84	4.3	7.4	17.5	8.0	45.2	13.0
Norway						
1970−72	6.2	0.8	21.8	11.1	44.5	12.5
1982−84	3.9	17.3	13.8	10.5	39.5	14.0
USA						
1970−72	2.7	1.7	25.1	7.4	49.8	13.5
1982−84	2.3	3.9	21.0	7.0	53.9	13.0

Source: UNCTAD (1986)

GDP. Exports form about 15 per cent of GDP so that Australia is a relatively insular economy (Table 10.2).

How then can we account for the relatively slow growth of the Australian economy? According to Denison (1967) the rapid growth of the US and European economies in the 1950s and 1960s could be explained as a result of the increase in labour released from the agricultural sectors. But Australia, like the UK, had an efficient agricultural sector and there was little surplus labour to release to industry. Yet Australia had a small public sector and therefore did not run the risks of public employment crowding out private employment (Table 10.3). What is perhaps of greater significance is the low total productivity of the Australian economy. In other words, Australian industries tend to use more of all inputs per unit of output than do comparable foreign industries. To explain this low productivity we need to consider three factors: the structure of industry and the influence of the tariff; the effects of natural resource exploitation and the expansion of the non-trading sector; and the effects of the industrial relations system.

The Changing Structure of Industry

The main changes in economic activity since the 1950s have been the relative decline in manufacturing and agriculture and the growth in mining and services. Before the Second World War manufacturing accounted for less than 25 per cent

Table 10.3 Selected Economic Indicators: Australia and Canada

	Australia	*Canada*
Population		
1983 (millions)	15,297	24,891
growth 1970−83 (%)	1.5	1.2
urban population percentage	85.5	75.9
GDP 1985 (million dollars)	323,595	156,542
GDP per capita	13,000	10,324
GDP growth rate		
1960−70	5.7	5.6
1970−80	3.1	4.1
1980−86	1.4	2.1
Inflation rate		
1960−70	7.3	
1970−80	9.3	9.3
1980−84	7.5	8.7
Unemployment rate		
1960−70	1.8	4.7
1970−80	3.6	6.6
1980−84	7.2	9.8
Balance on current account (% GDP)		
1960−70	−3.3	−2.0
1970−80	−2.1	−0.8
1980−84	−3.8	−0.1

Source: OECD (1950−87)

of total output. As a result of tariffs and import controls manufacturing was expanded and became 30 per cent of total output at the end of the 1950s. In the 1960s manufacturing's share remained constant but during the 1970s and 1980s it declined. Over the same period the share of agriculture fell from about 20 per cent in the 1950s to under 5 per cent in the 1980s.

These changes in industrial structure have been associated with changes in the pattern of trade. Because of its distance from major markets and because of the existence of the tariff, the Australian economy has been relatively insulated from the world economy. Exports as a percentage of total output were about 9 per cent in the 1950s, 16.5 per cent in 1970 and 17.1 per cent in 1983. The results of the relative insularity were two-fold. First, manufacturing industry was broad based and probably slow to respond to advances in technology and changing tastes; it also lacked a large internal market. Because industry did not have high skill requirements, the percentage of the population in higher education tended to be smaller than in most advanced countries. Second, the result of the tariff was, as the Stolper−Samuelson theorem predicted, to increase the reward to labour and make manufacturing a high-cost industry because it protected Australian labour from foreign competition.

The emergence of the tariff may have had its origins in the political structure of Australia where everyone had the vote and the urban working class outnumbered and were more socially cohesive than the farming communities. Import substi-

tution, as a result of the tariff, may have pushed Australia along the same path
as many Latin American countries, especially Argentina. Indeed, the similarities
with Argentina are striking because both countries enjoyed high living standards
at the turn of the century and both embarked upon import substitution policies
in the inter-war years.

But the tariff wall has been falling since the 1950s because it has been insufficiently protective and because it lacked selectivity. The fall in transport costs at
the end of the 1950s and the emergence of low wage cost industries in South-east
Asia meant that the tariff no longer afforded the protection it used to give and
it was replaced by more discriminating measures. However, protection was not
confined to Australia and the creation of the EEC and the UK's decision to join
the Common Market meant that Australia lost its most lucrative selling outlets.
Indeed, most of Australia's slippage down the real income league table has taken
place in the 1950s and 1960s.

Agricultural goods and minerals still account for about 80 per cent of exports
but the composition has been changing. Agriculture accounted for 65 per cent
of exports in the 1950s but declined to 10 per cent in 1980. In contrast, mining
exports rose from 10 per cent in 1950 to 36 per cent in the 1980s, with most
of the expansion coming in the late 1960s and early 1970s. In the 1980s Asian
markets have accounted for 40 per cent total sales and the UK, which had taken
some 26 per cent in the 1950s, was taking only 3 per cent in the 1980s. Yet despite
these changes the Australian economy has not moved into high technology industries. The shift into mining has resulted in an exchange of minerals and metals
for manufactures and permitted an expansion of the non-trading private sector
— which is not exposed to the forces of competition. Furthermore, the difficulties
of moving resources out of declining industries have probably been aggravated
by the workings of the industrial relations system.

The Industrial Relations System

Mining is not a labour-intensive industry. It expanded by about 2,000 workers
between 1970 and 1980 but many activities involve strip (open cast) mining which
uses relatively more capital than labour. It has not absorbed all the labour displaced from manufacturing nor has it absorbed the influx of 'baby boom' labour.
Unemployment has increased, particularly youth unemployment.

At first sight it might seem surprising that unemployment should increase, given
the existence of a highly centralised system of wage determination which should
have produced an effective incomes policy along the lines of those operating in
Sweden, Austria and Japan. Thus, the Australian Conciliation and Arbitration
Commission has jurisdiction over disputes extending beyond one state and a set
of state tribunals and boards exist at regional level. What the Commission and
the tribunals have done in the past is to determine a basic wage and a skill margin.
Until 1953 wages were adjusted according to movements in the consumer price
index with infrequent adjustment of the basic wage and the margin for skill. In

1967 the basic wage and the skill margin were replaced by a total wage and a minimum wage. But throughout the 1950s and 1960s the tribunals tended to maintain real wages and wage differentials.

In the 1970s the uniform centralised wage system began to break down as inflationary pressures led to plant level bargaining with the tribunals tending to consolidate the increases in earnings. The 1980s saw an attempt — an Accord — to restore control over wages. However, anarchic tendencies still persisted and since the aim of the tribunals is to maintain industrial peace and not implement government economic policy there is no guarantee that the labour market will respond to monetary and fiscal weapons or that governments are intent on using unemployment to control wage movements.

Monetary and Fiscal Policies

All of this has a bearing upon the adjustment of the Australian economy to the oil shocks of the 1970s and the rise and fall of mining exports. In the early 1970s Australia suffered from the worldwide inflation and between 1974 and 1975 prices rose by 17 per cent following a 25 per cent increase in the money supply. Stringent monetary and fiscal policies in 1976 brought the inflation rate down to 10 per cent in 1978, but it rose again in 1980 as monetary policy was relaxed and the effects of the second oil shock worked through. The result has been stagflation in the 1980s with the authorities finding it difficult to control the economy because of: (1) movements in overseas investment stemming from changing views about the value of Australia's natural resources; (2) the deregulation of financial markets which has eased capital flows; and (3) the reluctance of the authorities to allow the exchange rate to vary in order to absorb fluctuations in capital flows. Instead the exchange rate has tended to be used to control inflation; but given rigidities elsewhere in the economy the result has been a rise in unemployment.

Canada

The problem of the Australian economy is its dependence upon exporting goods to slow growing markets; the problem of the Canadian economy is its close proximity to the US market. The early development of the Canadian economy rested upon furs, timber for shipbuilding and, in the middle of the nineteenth century, the sale of sawn timber. The hopes of becoming the outlet for the farm products of the American Mid-West led to a spate of canal and railroad construction but these ideas were dashed by the construction of the American railroads. Yet until the American Civil War the links with the United States were being strengthened. After the Civil War the American economy developed its own dynamism and threatened Canadian agricultural interests. Thereafter, Canadian industry developed behind tariff walls and at the turn of the century wheat production expanded and exports to Europe rose.

But the problems of the relationship of Canada and the United States returned after the Second World War. It was not merely the fact that there was a considerable amount of US direct foreign investment in Canada, but that the structure and destination of Canadian exports were changing. Table 10.4 shows the increasing importance of the American market and the decline of sales to the UK and European. The fall in the European markets seems to have been the result of increasing protectionism, especially by the EEC. Table 10.5 indicates the growth in importance of exports of manufactures as opposed to primary products and Table 10.6 draws attention to the increasing importance of the home and export markets for some key industries.

The growth of trade, especially intra-industry trade between Canada and the United States, was stimulated by the automotive pact in the 1960s and was gradually extended to other trades. And an increase in trade between the two countries is now seen to be capable of bringing many advantages to both countries. For the USA, faced with the rise of protectionism in Europe and Japan, a reasonably homogeneous market of 25 million, with high incomes, offers opportunities for the introduction and testing of new products and the exploitation of

Table 10.4   Destinations of Canadian Exports 1960–84

	1960	1970	1984
USA	55.8	64.4	75.6
UK	17.4	9.0	2.2
Other Western European	11.3	9.8	5.0
Japan	3.4	4.9	5.1
Other Asian	2.2	2.9	3.8
Other countries	9.9	9.0	8.3
Total	100.0	100.0	100.0

Source: UNCTAD (1986)

Table 10.5   Canadian Exports by Main Categories

	1970	1975
All food items	12.20	9.29
Agricultural raw materials	10.17	8.15
Fuels	6.04	13.93
Ores and metals	22.91	10.44
Manufactures	48.07	57.64
Unallocated	0.60	0.56
	100.00	100.00

Source: UNCTAD (1986)

Table 10.6 Percentage of Manufactured Goods Exported

	1960	*1984*
Transport equipment	60.4	68.4
Electrical	13.0	24.4
Machinery	37.8	54.4
Chemical	15.3	29.0
Wood	43.3	47.0
All manufacturing	24.3	30.0

Source: UNCTAD (1986)

mass marketing techniques. For the Canadians the attractions lie in the existence of a market of some 200 million and the opportunity to shift away from the low technology industries which are being taken over by the newly industrialising countries. But a move towards closer economic cooperation carries two possible dangers: one economic, the other political.

The economic danger can be quickly dismissed. Fluctuations in economic activity in the Canadian economy already coincide closely with those in the United States. There was a divergence in unemployment rates in the early 1980s but that can be explained away by the unusually severe effects of the recession on the Canadian mining sector and the fact that the Americans had moved to deregulating their economy and introducing greater price flexibility. But in all other respects their economies are already closely integrated and their industrial structures are very similar. The problems of further integration are likely to be political. The United States emerged as a reaction to British political and social attitudes — what Burke called 'salutary neglect' — and it was in the process enlivened by ideas disseminated from the French Revolution. In contrast, the United Empire Loyalists left the thirteen colonies in order to perpetuate British ideals and they came into contact with French settlers who were neither enamoured with the ideals of the French Revolution nor with the British way of life. Given the conflicts within Canada between the English and the French it is not difficult to see the threat posed to two fragile cultures by the more vigorous American way of life. The problem for the Canadians is that closer economic association with the United States carries with it the dangers of political dependence. Yet detachment and the failure to find new markets could lead to an Australian way of life in which the sale of minerals provides a means of purchasing manufactures and permits a life of enforced leisure.

Bibliography

Denison, E.F. (1967) *Why Growth Rates Differ*, Brookings Institution.
Lewis, W.A. (1978) *Growth and Fluctuations in the World Economy*, Allen and Unwin.

Norton, W.E. and Kennedy, P.J.C. (1986) *Australian Economic Statistics*, Reserve Bank
    of Australia.
OECD (1950—87) *Country Reports: Australia, Canada*, OECD.
Summers, R., Kravis, I. and Heston, A. (1986) 'Changes in world income distribution',
    Journal of Policy Modelling, vol. 6, pp. 237—269.
UNCTAD (1986) *Handbook of International Trade and Development Statistics, Supplement*,
    United Nations.

11

The USSR and Eastern Europe

The Russian Revolution led to the formation of the centrally planned economies. The origins of the revolution were complex. Marxism, a system of thinking derived from the advanced industrial countries in Western Europe whose evolution was assumed to proceed from feudalism through capitalism and socialism to communism, was one. But prerevolutionary Russia was not an advanced industrial country. There was some industry, but the mass of people still lived in rural areas. Indeed, the bourgeoisie seemed incapable of making a revolution and without a bourgeois revolution there could be no increasing concentration of capital, no increasing immiserisation of the proletariat and no heightening of the consciousness of the industrial proletariat, all stages predicated by Marxism. In short, there could be no proletarian revolution.

In the late nineteenth century Russian radical thought was represented by the *narodniks* who believed in a theory of peasant revolution which would remove the aristocracy and solve the problems of an overpopulated agrarian economy. For Plekhanov and later, Lenin, the revolution had to come from without rather than from within. Marx and Engels welcomed the incursions of Western capitalism into the East: they were seen as a means of displacing feudalism. Immediately after the revolution there were hopes that other Western workers would overthrow their capitalist masters and offer socialist support to the USSR. But Western capitalist societies proved to be remarkably resilient and hopes of revolutions in Poland, Hungary, Austria and Germany gradually ebbed away.

Some unusual features of Russian society both before and after the Revolution dominated Lenin's thinking. Given the absence of a capitalist society there had to be a revolution from without, brought to the embryonic proletariat by the party, which was to be the vanguard of the Revolution. In other words, a distinction was drawn between class, the economic unit, and party, the political unit. The hostility of West capitalist societies compelled the creation of socialism within one country. The Comintern (Communist International) had to be restructured and the policies of communist parties in other countries had to be redefined. This redefinition included a shift away from destructive divisions within and between socialist groups and towards the creation of popular fronts. Fear of the West (originating from earlier invasions of Russia by the Swedes, the French, the Germans and even the Japanese) accounted for the Nazi—Soviet non-aggression pact and, after the Great Patriotic War, the creation of a socialist zone in Europe and Asia which, until the death of Stalin, contained only two weak links — Yugoslavia and China. Cuba was later to create a further distinct socialist model embracing Afro—American traditions within an Hispanic-Marxist-Leninist ideology.

The Russian Revolution was two revolutions. The first, a peasant revolution, redistributed land to the peasants and created a free market in land and food. The succeeding proletarian revolution nationalised the puny commanding heights of the economy. These two revolutions conflicted since the party required that the agricultural surplus be enlarged and made available to finance industrialisation — Stalin was later to resolve this conflict by forced collectivisation. This is the major difference between the Russian and subsequent revolutions. In the USSR the task of enlarging and obtaining the surplus was carried out by recreating the farm in an industrial image; that is, by the creation of large-scale farms. But other peasant-led revolutions, in China, Africa and Latin America, had to create industrial development with minimal industrial expertise.

Industrial Production

Figure 11.1 shows the movement of annual changes in industrial production between 1930 and 1985. The data fall into three, possibly, four, distinct periods. First, there is the pre-war period of high and violently accelerating and decelerating growth. Second, there is the period of the Second World War and for which there is no available information but during which there were tremendous losses of both capital and labour. Third, there is the deceleration of growth from 1950 onwards, which possibly becomes even faster after 1975.

The pre-war high growth rates attracted contemporary attention because they were in sharp contrast to the slump conditions in the West. However, as Seton (1958) later observed, these apparent differences may have been due to differences in the composition and weights attached to industries in the indices of industrial production. (And, of course, there were inevitable gains in 'catching up' with the West.)

But it is the post-war deceleration, revealed also by the other indicators in Table 11.1, which has attracted the greatest attention. Such a slowing down implies the possibility that the USSR will never catch up with the West and is doomed for ever to export raw materials for Western technology. It also sheds light upon the attempts by successive political leaders, from Khrushchev to Gorbachev, to change the politico-economic structure of the Soviet Union.

Among the causes of the deceleration which have been isolated are: (1) the long lead times for inventions and innovation; (2) overmanning and underutilisation of both capital and labour; (3) a slowing of population growth; (4) lack

Table 11.1   Selected Economic Indicators of the Socialist Countries of Eastern Europe
(Average Annual percentage Change)

	1956–60	1961–65	1966–70	1971–75	1976–80	1981–85
Bulgaria						
NMP[a]	9.1	6.2	7.2	6.2	6.1	3.7
Plan target			(8.5)	(8.1)	(7.7)	(4.1)
Industrial output	6.2	11.7	11.2	8.9	6.0	4.3
Investment	14.9	12.4	13.1	8.6	4.5	4.7
Real income per head	7.9	2.5	5.0	2.0	0.4	2.4
Balance of trade ($bn)	n.a	n.a	n.a	51	–0.1	0.2
Czechoslovakia						
NMP	7.5	1.2	6.6	5.7	3.7	1.8
Plan target			(4.2)	(5.1)	(4.9)	(1.8)
Industrial output	10.5	5.2	6.3	6.7	5.2	4.6
Investment	13.6	1.1	6.4	4.2	4.1	1.0
Real income per head	4.8	1.6	3.6	4.5	1.4	1.1
Balance of trade ($bn)	0.1	–0.5	–0.7	0.1	0.2	0.0
German Democratic Republic						
NMP	7.7	2.6	5.6	5.4	4.1	3.5
Plan target			(5.4)	(4.9)	(5.3)	(5.1)
Industrial output	9.2	5.9	6.4	6.3	4.9	
Investment	11.7	3.4	13.0	4.4	3.5	–1.5
Real income per head	6.0	12.5	2.8	4.6	1.8	1.6
Balance of trade ($bn)	n.a	n.a	n.a	0.02	–0.3	1.7
Hungary						
NMP	5.8	4.5	6.5	6.2	3.2	1.3
Plan target			(3.7)	(5.7)	(3.2)	(2.9)
Industrial output	7.5	8.1	6.1	6.5	3.4	
Investment		7.2	16.2	7.0	4.2	–3.2
Real income per head	8.4	3.6	4.8	4.6	1.8	1.6
Balance of trade ($bn)	n.a	n.a	n.a	0.05	–0.4	0.4
Poland						
NMP	6.6	6.0	5.7	9.8	1.6	–0.5
Plan target			(6.0)	(7.0)	(7.0)	(3.5)
Industrial output	9.9	8.6	8.3	10.6	4.5	
Investment	10.7	7.9	8.6	18.4	0.5	–1.5
Real income per head	6.0	1.6	1.4	7.6	3.0	–1.3
Balance of trade ($bn)	n.a	n.a	n.a	–0.6	–2.2	1.3
Romania						
NMP	10.8	8.9	7.7	11.3	7.1	4.4
Plan target			(7.0)	(11.5)	(10.5)	(7.1)
Industrial output	19.9	13.0	11.8	13.2	9.5	
Investment	12.6	7.9	8.6	18.4	9.8	–1.5
Real income per head	9.6	4.4	2.6	1.7	5.6	0.9
Balance of trade ($bn)	n.a	n.a	n.a	0.1	0.2	1.8
USSR						
NMP	8.7	6.4	7.6	5.7	4.4	3.6
Plan target			(6.8)	(6.8)	(4.7)	(3.8)
Industrial output	10.4	8.6	8.5	7.4	4.5	
Investment	12.5			7.0	3.9	3.6
Real income per head	3.0	3.0	4.6	4.4	3.4	2.2
Blance of trade ($bn)	n.a	n.a	n.a	0.3	6.2	7.0

Note: (a) NMP (Net Material Product). This is the centrally planned economy equivalent of national
       income and differs in the treatment of services and depreciation.
Source: UN (1960–87)

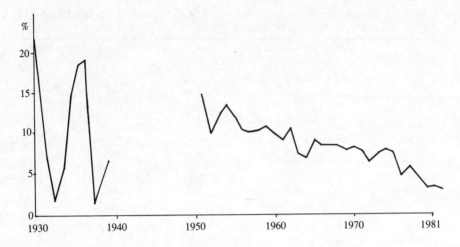

Sources: Mitchell (1981), UN (1960−87)
Figure 11.1   Annual Changes in Industrial Production: USSR 1930−85 (%)

of incentives for greater efficiency; and (5) the poor morale of Soviet workers. The slowing down of population growth highlights the problem that much Soviet economic development has been *extensive,* involving proportional increases in both labour and capital rather than an *intensive* use of capital. But with the exception of central regions of the USSR — Muslim regions — there are no labour reserves and birth rates are declining. There is therefore a need to use the available supplies of labour more efficiently. The long lead times in invention and innovation do not apply in all spheres of activity. In defence, for example, space rocketry has been as advanced as that of the United States. But in many other industries there are unnecessarily long lead times.

Planning

The question must be whether central planning is inferior to the market in the allocation of resources. Have the critics of socialism, such as Mises and Hayek, been vindicated? Planning is a matter of degree and at its simplest may take the form of indicative planning, as practised by the French and the Japanese, and once attempted (in the National Plan) by the British. Under indicative planning the central bureau asks all economic agents to submit details of their plans for future consumption and production and then attempts to consider whether they are reconcilable with available supplies. The problems with such a procedure are twofold. First, each economic agent may have more than one plan; fulfilling today's plan may open a variety of options for tomorrow. In short, there may be a decision tree and given a multiplicity of plans there is a need to impose order and eliminate some possibilities, perhaps unwisely.

Second, there is the problem of whether agents will release information. Since indicative planning tends to be practised in market economies there is a presumption that agents will be willing to release information in order to supplement that provided by markets. But if markets are dominated by oligopolists then they may not disclose information for fear of giving rivals an advantage.

Soviet planning is central planning: it tends to be top down in contrast to the bottom up procedure adopted in indicative planning. But the distinction is often a matter of degree and both types of planning require agents to provide information. It is this general question of information collation and processing which has been at the centre of the discussions about central planning since Barone first raised the issue. Hayek and Mises later questioned whether a socialist commonwealth could make rational economic decisions because the information which planners required related to time, place and circumstance and could not be quantified in a form suitable for planners. Only a price system, they argued, could collate and transmit disparate bits of information. However, Lange (1938) suggested that there was no need for planners to dispense with the price mechanism because they could use taxes and subsidies to adjust accounting prices. But his solution did presuppose that the planners possessed a social welfare function or rule which could tell them in which direction and by how much prices should be adjusted.

We can now turn to a more detailed consideration of Soviet planning, which starts with the laying down of targets for each sector by the State Planning Committee (*Gosplan*), and to the examination of those plans by the State Committee on Materials Technical and Supply (*Gossnab*) to assess the intersectoral flows of goods and inputs required to execute those plans. More detailed analysis of the plans involves consultations with ministries, trade associations and enterprises. What is involved therefore is a resolution of the centralisation—decentralisation debate. The reconciliation of the plans for all enterprises involves coordination; but coping with the complexity of detailed planning requires decentralisation.

Foreign Trade

The USSR is not self-sufficient and there is trade both with the market economies and with the other planned economies. Such trade is dictated by the planning process and gives rise to problems. The planners attempt to balance demand and supply. When imbalances occur trade is required. But trade cannot take place on the basis of domestic prices because they reflect only planners' priorities. As a result of the emphasis upon industrialisation the prices of consumer goods tend to be lower and the prices of capital goods higher than in the West. Trade with market economies could therefore lead to consumer goods being offered in exchange for capital goods — a procedure which would frustrate the aims of the planners. Trade has therefore to be conducted through a government agency with raw materials being exchanged for Western manufactures and high technology — a procedure which rests upon comparative advantage. Despite the restrictions upon trade there has been a considerable expansion of East—West trade over the last two decades.

Trade with the other planned economies is much more complicated. The Council for Mutual Economic Assistance (CMEA or Comecon) was set up in 1949 in response to Western efforts at closer economic cooperation. Comecon includes all the planned economies of Eastern Europe, except Yugoslavia, plus Cuba, Mongolia and Vietnam. But at what prices should trade take place, given that not all planned economies use market clearing prices? The practice is to use world prices. This works well with raw materials but not with manufactures, for which there are considerable quality differences between Western and Eastern goods.

Unfortunately the use of world prices does not overcome a second trading problem which arises because currencies are not convertible. If Poland sells goods to the USSR then the Poles must use roubles to buy Soviet goods and cannot convert them into, say, marks with which to purchase East German goods. The result is that Comecon tends to encourage trade diversion rather than trade creation because it prevents multilateral trading.

The Objects of Planning

Planning deals with growth and distribution. Under war communism planning was concerned with distribution: with the problems of feeding and equipping the Red Army in its attempts to defend the frontiers of the USSR. Factories and mines were nationalised and by degrees the rest of industry and commerce was brought under government control. Foreign trade was monopolised. Consumer goods were rationed, output norms were set for factories and the peasants were forcibly compelled to deliver crops. War communism was undermined by peasant uprisings and by the Kronstadt mutiny. The market was then re-established under the New Economic Policy. But the policy was short lived and controls were re-introduced in 1924.

After Lenin's death, Stalin extended the scope of planning and made its objective growth with an emphasis upon heavy industry. The USSR was to be protected against foreign encirclement and was to 'catch up' with the advanced capitalist countries. All industries and trades were renationalised and farmers were concentrated in collective farms. The price mechanism as a means of reconciling supplies and demands was abandoned. Many of the objectives were achieved, although the cost in human life was enormous. It was Stalin's political legacy which was the primary objective of Khrushchev's denunciation in 1953, but the economic failings were not overlooked. Agricultural production, Khrushchev argued, had been lower under Stalin than under the tsars. Khrushchev attempted to boost agricultural production by several methods: the virgin lands of the central USSR were exploited and wheat acreage was doubled. But the effects were short-term. Lack of fertilisers, failure to rotate crops, soil erosion and bad harvests led to falling yields. Shortages of fodder for livestock as well as food shortages led to decisions to import grain from the United States and Canada. The attempts to increase the incentives to peasants by raising procurement prices did not succeed, nor did attempts to reduce the size of the private agricultural sector. Problems with agriculture and attempts to rationalise the centralised economy therefore led to Khrushchev's downfall.

Khrushchev was succeeded by Brezhnev who, between 1964 and 1984, sought to introduce greater devolution. Unfortunately, the Prague Spring (1968) forced a retreat to the command economy. But there was no restoration of Stalin's emphasis upon growth: instead, there was an attempt to build up defence and to improve distribution. The objectives of Brezhnev's policy were to: (1) achieve military parity with the United States; (2) exploit the mineral resources of Siberia through the construction of railways and oil pipelines; (3) increase money wages in an attempt to expand consumption; and (4) reduce income differentials between town and countryside. The attempts to achieve this programme were frustrated by labour shortages (the legacy of the war), by a failure to expand higher education and an undue concentration upon general education and by a failure to improve productivity. Instead of raising farm incomes by raising productivity food was subsidised while the incomes of low paid workers were raised. The result was that the demand for food and manufactures increased faster than supplies. Despite the obvious shortages — the oil crises, the bad harvests and the fluctuations in economic activity — the cost of living index remained obdurately constant. On the Moscow Metro prices remained set at the levels established in the 1930s. Shortages led to queues and workers absented themselves from factories to join them. As a result productivity fell. But productivity also fell because of a lack of investment and because defence absorbed highly skilled people.

Although Andropov and Chernenko tried to change the system, their periods of office were too short lived to achieve much by way of reform. The economic system that Gorbachev inherited, therefore, was to all intents and purposes the one that Stalin created. The reforms proposed by Gorbachev involve the replacement of central planning by a form of indicative planning and the construction of a new set of incentives and signals through the greater use of the price mechanism. The state will no longer bear responsibility for day to day planning but will confine its attention to identifying required structural changes and determining investment within broad sectors. In the state sector the intention is to introduce a dual system. Factories will continue to use some 50 to 70 per cent of their capacity to produce goods for government orders, but will be allowed to use their remaining capacity to produce for the market. Profits can be ploughed back or used to provide employees' welfare services. If no profits are earned then plant can be closed down and managers will have the right to dismiss (as well as hire) workers. This will mean a shift from achieving output norms to the fulfilment of contracts, which may place emphasis upon quality as well as quantity. Workers will be provided with individual incentives.

Side by side with the reform of the public sector there is to be an expansion of the private sector with greater opportunities for peasants and craftsmen and an increase in joint ventures with foreign firms. Finally, there is to be a realignment of domestic prices with foreign prices, implying a revaluation of the rouble. If the reforms are achieved then the USSR's dependence upon the exchange of raw materials for Western technology will be diminished. But major economic reforms usually require political revolution and the USSR has had no political disturbances comparable to those experienced by China, Poland, Hungary and Cuba since 1917. The attempt to achieve an economic revolution without bullets may therefore depend upon the willingness of the bureaucracy to accept new ways of managing the economy.

Eastern Europe

The problem of what reforms should and could be undertaken becomes acute when attention is directed to the alternatives suggested by other East European countries. During the 1950s they attempted to model themselves on the Soviet model, although the creation of Comecon allowed for some trade specialisation. Yugoslavia was the exception, for two reasons: it had not been occupied by Soviet troops nor had its leading politicians been domiciled or educated in the USSR during the 1930s and 1940s. Second, Tito insisted upon the importance of nationalism, broke with the USSR in 1948 and, subsequently, became involved in the creation of a politically neutral group of countries which came to be known as the Third World.

What emerged in Yugoslavia was a system of workers' cooperatives combined with central control over investment. Much has been written about the cooperatives and the tenor of the discussion has been that they may be efficient where there are few economies of scale and, as a consequence, freedom of entry is relatively easy. The reasoning behind this conclusion is as follows. A cooperative attempts to maximise the income per head of its members. Faced with an increase in demand it will therefore restrict its output rather than increase its membership and expand. It will not increase its membership because the marginal product of labour being less than the average product, it would have to redistribute income from existing members to new members. The overall effects of cooperatives on the economy would therefore depend upon whether or not there is freedom of entry and whether or not there is a capital market. Given that an individual's income is derived from his membership of a cooperative and that the derivation of income from the possession of shares in other cooperatives is frowned on, then it seemed likely that the capital market would be imperfect. By preventing members from diversifying their risks through the capital market the cooperative system leads workers to increase their consumption and the growth rates of capitalist cooperative firms will therefore be lower than those of capitalist firms.

Many of these criticisms did not apply to Yugoslav enterprises in their early phase because decentralised decision making about prices and production was combined with some degree of centralisation of investment financed through turnover taxes on the enterprises. But in the mid-1960s the cooperatives were given greater freedom and, as a consequence, the performance of the economy became less impressive and severe unemployment was alleviated only by the flow of guest workers to West Germany.

But compared with Poland's economic performance Yugoslavia's has been satisfactory. At the end of the Second World War the Polish economy was geared to grow along the lines laid down by the Soviet model. However, the investment plans were never adjusted when the Cold War began and defence spending was added to investment priorities. As a result consumption and real wages were held down and bureaucratic controls became more burdensome. In 1956 there was an outburst caused by the high level of investment in the previous period and Gomulka came to power on a wave of popular support. Works' councils were then introduced. But investment was again increased and the economic controls became tighter. In 1970 there was an attempt to increase food prices which led to riots and Gomulka resigned.

Under the new prime minister, Gierek, there was an attempt to increase both investment and consumption. Between 1971 and 1975 investment rose by over 18 per cent per annum and over the whole period money wages were increased by 65 per cent — all financed by foreign borrowing. In 1976 there was an attempt to change course and food prices were raised in an attempt to reduce the high level of subsidised consumption. This led to riots and a drift into disaster with ever increasing debts, food shortages and imbalances in various sectors of the economy. In 1980 there was a further attempt to raise food prices which resulted in a collapse of authority and the rise of the trade union Solidarity. For the Soviets the problems of securing political stability were made acute by the obvious lack of politicians who would be acceptable to the people. In the end the problem was solved, not by Soviet occupation, but by the installation of a Polish military government — acceptable to the USSR yet still Polish.

Hungary has experimented with the use of the market combined with some bureaucratic controls. In the 1950s the country experienced the typical problems of centrally planned economies, with demand deficiency being forestalled by soft budgets which resulted in a supply constrained economy, persistent shortages and the development of black markets. After the Hungarian uprising of 1956 there was a move to abolish agricultural procurements. The major reform steps were taken between 1968 and 1979 when a package of reforms was introduced which included the linking of domestic prices to world prices; the financing of investment by interest bearing loans with enterprises being responsible for about half of all investment; the linking of managerial bonuses to profits; and the permitting of small-scale private enterprise. Central planning was confined to such macroeconomic variables as energy policy.

The New Economic Mechanism, as it has been called, is not market socialism of the type written about by Lange and Lerner, because it does embody a considerable amount of planning from the centre. And there are still shortages of consumer durables, such as cars and telephones and imported goods. But the reforms have resulted in an improvement of agriculture, which has traditionally been a weakness in centrally planned economies, and in the elimination of food shortages.

Yet in 1986 Hungary was in severe financial difficulties as a result of overseas borrowing and new economic reforms were introduced, including the raising of food prices.

Elsewhere economic reforms have been sparse. Romania has a highly centralised economy and a dubious administration. Its agriculture is backward and contributes about 50 per cent of total output; the standard of living is the lowest in the Eastern bloc. In so far as it has an economic policy then it has been one of heavy industrialisation with demand management being subject to the constraint of the current balance. Bulgaria, like Hungary, enjoys plentiful supplies of food and cheap oil from the USSR. It has also emphasised small projects. In 1982 it attempted to decentralise and introduced a New Economic Mechanism with a stress on creating a better trained labour force, as a result of which the growth rate has improved. Since 1968, the Prague Spring and the Soviet intervention, Czechoslovakian decision making has become more centralised. However, the industrial base is energy-intensive and is ageing. Finally, East Germany is the most heavily industrialised country in the Eastern block, with some 70 per cent of its net material product coming from manufactures. Not only does it enjoy the highest living standards of the planned economies but the gap between it and the other members of the group has been tending to widen (Table 11.2).

But the important point to note about the planned economies is that despite their attempt to insulate themselves from the capitalist economies they have turned out to be vulnerable to world economic crises. Before the 1970s growth rates were impressive but not unusual. As Table 11.2 reveals, Greece and Portugal have done as well as Bulgaria and Romania. When compared with the performances of Japan and the smaller economies of South-east Asia the results are unimpressive. Only when the comparisons are extended to include the Latin American do the planned economies appear to have performed well. But the growth rates of the Eastern European countries depended upon Soviet energy supplies and diminishing supplies forced the Soviet Union to turn to Siberia and to the West for imports of heavy machinery. When the oil shocks of the 1970s came Eastern Europe was forced to consider three possibilities: (1) reduced dependence upon the Soviet Union and increased reliance upon the Middle East which would have meant an increase in exports; (2) reduced consumption and growth; or (3) expansion of domestic energy supplies using Western technology and increased exports. Whether the fall in oil prices in 1986 and 1987 will relieve them of these dilemmas remains to be seen.

Summary and Conclusions

Given that the target was to catch up with the West, why has central planning been so unsuccessful? What are the arguments upon which apology might be constructed? Looking back to 1917 the results of Soviet planning appear to be suc-

Table 11.2 Per Capita GDP in Centrally Planned Economies, Southern European Economies and the United States, 1950–80 (USSR=100)

	1950	1960	1973	1980
Bulgaria	66	79	87	87
Czechoslovakia	159	153	126	124
East Germany	108	144	129	140
Hungary	112	109	98	98
Poland	110	96	95	89
Romania	54	57	63	70
China	22	24	24	29
Yugoslavia	56	60	65	84
Greece	66	67	97	100
Portugal	53	56	77	77
Spain	85	83	96	106
Turkey	51	50	45	52
USA	331	252	207	205

Source: Summers, Kravis and Heston (1986)

cessful. In 1917 some three-quarters of the population were employed in agriculture: today about two-thirds live in towns. The other East European countries show similar reductions in the agricultural labour force. Then there are the effects of the Second World War to be considered. The USSR lost some 20 million people and although it emerged from the war as a great military power it was economically weak. Marshall Aid was denied because of the Cold War and Europe was split into two. More resources were as a result devoted to defence: atomic weapons were developed; space rocketry was devised; the navy was enlarged and military and political influence was extended to various parts of the world. Yet economic growth rates have declined.

But socialism was supposed to facilitate 'catching up'. What went wrong was that the planning system failed to provide the appropriate signals. To keep the population happy food prices have been kept low, with the result that it became cheaper to feed bread rather than unprocessed grain to livestock. Of course, the USSR's agricultural lands lie further north than those of Canada and the United States and harsher climates prevail; but similar agricultural weaknesses in pricing can be observed in the other planned economies. Despite the successes of the Chinese agrarian reforms there have been no attempts at emulation in the USSR. Similar weaknesses can be found in industry. And finally, there is the problem of an ageing population.

The problem is to identify the optimal policy to be pursued in a depressed world economy. In Hungary market socialism has led to increased consumption and a low growth rate. In Yugoslavia economic devolution has accentuated regional differences in incomes per capita. In Poland import-led growth has led to disaster. Only East Germany has managed to achieve high growth rates, but upon the basis of factors not available elsewhere in the Eastern bloc, such as higher educational standards, a more efficient agriculture and the benefits of close proximity to the West.

Can the market economies of South-east Asia offer any guidelines? Land reform has improved their agricultural productivity and led to greater income equality. Educational reforms provided the basis for an industrial labour force and also contributed to reducing income inequality. Planning has made a judicious use of market signals and been less tied to dogma. But the implementation of such economic reforms in Eastern Europe might pose political problems which the party machines may find unacceptable.

Bibliography

Abouchar, A. (1979) *Economic Evaluation of Soviet Socialism*, Pergamon.

Adam, J. (1984) *Employment and Wage Policies in Poland, Czechoslovakia and Hungary since 1950*, Macmillan.

Adam, J. (ed.), (1986) *Employment Policies in the Soviet Union and Eastern Europe*, Macmillan.

Amann, R. and Cooper, J. (1986) *Technical Progress and Soviet Economic Development*, Macmillan.

Balassa, B. (1983) 'Reforming the New Economic Mechanism in Hungary', *Journal of Comparative Economics*, vol. 7, pp. 253–76.

Balassa, B. and Bertrand, J.T. (1970) 'Growth performance of East European economics and comparable Western economies', *American Economic Review, Papers and Proceedings*, vol. 69, pp. 314–320.

Barone, E. (1908) 'Il ministero dello produzione nello stato colletivista', *Giornale degli Economisti e Rivista di Statistica'*, vol. 37, pp. 267–293 and 391–414. A translation appeared in Hayek (1935).

Berend, I.T. and Ranki, G. (1985) *The Hungarian Economy in the Twentieth Century*, Croom Helm.

Bergson, A. and Levine, H.S. (1983) *The Soviet Economy: Toward the Year 2000*, Allen and Unwin.

Bialer, S. (1987) *The Soviet Paradox: External Expansion and Internal Decline*, Tauris.

Cameron, N.E. (1981) 'Economic growth in USSR, Hungary and East and West Germany', *Journal of Comparative Economics*, vol. 5, pp. 24–42.

Cole, J. and Buck, T. (1985) *Modern Soviet Economic Performance*, Macmillan.

Csikos-Nagy, B. (1984) 'Further development of the Hungarian price system', *Acta Oeconomica*, vol. 32, pp. 21–37.

Desai, P. (1986) 'Soviet growth retardation', *American Economic Review, Papers and Proceedings*, vol. 76, pp. 175–186.

Economist Intelligence Unit (1960–87) *Country Reports*.

Ellman, M. (1986) 'The macroeconomic situation in the USSR', *Soviet Studies*, vol. 38, pp. 530–542.

Freris, A. (1984) *The Soviet Industrial Enterprise: Theory and Practice*, Croom Helm.

Goldman, M.J. (1983) *USSR in Crisis*, Norton.

Gomulka, S. (1985) *Growth, Innovation and Reform in Eastern Europe*, Harvester.

Gomulka, S. (1986) 'Soviet growth slowdown: duality, maturity and innovation', *American Economic Review, Papers and Proceedings*, vol. 76, pp. 170–180.

Hartford, K. (1985) 'Hungarian agriculture: a model for the socialist world', *World Development*, vol. 13, pp. 123–150.

Hayek, F. (ed.) (1935) *Collectivist Economic Planning*, Routledge and Kegan Paul.

Hayek, F. (1949) *Individualism and the Economic Order,* Routledge and Kegan Paul.

Houston, D.B. (1984) 'Poland's economic crisis', *European Economic Journal,* vol. 10, pp. 441–454.

Ickes, B.W. (1986) 'Cyclical fluctuations in centrally planned economies', *Soviet Studies,* vol. 38, pp. 36–52.

Kaser, M.C. (1981) 'Economic reform in Eastern Europe', *Acta Oeconomica,* vol. 31, pp. 28–36.

Kaser, M.C., and Radice, C.A. (1986) *Economic History of Eastern Europe,* Oxford University Press.

Kornai, J. (1985a) 'Adjustment to price and quantity signals in a socialist economy', *Economic Appliquée,* vol. 25, pp. 503–524.

Kornai, J. (1985b) *Contradictions and Dilemmas,* MIT Press.

Kornai, J. (1986) 'The Hungarian reform process', *Journal of Economic Literature,* vol. 18, pp. 38–57.

Landau, Z. and Tomaszewski, J. (1985) *The Polish Economy in the Twentieth Century,* Croom Helm.

Lane, D. (1985) *Soviet Economy and Society,* Blackwell.

Lange, O. (1938) 'On the economic theory of socialism', in B.E. Lippincott (ed.) *On The Economic Theory Of Socialism,* University of Minnesota.

Lerner, A.P. (1944) *The Economics of Control,* Macmillan.

Lydall, H.F. (1984) *Yugoslav Socialism: Theory and Practice,* Clarendon Press.

Mises, L. von (1935) 'Economic calculation in the socialist commonwealth', in Hayek (1935) *op. cit.*

Mitchell, B.R. (1981) *European Historical Statistics,* Cambridge University Press.

Nove, A. (1983) *The Economics of Feasible Socialism,* Allen and Unwin.

Nyitrai, V. (1983) 'Industrial structure and industrial change in Hungary', *Acta Oeconomica,* vol. 31, pp. 175–195.

OECD (1960–87) *Country Reports: Yugoslavia,* OECD.

Ofer, G. (1987) 'Soviet economic growth 1928–1985', *Journal of Economic Literature,* vol. 25, pp. 1767–1833.

Sapir, A. (1980) 'Economic growth and factor substitution: what happened to the Yugoslav miracle?', *Economic Journal,* vol. 90, pp. 294–313.

Seton, F. (1958) 'On the tempo of Soviet expansion', *Bulletin of the Oxford University Institute of Statistics,* vol. 18, pp. 214–225.

Smith, A.H. (1983) *Planned Economies of Eastern Europe,* Croom Helm.

Summers, R., Kravis, I.B. and Heston, A. (1986) 'Changes in world income distribution', *Journal of Policy Modelling,* vol. 6, pp. 207–262.

UN (1960–87) *Economic Survey of Europe,* United Nations.

Vissi, F. (1983) 'Major questions of the improvement of economic control and management in Hungary', *Acta Oeconomica,* vol. 30, pp. 325–339.

Walker, M. (1987) *The Waking Giant: Soviet Union under Gorbachev,* Michael Joseph.

Winiecki, J. (1986a) 'Are Soviet-type economies entering an era of long term deline?', *Soviet Studies,* vol. 38, pp. 325–348.

Winiecki, J. (1986b) 'Soviet-type economies: consideration for the future', *Soviet Studies,* vol. 38, pp. 534–561.

Zaleski, E. (1980) *Stalinist Planning for Economic Growth, 1933–1952,* University of North Carolina Press.

12

China and India

China and India share many characteristics. Both are populous countries. Together the estimated 1 billion Chinese and 730 million Indians account for some 40 per cent of the world's population. Both countries achieved independence/revolution within a few years of each other: India in 1947 and China in 1949. In the process both lost some territory: India forfeited Pakistan (which later disintegrated into Pakistan and Bangladesh) and China never regained Taiwan. And in both countries successive governments have tried to raise living standards. But the similarities end there. China has followed the socialist path to development whereas India has adopted the model of a mixed economy. Ostensibly paying lip service to the Soviet model, China has been notable for some spectacular experiments in social engineering: the Great Leap Forward in (1958—60) attempted bold schemes of reallocation and distribution and emphasised the importance of basic needs. It was followed by serious drought, starvation and famine between 1959 and 1961. In 1964 there was another great attempt, the Cultural Revolution, to revive and recreate the economy, but after 1978 there was a return to more market-oriented policies and a greater use of market incentives. In contrast, India's policies have been marked by the use of five-year plans, a greater emphasis upon heavy industry in the early years and a greater use of the market than in China.

The contrasts in performance are also revealing (Table 12.1). China enjoys a higher real per capita income than India and its growth rate has been higher. The non-economic indicators also compel attention. Life expectancy is higher and the mortality rate is lower in China than in India. China has concentrated on mass education whereas India has been preoccupied with the maintenance of an elite. But democratic societies are supposed to be more responsive to changing circumstances than planned economies and, as Sen (1984) has observed, Indian governments, under pressure from a free press, respond more quickly to famine than do monolithic, socialist governments — outcomes which must be set against the fact that most Chinese go to bed reasonably well nourished while many Indians

Table 12.1 Basic Indicators of Development: China and India

	China	India
Population (1983) (000)	1,021,000	730,900
Growth rate 1970–83 (%)	1.8	2.1
GDP per capita growth rate (%)		
1960–84	5.5	1.3
Increase in per capita food production (%)		
1961–70	3.8	–0.5
1970–80	1.4	0.3
1980–85	5.0	2.3
Crude birth rate per 1,000	18.4	25.5
Crude death rate per 1,000	6.6	28.1
Life expectancy	69.4	57.9
Illiteracy rate (%)	30.7	56.5

Source: UNCTAD (1986)

remain undernourished. Which leaves the unanswered question: development for what?

Population

It is in coping with their large and growing populations that the two countries have revealed significant differences. Marx did not accept the Malthusian postulate that living standards would be pulled down by overpopulation; it was Marx's theory that Mao Zedong followed in 1949 when he stated that

> A large population in China is a very good thing. With a population several-fold we still have an adequate solution. The solution lies in production. The fallacy of Western capitalist economists, like Malthus, that the increases in food lag behind the increase of population was long ago refuted in theoretical reasoning by Marxists; it has also been disproved by the facts existing after the revolution of the Soviet Union and in the liberated region of China.

Anti-Malthusianism persisted in China until the 1970s.

In 1953 the population of China was some 583 million and by 1984 it was over one billion. The population increase was strongly influenced by changes in the birth and death rates. Death rates have shown a continuous fall whereas birth rates have undergone fluctuations. In 1953 the birth rate was 34.3 per 1,000 and it remained constant until about 1958. Thereafter it fell dramatically in the early 1960s and then rose again in the late 1960s. This rise and fall seems to have been influenced by the economic reversals following the Great Leap Forward. From the 1970s onwards the birth rate started to decline and it has continued to fall in the 1980s. Throughout the last period successive governments have actively advocated family planning and the policy of one child families was being propagated in the mid-1980s.

In India preoccupation with population control was emphasised in the Sixth Five-Year Plan (1981) when the long-term goals were set of reducing the birth rate from 33 per 1,000 in 1980 to 25 per 1,000 by 1996 and the death rate from 13.2 per 1,000 to 9.4 per 1,000 in order to obtain a population of 864 million in 1996. However, to achieve this target — and the comparable Chinese goal — requires considerable change in social structure as well as in economic performance. In the absence of social security systems, children are regarded as an investment and yield an income for ageing parents. Despite Cassen's (1978) empirical work, which demonstrates that such a belief may rest on extremely fragile foundations, it is a belief which persists.

Agriculture

In both China and India agricultural policy has had to serve two ends — feeding the masses and providing a surplus to finance industrial development. Chinese economic policy has attempted to restrict the movement of labour between urban and rural areas and between the communes in rural areas. Such a policy may have the laudable aim of preventing a drift to the towns and the creation of urban unemployment on the scale observed in many Indian cities, but it can also result in a misallocation of resources.

In China the index of agricultural production stood at 100 in 1952 and rose to 269 in 1985. This rise was brought about mainly by increases in labour and current inputs. The amount of land under cultivation increased by about 3 per cent; there was no dramatic increase in the extensive margin of cultivation. The contribution of capital was also slight because most farmers did not possess savings. There was an increase in the surplus from agriculture but this was largely appropriated by the state. Agricultural savings, as a percentage of total savings, rose from 6.7 per cent in 1957 to 13.5 per cent in 1965 and then fell back to about 8 per cent in 1980. This must be seen in the context of the attempt to finance and build up heavy industry and to subsequently generate savings in urban areas (as well as coping with a rising population). In 1952 agriculture was responsible for about 60 per cent of total output; by 1985 its contribution had fallen to about 40 per cent. Yet over the same period the ratio of peasants supporting urban workers remained roughtly constant, a testimony to the importance of human effort and ingenuity in devising different socio-economic arrangements to raise output.

Before the revolution landholdings were extremely concentrated: some 10 per cent of the rural population held between 70 and 75 per cent of the land. A series of land reforms between 1949 and 1952 resulted in wholesale redistribution. But this extensive redistribution meant that most peasants could not work their land economically on an individual basis and cooperatives (mutual aid teams) were established in a second stage of agrarian reform. But these groupings were still too small to be effective and the Great Leap Forward was begun in 1958. Under this ambitious attempt to accelerate the pace of development communes were introduced as administrative as well as production units. Between 1958 and 1959 some 99 per cent of all peasant households were organised into 26,425 communes. The sales of the communes were subject to a government procurement tax which fixed prices on a quota basis and attempted to ensure a supply of agricultural goods to the urban areas. Within the communes there was an attempt to distribute net revenue on the basis of needs rather than abilities.

The social experiments of the Great Leap Forward were, however, disrupted by drought and famine during 1959 and 1961 and by the upheavals attendant upon the Cultural Revolution; the communes were eventually abolished after 1978. It is nevertheless worth reflecting upon some of their achievements. In 1957 agricultural savings as a percentage of total savings were 6.7 per cent. They rose to 13.5 per cent in 1965 and then fell back to 7.8 per cent in 1980. In 1952 agriculture was responsible for about 60 per cent of total output; by 1980 its contribution had fallen to 40 per cent — thereby revealing its success in financing the expansion of industry. Terms of trade steadily turned in favour of agriculture; the figure for 1950—56 was 25 per cent and this rose to 32 per cent between 1956 and 1970 (Table 12.2).

The agricultural reforms of 1978 abolished the communes and shifted the bases of incentives and responsibilities on to households. The unit tax procurement price was replaced by a lump sum tax and there were increases in the prices of many commodities. However, there were still restrictions upon the mobility of labour.

In India agriculture accounted for some 50 per cent of the national income in 1950 but its contribution fell to 35 per cent in 1980. In the first Five-Year Plan (1951—55) agriculture was accorded top priority and received 30 per cent of the investment funds. However, the second Five-Year Plan (1956—61) brought a shift

Table 12.2   Terms of Trade between Agriculture and Industry, China 1950—70

	Agricultural purchase price index	Industrial retail prices in rural areas index	Terms of trade 1/2
	(1)	(2)	(3)
1950	100.0	100.0	100.0
1951	119.6	110.2	108.5
1952	121.6	109.7	122.4
1953	132.5	108.2	122.4
1954	136.7	110.3	123.9
1955	135.1	111.9	120.7
1956	139.2	110.8	125.6
1957	146.2	112.1	130.4
1970	—	—	166.7

Source: Gurley (1974)

in emphasis to heavy industry and import substitution, with the result that investment in agriculture fell to 20 per cent of total investment. But unlike Chinese agriculture, Indian farming was characterised by the use of fertilisers as well as by new varieties of grains and the high procurement prices turned the terms of trade in favour of agriculture.

Yet despite the innovations, agricultural output only kept pace with population growth. The introduction of high yielding varieties of grain — the so-called Green Revolution — was mainly a revolution in wheat production and to a lesser extent in the staple crop, rice. The varieties developed tended to be adopted by the rich farmers, who had easier access to sources of credit and finance and could afford the expensive imputs the new varieties needed. Indirectly, therefore, the new wheat varieties tended to redistribute income. This income redistribution was accentuated by the procurement prices which favoured the richer farmers. In the 1970s some 3 per cent of rural households owned 26 per cent of the cultivable acreage and about 63 per cent of all farms had less than 5 acres. The problems of efficiency and equity were, of course, intertwined and not clear cut. Redistributing land to the poorer farmers and landless may have led to the problems encountered in China in the early 1950s. Criticisms of land tenure systems, especially sharecropping, turned out upon inspection to lose their force and gave way to a greater appreciation of the problems of providing incentives and of the interrelations of wage and credit systems. Nevertheless, the Indian record of slow improvement stands in sharp contrast to Chinese endeavours.

Industry

Between 1952 and 1957 Chinese industry tended to follow the Soviet model with an emphasis upon central planning. Profits were handed over to the state and wages were determined on the basis of grade scales which emphasised the importance of ability. The Great Leap Forward shifted the stress in distribution to need. Following the collapse of The Great Leap Forward there was a return to more conventional methods of remuneration, but it was not until 1978 that there was any attempt to organise industry along market lines. Between 1978 and 1980, 6,000 state enterprises, accounting for 60 per cent of total output, were selected as experimental enterprises. These enterprises were allowed to retain some portion of their profits and produce their own marketing and production plans.

There were three reasons why the experimental, or responsibility, system did not resolve the efficiency problem. First, some enterprises gave up because the percentage of profits which had to be handed to the state went up year by year. Second, only the profitable enterprises were involved in the scheme. Third, in distributing part of the profits as wages there was still an emphasis on needs. In 1983 four changes were therefore made in the responsibility system. The enterprises were leased from the state and the leasing fee became a lump sum payment rather than a unit profit tax (a change in the system of taxation similar to that introduced into agriculture). The amount of output which could be sold in private markets was increased; the establishment of collective ownership of enterprises was introduced and there was an improvement in the administrative system governing taxes and leases.

Despite these changes, there has not been a great improvement in output. One factor which may account for the disappointing results is the change in the composition of output. But there may be more fundamental problems. A decentralised market system requires greater expertise at all levels. The fact that China has a low percentage of its population in higher education may therefore be a factor contributing to the difficulties of enterprises in carrying out marketing, production and financial decision making. The availability of such skills may be more plentiful in those East European countries, such as Hungary, which have been pursuing a similar policy of market socialism. They may also be more plentiful in India.

However, Indian manufacturing industry has also had its weaknesses and the growth in the size of the manufacturing sector has not been matched by a corresponding increase in output. This apparent lack of efficiency has been linked to the policy of import substitution with its concomitant apparatus of tariffs, quotas and licences. The effect of these policies can be defined and measured by the effective rate of protection and the domestic resource cost. The effective rate of protection is defined as the ratio of value-added measured in domestic prices to the value-added in international prices. According to Bhagwati and Srinivasan (1983) these ranged from 27 per cent to 3,354 per cent; or these may be compared with the estimates of ERPs for other countries contained in Table 12.3.

The domestic resource cost (DRC) is defined as the ratio of value-added in an industry in domestic prices to the value-added in domestic prices. In other words, the DRC measures the cost or benefit (measured in foreign exchange) of a domestic activity and as such is related to the ERP. In 1968−69 the official exchange rate was Rs 7.50 per dollar and in 34 industries the DRC was greater than Rs 15. Such high rates of protection led to evasion, smuggling, under- and

Table 12.3   Range of Effective Rates of Protection for Manufacturing Industries in Some Developing Countries

Country	Year	Range of ERPs
Brazil	1958	17− 502
	1967	4− 252
Chile	1967	−23− 1,140
Indonesia	1971	−19− 5,400
Pakistan	1970	36− 592
South Korea	1968	−15− 82
Tunisia	1972	1− 737
Uruguay	1972	17− 1,014

Source: Krueger (1983)

over-invoicing of exports and the emergence of black markets. The fact that manufacturing industries were import-intensive led to further complications and aggravated the shortage of foreign exchange.

Foreign Trade and Investment

The effects of import substitution policies necessitate an examination of the importance of foreign trade to both China and India. Chinese foreign trade constituted about 10 per cent of national income in 1950 and rose to 18 per cent in the 1980s. But in the 1960s it fell to as low as 6 per cent because of the pursuit of self-sufficiency, hostile relations with the United States and the effects of the Cultural Revolution. There were significant changes in the commodity composition of exports and imports and in the trading partners. In the 1950s agricultural goods formed 60 per cent of exports; by 1980 they had fallen to 20 per cent. Over the same period there was a switch in imports from capital goods to consumer goods. In the 1950s foreign investment took the form of loans from the Soviet Union; in the 1980s there was a switch to seeking loans from the USA, Japan and West Europe as a result of the desire to import high technology from the advanced countries.

In India there was also a low dependence upon foreign trade through the 1950s and up to the 1970s and Indian trade policy was strongly influenced by elasticity pessimism — the belief that exports and imports would not respond to price changes. But foreign trade could not be forgotten because of the need to import capital goods and because protection policies tended to reduce the efficiency of domestic industries and increase the incentive to engage in illicit activities. By the 1980s India, as well as China, was beginning to pursue more outward looking policies.

Income Distribution and the Scissors

So far we have looked at agriculture and industry in isolation from each other. But both successive Chinese and Indian governments have sought to use agricultural surpluses to finance development. The question therefore is what effect have such policies had upon the distribution of income. The existence of rationing and the restrictions upon the mobility of labour complicate the answering of this question in the case of China.

Between 1952 and 1980 real wages in both agricultural and urban areas declined slightly as a result of the emphasis upon industrialisation. Urban consumption increased as a result of an increase in the employment rate with more and more household members obtaining work. In the rural areas there was no comparable increase in the employment rate. But these changes need to be qualified by two factors. First, the increase in urban employment may have meant a reduction in (unwanted) leisure. Second, the existence of rationing meant that workers may not have been free to spend their incomes on the goods they wanted. But after the 1978 reforms there may have been a narrowing of the gap between rural and urban incomes.

In India the problem of income distribution has been dominated by the issue of poverty. Thus, Bardhan (1986) estimated that in 1961, 38 per cent of the rural population and 32 per cent of the urban population were living below the poverty line; the respective proportions rose to 53 and 41 per cent in 1969. Studies, in the 1970s suggested that there was no marked change in the extent of absolute poverty.

Final Observations

The contrasts between the performances of the Chinese and Indian economies to which we drew attention at the beginning of this chapter were strong and stemmed from differences in policies. China sought a socialist route for development which bore some resemblances to that pursued by the USSR. The communes were to some extent the successors of the collective farms of the 1920s and 1930s. But there have been significant differences. In China there has been a more conscious attempt to alter the superstructure of society without waiting for changes to emerge naturally from altered infrastructure. The stress of needs has been much stronger than in the USSR where, in the comparable period, the emphasis was on scientific management, piece rates and ability. China seems to have been able to maintain growth with distribution for a longer period than did the USSR and redistribution may have helped to maintain the momentum of the economy.

But the comparison with India needs further consideration. According to Bardhan (1986) India inherited an efficient bureaucracy and a national leadership with moral stature. Bearing this inheritance in mind the record seems disappointing. The growth rate has been low and poverty has been persistent. Yet there have been changes in the composition of business firms and very few foreign firms have been involved in the economy. And India has not suffered, since partition, the upheavals and deaths from famine that China has been subject to.

Bibliography

Ahluwalia, L.J. (1985) *Industrial Growth in India: Stagnation since the Mid-Sixties,* Oxford University Press.

Baggchi, (1982) *Political Economy of Development,* Cambridge Universtiy Press.

Bardhan, P. (1986) *The Political Economy of Development in India,* Cambridge University Press.

Bergson, A. (1985) 'A visit to China's economic reforms', *Comparative Economic Studies,* vol. 15, pp. 16–23.

Bhagwati, J.N. and Srinivasan, T.N. (1983) *Lectures on International Trade,* MIT Press.

Bhalla, A.J. (1974) 'Technological choice in construction in two Asian countries: China and India', *World Development,* vol. 2, pp. 65–74.

Bliss, C. and Stern, N.H. (1982) *Palanpur: The Economy of an Indian Village,* Clarendon Press.

Cassen, R. (1978) *India: Population, Resources and Development,* Macmillan.

Chan, K.W. and Xu, X. (1985) 'Urban population growth and urbanization in China since 1949: reconstructing a baseline', *The China Quarterly,* vol. 104, pp. 583—613.

Chossudovsky, M. (1986) *Towards Capitalist Restoration,* Macmillan.

Conroy, R. (1984) 'Technological innovation in China's recent industrialization', *The China Quarterly,* vol. 97, pp. 1—23.

Croll, E. (1983) 'Production versus reproduction: a threat to China's development strategy', *The China Quarterly,* vol. 102, pp. 467—483.

Derberger, R.F. (1980) *China's Development in Comparative Perspective,* Harvard University Press.

Farmer, B.H. 'Perspectives on the Green Revolution in South Asia', *Modern Asian Studies,* vol. 20, pp. 175—199.

Feuchtwang, S. and Hussain, H. (1983) *The Chinese Economic Reforms,* Croom Helm.

Gray, J. and White, G. (1983) *China's New Economic Development,* Academic Press.

Griffin, K. (1984) *Institutional Reform and Economic Development in the Chinese Countryside,* Macmillan.

Griffin, K. and Khan, A.R. (1973) *Growth and Inequality in Pakistan,* Macmillan.

Gurley, J.G. (1974) 'Rural development in China: 1949—1972 and lessons to be learned from it', in Edwards, E.O. (ed.) *Employment in Developing Nations,* Columbia University Press.

Gurley, J.G. (1978) 'The dialectics of development: USSR v. China', *Modern China,* vol. 4, pp. 123—156.

Ishik, Y. (1983) 'Chinese economic system reform', *World Development,* vol. 25, pp. 647—658.

Koziara, E.C. and Chiou-Shuag, Y. (1984) 'The distribution system for producers' goods in China', *The China Quarterly,* vol. 97, pp. 689—702.

Krueger, A. (ed.), (1983) *Alternative Trade Strategies and Employment,* vol. 3, *Synthesis and Conclusions,* Chicago University Press.

Kueh, Y.Y. (1983) 'Economic reform in China at the xian level', *The China Quarterly,* vol. 102, pp. 665—688.

Kumar, D. (1985) *The Cambridge Economic History of India,* Vol. 2, *1757—1970,* Cambridge University Press.

Lardy, N.R. (1983) *Agriculture in China's Modern Economic Development,* Cambridge University Press.

Oke, S. (1983) 'China's relations with the world economy', *Journal of Contemporary Asia,* vol. 22, pp. 237—246.

Ravallion, M. (1985) 'The Performance of rice markets in Bangladesh during the 1974 famine', *Economic Journal,* vol. 95, pp. 15—29.

Schram, S.R. (1984) ' "Economics in command?" Ideology and policy since the Third Plenum 1978—84', *The China Quarterly,* vol. 103, pp. 417—461.

Sen, A.K. (1984) *Resources, Value and Development,* Blackwell.

Streeten, P. and Lipton, M. (eds), (1968) *The Crisis of Indian Planning,* Oxford University Press.

Sui-Lun, Wong (1984) 'The consequences of China's new population policy', *The China Quarterly,* vol. 103, pp. 220—240.

UN (1960—86) *Economic Survey of Asia and the Pacific,* United Nations.

UNCTAD (1986) *Handbook of International Trade and Development Statistics, Supplement,* United Nations.

13

Latin America

The countries of Latin America have a shared history, shared problems and shared solutions. They are all the legatees of the Hispanic Empire which began to break up when Napoleon invaded Spain. But the removal of the monarchies did not result in the abolition of the bureaucratic controls through which they had ruled — a state of affairs which might seem surprising given that the early development of Latin America was influenced by the ideas of the French and American revolutionaries and that their later evolution has been susceptible to the thought of Marx, Trotsky and Mao Zedong as well as a group of indigenous thinkers of whom Prebisch and Cardoso must be singled out for attention.

Table 13.1 draws attention to some economic and social indicators. Population growth is noticeably high, the average age is low and levels of illiteracy are in some instances very high. Among developing countries and continents, Latin America is unusual for having the lowest percentage of its population in agriculture and the highest percentage of wage labour in agriculture. Much agricultural land is held in large estates, in part a legacy of the Spanish and Portuguese empires and in part a result of land mergers in the nineteenth century. Latin America attracted the Spanish and Portuguese because of its mineral wealth and it still accounts for one-quarter of the world's output of silver and one-sixth of the world's production of copper and tin. Its manufacturing industries have developed behind tariff walls as a result of experiences during the slump of the 1930s. One consequence of industrialisation has been urbanisation. Latin America is highly urbanised and it contains some of the largest cities in the world. This urbanisation has made Latin America different from Africa and Asia. It has given rise to an internal colonialism in which the urban working class has become detached from the peasantry; the intellectual class hovers between them. Latin America has become a synonym for political instability, with colonels and politicians alternating in government, with inflation and foreign debt. Issues requiring special attention are: (1) dependency theory; (2) import substitution; (3) inflation; (4) foreign debt; and (5) land reform.

Dependency theory — the notion that Third World countries are tied to the ad-

Table 13.1 Latin America: Selected Economic and Social Indicators

| | Population | | Median age | Life expectancy | Urban population (%) | Illiteracy rate (%) | GDP per capita (dollars) 1983 |
	Total (millions) 1983	Annual average growth rate 1970–83 (%)					
Latin America	386,700	2.4					
Argentina	29,637	1.6	27.3	74.0	84.6	4.5	2,263
Brazil	128,853	2.4	21.6	64.9	72.7	22.3	1,605
Chile	11,674	1.6	24.7	70.7	83.6	5.6	1,692
Mexico	75,154	3.0	18.4	67.2	69.6	9.7	1,899
Paraguay	3,476	3.3	18.8	66.1	44.4	11.8	1,868
Uruguay	2,971	0.4	29.8	71.0	84.6	6.1	1,837
Bolivia	6,050	2.7	19.5	53.1	47.8	16.2	1,089
Colombia	27,546	2.6	20.7	64.8	67.4	11.9	1,406
Ecuador	8,876	2.2	18.7	65.4	52.3	17.6	1,419
Peru	18,737	3.0	19.4	61.4	67.4	14.3	862
Venezuela	16,440	2.7	19.5	69.7	86.6	13.1	4,122
Cuba	9,915	1.1	29.6	74.4	71.8	4.6	—
CACM[a]	22,438	3.0					1,080
CARICOM[b]	5,517	1.5					2,949
OCES[c]	557	1.1					1,093
Other America	29,276	1.8					1,185

Source: UNCTAD (1986)
Notes: (a) CACM (Central American Common Market): Costa Rica, El Salvador, Guatemala, Honduras, Nicaragua.
    (b) CARICOM (Caribbean Community): Bahamas, Barbados, Belize, Guyana, Jamaica, Trinidad and Tobago.
    (c) (Organisation of Eastern Caribbean States): Antigua, Dominica, Grenada, Montserrat, St Christopher, St Lucia, St Vincent, Grenadines.

vanced countries and cannot easily escape from the pattern of trading determined by the policies of the latter — was first developed in Latin America and arose out of the work of Prebisch. It subsequently took root in parts of Africa. Along with the theory of hegemonic stability (the idea that the world has always required a leader — be it the UK, USA or Japan) and with the new protectionism, it has formed an important strand in the political economy of international trade.

Dependency Theory

Dependency theory had its origins in Latin America and it began with Prebisch's observations on the secular and cyclical behaviour of the terms of trade of primary producers, from which he concluded that primary producers faced a secular decline in their terms of trade and that in the short run the prices of their products showed greater instability than the prices of advanced countries' manufactures. But the theory evolved, partly as a result of changes in the international economy in the post-war period when, for example, multinational corporations began to emerge in manufacturing, and partly as a result of the elaboration of the theory by writers in other countries who observed dependency in Asia and Africa. Myrdal (1957), for example, emphasised the importance of spread and backwash effects. Spread effects were deemed to be beneficial: ideas, goods and processes spread out from the advanced regions to the periphery. Backwash effects were malignant: skilled labour migrated from backward regions to the centre leaving the periphery devoid of talent. Myrdal was strongly influenced by developments in India and Southeast Asia. Amin (1976) provided African insights and Emmanuel (1972) shifted the emphasis from production to exchange — unequal exchange. Whereas Prebisch had taken the condition of less developed countries as given, Marxist writers, such as Baran and Sweezy (1968), Wallerstein (1979) and Frank (1972) suggested that their condition was imposed by an initial core of advanced countries. These writers went on to explore class relations underlying the conditions of production and exchange and to provide a systems framework for analysing the evolution of the world economy.

The starting point of dependency theory is the first move assumption of game theory: it is assumed that the nature and development of an economy is determined by the time of its insertion into the world economy. The second assumption is that a distinction can be drawn between the centre of advanced countries (first movers) and the periphery of late entrants. The third assumption is that technological dependence is crucial to economic development. The advantage of the first move may be important in manufacturing, which is subject to economies of scale and the advantages of learning by doing. If we consider two time periods the following scenario obtains. In the first period country A sets up manufacturing. In the second period country B enters the world economy but is constrained to offer agricultural goods because it cannot compete in manufactures: it cannot instantly obtain all the advantages which A obtained in the first period. B's inability to set up in manufacturing then persists through successive periods. There is a further reason why B's disability may increase over time. Inventions tend to be random in their incidence, though this does not mean that they are due to chance: larger expenditures on research and development increase the likelihood of capturing new ideas.

But a competitive economy might lead to B obtaining some of the benefits of A's technology through offering manufactures at lower prices. There are two obstacles here. First, agricultural goods might have low income elasticities of demand so that the growth in country A might lead to greater domestic consumption of manufactures. B would not then obtain the benefits of progress but would always remain underdeveloped; B might grow but would never catch up with A. Second, the existence of monopolies and trade unions in country A might restrict the output of manufactures and prevent price reductions. Indeed, the existence of restrictive practices could accentuate the losses sustained by B during cyclical fluctuations. In slumps A's prices would not fall because of unions' resistance and in booms output might not expand greatly because of monopolies. In contrast, B's prices would fall precipitously in slumps and its output would be constrained in booms by monopolists in A.

Dependency theory is an attack on one of the oldest parts of economic theory; the doctrine of comparative advantage. In the hands of the classical economists the theory had suggested the possibilities of mutual gains from trade which could be measured in terms of the amounts of labour saved in production. In so far as there was a suggestion of unequal gains then classical theory predicted that the benefits would accrue to the landlord (the primary producer) rather than the manufacturers. Interestingly, Marx deduced from the classical analysis the possibility that trade would lead to the destruction of feudal economies and accelerate the movement to socialism. Neoclassical economists did not overthrow the classical emphasis upon comparative advantage but extended it, through the concept of opportunity cost, to embrace more factors than labour. Indeed, at the precise moment when dependency theory was first being propounded, Samuelson (1949) was extending the theory by suggesting that under certain conditions (which included the absence of increasing returns) trade would lead to the equalisation of factor rewards. However, Samuelson's analysis was concerned with functional factor rewards and did not embrace personal income distribution. Nevertheless, the emphasis in Samuelson's analysis upon the production function and the tendency of some writers such as Solow (1961), for example, to stress that the production function was a technical relationship led to the Cambridge critique of neoclassical theory and caused Cardoso (1977) to draw attention to the relevance of the Cambridge strand of neo-Keynesian theory for dependency theory. If income distribution was not determined by technical relationships then the way was open for bargaining power to be incorporated into dependency theory. And curiously, at the same time as dependency theory was being attacked by Viner (1953) and by Haberler (1950), Hicks (1953) was developing a neoclassical model of growth and trade which accounted for underdevelopment. The post-war dollar shortage had raised questions about the origins and persistence of underdevelopment. Hicks demonstrated that there could be a long-run dollar shortage if the USA's productive superiority was in import competing industries. However, Hicks's analysis was overlooked by both advocates and critics of dependency theory.

Dependency theory provokes several questions. Could the dependent economies use some of the proceeds from agricultural exports to subsidise the development of manufacturing? This was the line of advance adumbrated in staple theory and adopted by Australia, which at the end of the nineteenth century had a manufacturing industry comparable in size with those of France and Germany. The answer to the question may lie in contrasting theories — Ricardian, Marxist (Leninism) and Malthusianism. If landlords own most of the land and choose to spend most of their incomes on imported luxuries then there will be a persistent failure to develop industry. A penchant for luxury goods has been a characteristic of Latin American countries and this constitutes the Leninist (and of course Ricardian landlord) contribution to dependency theory. Unlike Marx, Lenin drew attention to the possibilities of alliances between manufacturing capitalists and feudal landlords. Even if some of the profits were to trickle down to the peasantry then higher real incomes might be translated into more children. A low level Malthusian equilibrium trap might then arise. In Latin America the attempt to avoid both dependency and Malthusianism led to import substitution industrialisation. Imports of manufactures were discouraged by the use of tariffs and behind the tariff walls manufacturing industries were developed. But because the distribution of income was so unequal, it was impossible to develop mass markets from which industrial plants could derive economies of scale.

The second issue is this. If the dominant ruling class will not invest in manufactures, then an alternative strategy might be to allow foreign firms to establish production units; this has given rise to transnational firms. The objection to such a policy is that the distribution of gains may be biased in favour of the transnational corporations who, through transfer pricing policies, can conceal their profits. The difficulties of controlling transfer prices is one reason why many governments have favoured borrowing rather than foreign direct investment and why they have pursued public rather than private investment.

The Record of History

Dependency theory is not a mere abstraction: it has its roots in experience. But has the record been analysed carefully enough? Dependency *may* have its roots in colonialism, in the social structure established by the Spanish and Portuguese which have dictated the subsequent evolution of an apparently independent periphery. In the period following independence were the Latin American states still bound to Europe through an informal empired based upon trade? In what sense, if any, did Latin America become dependent upon Europe and the USA in the nineteenth century? What were the effects of policies pursued during the slump of the 1930s?

There can be no doubts concerning the extent of European involvement in the independence movements in Latin America. British merchants helped to finance Bernardo O'Higgins's navy. But what happened after independence? O'Brien (1975) maintains that in the context of the world economy, the periphery was peripheral. Latin America dropped out of mind as well as out of sight. After the Napoleonic Wars Europe was preoccupied with internal political stability and internal growth and trade and the USA was obsessed with its own frontier of development. And even Cardoso and Faletto (1979) concluded that there was no substantial investment in the newly independent Latin America. In so far as there was an informal empire — a form of neocolonialism — through which Latin America was bound to Europe through trade, then that trade was insignificant

(which is not to deny that it was significant that Latin America was unable to develop until Europe wanted its exports.)

In the third quarter of the nineteenth century the outlook for dependency theory appears more promising. There was a considerable amount of British investment. The railway network was created and the export of agricultural goods and minerals became important. There was also labour migration from Southern Europe into the Southern Cone. This was the period in which the export cycle emerged not only in terms of fluctuations in fixed capital investment in Europe leading to variations in exports from Latin America, but in long swings in technological progress and development. Thorp and Bertram (1978) have drawn attention to three waves in Peruvian development: from 1830 to 1881 there was a wave associated with exports of minerals, notably guano; from 1881 to 1929 there was a swing which could be related to the exports of other minerals and agricultural goods; and from the 1930s there was another long wave which could be linked to the tempo of economic activity in the advanced countries.

Nevertheless, there are qualifications to dependency in the latter decades of the nineteenth century. Before the First World War Argentina was producing a wide range of manufactured goods which were locally produced: 70 per cent of furnishings were produced domestically as were 38 per cent of chemicals and 22 per cent of textiles. Argentina's dependence was qualified by the fact that it was the most important, and cheapest, producer of chilled beef. Its decision to allow private investment in railways was dictated by cost considerations and not by the power of foreign capitalists. Mexico, for example, borrowed to build its railways and loans were relatively easy to raise.

However, it is the inter-war years which have attracted the greatest attention. Although the terms of trade of the Latin American countries fell precipitously and there were severe reductions in GNP per capita, there were varied reactions to the slump which led, in some instances, to a softening of its intensity. Not all countries reacted sharply to the recession. Industrialisation had been proceeding before 1929 and some observers have drawn attention to the continuity of economic activity between the 1920s and 1930s. But in some countries there was a perceptible quickening of industrial activity. Diaz Alejandro (1970) suggested that a distinction could be drawn between those countries which maintained fixed exchange rates and those which adopted floating rates or managed currencies. Devaluation with an unchanged money supply gave rise to expenditure reducing and expenditure switching effects which reduced the pressures upon prices and wages — although in some countries the adjustment processes were powerfully assisted by price and wage flexibility. Countries which maintained fixed exchange rates threw the burden of the adjustment on to wages and provoked the greatest resistance to wage cuts, delaying the restoration of equilibrium.

In Brazil the slump led to a contraction of export revenues and to a fall in capital inflows. The authorities interposed with measures designed to devalue the currency, imposed exchange and import controls and introduced a coffee support scheme. But whereas Brazil benefited from US leniency, Argentina was confronted by the British policy of imperial preference — a policy that was to have repercussions in the Second World War and its aftermath. Nevertheless, the recovery in Argentina, as in Peru and Cuba, was in advance of the recovery of exports. It occurred because government spending did not fall as much as might have been expected and because of wage and price flexibility. But the fact that domestic policies could soften recessions, as in advanced countries, was to have a decisive influence upon thinking in Latin America. It contributed to the theories of import substitution and to the need to create an infrastructure within which firms could grow. It also pointed to the importance of linkages between firms.

Import Substitution

Through the 1950s and 1960s most Latin American countries pursued import substitution policies. The instruments used to carry out such policies were tariffs and exchange rate controls, special preferences for firms importing goods for new industries, cheap loans for special industries, direct government involvement in heavy industry where neither domestic nor foreign capital was available and government construction of infrastructures. But the policies were not selective nor were they always directed at industries in which the countries might have a comparative advantage — unless it was admitted that industries producing consumer goods with simple technologies were the simplest to promote.

How successful were these import substitution policies? Between the 1930s and 1960s the contribution of agriculture to GDP fell by 10 per cent in Argentina, by 7 per cent in Mexico and by 8 per cent in Brazil. Taking Latin America as a whole, the contribution of agriculture fell by about 10 per cent and, as a consequence, Latin America's exports as a percentage of world exports fell by about 5 per cent by the end of the 1960s.

But mere changes in the composition of output are not in themselves a sufficient comment upon the appropriateness of the import substitution policies. What is needed is some evidence about the relative costs of domestic production versus imports. Table 13.2 throws some light upon the question by indicating the magnitudes of effective rates of protection in Latin American countries; that is, the ratios of value-added in domestic prices to value-added measured in international prices. What the table reveals is the wide spread of effective protection rates. In the case of Brazil the lower rates for 1968 are the result of policies designed to reduce protection. But not all distortions are due to tariffs and Table 13.3 attempts to throw some light upon distortions in capital and labour costs resulting from trade policies, credit rationing and minimum wage legislation. In the absence of distortions it has been estimated that labour inputs would have increased by about 10 per cent in Argentina and 15 per cent in Brazil. Additional evidence comes from studies which suggest that multinational corporations tend to have fewer plants, higher ratios of value-added to output, to engage in more advertising, to export more goods, to have greater capital intensity, higher labour productivity and to pay higher wages than comparable indigenous firms.

And yet, was it all a waste of resources? How much stress can we place on

Table 13.2 Range of Effective Rates of Protection for Manufacturing Industries in Some Developing Countries

Country	Year	Range of ERPs
Brazil	1958	17−502
	1967	4−252
Chile	1967	−23−1,140
Indonesia	1971	−19−5,400
Pakistan	1970	36−592
South Korea	1968	−15−82
Tunisia	1972	1−737
Uruguay	1972	17−1,014

Source: Krueger (1983)

Table 13.3 Brazil: Selected Economic Indicators

	1960−70	1970−80	1980−85
Increase in GDP per capita (%)	2.7	0.6	−2.8
Increase in food production per capita (%)	0.0	0.9	0.3
GDP by type of economic activity (%)			
	1970	*1980*	*1984*
Agriculture	10	13	13
Industry	26	28	29
Construction	5	5	4
Services	58	54	55
Export structure (%)			
	1970	*1980*	*1984*
Food	63.25		40.31
Manufactures	9.66		31.94
Minerals	13.68		17.12
Agricultural raw materials	11.90		4.03
Fuels	0.58		5.29
Unallocated	0.93		1.31
	100.0		100.0
Illiteracy rate (%)	22.3		

Source: UNCTAD (1986)

nominal tariff rates? Was the Brazilian surge in growth in the mid-1960s a result
not merely of the abandonment of import substitution but a consequence of investment in capacity in the previous period; and was the slackening of growth in the
1980s a consequence of factors outside the control of the Brazilians (Table 13.3)?

Inflation

Latin American inflation is assumed to possess two characteristics which
distinguish it from inflation in advanced countries: inflation rates tend to be higher
and give rise to hyperinflation and the causes are deemed to be structural rather
than monetarist. Table 13.4 suggests that the first assumption is not correct. In
the post-war period inflation in Latin America has followed the world trend, being
low in the 1950s and high in the 1970s and 1980s. It has been a trend which

Table 13.4 Inflation Rates in Latin American Countries and the World, 1953–85
(Average Annual Percentage Changes in Consumer Prices)

	1953–60	1961–73	1974–80	1981–85
Argentina	26.3	43.5	178.3	38.4
Bolivia	n.a	7.5	19.6	144.2
Brazil	n.a	38.5	45.7	132.8
Chile	n.a	65.7[a]	184.1	21.5
Colombia	7.9	12.1	24.0	22.4
Ecuador	0.6	5.6	13.8	27.4
Mexico	6.1	3.7	21.2	62.4
Paraguay	22.0	4.7	15.3	15.9
Peru	7.7	9.0	42.5	104.9
Uruguay	18.1	52.1	60.1	45.9
Venezuela	1.3	1.6	10.7	11.2
Costa Rica	1.8	3.6	12.6	37.4
El Salvador	2.1	1.2	14.7	14.7
Guatemala	0.8	1.7	11.7	7.7
Honduras	0.7[a]	2.6	8.0	9.3
Nicaragua	n.a	n.a	16.7	66.9
Panama	−0.3	2.1	8.2	3.3
Bahamas	n.a	5.9[a]	8.3	6.0
Barbados	n.a	8.6[a]	15.7	6.7
Dominican Republic	−0.4	3.7	11.1	16.9
Guyana	1.4[a]	2.8	12.8	16.0
Haiti	0.3[a]	4.9	10.2	9.3
Jamaica	2.4[a]	5.5	21.9	16.9
World	2.6	5.1	12.2	14.1

Source: IMF (1987)
Note: (a) Incomplete series.

has run parallel to, but at a higher level, than that of the rest of the world. However, the Latin American average conceals many variations. In some countries, and on some occasions, inflation rates have been negative.

What Table 13.4 suggests is that countries can be grouped according to their inflation rates and known industrial and political characteristics as follows.

1. *Large industrialising countries (Argentina, Brazil and Mexico).*   These countries tend to have the high inflation rates that characterise European beliefs about Latin America. In these countries governments have rigorously pursued industrialisation through the use of import substitution policies. High rates of inflation have tended to be fuelled by the forced growth of industry which is often state owned and financed by the state and through borrowing. The controls over imports have meant that there has been no compulsion by firms to curb prices and ensure efficiency.

2. *Medium sized industrialising countries (Chile, Peru, Colombia and Uruguay).*   Although some of these countries have sophisticated economies in which workers enjoy relatively high living standards, they rely heavily upon the export of a few primary products, such as coffee and copper, and do not possess much heavy industry. Government expenditure tends to be a large part of national income and workers are usually well organised in trade unions. Consequently, when export prices fall or when import prices rise then there is an intense struggle to maintain their living standards.

3. *Oil economies (Venezuela, Mexico, Ecuador and Peru).*   With the exception of Peru, these countries have tended to have low inflation rates — possibly because governments have managed to control the speed at which oil revenues have been allowed to filter into the domestic economies. The exception has been Mexico which went on a spending spree in the 1970s.

4. *Small open economies.*   The small open economies comprise two groups: (1) those which concentrate on primary products for export, such as Honduras and the Bahamas; and (2) those which have some light industry, such as Nicaragua and Jamaica. In the first group inflation may be imported, as it was in 1973 and 1979. However, price rises tend to be modest — possibly because the monetary and fiscal systems are not sophisticated and there is no deficit spending. In the second group there may be resistance to real wage cuts but the small size of the industrial sectors means that the inflation tends to be moderate.

5. *Dependent economies (Martinique and the Virgin Islands).*   Some countries are economies still dependent on metropolitan powers and their rates of inflation tend to be similar to those of the metropolis.

Table 13.4 introduces our discussion of the competing claims of monetarists and structuralists. Of course, all sustained inflation requires some increase in the money supply: what the monetarist versus structuralist debate is about is the nature of the economy in which inflation occurs. The monetarist model assumes that the demand for money is a function of a few key variables, such as wealth, and distinguishes between anticipated and unanticipated changes in the money supply and real forces (such as the price of oil).

Anticipated changes in the money supply are assumed to have no effect upon relative prices and outputs but merely cause a rise in the general level of prices, whereas unanticipated changes in the money supply are assumed to cause, first, an increase in output and, second, an increase in the price level. Hanson (1980) found that a significant relationship existed between output and unanticipated inflation in Brazil, Chile (before Allende), Colombia, Mexico and Peru with, on average, a 10 percentage point in unanticipated inflation leading to 1 extra percentage point increase in growth. And in an analysis of inflation in 16 different countries between 1950 and 1969 Vogel (1974) found that the differences in inflation rates could not be explained by differences in economic structures but by differences in the behaviour of money supply — a conclusion which might seem at variance with our initial comments on the inflation rates revealed in Table 13.4. However, Vogel did make three concessions. First, that it was important to explain why differences in the behaviour of the money supply occurred. Second, that small open economies on fixed exchange rates might not have exogenous money supplies. Third, that purely monetarist conclusions for stabilisation policy could not be derived from his model since inflation rates required up to two years to adjust to changes in the money supply and this might be a longer period of austerity than most Latin American regimes could tolerate politically.

This brings us to a consideration of the structuralist explanation and its emphasis upon the political aspects of inflation. The structuralist model may be regarded as an outcome of dependency and import substitution. The urban population increases because of import substitution, and the demand for foodstuffs rises. But because agriculture has been neglected, the supply of food does not increase rapidly and food prices also rise. In the towns the fall in real wages may provoke unrest and governments may react by introducing food subsidies financed by borrowing and the printing press. A second route via which inflation feeds into the economy arises from the shortage of foreign exchange. Although import substitution policies are designed to reduce imports, their initial effect is to increase the import of capital goods. Unfortunately, the ability to purchase foreign currencies is constrained by the lack of incentives to farmers to produce more output. In order to correct an adverse balance of payments, governments are then forced into devaluations which raise import prices, reduce real wages and create demands for increases in wages and prices. The third source of inflation is deficit financing. Because of the smallness of the tax base and the unequal distribution of income and wealth in Latin America, governments are obliged to borrow in order to finance their development programmes.

Structuralist models of inflation bear a close resemblance to the Keynesian models of inflation and unemployment discussed in advanced countries: that is, there is an emphasis upon the supply-side problems which must be tackled in pursuing a deflationary policy. Of course monetarists have not neglected the supply side — at least since the end of the 1970s. The difference may therefore be one of emphasis, with the structuralists tending to pay more attention to the distribution of income and wealth and the importance of incomes policies.

Combating Inflation

Some light is thrown upon the relative merits of the respective approaches to inflation by the attempts to achieve economic stability in the Southern Cone (Argentina, Chile and Uruguay) in the 1970s. The experiments failed; but their failure drew attention to the problems of exchange rate management, the deregulation of financial markets and the relative speeds of adjustment of financial and real markets. The most widely analysed country has been Chile. In 1970 Salvadore Allende became the first Marxist to be elected head of state by a democratic vote in the Western world. In 1973 he was overthrown by a military coup in which the CIA and US multinationals were implicated — although it must be conceded that his election was more surprising than his deposition. Allende promised too many interest groups too much. With inflation approaching 400 per cent, the fiscal deficit reaching 30 per cent of GDP and an undercapitalised economy where savings were 2 per cent of GDP, the new regime introduced deflationary measures and proposed a reform of the financial sector as well as the opening of the economy to foreign trade. In a nutshell, the post-Allende government proposed to control aggregate money demand and to prevent unemployment by improving the supply side of the economy.

The fiscal measures resulted in the elimination of taxes on wealth and capital gains and the adoption of a value-added tax from which consumer goods were exempt. The reduction in taxation was accompanied by cuts in public expenditure, especially on social benefits. In an endeavour to improve the efficiency of the monetary and financial systems the banks were denationalised, exchange controls were eased and tariffs were reduced, with the result that Chile was less protected than most advanced countries.

Deregulation of the financial system without any checks upon the credibility of institutions led to an expansion of credit. The increase in credit was assisted by the removal of price controls which led to the emergence of profitable opportunities — as well as a rise in inflation. The new profitable opportunities seem to have accrued mainly to the larger firms — the so-called *groupos* — concentrating wealth and power in their hands. In an endeavour to control the rate of inflation the exchange rate was pegged at too high a rate with the result that substantial capital inflows assisted the expansion of credit. Because the currency was overvalued there was an incentive to increase real consumption (Table 13.5). Index linked wages tended to lag behind the rate of change of prices and hindered the adjustment of the real sector, which did not respond readily to profitable opportunities and began to disappear as firms started to fail. In some cases banks were bailed out and the threat of bankruptcy no longer acted as a spur to efficiency — people were prepared to engage in risky ventures.

Table 13.5 Chile: Selected Economic Indicators, 1973−84

	Terms of trade[a]	Real exchange rate[b]	Index of real private consumption[c]	Annual change in real wage[d] (%)	Trade balance ($ million)[e]	Unemployment (%)[f]
1973	195	44.3	n.a	−34.0	−13.1	n.a
1974	164	86.7	n.a	−9.1	250.0	9.2
1975	122	113.2	n.a	−3.3	−70.4	14.7
1976	118	99.4	n.a	0.5	643.0	13.0
1977	105	92.7	n.a	12.9	35.0	11.6
1978	100	107.8	100	6.4	−426.0	14.2
1979	101	98.5	119	8.3	−355.0	13.6
1980	83	83.8	122	9.0	−764.0	10.4
1981	66	75.3	132	9.1	−2,678.0	11.3
1982	62	83.9	93	−0.4	63.0	19.6
1983	75	90.5	90	−10.6	987.0	14.6
1984	n.a	91.4	90	n.a	293.0	14.0
1985	n.a	103.8	90	n.a	789.0	n.a

Sources: (a) UNCTAD (1986)
   (b) Balassa *et al.* (1986) (average 1976−78=100)
   (c) IMF (1987)
   (d) UN (1983)
   (e) UNCTAD (1986)
   (f) ILO (1985)

A similar state of affairs can be discerned in Argentina between 1976 and 1982 (Table 13.6). There was an attempt to control the money supply and wages through indexation; there was also an attempt to influence expectations by the establishment of a pre-announced schedule of reductions in the exchange rate supposedly accompanied by fiscal measures to reduce the public sector deficit. Following a financial crisis in 1980, the stabilisation policy was abandoned in 1981 and in 1982 there was a virtual nationalisation of bank deposits. In Uruguay the currency was linked to the dollar via the Argentine peso and as long as the Argentina currency was overvalued the influence on expectations was probably favourable. But when Argentina devalued, Uruguay faced a crisis.

The policies pursued in the Southern Cone have been considered monetarist in inspiration. How is their failure to be explained? Governments did not lack resolution: military regimes can by and large set aside fears of being voted out at elections. It is possible to explain some of the problems by reference to unforeseen circumstances such as the fall in the price of copper, which had a serious effect upon the Chilean economy, and the rise in the value of the US dollar. None the less many areas were within the control of the authorities; it is policy inconsistencies which created the major problems. The attempt to manage the exchange rate was an attempt to influence expectations without the loss of output and in-

Table 13.6 Argentina: Selected Economic Indicators, 1973−85

	Terms of trade[a]	Real exchange rate[b]	Index of real private consumption[c]	Annual change in real wage[d] (%)	Trade balance ($ million)[e]
1973	177	98.6	108	n.a	1,288.7
1974	164	87.2	132	n.a	714.0
1975	159	118.9	126	n.a	−548.8
1976	139	90.3	125	n.a	1,153.0
1977	119	110.2	112	−10.4	1,852.0
1978	109	99.4	100	−13.4	2,925.9
1979	103	75.7	111	−14.8	1,797.2
1980	100	67.5	109	12.0	−1,378.3
1981	102	75.6	107	−10.2	712.0
1982	91	115.2	109	−10.5	2,764.0
1983	90	103.6	118	22.6	3,716.0
1984	102	95.7	n.a	n.a	1,809.0
1985	93	129.4	n.a	n.a	1,931.0

Sources: (a) UNCTAD (1986)
(b) Balassa *et al.* (1986) (average 1976−78 = 100)
(c) IMF (1987)
(d) UN (1983)
(e) UNCTAD (1986)
(f) ILO (1985)

crease in unemployment predicted by monetarists. Exchange rate management was an alternative to the structuralist's incomes policy. But it failed because of a lack of appreciation of how slowly real forces, such as the labour market, respond to changes, as compared with financial markets. The exchange rate cannot therefore be isolated from what is happening to the money supply and to wages and production. Overvalued currencies must at some stage be devalued to avoid the persistence of unemployment. The possibility of future devaluation should therefore encourage people to save and not spend; but such an argument assumes that the generation who are in effect borrowing will be the generation who will pay the tax (the depreciated currency). It is, however, conceivable that one generation is myopic or that it assumes that the next generation will pay the tax. In Latin America the evidence suggests that when currencies were overvalued real consumption increased.

External Debt

The external borrowing problems of Latin American countries began in the nineteenth century, revived in the 1940s and 1950s and became acute in the 1980s. In the nineteenth century borrowing took place to develop and exploit the natural resources of the continent. In the 1940s and 1950s borrowing was associated with the policy of import substitution; industrialisation required finance but exports of primary products were unable to supply the finance — for two reasons. Price controls on agriculture and subsidies to industry discouraged agricultural production; and agriculture's share of world trade declined, partly because of protection and agricultural innovation in the advanced countries and partly because rising real incomes were devoted to manufactures and services.

The problems created by borrowing intensified in the 1970s and 1980s. Oil supplied 70 per cent of the region's energy requirements so that the first oil shock placed an enormous burden upon Latin American countries. After the second oil shock advanced economies deflated and the resulting world recession led to a decline in world trade and a collapse in the exports of the Latin American countries. The price of sugar (exported by most Latin American countries) fell by 82 per cent between 1980 and 1984, coffee by about 12 per cent, copper by 35 per cent and tin by 27 per cent.

The terms of trade of Latin America fell and the real interest rates on debt rose. After 1979 the advanced economies — especially the United States — pursued a combination of restrictive monetary policies and expansionary fiscal policies. Inflation had to be checked, so the burden of deflation was conducted through monetary policies. As a result real interest rates rose from 2 per cent in 1980 to 6.9 per cent in 1981. Since most of Latin America's debt was linked to bank lending there was an automatic rise in debt service charges. Here was the scissors effect — not in terms of the ratio of the prices of manufactures to the prices of agricultural goods — the model of Soviet economic development in the 1920s — or of the Prebisch model discussed in Chapter 5 and earlier in this chapter, but in terms of the prices of loans from advanced countries and the prices of primary products from developing countries. Table 13.7 measures the widening of the scissors in terms of the number of imports represented by international reserves and Table 13.8 measures long-term servicing as a percentage of the exports of goods and services. For Latin America the percentage of exports required to service long-term debt rose from 26 per cent in 1980 to 35.4 per cent in 1982. The experiences of individual countries are more revealing: for Argentina debt servicing rose from 25.1 per cent to 64.4 per cent. In the case of Brazil the debt charge rose from 57.1 per cent to 77.0 per cent and for Chile it climbed to 45.8 per cent from 35.2 per cent. An alternative way of measuring the impact of the slump is to look at the impact on international reserves. In the case of Argentina the purchasing power of reserves was reduced by about two-thirds. Mexico was almost bankrupt in 1980 and had to be bailed out because the reserves fell to less than two months' command over imports. (African countries experienced similar and, in some instances, more severe problems, but African debt has always tended to be regarded as aid rather than loans.)

The demand for loans came from countries which were attempting to continue with development programmes and were reluctant to cut back sharply on policies which they perceived would bring long-run benefits. The supply of loans came

Table 13.7 Number of Months of Imports Represented by International Reserves[a]

	1970	1980	1983
Latin America	3.8	4.2	4.2
Argentina	4.5	8.3	3.5
Brazil	4.3	2.9	3.5
Chile	4.8	6.7	7.8
Mexico	3.9	1.7	4.9
Paraguay	3.2	17.9	15.3
Uruguay	9.1	3.9	4.6
Bolivia	3.3	2.1	4.0
Colombia	2.8	12.1	5.5
Ecuador	2.9	5.5	5.0
Venezuela	7.1	7.6	13.3
Africa	5.0	5.3	2.3
Egypt	2.2	2.0	2.4
Sudan	0.8	0.4	0.2
Benin	2.7	0.2	0.2
Congo	3.6	0.6	0.2
Senegal	1.3	0.1	0.2
Tanzania	2.2	0.2	0.3
Asia	4.9	4.2	4.6

Source: IMF (1987)
Note: (a) International reserves consist of a country's holdings of monetary gold, Special Drawing
Rights (SDRs), as well as its reserve position in the International Monetary Fund.

Table 13.8 Long-term Debt Service as a Percentage of Exports of Goods and Services
1975−85

	1975	1980	1982	1982	1983	1984	1985
Latin America	18.6	26.0	35.4	32.0	29.6	26.0	30.0
Argentina	27.7	25.1	64.4	41.9	30.2	28.8	63.6
Brazil	40.1	57.1	77.0	69.6	60.7	31.7	35.2
Chile	34.5	35.2	45.8	63.4	52.3	53.2	46.7
Mexico	39.0	38.8	43.2	39.8	38.7	36.3	38.2
Paraguay	12.0	16.6	20.7	16.5	30.0	17.5	15.0
Bolivia	18.8	28.1	33.6	33.0	33.5	40.9	27.8
Colombia	13.0	12.8	23.2	23.0	28.3	25.6	34.2
Ecuador	7.6	18.7	36.3	34.7	31.2	33.2	23.1
Venezuela	5.0	21.2	25.7	21.0	18.0	16.2	15.4
Africa	9.2	12.6	20.1	20.8	24.5	23.3	27.1
Asia	5.0	5.4	7.5	7.2	9.0	9.0	11.5

Source: UNCTAD (1986, 1987)

from commercial banks. Before the oil crises commercial banks were seldom
involved in lending to Latin America. In the 1950s and 1960s the bulk of annual
capital inflows took the form of official credits and foreign direct investment.
This state of affairs changed at the end of the 1970s. Because the Arab oil states
had small populations and low consumption levels, the profits from higher oil
prices were recycled to the rest of the world economy through commercial banks.
The banks were encouraged by Western governments to lend to developing countries. This satisfied the consciences of the Arab oil states who were able to feel
that they were assisting the less developed countries; it also satisfied the advanced
countries who were able to feel that they were 'doing something' for the Third
World. Taken in conjunction with a rise in OPEC imports and a fall in the real
price of oil, the policy of recycling proved a successful method of coping with
the first oil price rise: the burden of debt even tended to fall as world inflation
continued.

The success of recycling after the first oil shock led to a belief that developing
countries could repay their debts. But circumstances changed after the second
oil shock. There was a world slump and a rise in real interest rates. As interest
rates rose the less developed countries found it more convenient to shift to short-
term debt — a policy the banks encouraged because they thought that it would
reduce risks. By 1982 one-quarter of Latin America's debt was short-term debt
and some countries were having difficulties repaying the interest on it. In 1982
Argentina was forced to admit that it could not continue to service its debt as
a result of the embargo on new loans imposed during the Malvinas War. Mexico
was also forced to admit that it could not service its debt in 1982. The result
was a cut back in lending. In 1985 President Perez told the United Nations that
his country faced a choice between servicing its debt and democracy and that
he therefore proposed to restrict debt servicing. In 1987 Brazil ran into difficulties.
Nor have the problems of Latin America's debt been confined to the financial
institutions of the advanced countries. As a result of the IMF conditions imposed
upon countries many found that they had to reduce their imports from the advanced
countries: US exports to Latin America fell by 25 per cent between 1981 and 1985.

The initial response to the crisis was *ad hoc*; the IMF analysed countries on
an individual basis and proposed rescheduling of their debts. Underlying the proposals was the objective of reducing the growth of debt to a level which would
balance the willingness of lenders to continue lending with Latin America's capacity to borrow. The way forward was usually an approach to the IMF. Taken
in isolation each of the IMF's proposals could seem reasonable; taken in combination they were unusually harsh, involving rapid adjustment and provoking
a clash between debt servicing and democracy where the bases of democracy were
fragile and there was a tendency to slide into authoritarian and military regimes.
But given the vulnerability of the commercial banks, the threat to suspend payments
could be a strong bargaining counter. For even if the banks were to threaten to
make no further loans there is no evidence that they could afford to enforce such
a policy.

One solution would be to introduce partial and selective debt forgiveness on the grounds that it would be foolish to destroy fragile democracies. The case for such a policy is further strengthened by the fact that the financial markets have, in their wisdom, discounted the commercial banks' nominal claims on the debtor countries. But debt forgiveness is only a partial solution and attention needs to be paid to the economic policies within the countries. There is a need, for example, to resolve the relationship between macroeconomic and microeconomic policies. As we noted above, some countries have pursued inconsistent micro- and macroeconomic policies. One way out of this impasse would be to concentrate initially on the macroeconomic objectives of stability, with an emphasis on the money supply and the exchange rate. Most Latin American countries have tended to have overvalued currencies, which has encouraged a growth in consumption and the flight of capital. Such a policy would leave the issues of deregulation of markets to a later stage on the grounds that they might be much slower to change. There is, however, a need to control the size of public sectors on the grounds that a considerable amount of debt has been incurred as a result of excessive government spending.

But prescriptions to Latin American countries rest upon some view of how the world economy will develop. Will there be an expansion of world trade or greater protectionism? The behaviour of the world economy is the great uncertainty: the nostrums of the international agencies have failed because none of their forecasts has been reliable.

Land Reform and Agricultural Productivity

So far we have concentrated upon the problems created by import substitution, inflation and external debt. But, as Table 13.9 indicates, improvements in agricultural productivity have been meagre.

One solution to the problem of low agricultural productivity would be land reform. Land distribution in Latin America is highly concentrated. The Gini coefficient is about 0.84, as compared with 0.72 for the United States, 0.71 for the United Kingdom and 0.51 for India. Large tracts of land appear to be underutilised. However, previous land reforms have not been entirely successful.

Between 1915 and 1968 over one-half of the land in private ownership in Mexico

Table 13.9 Annual Average Growth Rate of Per Capita Food Production, 1960−85

	1960−70	1970−80	1980−85
Latin America	0.3	−0.5	−2.2
Developed market economies	0.8	0.9	0.8

Source: UNCTAD (1986)

was redistributed and the result seems to have been that Mexico became self-sufficient in food. But land reform does not appear to have satisfied many of the other aspirations of the people and many of the old power groups still persist. In Bolivia the 1953 land reform reduced the appeal of Guevara and his Cuban revolutionaries to the populace; but landholdings are still unequal in size and there is still a need for finance and credit to assist the peasant farmers. In Cuba the revolution was intended to satisfy many aims. It represented not merely an attempt to redistribute land but also an attempt to reduce dependence upon sugar production and therefore the United States; it was also hoped to reduce the importance of Havana and its domination of the economy. But the attempt to reduce sugar production led in the early years to a lack of finance and subsequently, when the Americans removed the preference quota, to a dependence upon East European countries. Land reforms elsewhere have been applied fitfully and most landowners have managed to circumvent the legislation.

There is, however, a more fundamental problem. In Europe and Asia there has always been a tradition of peasant farming, with skilled labour working under the direction of landlords or tribal chiefs. After land reforms were introduced the agricultural workers were able to continue production without encountering severe problems. The main difficulty was commerce, in which they had no experience. But, in sharp contrast, many agricultural workers in Latin America tend to be migrant workers, living not on plantations but outside them, hired for only short periods to work on tasks which vary with the nature of the crops. They do not have the opportunity to become skilled farmers. But farming is not like engineering: farming skills cannot be taught in schools. The success of Asian land reform rested upon the existence of skilled labour and an increase in agricultural education. The weakness of Latin American land reforms has stemmed from the lack of skilled labour and the lack of provision for educational assistance, as well as the opposition of the landlords. Skills cannot be acquired in schools because farming is not like factory work: skills must be acquired in the field.

Comparative Performance and Conclusions

Latin America's performance needs to be seen from a proper perspective. Should we compare small economies with large ones? Have all the Asian countries been successful, have all the Latin American countries been so bad? Table 13.10 attempts to answer these questions by detailing the comparative performances of different Latin American and Asian countries. There has been considerable variation in the performances of countries. Many Latin American countries performed well in the 1960s and tended to deteriorate in the 1970s and especially in the 1980s. In the 1970s many Latin American countries borrowed on the expectation that the earnings from their natural resources would eventually rise. But behind these figures lie differences in philosophy and accidents of timing. Latin America attempted import substitution because of the experiences of the 1930s

Table 13.10 Comparative Economic Performance

| | Growth Rates of GDP | | | Inflation | | |
	1965–73	1970–80	1980–85	1965–73	1970–80	1980–85
Latin America						
Argentina	4.3	2.2	−1.4	24.1	130.8	342.8
Brazil	9.8	8.4	−1.3	23.2	36.7	147.2
Chile	3.4	2.4	−1.1	50.3	185.6	19.3
Colombia	6.4	5.9	1.9	10.8	22.0	22.5
Mexico	7.9	5.2	0.8	4.8	19.3	62.2
Peru	3.5	3.0	−1.6	10.1	30.7	98.6
Venezuela	5.1	5.0	−1.6	3.3	12.1	9.2
Asia						
Indonesia	8.1	7.6	3.5	63.0	20.5	10.9
Korea	10.0	9.5	7.9	15.5	19.8	6.0
Malaysia	6.7	5.5	5.5	1.2	3.1	0.1
Philippines	5.4	6.3	−0.5	8.8	13.2	19.3
Taiwan	10.4	9.2	5.4	5.7	9.5	5.6
Thailand	7.8	7.2	5.1	2.5	9.9	3.2
Bangladesh	—	3.9	3.6	7.3	11.5	0.1
India	3.9	3.6	5.2	6.3	8.5	7.8
Pakistan	5.4	4.7	6.0	4.8	13.5	8.6
Sri Lanka	4.2	4.1	5.1	5.1	12.6	14.7

Source: World Bank (1982, 1985, 1987)

and because of its abundant raw materials. South-east Asia sought to use trade as an engine of growth because of its small populations and fewer resources. For Latin America trade was not to be an engine of growth so much as a means of obtaining foreign exchange with which to buy some essential capital goods. In the 1960s there was a switch to expanding trade and growth rates increased. In the 1970s there were problems stemming from over-borrowing which intensified in the 1980s. But to suppose that the Asian successes could have been replicated in Latin America may be a mistake when we consider differences in political structure and the distribution of income and wealth.

In spite of their abundant resources the record of the Latin American countries has been poor. In some respects they have been unfortunate. They pursued, on the basis of experience, import substitution at a time when world trade was expanding. But even if they had stuck to their comparative advantage they would have found markets contracting because Europe was becoming self-sufficient in food and the prices of minerals fell in the late 1950s. But it is their underlying political and social structures which have been responsible for a failure to capitalise on their comparative advantage. Failure to carry out land reform has resulted in low levels of productivity which have set the standard for industry. Lack of literacy has also been a contributing factor, while the uneven distribution of income and wealth has inhibited the development of mass markets.

Bibliography

Alejandro, C.D. (1970) *Essays on the Economic History of the Argentine Republic,* Yale University Press.

Amin, S. (1976) *Unequal Development,* Harvester Press.

Baer, W. (1973) 'The Brazilian boom 1968–72: an explanation and an interpretation', *Journal of Development Studies,* vol. 1, pp. 1–16.

Baer, W. and Gillis, M. (1981) *Export Diversification and the New Protectionism: The Experiences of Latin America,* National Bureau of Economic Research.

Balassa, B. *et al.* (1986) *Toward Renewed Economic Growth in Latin America,* Institute for International Economics, Geneva.

Baran, P. and Sweezy, P. (1968) *Monopoly Capital,* Penguin.

Bath, C.R. and James, D.D. (1985) 'Dependency analysis of Latin America: some criticisms, some suggestions', *Latin American Research Review,* vol. 11, pp. 3–54.

Bethell, L. (ed.), (1986) *Cambridge History of Latin America,* vol. V, *1870–1930,* Cambridge University Press.

Cardoso, F.H. and Faletto, E. (1979) *Dependency and Development in Latin America,* University of California Press.

Conroy, M.E. (1974) 'Recent research in economic demography related to Latin America: a critical survey and an agenda', *Latin American Research Review,* vol. 9, pp. 3–21.

Corbo, V. and Mellor, P. (1979) 'Trade and employment: Chile in the 1960s', *American Economic Review, Papers and Proceedings,* vol. 69, pp. 134–139.

Economic Commission for Latin America (1950–86) *Cepal Review,* United Nations.

Elias, P. (1978) 'Sources of growth in Latin America', *Review of Economics and Statistics* vol. 32, pp. 7–15.

Emmanuel, A. (1972) *Unequal Exchange,* NLB.

Erikson, K.P. *et al.* (1974) 'Research on the urban working class and organized labor in Argentina, Brazil and Chile: what is left to be done', *Latin American Research Review,* vol. 9, pp. 115–142.

Finch, M.H.J. (1981) *A Political Economy of Uruguay,* Macmillan.

Fitzgerald, E. (1980) *The Political Economy of Peru 1956–78,* Cambridge University Press.

Foxley, A. (1987) *Latin American Experiments in Neo Conservative Economics,* University of California Press.

Frank, A.G. (1972) *Dependence and Underdevelopment,* Doubleday.

Gereffi, G. and Evans, P. (1981) 'Transnational corporations, dependent development and state policy in the semi-periphery: a comparison of Brazil and Mexico', *Latin American Research Review,* vol. 16, pp. 31–64.

Glezakos, C. and Nugent, J.B. (1984) 'Price instability and inflation: the Latin American case', *World Development,* vol. 12, pp. 755–758.

Griffith-Jones, S. (1984) *International Finance and Latin America,* Croom Helm.

Haberler, G. (1950) 'Some problems in the pure theory of international trade', *Economic Journal,* vol. 60, pp. 201–205.

Hanson, J.A. (1980) 'The short-run relationship between growth and inflation in Latin America: a quasi-rational or consistent expectations appraisal', *American Economic Review,* vol. 70, pp. 275–289.

Harberger, A.C. (1985) 'Observations on the Chilean economy, 1973–78', *Economic Development and Cultural Change,* vol. 33, pp. 451–462.

Hewlett, S.A. and Weinert, R.S. (1984) *Brazil and Mexico: Patterns in Late Development,* Institute of Human Issues.

Hicks, J.R. (1953) 'An inaugural lecture: the long run dollar problem', *Oxford Economic Papers,* NS, vol. 5, pp. 1–12.

Iglesias, E.V. (1984) 'Latin America: crisis and development options', *CEPAL Review,* vol. 23, pp. 7–28.

ILO (1985) *Yearbook of Labour Statistics*, ILO.

IMF (1987) *International Financial Statistics*, United Nations.

Janvry, A. de (1986) *The Agrarian Question and Reformism in Latin America*, Johns Hopkins University Press.

Jenkins, R. (1985) *Transnational Corporations and Industrial Transformation in Latin America*, Macmillan.

Krueger, A. (ed.), (1983) *Alternative Trade Strategies and Employment*, vol. 3, *Synthesis and Conclusions*, Chicago University Press.

Leff. N. (1982) *Underdevelopment and Development in Brazil*, Allen and Unwin.

Lopen. J.G. (1983) 'The Mexican economy: present situation, perspectives and alternatives', *World Development*, vol. 11, pp. 455–465.

Muñoz, H. (1981) 'The strategic dependency of the centres and the economic importance of Latin America', *Latin American Research Review*, vol. 16, pp. 3–29.

Myrdal, G. (1957) *Economic Theory and Underdeveloped Regions*, Duckworth.

Nunnekamp, P. (1986) *The International Debt Crisis of the Third World*, Wheatsheaf.

O'Brien, P.J. (1975) 'A critique of Latin American theories of dependency', in I. Oxaal *et al.*, *Beyond the Sociology of Development*, Routledge.

Prebisch, R. (1950) *The Economic Development of Latin America and its Principal Problems*, United Nations.

Rock, D. (1980) *Argentina 1850–1980*, Tauris.

Samuelson, P.A. (1949) 'International factor-price equalisation once again', *Economic Journal*, vol. 58, pp. 163–184.

Seers, D. (1982) *Inflation: A Sketch for a Theory of World Inflation*, Institute of Development Studies.

Solow, R. in D.C. Hague (ed.), (1961) *Theory of Capital*, Macmillan.

Symposium (1980) 'Stabilization in Latin America', *World Development*, vol. 8.

Symposium (1981) 'Latin America and trade liberalization', *Quarterly Review of Economics and Business*, vol. 34.

Symposium (1985) 'Liberalization with stabilization in the Southern Cone of Latin America', *World Development*, vol. 13.

Symposium (1986) 'Growth reform and adjustment in Latin America's trade and macroeconomic policies in the 1970s and 1980s', *Economic Development and Cultural Change*, vol. 34.

Symposium (1987) 'The resurgence of inflation in Latin America', *World Development*, vol. 15.

Thorp, R. (ed.), (1984) *Latin America in the 1930s: The Role of the Periphery in World Crisis*, Macmillan.

Thorp, R. and Bertram. G. (1978) *Peru, 1890–1977*, Macmillan.

Thorp, R. and Whitehead, L. (1979) *Inflation and Stabilisation in Latin America*, Macmillan.

Thorp, R. and Whitehead, L. (1987) *Latin American Debt and the Adjustment Crisis*, Macmillan.

UN (1983) *Economic Survey of Latin America*, United Nations.

UN (1960–83) *Economic Bulletin for Latin America and the Caribbean*, United Nations.

UNCTAD (1986, 1987) *Handbook of International Trade and Development Statistics*, United Nations.

Viner, J. (1953) *International Trade and Economic Development*, Oxford University Press.

Vogel, R. (1974) 'The dynamics of inflation in Latin America, 1950–1969', *American Economic Review*, vol. 64, pp. 102–114.

Wallerstein, I.M. (1979) *The Capitalist World Economy*, Cambridge University Press.

World Bank (1982, 1985, 1987) *World Development Reports*, United Nations.

14

Africa

Although the Mediterranean shores of Africa had long been familiar to Europeans and settlements were established along the coastline of West Africa in the fourteenth century, the interior was largely unknown until the last quarter of the nineteenth century, when the scramble for Africa provided evidence for the theory of imperialism. Africa was the stage for the last act of European colonisation. Not only was Africa the last continent to be colonised, it was also the last to be decolonised — largely as a result of a series of struggles for independence between the late 1950s and early 1960s (although the status of South Africa has still to be determined). As a result of European settlement, African variety and complexity — political and economic, religious and ethnic — have largely been obscured by colonialism. Egypt and Ethiopia are the only long established states. With the exception of the disputed area of the western fringe, North Africa consists mainly of large states with relatively settled boundaries. But elsewhere a *mélange* of states has emerged whose boundaries reflect a division of spoils agreed in the nineteenth century. States have emerged and have been internationally accepted despite their lack of internal coherence. The boundary between Islam and Christianity runs through Ethiopia, the Sudan and Nigeria; the creation of Islamic states threatens to disrupt the neat European distinction between church and state. Elsewhere political boundaries are bisected by ethnic divides. The pattern is further complicated by variations in population sizes and real incomes per head. Libya is a large country but has a small population. Despite the high incomes yielded by its oil reserves and despite the religious zeal of its leaders, it has not been able to pursue its stated external policies with the desired success. Between the large northern states and South Africa lie many small countries, some rich and some extremely poor. And at the tip of Africa lies South Africa, the last remnant of colonialism.

The varied pattern of shapes and sizes is complemented by differences in policies, despite the existence of some common themes and problems. Many states have expanding populations and scarce agricultural resources. Many have

increased the production of cash crops in order to create export surpluses with
which to finance manufacturing industry. Some have sought assistance in continued association with France, through the acceptance of General de Gaulle's
offer of *communauté* to former colonies, an offer which has delayed and frustrated
the attempts at African unity. In some isolated instances — Tanzania, for example
— there has been an attempt at self-help, at socialist independence. Confronted
by so much variety we seek refuge in selection, choosing as the important issues
the relationship between famines and economic development, the relative lack
of development of Sub-Saharan Africa and the economic analysis of apartheid.

Malnutrition and Famines

In the 1970s and 1980s attention was directed at the problems created by famine
in Africa. In 1973 the Wollo Famine in Ethiopia was responsible for the deaths
of about 200,000 people out of a total population of 27 million. In 1984 some
30 million people in 21 African countries were exposed to starvation and 20 per
cent of of population of Ethiopia was destroyed by famine. The 1984 famine
brought a generous charitable response from the rest of the world. Yet 1984 was
a year of agricultural abundance and world production of cereals was up by 10
per cent to an all time record. Out of the increased supplies and large stocks 5.3
million tonnes of grain were imported into Sub-Saharan Africa of which 2.9 million
tonnes were contributed by relief agencies. The paradox of poverty in the midst
of plenty continued in 1987 when drought in Ethiopia threatened further starvation while a drought in India did not lead to famine because of the availability
of stocks.

But malnutrition in Sub-Saharan Africa is persistent and severe. Unfortunately
it is not easy to measure either malnutrition (lack of protein or calories) or undernutrition (lack of food) and no single measure can provide firm conclusions about
nutritional standards. The simplest method, the dietary approach, involves
estimating an individual's food intake, calculating the nutritional content of the
food eaten and comparing this with the intake an individual would require to function effectively. A second approach is to use evidence such as height, weight and
morbidity for various age groups and compare them with data for other countries. It is also possible to observe the relative importance of an individual's demand
for food as opposed to other goods.

Each procedure has its own pitfalls. The dietary approach can be costly because
an observer has to weigh all the different items of food consumed by the individual
and this may be impossible when all the members of a household eat out of a
communal pot and odd meals are taken away from home and in towns or in the
fields. An alternative method of estimating aggregate food production, consumption and stocks runs into similar difficulties when most people are self-employed
and direct observations are difficult.

The second approach is to use anthropomorphic evidence on height, weight, age and the prevalence of diseases and other medical symptoms associated with undernutrition and malnutrition. The problem then becomes one of finding an appropriate yardstick against which to measure the evidence. It may not be the case that well nourished Africans would have the same height and weight as comparably aged Europeans. An alternative procedure is to use the per capita calorie availability data provided by the FAO. These suggest that in the 1980s there were about 30 Sub-Saharan countries with a per capita calorie intake below the required nutritional levels and that the region appeared to fare badly as compared with some Asian and Latin American countries. However, Table 14.1 indicates that many African countries have relatively high food availability.

The third approach of observing preferences does indicate that there are instances of people purchasing expensive foods (such as meat and fish) when cheaper foods (such as roots and tubers) would yield the same or greater nutritional value. The difficulty with this type of evidence is that its interpretation involves value judgements. But one important piece of evidence to emerge from Africa is that there does not appear to be a sex bias in the distribution of food; nor is there much evidence indicating that children fare badly as compared to adults. These findings run counter to those obtained for India where there does appear to be a sex bias in food distribution (Sen 1987b).

Entitlement

Setting aside the statistical evidence on the extent of undernutrition and famine, what are their causes? It is tempting to attribute the problems to climatic changes. Rainfall has been lower throughout the 1980s: the 1984 rainfall was 60 per cent of the 1931—60 mean rainfall and the climatic zones appear to have shifted some 200 to 300 kilometres south of their position in the middle of the century. Desertification has led to dust storms which have created temperature inversions and may have affected yields. But drought does not cause a famine. It is possible to provide alternative employment and to respond to drought by transporting food to famine stricken areas. It is also possible to establish advance weather forecasting services and to stockpile food.

A second possible cause of malnutrition and famine is low agricultural productivity. Table 14.2 provides details of output per head in Africa as well as other parts of the world. What stands out here is the slow growth and, in many instances, decline in African productivity. Yet despite the poor performance food availability is often higher than in many non-African countries. But India has had relatively few famines, China had only one famine, in 1965, and there are no recorded famines in Latin America. Climatic changes can reduce food supplies but the problems of nutrition and famine owe much to the nature of the institutional arrangements for the allocation of food. This brings us to an examination of Sen's theory of entitlement, a theory which directs attention away from the Malthusian emphasis upon output per head to the problems of distribution. According to Sen

Table 14.1 Comparative Food Availability Per Head, 1981–83, Expressed in Daily Calories

Sub-Saharan Africa		Asia		South America	
Ghana	1,621	Bangladesh	1,878	Ecuador	2,052
Mozambique	1,735	India	2,008	Bolivia	2,061
Guinea	1,827	Thailand	2,313	Peru	2,150
Mali	1,889	Indonesia	2,401	Chile	2,564
Zimbabwe	1,890	Philippines	2,411	Guyana	2,334
Zambia	2,008	Burma	2,464	Surinam	2,421
Sierra Leone	2,010	Malaysia	2,554	Colombia	2,534
Kenya	2,026	China	2,602	Brazil	2,564
Benin	2,073	Mongolia	2,744	French Guiana	2,064
Cameroon	2,106	Japan	2,858	Venezuela	2,664
Central African				Paraguay	2,817
Republic	2,106			Argentina	3,195
Burkina Faso	2,137				
Botswana	2,152				
Zaire	2,157				
Mauretania	2,162				
Rwanda	2,207				
Togo	2,103				
Sudan	2,246				
Uganda	2,320				
Lesotho	2,322				
Tanzania	2,353				
Liberia	2,368				
Niger	2,380				
Burundi	2,390				
Malawi	2,423				
Congo	2,480				

Source: FAO (1986)

(1984) 'starvation is a matter of some people not *having* enough food to eat and not of there not *being* enough food to eat'. But beyond that proposition the theory of entitlement does not specify the particular causes of famines. Instead, the theory distinguishes between two general causes of entitlement failure: a failure of the initial endowment of goods and a failure to obtain through exchange a bundle of goods which will permit survival.

Sen used the distinction to examine three famines: the Bengal famine of 1943, the Wollo (Ethiopian) famine of 1973 and the Bangladesh famine of 1974. Although two of these famines occcurred in the Indian sub-continent they are worthy of analysis because of the light they throw upon the nature of famines. The Bengal famine was associated with: (1) a cyclone in 1942; (2) disruption of food supplies from Burma because of the Japanese invasion; (3) restrictions on the movement of grain between provinces; and (4) the removal of stocks from

Table 14.2 Annual Average Growth Rates of Per Capita Food Production, 1961−85

	1961−70	1970−80	1981−85
Africa	0.2	−1.3	0.2
Cameroon	1.9	−0.4	−0.8
Central African States	0.8	−0.1	−0.5
Chad	−1.0	−0.5	−0.6
Congo	−0.5	−0.2	−1.9
Gabon	−0.3	−0.8	−0.5
Kenya	0.0	−0.9	−1.1
Mali	0.7	0.8	−1.1
Mozmbique	1.1	−4.6	−3.9
Mauretania	−0.7	−0.3	1.3
Senegal	−2.2	−1.8	0.1
Somalia	1.5	−3.3	−2.6
Sudan	0.4	0.5	−0.6
Socialist countries			
Eastern Europe	2.5	0.8	1.2
Asia	3.0	1.5	4.7
China	3.8	1.8	5.0
India	0.0	−0.7	−0.6
Latin America	0.3	0.5	−0.5
USA	0.5	0.8	0.6
Canada	0.6	0.8	−1.7
Australia	1.1	0.4	1.9

Source: UNCTAD (1986)

coastal areas because of the fear of a Japanese invasion. Yet despite these adverse factors the food supply was greater in 1943 than in 1941 when there was no famine. When famine victims were classified, it was found that the destitute were mainly rural labourers, that the peasants and sharecroppers were least affected and that urban dwellers were protected by rationing. Sen concluded that the famine was a boom famine precipitated by a wartime expansion of demand which led to an increase in incomes for urban workers but not for rural labourers, so that the latter were crowded out of food markets. The rise in prices and the change in the terms of trade led to a failure of exchange entitlements rather than a failure of endowments. The Bangladesh famine was similarly associated with macroeconomic factors which led to a rise in prices even though there was an increase in food supplies.

The Asian famines underline the fact that famine need not be associated with a fall in output per head. The Ethiopian famines highlight another paradox: food prices may not rise during a famine. The Ethiopian famine of 1973 was associated with a drought and some 200,000 people out of a population of 27 million were estimated to have died. But the availability of food was only slightly lower than the preceding year and was higher than for most of the preceding decade. Indeed, there was the curious phenomenon of food being moved out of the Wollo region — a state of affairs which paralleled the movement of grain out of Ireland during the potato famine. Nor could it be argued that there was an inability to move food into the area because of the poor quality of roads. What seems to have happened is that the low food yield prevented farmers from selling some of their produce for other foodstuffs which would have balanced their diets. It was the farmers, rather than the non-farmers, who were most affected by crop failure. Food prices did not rise because the farmers had nothing to sell.

Sen's analysis serves to draw attention to the wider institutional aspects and particular circumstances surrounding the Ethioipian famines since 1974. Ethiopia is unique among the African states in having had a relatively short period of foreign domination from 1936 to 1941 and in being a very old Christian country. Its long period of political stability allowed feudal structures to persist, although cautious progress was made under Haile Selassie, who become emperor in 1931. But progress was slow and the 1974 rise in raw material prices acted as a catalyst for the dissident and disaffected groups of students, peasants and military personnel who finally deposed the ageing Emperor and created a republic. In 1975 the first steps towards land reform were attempted. However, moves towards further development have been impeded by internal dissension, wars with Somalia and Eritrea, intervention by the superpowers, more climatic disturbances and the uneven distribution of rich and poor land.

In the Horn of Africa races and religions intermingle and disputes have arisen between Kenya, Ethiopia, Somalia and Eritrea (the last two having have an uneasy history of colonisation by the British, French and Italians). The disturbed situation has been further complicated by the changing superpower policies. Before 1974 the USSR supported Somalia and the USA favoured Ethiopia. After the fall of Selassie and the emergence of a Marxist government the USA pulled out of Ethiopia and established a nuclear submarine base on the island of Diego Garcia which gave them control of the Indian Ocean as well as a means of launching missiles at various regions in the USSR. The USSR tried to have the Indian Ocean declared a nuclear free zone but failed and then decided to support the new regime in Ethiopia. The political problems have been further aggravated by uncertain climatic changes in some of the marginal areas of settlement. In 1975 and 1980 rainfall was low. In 1981 there was a poor harvest. In 1982 and 1983 there were food shortages. In 1984 and 1985 severe drought were followed by widespread famine. In 1987 there was a further threat of famine.

Many of the features of the Ethiopian situation are therefore either unique or intensified versions of situations present in other parts of Africa. But they do underline the problems of coping with famines. Per capita food production in Sub-Saharan Africa, India and most Latin American countries has shown little or no increase over recent decades; yet we are confronted with famines in Africa but not elsewhere. Elsewhere there appears to be quiet hunger, although there are some noticeable exceptions in Asia. South Korea and Malaysia have both managed to increase per capita food production and even China has been successful in feeding its billion. How can we explain differences in famine management? A failure to produce new varieties of crops capable of withstanding the drier climates of Africa is one obvious difference in food production. The Green Revolution in wheat and rice in South-east Asia depended upon the successful introduction of grains suitable for the climatic conditions. This brings us to a second factor: the relative importance attached to food production. A third cause of disparity is the nature of political systems. Sen has drawn attention to the contrasting political structures of China and India. In China most people go to bed reasonably well fed and the life expectancy is high; in India most people experience hunger. But the Chinese system appears to be slow to respond to famine (although the circumstances surrounding the Great Leap Forward and the Cultural Revolution make firm statements difficult) whereas India possesses a vocal and voluble press which will tolerate quiet hunger but becomes a powerful opposition of government during famines. Now most African states are, like China, one party states which lack a vocal political opposition to prod the government into action.

The management of famine has been the subject of international aid and the question arises: what form should aid take? Should it be in kind or cash? Aid to famines naturally takes the form of food donations and in most circumstances this can be effective. It also has the advantage of providing effective propaganda for charities because it can be highly visible, supplying pictures of planes, ships and trucks being loaded with grain. But food aid raises difficult logistical problems of planning and directing distribution and obtaining transport. The need to set up relief centres to which people have to walk to obtain food can be disruptive of communities. The alternative is to provide cash or, rather, cash in return for work. The evidence of famine management in other countries, especially India, is that the payment of wages for relief work on building roads and irrigation ditches can be an effective method of restoring the monetary economy and ensuring the maintenance of distribution networks.

Agriculture

Famines might result from a lack of transport; but even if good roads and trucks were available the peasants might not be able to purchase food. Famines might result from a lack of entitlement but when famines persist then the causes of prolonged lack of entitlement deserve attention. We return therefore to the causes which lie behind the falling rate of agricultural productivity.

The first factor which deserves attention is the switch of land use from food growing to cash crops. In the 1970s in Senegal half the available land was used for growing peanuts; cotton cash cropping was introduced in that decade. In Mali peanut production rose by 70 per cent and cotton growing increased by 400 per cent in the 1970s. Cash crops were promoted in order to earn foreign currency;

but they have encroached on marginal lands and expelled grazing animals. Even where animals were still raised there has been a switch from milk to meat production and cattle ranching. The overall effect has been to eliminate crop rotation and the practice of leaving land fallow.

A second factor has been that food prices have been kept down in order to pacify the urban dwellers. But since farmers are responsive to changes in prices, the result has been a reduction in food production and an increase in cash crops (which attract subsidies) as well as an enhanced drift to the towns. The rise in the numbers of town dwellers has led to an increase in the demand for fuel and to deforestation. The consequent reduction in woodland has exposed the top soil and intensified erosion. A further effect of urbanisation has been the importing of prestige foods, such as wheat and rice. Unfortunately the resulting change in tastes has reduced self-sufficiency because wheat and rice cannot be grown in arid regions. Nutritional problems are intensified by aid programmes which supply unsuitable foodstuffs, such as dried milk, which when mixed with local water supplies lead to diarrhoea and infant mortality. Aid programmes have often been perverted by the sale of food to balance budgets and the inability to transport supplies to areas of need.

The reduction or restriction of food production has been aided and abetted by the agricultural policies of the advanced countries. The pursuit of self-sufficiency through the use of farm support programmes in the United States and Western Europe has led to overproduction. In some instances the expansion of supply has led to the undermining of cash crop production by developing countries. In other cases it has led to a reduction in the acreage devoted to food production. In effect, the advanced countries and their spokesman, the World Bank, have encouraged the developing countries to rely upon food imports despite the risks that can attend such a policy. Its success depended upon the developing countries being able to find markets for their cash crops and being able to find markets for manufactures — both of which tended to disappear in the 1970s.

Wider Issues

Famines indicate a significant and dramatic failure of economic systems to cater for the wants of people; but they also distract us from examining the overall performance of Sub-Saharan Africa since independence. One explanation for the disappointing results was that there was too much optimism and insufficient attention was paid to the trends in the various economies. Too much hope was placed in the continuation of the high commodity prices which prevailed in the decade immediately after the Second World War. When those prices collapsed the early momentum could not be sustained. Another explanation is that there was too much preoccupation with central planning and not enough attention paid to the use of markets as allocators of resources. This is a criticism which has been applied not only to Africa but to Latin America; it could also be applied to the advanced countries.

Planning produced the notion of a big push, of mobilising resources to leap into the world of developed countries. If savings were a higher percentage of income then development could be assured. A few big projects would create linkages and spill overs with various sectors of the economy and generate the momentum for advancement. There were big projects and there were big failures — the Volta Dam, for example. Disillusionment set in. But planning was not so much an economic inevitability as a political necessity. Those states which emerged in Africa had had their previous cohesion guaranteed by the imperial powers. Once they departed then there was no reason why the heterogeneous groups left behind should persist in their alliances. What was to guarantee cohesion was patronage.

It is, of course, tempting to attribute weaknesses to movements in the international economy, to the dependence of the African states on Europe and the United States. But the effects of this dependence were not all bad. The majority of African states had their greatest period of expansion in the post-war decades. It was not until the 1970s that circumstances changed, as they did for all countries. During the 1960s the terms of trade moved in their favour and they enjoyed access to the EEC. What is more significant is that they did less well than other parts of the Third World. So part of the explanation for failure must lie in the policies which the states adopted.

A factor causing arrested development was a preoccupation with import substitution. Elasticity pessimism, the belief that demand elasticities were too low and no benefits could be obtained from exchange rate adjustments, underlay much economic analysis in the 1940s and 1950s. Import substitution became the order of the day and it resulted in the creation of industries which were condemned to be inefficient because markets remained small.

Generalisations admit of exceptions and there have been variations in the performances of the different states. Ghana was the first country to become independent and it was the first to adopt central planning and the first country to suffer disastrously from its effects. Public employment as a percentage of wage employment reached 74 per cent in 1972. Allied with the large public sector was an elaborate system of price controls and import licences which led to the development of a black economy. When cocoa prices began to collapse in the 1960s living standards collapsed. There was an attempt at rapid industrialisation but little effort was made to improve agriculture. Between 1960 and 1970 imports of consumer goods as a percentage of total private consumption fell by some 10 per cent. But domestic industries could survive only behind high tariff walls and even then there was considerable underutilisation of capacity. When the economy collapsed in the 1960s external debt rose to 35 per cent of GDP.

South Africa

South Africa is the last remnant of colonialism and the home of apartheid. Some 72 per cent of its population are blacks and have little capital; 12 per cent are classed as coloureds or Indians and possess some capital and the remaining 16 per cent are white and possess most of the capital. In an 'ideal' economy white capital and black labour would be combined to yield the greatest output. But such a result would push down the wages of white labour to levels which would be unacceptable to the white community. Apartheid is a doctrine concerning the abilities and cultures of blacks and whites and has resulted in segmentation (whereby blacks are confined to their 'homelands' or bantustans) and discrimination in terms of education, health and jobs. The terms on which white capital and black labour combine are controlled and the mobility of blacks and their opportunities to live in white towns are strictly controlled. Apartheid has led to the following patterns of employment.

1. The homelands or Bantustans are where the majority of blacks are confined and in which they practise communal, subsistence agriculture and use very little capital. An attempt has been made to stem the flow of black labour to the towns by the creation of industries in the homelands but this has not been successful because of the economies of scale and access to markets accruing to manufacturing industry in the white towns.
2. A commercial agricultural sector in which white capital employs black labour.
3. A mining sector in which white capital employs both white and black labour.
4. A manufacturing sector in which white capital employs both white and black labour (Table 14.3).

Despite attempts to control the employment opportunities of blacks, market imperatives can sometimes break through and, as in the case of commercial

Table 14.3 Racial Distribution of the Labour Force between Industries, 1980 (000)

	Whites		Coloureds	Indians	Total
Agriculture	102	1,673	149	7	1,931
Mining	90	768	13	2	873
Manufacturing and construction	403	1,103	307	108	2,011
Services	1,202	2,229	375	124	3,930
Unclassified and unemployed	41	735	84	15	291
Total	1,928	6,523	928	256	9,635

Source: Central Statistical Agency (1982)

agriculture, white labour ceased to be employed at an early stage in the development of cash crops. The reason for the early use of black labour lay in the existence of poor soils, erratic rainfall and poor natural irrigation which meant that commercial farming could be successful only if wages were kept to low levels. Elsewhere, in mining and manufacturing, a job colour bar has tended to prevail with the high wage jobs being controlled by white labour. In addition to discrimination there has been exploitation (defined as the payment of a wage less than the marginal revenue product).

Exploitation can occur where there is a pool of immobile labour and lack of competition between employers. Black labour tends to be immobile; if it refuses jobs in the towns and mines it is left with a choice of remaining in the homelands at extremely low incomes or remaining, in the case of migrant labour, in the surrounding countries. The existence of jobs in the homelands and in countries such as Botswana establishes a reservation wage. Lack of competition between employers has tended to be most conspicuous in mining where the great depth of workings has meant the need to raise large amounts of capital and restricted entry to the industry. In 1980 some 90 per cent of the 700,000 workers were recruited through agencies licensed by the Chamber of Mines to which all the mining companies were affiliated. In the diamond industry in South Africa, de Beers enjoy a virtual monopoly. Employers have a monopsony position and face an upward sloping supply curve whose elasticity may be very low. Between 1934 and 1970 the price of gold remained constant, at 35 dollars an ounce. The ability to maintain such a low and constant price owed much to the limited industrial uses of gold, as compared with silver, but was primarily due to the ability of the employers to maintain low wage costs in an industry subject to diminishing returns. Within mining and manufacturing unions of white workers have tended to restrict the high wage jobs to their members. Black labour thus tends to be underpaid by being deprived of its rents and white labour tends to be overpaid and obtains large rents in excess of its opportunity cost (Table 14.4).

Table 14.4   Wages of Africans as a Percentage of White Wages in Various Sectors, 1952−82

	Manufacturing and construction	Gold mines	White agriculture
1952−53	19.7	6.5	—
1969−70	16.8	4.8	7.3
1975−76	20.5	11.9	12.2
1982−83	22.7	18.3	14.9

Source: CSA (1984)

The Burden of Discrimination

Discrimination involves the exercise of preferences. The person who chooses apples when oranges are available may be said to discriminate in favour of apples and against oranges. In doing so the individual indicates that he is prepared to pay a higher price to get apples than he would to get oranges. In the job market the desire of whites to work with each other and not with blacks should reveal itself in a willingness to pay a price for the privilege of exclusion. However, we do not observe whites earning less than blacks and the burden of discrimination is partly borne in a lower national income and partial redistribution from white capital and black labour; the wages of black labour and the returns on white capital are both lower because of discrimination.

The burden of discrimination exhibits itself in a variety of ways. Because manufacturing cannot have access to cheap labour, it needs protection. Manufacturing started to grow during the Second World War when South Africa was cut off from American and European goods. In the post-war, worldwide boom it prospered and by 1970 accounted for some 24 per cent of the GDP. But after 1970, in a harsher economic climate, South African manufacturing became relatively expensive. The immediate effect was to cause further distortions in the allocation of resources. To overcome the shortages of skilled labour there was increased mechanisation which had the undesirable effect of displacing more labour, especially unskilled labour and, paradoxically, increasing the demand for skilled labour still further. To reduce the competition from foreign goods, manufacturing was given further protection which led to further inefficiency and a stifling of competition. There was therefore pressure to relax the job colour bar.

Market forces are tending to break through and it is a moot point how long they can be contained. Support for apartheid has tended to come from white farmers and white labour and from the Afrikaans rather than the 'English'. Class interests have therefore tended to combine with national as opposed to foreign ('English') interests and led to the preservation of apartheid until the 1960s. But from the 1960s onwards other forces began to exert an influence on the South African economy. The political independence of the surrounding, front line states led to a growth in hostility which received support from the international community. Guerrilla forces based in Angola, Mozambique and Zimbabwe received arms from the USSR and other Eastern European states. In the 1970s there was an OPEC ban on oil exports to South Africa which led to attempts to refine oil from coal. There was a growing radicalisation of young blacks following such incidents as Sharpeville and Soweto. Finally, there was a growing reluctance of foreign firms to invest in South Africa. Judged in military terms, the South African regime could persist for a considerable number of years. Its overwhelming military superiority could resist invasion from the surrounding states and the mutual suspicions of the Americans and Soviets would stifle any international intervention.

Summary and Conclusions

At the end of the Second World War the prospects for many African states looked good. Primary commodity prices had risen during the War and were sustained through the Korean War. There seemed to be no reason why the metropolitan powers should relinquish their hold on colonies which were important sources of revenue and were also becoming useful markets for consumer goods. The motives for conceding independence were therefore complex. There was pressure from the Americans. There was a feeling that a quick release might foster good will. There was a growing preoccupation with the developing European market.

But the timing of decolonisation was unfortunate. In the colonies there was a distinct lack of people with political and administrative skills. Lack of skill and low levels of literacy were a colonial inheritance. Harsh climatic conditions were a perennial problem. The new governments carried over some of the features of the colonial agricultural system but changed their goals. Marketing boards were retained and a surplus was extracted but was then put to government use. Public consumption was increased (some of it inevitable). There was a need to finance defence in politically unstable systems and public consumption served as a means of maintaining power. But there was a tendency to squeeze agriculture whereas the colonial powers had been careful not to destroy the goose that laid the golden eggs. Import substitution became fashionable but the markets were too small to obtain economies of scale and agriculture was left to languish. There was a failure to carry out land reforms and a failure to encourage new varieties of crops which would suit the harsh climate. There was a reliance upon the United States and Europe for foodstuffs and a preoccupation with cash crops. It was a policy which contrasted with the American and European emphasis upon self-sufficiency in food. In the 1950s and 1960s most states could manage by taxing agriculture and by borrowing; in the 1970s exports started to fail and borrowing became prohibitive.

Sub-Saharan Africa is a picture of failure. Probably too much was expected. In contrast South Africa has flourished through the presence of an educated white labour force, abundant raw materials and cheap black labour which has had its wages held down by racial discrimination.

Bibliography

Bates, R.H. (1983) *Essays on the Political Economy of Rural Africa,* Cambridge University Press.

CSA, *South African Statistics,* (1982, 1984), Central Statistical Agency.

Cooper, F. (1981) 'Africa and the world economy', *The African Studies Review,* vol. 24, pp. 3–18.

Coulson, A. (1982) *Tanzania,* Oxford University Press.

..H. (eds) (1975) *The Economics of Colonialism*, Cambridge

Yearbook, FAO

IMF and Stabilisation in Sub-Saharan Africa: a Review, Discus-
ute of Development Studies.

asuring Undernutrition, WP8, The World Institute for Develop-
earch, United Nations University.

an Famines 1973—1985: A Case Study, WP26, The World Institute for Development Economics Research, United Nations University.

Leys, C. (1975) *Underdevelopment in Kenya,* Heinemann.

Osmani, S.R. (1987a) *Controversies in Nutrition and their Implications for the Economics of Food,* WP16, The World Institute for Development Economics Research, United Nations University.

Osmani, S.R. (1987b) *The Food Problems of Bangladesh,* WP29, The World Institute for Development Economics Research, United Nations University.

Riskin, C. (1987) *Feeding China: The Experience since 1949,* WP27, The World Institute for Development Economics Research, United Nations University.

Sen, A. (1984) *Resources, Value and Development,* Blackwell.

Sen, A. (1987a) *Gender and Cooperative Conflict,* WP18, The World Institute for Development Economics Research, United Nations University.

Sen, A. (1987b) *Africa and India: What Do We Have to Learn From Each Other?,* WP19, The World Institute for Development Economics Research, United Nations University.

Svedberg, P. (1987) *Undernutrition in Sub-Saharan Africa: A Critical Assessment of the Evidence,* WP15, The World Institute for Development Economics Research, United Nations University.

UNCTAD (1986) Handbook of Trade and Development Statistics, United Nations.

15

A Summing Up

The sharp rise in raw material prices in the 1970s and the subsequent slump raised many questions. Did the 1970s mark the breaking of a Kondratieff long wave and the emergence of Keynesian secular stagflation? The 1970s also focused attention upon the problems of the Third World. Why did so few countries manage to 'take off' in the long boom? Why was there no apparent closure of the gap between rich and poor? And why were the centrally planned economies so unsuccessful? Why was there a failure of so many countries to engage in international trade? Was there a simple connection between trade and development? Were there significant limitations upon the terms offered to those countries which wished to trade?

Evidence for long waves was detected by Kondratieff in nineteenth-century price data. He suggested various causes: overinvestment; technological change; wars; the opening up of new territories; and variations in the money supply. Schumpeter subsequently elaborated the place of technological change by postulating a clustering of innovations in recessions stimulated by the pressure to cut costs. The link between investment and the opneing of new territories was examined by Rostow who suggested that the growth of the advanced countries might be halted by a raw materials ceiling which would cause a fall in profits and induce a switch of resources into expanding supplies of raw materials. Rostow was writing in the context of the price rises of the 1970s. However, Lewis did draw attention to the possibilities of a Kondratieff price swing in the 1880s. Both Rostow and Lewis have therefore provided some evidence for the movement of wholesale prices as an indicator of the terms of trade between manufactures and raw materials. Synthesising the evidence we can produce a long wave model, where the lower turning point of a wave arises through the clustering of innovations assisted by an expansion of the money supply and low raw material prices. Money supply changes might operate autonomously through, for example, gold discoveries or unexpected credit expansions. The upper turning point would arise as a result of overinvestment brought on by rising raw material prices, wages increasing at the expense of profits or a credit sqeeze.

Evidence on the movement of output was missing in the early discussions. Solomou found no evidence of this in the second half of the nineteenth century or in the twentieth century. He concluded that long swings were generated by the statistical procedures adopted and by the differential growth rates of the advanced economies. He found evidence of a swing longer than the Kondratieff wave in the third quarter of the nineteenth century which he attributed to a shift (traverse) from one equilibrium growth path to another. In the post-World War II period he attributed the long boom to a favourable conjuncture of circumstances: pent up demand, a backlog of innovations, plentiful labour supply and cheap raw materials. But he found no bunching of innovations.

Some of Solomou's findings can be reconciled with those of earlier writers: Rostow, for example, had suggested that the post-war boom might not be a separate Kondratieff but merely the delayed diffusion of US innovations of the inter-war years. Lewis had drawn attention to the influence of differential growth rates upon the behaviour of the world economy. It seems intuitively plausible that two world wars would have had a general and long lasting effect upon economic activity, although economists have tended to avoid incorporating wars into their analysis.

Solomou did find evidence, however, supporting the existence of Kuznets long swings. In the ninteenth century the Atlantic economy exhibited an alternating pattern of domestic and foreign investment in the construction industries. This pattern has disappeared in the twentieth century partly because of the closing of the American frontier and partly because two world wars placed the advanced economies on the same footing. The universal construction boom of the post-war period began in the 1940s, started to peter out in the 1960s and was a factor contributing to the expansion of money supply in an effort to maintain the long boom.

The lack of conclusive evidence on the Kondratieff wave and the support for the Kuznets long swing have focused attention on population movements. Family formation decisions are typically long-run decisions involving the lifecycle and having long-run effects. As such they can give rise to lengthy lags and to fluctuations which underlie Kuznets swings.

Although evidence for Kondratieff waves is tenuous, the effects of various shocks on the pattern of international trade and development still need to be unravelled. Prominent among these shocks have been wars: Napoleonic, Crimean, the American Civil War, the Prussian Wars which unified Germany and two world wars as well as the Korean and Vietnam Wars. The second half of Chapter 1 used wars as a means of demarcating periods. Britain's naval supremacy after the Napoleonic Wars influenced Europe's trade with the rest of the world and the alliance of Britain, Austria and Russia served to determine the political framework within which trade and industrialisation took place. The Crimean War similarly enabled the unification of Germany and Italy to begin and the American Civil War allowed the American sub-continent to develop as one trading area. The two world wars exercised a profound influence upon the pattern of world trade and drew attention to the problems of uneven economic development; a byproduct of the discussion of wars and trade was the emergence of a political economy (hegemonic) theory of world trade.

The political economy of the post-war world has been dominated by a number of factors.

Bretton Woods. At Bretton Woods the Americans set out the rules which were to govern international trade. These were:

1. an international agency to ensure exchange rate stability and to adjudicate on balance of payments difficulties;
2. an international organisation to influence long-term investment;
3. an international agreement to deal with commodity price stabilisation;
4. international procedures to bring about reductions in trade barriers;
5. international organisation of relief and reconstruction; and
6. an international commitment to maintain full employment.

Although (3) and (6) were never ratified they influenced subsequent actions of the advanced countries.

The Marshall Plan and Marshall Aid were designed to reconstruct Europe; the USA devoted 1 per cent of GNP to aid in each year between 1948 and 1952.

Methods of Production. Increasing returns in manufacturing require the development of new techniques of production and human resource management. There was an attempt to introduce American techniques into Europe. These were known variously and misleadingly as Taylorism and Fordism but Taylorism had been introduced into Europe in the inter-war years and Ford had already established factories in Europe. American production management had been strongly influenced by the human relations school. The methods of diffusion of American knowhow ranged from direct involvement by Americans, especially in the occupied countries of West Germany and Japan, to visits to American firms and the issuing of reports by, for example, the Anglo-American Productivity Council. The success of the ventures varied. In the UK the research body of the cotton industry, the Shirley Institute, popularised statistical techniques for quality control but the industry catered for the diverse markets of the former empire and American mass production methods were not appropriate. What was true of cotton was also true of other industries. US methods presupposed mass markets, something which the Marshall Plan was designed to bring about in Europe but which was frustrated by British and French policies. Another major obstacle in the UK was the absence of trained managers. The British system of industrial relations rested upon the concept of managerial prerogatives; but British managers had no ideas to implement. The implementation of ideas presupposed their acceptance by workers; with managers locked into managerial prerogatives and workers into workers' rights there was an impasse until the productivity bargaining of the 1960s. In other countries where unions were less strong American ideas were more readily accepted.

Nationalisation, Public Sectors and Welfare States. In the post-war period many European countries solved the problems of income distribution and income instability by nationalising industries, such as coal, railways, iron and steel, as well as by promoting state education, health and social security. The concept emerged of a welfare state as a provider of basic needs and an instrument for reducing income inequalities. The welfare states brought about that greater equality of incomes in advanced countries which we noticed in Chapter 2 and they provided a strong basis for consumption without reducing profits by their emphasis on fairness and consensus.

Productivity, Wages and Profits. Because the welfare states introduced fairness they enabled capital accumulation to take place on a massive scale in the early post-war period. Real wages and productivity moved together and profits were maintained. It was not until the 1960s that the post-war international order broke down because of the uneven development of countries, the inability of the USA to finance the system, tight labour markets which led to increasing union militancy and the encroachment of public consumption on private consumption.

Our second question was why so few countries took off into self-sustaining growth in the long boom. To answer this question we need to establish the size of the income gap between countries and whether there was any convergence. In Chapter 2 we distinguished three groups of countries. In the first group, the advanced market economies, there was evidence of convergence, with its speed being determined by the size of the initial income gap. Convergence was then related to the Ramsay model of capital accumulation and the diffusion of technologies by aid, emulation and movements of capital and labour. Convergence was responsible for the relative decline of the United States, although that decline was intensified by USA's role as the world peacekeeper. Convergence was also noted in the second group, the centrally planned economies; but this was not a convergence upon the norm of the market economies. The developing countries showed no such signs of closing the gap.

Was convergence assisted by inequality in the distribution of income? This is the substance of the Kuznets thesis which states that economic development is initially associated with increasing income inequality and subsequently with greater equality. The thesis was produced on the basis of cross-section data. The data presented in Chapter 2 provided some evidence that the advanced countries showed greater equality than the less developed countries but there were some interesting variations — France, for example, was less equal than the other advanced countries and more importantly, the Asian countries showed greater equality than the African and Latin American countries. Arguments were then presented to suggest that the Kuznets thesis need not always hold.

Leaving aside for the moment the centrally planned economies, the problem of the developing countries and their failure to catch up with the advanced countries suggested several other questions. Was the failure of the primary producers due to their own inefficiency or was it due to poverty? Was their failure due to factors operating through the terms of trade between advanced countries and less developed countries? Chapter 3 drew attention to the problems faced by primary producers and their methods of coping with risk. It was suggested that many of the features of agrarian contracts (sharecropping, tied contracts) represented attempts to cope with risks in situations where there was not a complete set of markets. Attention was also drawn to the pursuit of self-sufficiency in food production in the advanced countries.

Chapter 4 examined the nature and implications of manufacturing economies. Attention was drawn to the fact that manufacturing enabled increasing economic returns to be realised through the operation of hitherto sequential operations in parallel; such splitting of operations was dependent upon the expansion of the market. Manufacturing may give rise to further economies of volume and of agglomeration. (Doubling the area of cylinder may cube its volume without any corresponding increase in production or usage costs.) Manufacturing economies may also be realised through the close geographical concentration of activities and account for the development of urban centres and regional concentrations. Increasing returns (which are not present in agriculture) carry further implications: if demand falls then costs may rise; a stable equilibrium may not be possible unless the demand curve cuts the supply curve from above; and in the presence of increasing returns there may be protectionist pressures to realise them and protectionist pressures to maintain them. We may finally observe that industrial economies tend to exhibit price and wage rigidity and adjustments take place through variations in stocks.

Separate analysis of agrarian and manufacturing economies leads on to a consideration of their interaction. Prebisch and Singer suggested that there was a long-run decline in the terms of trade of primary producers and that the amplitude and duration of fluctuations in the prices of primary products were greater than those for manufactures. The Prebisch–Singer thesis suggested a possible reason why developing countries might fail to take off. Cyclical fluctuations pointed to the debt problems which might be incurred during recessions (as in Latin America in the 1930s and 1980s) and to the possible effects that population increase might have in eliminating the benefits of price rises. Evidence for the Prebisch–Singer thesis was provided by Evans, Thirlwall and Bergevin. The secular evidence did not, however, support the notion that productivity increases in manufactures were more important than in agriculture; but they did support the idea that the income elasticity of demand for manufactures was greater than for raw materials. The cyclical evidence was consistent with the view that price rigidities were greater in advanced countries than in developing countries and drew attention to the usefulness of commodity price stabilisation schemes in reducing the severity of cost-push inflation in advanced economies. It was noted that two-thirds of inter-

national trade was between advanced countries and that research and development and product differentiation were important determinants of trade patterns.

An important influence upon post-war economic activity, and a major factor
in creating the raw materials ceiling of the 1970s as well as prompting the discussions of long waves, were movements in the price of oil. Through the 1950s and
1960s the price of oil was strongly influenced by US foreign policy and policies
of the oil companies as well as the prices of other goods. In the late 1960s the
prices of oil forced a reduction in oil supplies. This reduction would have taken
place in the absence of a cartel (OPEC) since it was the optimum response for
independent competitive producers pursuing an optimum conservation policy. It
was intensified by the existence of a cartel, the fact that the Arab oil producers
had different time horizons from Western oil companies and by the eruption of
the Arab-Israeli war. That the cartel managed to hold prices up for some twelve
years was a testament to the dominant position in production of Saudi Arabia.
But high prices encouraged an expansion of alternate energy supplies and there
was some reneging within OPEC. In 1986 OPEC announced a cut in prices but
there was no immediate effect upon world economic activity.

The success story of the post-war period has been Japan. The Japanese response
to the oil prices is interesting because of the country's lack of natural resources,
especially energy. The success of the Japanese economy was partly due to US
aid and partly due to an ability and willingness to move into medium and high
technology industries and to couple those moves with innovations in the area of
workshop organisation which led to improvements in quality control, a reduction in the time lag between the introduction of new products and substantial reductions in costs. The maintenance of low unemployment after the oil shocks seems
to have been due to wage and price flexibility stemming from the use of an incomes policy and bonus schemes. As the 1980s draw to a close possible difficulties
may arise out of the fall in the price of the dollar and growing trade restrictions
in Europe.

The ability of the Japanese to catch up with the other advanced economies and
to weather the storms of the 1970s was conditional upon American economic
policy. While the Carter administration had tried to exercise some restraint upon
the economy, there had been a decisive switch of thinking under the Reagan
administration. Reaganomics blamed government regulation for the sluggish
behaviour of the economy. There was a movement towards deregulation, especially
in the fields of transport and communication. Incentives were boosted by reductions in income tax and it was predicted that lost revenue would be recouped by
the increased receipts resulting from the incentives. But these changes were overshadowed by an increase in government expenditure on defence which was
financed by borrowing. The effects of the budget deficit were to cause a rise in
domestic interest rates, a rise in the foreign price of the dollar and a trade deficit.
In order to borrow the Americans were obliged to raise interest rates; attracted
by high interest rates foreigners bought dollars to purchase American securities.
The rise in interest rates affected US industry and the rise in the dollar made

US exports uncompetitive and increased imports of manufactures. American resources switched out of low- and medium-tech industries and into high-tech industries and non-traded goods such as services. There was an acceleration of the movement of industries out of the Northern states and into the low wage areas of the South.

The rise in interest rates had worldwide repercussions. In effect, the Japanese and West Germans were obliged to finance some of the defence spending. The interest rate rise may have reduced investment in Europe and contributed to the debt problems of Latin America. Controversy raged about the ability of the Americans to manage the burden of the debt. Some observers were content to point out that American debt increased during recession; informed financial markets presumably took the economic implications into account. But rational expectations were severely shaken by the stock market crash of October 1987. No satisfactory explanation for the crash has yet been offered. If the markets had taken into account all available information then there should have been no crash. The only new 'news' was political disclosures about Irangate and Contra-gate and these may have served to cast doubt upon the general competence of the administration. The effects of the crash are likely to be a reduction in the growth of the American economy, an increase in the fall of the dollar and a diminution of the trade surpluses of Japan and West Germany.

Japan maintained low unemployment and the United States (subject to the trade deficit) increased the number of jobs. In contrast unemployment increased and stayed high in Western Europe, raising questions about the future of the European Community. During the 1950s and 1960s Western Europe had enjoyed high growth. The oil shocks and subsequent deflation then led to rising unemployment and sluggish productivity. The causes were located in wage rigidity, large public sectors and the lack of dynamism of the West German economy. However, the West Germans feared inflation and trade deficits. The persistence of unemployment and the uncertainties of geopolitics then led to plans to deregulate the Community's markets by 1992. But moves to improve efficiency are aggravated by the protection of agriculture and by attempts to enlarge the Community by the inclusion of Southern European agricultural countries.

Why were the planned economies unsuccessful? The USSR lost 20 million people in the Second World War and most of Eastern Europe was devastated. They received no American aid; they were not centrally involved in world trade. But socialism was supposed to be an alternative to market economics. The weaknesses of the planned economies have been attributed to the lack of signals for the efficient allocation of resources. In an endeavour to catch up with the West there was an emphasis upon industrialisation and consumer goods were rationed. But as incomes rose there was a lack of consumer goods. Problems of factory discipline then emerged: absenteeism, drunkenness, low productivity and poor quality control. In agriculture there was a failure to raise productivity. Attempts by Hungary and Yugoslavia to break away from the Stalinist model were not wholly successful. Hungary increased its supplies of consumer goods and introduced a form of market socialism but its growth rate declined. Yugoslavia introduced workers' cooperatives but in giving them greater autonomy faced a decline in employment and output. In 1987 attempts to increase efficiency posed many problems. Economic pluralism suggested the use of the price mechanism, with the uncertainty that some prices might rise. Economic pluralism threatened to undermine the role of the party and created the possibilities of political pluralism — which in the USSR might lead to the emergence of nationalist Islamic fundamentalism. In Yugoslavia there are already tensions between various regions.

Why did the developing countries meet with such little success? Why did they not follow the path of the advanced countries? In the nineteenth century Argentina and Australia had high real incomes per capita. In the twentieth century Argentina appears to have fulfilled the Prebisch—Singer prediction. Australia might have faced a severe decline when it lost its European agricultural markets had it not been able to switch into minerals; Argentina had no minerals.

China placed its emphasis upon growth and equitable distribution. Possibly it could have grown faster had it sacrificed equity, although the record of India is not convincing. Perhaps the less developed countries did follow the example of the advanced countries; but starting from low income levels they may have thought that the nineteenth-century industrialisation behind tariff walls was the most relevant example to follow. Not being under American rule they were not compelled to follow simple market rules; but then neither did the British after 1945, when they failed to absorb the lessons of the Anglo-American Productivity Council's reports.

The reluctance to follow the example of the market economies stems from a compound of historical experience in the Third World and preconceived ideas in the advanced economies. In Latin America there had been the experience of falling commodity prices and indebtedness in the 1930s. There was the apparent truth of the Prebisch thesis. In Africa there was the association of primary production with colonialism. Trade based upon current comparative advantage seemed to spell unstable incomes. These beliefs were intensified during and after the Korean War. In Latin America, therefore, later in Africa, there arose a belief in the powers of industrialisation and import substitution to break the dependence upon the advanced countries.

The reconstruction of Western Europe by Marshall Aid suggested that aid and planning could benefit the less developed countries. Practical experience received academic approval from the Keynesian growth models. These models suggested that growth was a matter of increasing the amount of capital (tractors) and that shortages of finance could be overcome by governments extracting a surplus from agriculture or obtaining aid from the advanced countries. The fact that the models assumed an absence of factor substitution fitted in with the prevailing notion that peasants were irrational and that developing countries were characterised by structural rigidities. The possibilities of generating savings through exports of raw materials was refuted by the prevailing mood of elasticity pessimism which believed that the demands for such goods were price inelastic. Industrialisation therefore meant restricting imports; this led to inflationary pressures, black markets and smuggling. Shortages of foreign exchange led to the development of two gap models in which development was constrained by a lack of domestic savings and by a lack of foreign exchange.

In the 1950s and 1960s the less developed countries began to discriminate against agriculture and the advanced countries began to discriminate in favour of agriculture. The combined effects of these were that the less developed countries received confirmation that there was no point in attempting to expand agricultural exports. But by discriminating against agriculture they increased the drift to the towns which, in turn, led to dependence upon food imports. The subsidisation of agriculture in the advanced countries created a surplus of foodstuffs which then found a market in the Third World, often in the form of aid. Countries which had previously been self-sufficient in food now became dependent upon imports from the advanced countries and attempts to improve their own agriculture were abandoned.

Pursuing a thesis advanced by Lewis it could be argued that the developing countries should have improved their agriculture before embarking upon industrialisation. But such a policy was not always easy. In South-east Asia it was possible because the Japanese occupation had loosened the social and political bases of the colonial powers; and in some countries American occupation forced the necessary land reforms. But the Latin American countries had never been invaded (since the sixteenth century), nor did they possess within themselves the impetus to effect social reforms. When land reforms did take place, as in Peru and Mexico, they were not carried through to completion. In Africa the conditions for land reform might have been present but decolonisation did not occur until the 1960s and the resulting political boundaries lacked any ethnic or religious rationale; the social cohesion needed for reforms was often lacking.

What, then, is to be the future of international trade and economic development? Hegemony theory would suggest that the present crisis stems from the lack of a world leader possessed of economic and political/military strength to recreate the rules of the game in terms of an international currency and ensure its value as well as defining the conditions for some form of free trade. In the nineteenth century Britain was the world leader. It created the international currency, sterling. It established the rules for free trade. And it was capable of enforcing the rules. These rules may, as List asserted, have worked to Britain's advantage by permitting its goods access to markets. Nevertheless, by its willingness to act as the world's banker, it did permit an expansion of world trade to take place. In the late nineteenth century Britain's position came under challenge from France, Germany and the United States. The First World War destroyed the ambitions of France and Germany and seriously impaired Britain's capacity to continue its former role. The United States was reluctant to take on the task and, so the argument runs, the world economy languished and protectionism increased.

After the Second World War the United States accepted the role of leader, defined the rules of the game (Bretton Woods) and the new international currency (the dollar) and provided the police force. In the 1970s the United States became unable and unwilling to continue in its role as the visible hand; an analogy was drawn between the 1930s and the 1970s and 1980s. But where is the new leader? Neither Japan nor West Germany seem willing or able to fill the role and their trade surpluses could disappear with a fall in the dollar. The rearming of either would arouse resistance from the USSR and China.

Will there be an increase in protectionism? There has been an increase in the use of subsidies and quotas in the 1970s and 1980s. World trade fell between 1980 and 1983 after the deflation of 1979, though there was a rebound between 1983 and 1986 (Table 15.1). The gains from trade for advanced countries are still considerable and the enlargement of the European Community will bring about an increase in trade, not only for its members but also for non-members as direct foreign investment occurs. The main problems for trade are likely to be that uneven economic development may threaten political stability and give rise to increased defence expenditure and wars. The political problem embraces not merely the United States, the USSR, the European Community and Japan but also China. But within the advanced countries, the engine of development, the problems are likely to centre around technological change and declining populations.

During the 1970s and 1980s there was a fear of technological unemployment. The wave of new processes which had started to emerge in the 1960s — auto-

Table 15.1 Annual Average Growth Rates of Exports and Imports, 1950−86 (%)

| | Exports fob | | | | |
	1950−60	1960−70	1970−80	1980−83	1983−86
World	6.5	9.2	20.3	−2.3	5.3
Developed market economies	7.1	10.1	18.8	−2.8	8.6
Developing countries and territories	7.3	25.9	36.0	−7.0	−2.8
Socialist countries					
Eastern Europe	10.8	8.7	18.1	4.6	2.6
Asia	2.0	20.0	28.3	5.8	11.3
	Imports cif				
World	6.5	9.1	20.3	−3.0	5.6
Developed market economies	6.5	10.2	19.5	−3.0	5.6
Developing countries and territories	4.3	6.5	23.8	−4.6	−2.5
Socialist countries					
Eastern Europe	12.0	8.1	18.4	1.7	4.1
Asia	12.6	3.0	22.4	2.5	26.0

Source: UNCTAD (1987)

mation — began to acquire a deeper significance. Economists have tended to be sceptical about the possibilities of technological unemployment although they have conceded that there may be short-run problems. At the height of the automation scare of the 1960s Meade (1964) drew attention to the similarities between over-populated agrarian countries, such as Mauritius, and the surplus labour problems which could arise in advanced countries. A high level of employment could be restored if wages were allowed to fall; but that might result in an unacceptable redistribution of income from wage earners to property owners. In order to solve both the problems of efficiency and equity Meade considered three alternatives: the trade union state (which later became the labour managed firm or the workers' cooperative); a revived form of capitalism; and socialism. The trade union state would, Meade suggested, lead to an increase in the incomes of its members but would restrict employment and was therefore rejected. Capitalism could be revived by redistributing wealth but this would need continual monitoring because the uneven distribution of abilities coupled with assortative mating (whereby property owners married property owners and households with few children acquired and passed on relatively large amounts of property). The weakness of socialism was that if it were introduced by purchasing private assets then it would lead to a situation in which the assets were nationalised but the income was still passed on to the former owners. Meade therefore favoured a wealth tax.

In the 1980s the advanced economies began to revive capitalism. Public sector assets were sold and markets began to be deregulated. But there has been little attempt to control the distribution of income; indeed, the emphasis has been upon widening differentials and removing social security benefits in an attempt to increase incentives. Meade had cautioned against the possible effects of improved welfare policies upon the level of immigration and suggested that a country might have to control the numbers of immigrants. But in the 1980s the problem is different. Most advanced countries have begun to exercise controls on migrants but they have also relaxed controls on capital movements. The Meade proposal for a wealth tax therefore faces the problem of a flight of capital and even increases in income taxes run the risk of brain drains. The problem for the advanced countries is to reconstruct their tax systems and to consider the level of government expenditure. In some countries tax reform has been achieved by broadening the tax base and reducing the number of allowances; in other countries there has been a distinct shift towards spending taxes — although there has been no attempt to introduce the Meade version of a spending tax which would be progressive and therefore equitable.

Technological change may be overshadowed by labour shortages resulting from falling birth rates and ageing populations. In the nineteenth century the growth of the advanced economies had been assisted by population increase and migration and by the release of labour from agriculture. The absorption of labour from agriculture, domestic service and other low wage, labour-intensive industries was checked by the inter-war years slump and then resumed after the Second World War. In the 1950s Western Europe drew on its reserves in agriculture and then turned to the pools of labour in Southern Europe. In the United States the numbers in agriculture were reduced and labour was pulled in from Mexico and Asia. Hiring standards were lowered, wage differentials were narrowed and dual labour markets became less distinct. The slump of the 1970s and 1980s halted the process but it will resume in the 1990s under the impact of falling numbers of young workers.

The response to falling numbers will be lowering of hiring standards. The age of retirement will be pushed up. The Japanese have raised their retirement age and in the United States it is illegal to discriminate against anyone on the grounds of age. With the enlargement of the European Community the flow of labour from Southern Europe will be accelerated.

The other response to labour shortages could be the setting up of industrial plants in the less developed countries. During the 1950s and 1960s the less developed countries grew at rates varying between 4 and 5 per cent. But they encountered three problems: the terms of trade; debt; and population increase. The terms of trade fell because food prices were generally falling. In the United States and Europe Europe agricultural productivity increased and pushed down food prices. But their farmers were protected by price support schemes and tariffs. Protection in the advanced countries then influenced the prices paid to farmers in less developed countries and attempts to introduce commodity price stabilisation schemes tended to founder. Only with the price rise of the 1970s was the process halted; in the 1980s terms of trade again declined.

The second problem has been the burden of debt. In the 1950s and 1960s much borrowing was spent unproductively. In the 1970s borrowing was undertaken to overcome the effects of the oil shock; but countries were then caught by the rise in interest rates. Population increase is a third problem. Falling death rates, with constant birth rates, have led to a population explosion. But discrimination against agriculture has meant falling productivity and a drift to the towns. The result has been both urban unemployment and a rise in food imports. What is required is an agricultural revolution stimulated by land reform and better prices for farm products. Improving agriculture would not only feed the increase in numbers but provide a base for industrial productivity. For without industrialisation the gap between the advanced and developing countries will persist.

Should the Third World detach itself from the global economy? Neoclassical trade theory rests upon competition, the absence of economies of scale and an ignorance of historical evolution. But there is no universal panacea. The relatively insulated Asian economies (China and India) have not fared any better than the smaller Asian countries. Liberalisation experiments in Latin America have proved disastrous. The centrally planned economies of Eastern Europe have had growth rates which have been on a par with those achieved by the less developed countries of Southern Europe. The smaller Asian countries achieved their main successes in the 1960s and 1970s when the advanced countries were growing rapidly; but expansion within the OECD countries now looks remote. And when we examine the relationship between growth and trade in the developing countries we find a bewildering variety of patterns. Small countries tend to be open economies.

Asian countries tend to export relatively more manufactures than the African countries which are still predominantly exporters of primary products. And it is doubtful whether the Asian countries would enter a common market with the African countries.

There are, in fact two problem areas with different problems. Africa has a food problem. It suffers from: (1) low quality and fragile soils and difficulties in obtaining cheap water supplies; (2) lack of technological breakthrough in producing high yielding crops such as the Green Revolution; (3) difficulties in making the transition from an extensive system of agriculture, to an intensive agriculture (which would involve changes in the structure of property rights); and (4) political instability resulting from colonialism. In Latin America the immediate issue is debt. But some Asian countries, notably South Korea, have incurred debt. However, they also have a large export to GDP ratio, something the Latin American countries do not possess. While protection and detachment may be required they need to be selective rather than universal and to operate with due regard for politics as well as economics.

Bibliography

Diaz-Alejandro, C. (1978) 'Delinking the North and South: unshackled or unhinged?', in A. Fishlow et al., Rich and Poor Nations in the World Economy, McGraw Hill.
Meade, J.E. (1964) Efficiency, Equality and the Distribution of Property, Allen and Unwin.
UNCTAD (1987) Handbook of International Trade and Development Statistics, United Nations.

Index